horse
behaviour

horse
behaviour

Don Harper

**MARKS &
SPENCER**

Marks and Spencer p.l.c.
Baker Street, London W1U 8EP
www.marksandspencer.com

Produced by The Bridgewater Book Company, UK

ISBN 1–84273–243–9

Printed in China

All pictures by Bob Langrish except;
p.12, The Ancient Art & Architecture Collection Ltd;
pp.14, 15, 30, Bruce Coleman Collection;
p.16 Bridgeman Art Library – (top) British Museum, London,
(bottom) Terme Museum, Rome, Italy

contents

introduction

Throughout the world today, horses still feature prominently in the lives of large numbers of people, just as they have done for thousands of years. But in the same way as our lives have changed over time, so has our relationship with the horse. From being essential on the battlefield and as a means of transport, horses are now kept largely as companions and often used for sporting purposes, ranging from horse racing to show jumping and polo to eventing.

Getting started

Even if you have never ridden before, it is generally quite easy to learn, with many reputable riding schools well established in numerous countries, teaching at all levels from novice to more advanced riding skills. You should, however, ensure that the school has a good reputation, with the instructors being suitably qualified in the area of riding that appeals to you. There is certainly no need or obligation to commit yourself to buying a horse at the outset, particularly since this will represent a substantial commitment – in terms of both finance and time. In addition, much of the equipment that you need can be borrowed or hired, although it is definitely a good idea to purchase your own riding hat. This always needs to conform to the latest safety standards. One of the great things about riding on this basis is that you can go as frequently as your schedule permits, and it will generally work out

much cheaper than owing your own horse. Problems are more likely to crop up if you want to start competing, however, and this is the stage when you will need to consider obtaining your own horse, rather than using one regularly ridden by other people as well.

As a novice begins to ride more horses, so it soon becomes apparent that each mount differs in character, and these differences apply just as much to horses of the same breed as between breeds. Such temperamental variances depend partly on the past experience of each horse. There has been growing interest in the psychological make-up of horses over recent years and the way in which their natural behaviour can influence their training, thanks partly to the popular film *The Horse Whisperer*. This interest has also led to a reappraisal of the best way to deal with horses suffering from behavioural problems, and experiments in novel ways of preventing these from arising in the first place. In turn, this has spawned developments such as stable toys, intended to keep horses from becoming bored in limited surroundings. Different treatments, often so-called alternative or complementary therapies such as acupuncture and Bach flower remedies, are also being used increasingly in the treatment of behavioural difficulties when they do arise in horses.

A number of these ideas, particularly relating to training, follow more intensive behavioural studies as to how horses behave naturally in herds, although there is actually no truly wild close relative of the domestic horse to be found in the world today. The last surviving species, Przewalski's horse (*Equus przewalski*) became extinct in the wild during the 20th century, but a well-coordinated captive breeding programme has ensured its continued survival.

Riding and friendship

Although the plight of wild equids attracts relatively little attention today, the number of people who ride regularly continues to increase. For most people, being able to go out on a hack through the countryside is a truly relaxing experience, especially in countries such as the British Isles, where there is a well-established network of special bridleways, allowing you to ride in safety away from roads and enjoy splendid scenery as well. If you are feeling more competitive, however, there are many events and activities, ranging from dressage to cross-country jumping, in which you can participate.

Another of the pleasures of being involved with horses is that it can easily expand your circle of friends, especially if you have your horse stabled at a yard or simply ride regularly at the same school. Having horsey friends often makes keeping your own horse easier and might even help you to reduce the cost of various activities. For example, you may be able to find someone to share a box or trailer to a show or similar event, and when you cannot get to the yard, or want to take a holiday, someone will almost certainly be prepared to look after your horse, as long as you are happy to return the favour in due course.

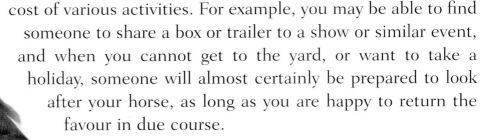

Horses and holidays

Horses can become a passion, a fact that has not escaped the attention of some of the more specialized holiday companies. If you fancy something different, you can go trekking among the spectacular volcanoes in Iceland, riding one of the hardy native Icelandic horses, or you might prefer to enjoy the spectacular landscape of the Rocky Mountains of North America from the back of a horse. There is an ever-growing number of such options on offer. Before you go, be sure that you are sufficiently fit for long days in the saddle, so that you do not become unduly saddlesore, which could spoil your holiday.

Should you be seeking a more leisurely break that includes horses, there are companies that will whisk you off to the awe-inspiring marshlands of the Camargue to track down the semi-wild grey horses that inhabit this unique area. Other options include tours to more formal settings in Austria, enabling you to gain insight into the famous Spanish Riding School of Vienna, including seeing the Lipizzaner stallions being put through their paces and visiting the stud farms.

You do not necessarily need to travel long distances to see horses at work, however. Even though they are no longer used routinely on farms, such is the current interest in working horses that they can be seen at many agricultural fairs and similar events, performing traditional tasks like ploughing or pulling carts. In such situations, they invariably prove to be a major attraction for people of all ages.

a horse's basic nature

Although the tasks they perform for humans have changed since they were domesticated centuries ago, horses still play a significant role in the lives of many people. The story of equine evolution reveals just how lucky horses have been to survive to the present day. Their existence in North America, where much of their early evolution occurred, came to a dramatic end about 8,000 years ago, and they have been restored there only comparatively recently. Climatic changes also led to a reduction in their distribution in Eurasia, and, had it not been for domestication, they could have become extinct here, too. While domesticated horses have since thrived under human care, their wild relatives have not fared so well, many species having been hunted into oblivion in both Africa and Asia. The last extinction occurred in 1927, with the disappearance of the Syrian onager.

evolution
of the horse

Horse lineage can be traced back over 60 million years to a small creature called *Hyracotherium*, which stood about 20cm (8in) tall at the shoulder and measured 60cm (2ft) in length. *Hyracotherium* had a wide distribution; its remains have been unearthed in localities as far apart as North America, Europe and Asia. Sixty million years ago these areas were largely forested, and *Hyracotherium* browsed on low-growing plants, having 44 teeth with low crowns for this purpose (the modern horse has only 36). Its number of toes also exceeded those of today's horse, with four on each of the front feet and three on both of the hind ones.

Climatic changes that occurred during the Oligocene Period, about 38 million years ago, saw the *Hyracotherium* lineage vanish entirely from Eurasia, but its descendants flourished in North America. Here, the forests were gradually replaced by more open areas of country and the lack of dense vegetative cover meant that speed became important as a means of defence against would-be predators: in order to survive, early horses were forced to start running. They also began to get bigger, and this is reflected in *Mesohippus*, which was more than double the size of *Hyracotherium*.

Fewer toes and bigger teeth

Mesohippus had three toes on each foot, with the middle toe being significantly longer than those on either side of it. Its head was longer as well, and its teeth also changed in shape, evolving a greater surface area for grinding purposes, although they were still set low in the jaw.

The development of high-crowned teeth confirms that from around this time horses began to switch from a browsing lifestyle to one that was based on grazing. This change becomes even more apparent in *Parahippus*, the successor to *Mesohippus*. The presence of hard silica in grasses, which had evolved by now, meant that its teeth would suffer heavy wear when grinding up this vegetation, in spite of the fact that they were additionally protected by a tough covering of cement.

Further development towards the modern horse can be seen in *Merychippus*, which followed *Parahippus*. Remains of herd members, dating back some 20 million years, have

The presence of horses in northern Europe led to them being portrayed in early cave art, and also reveals how they were initially hunted for food.

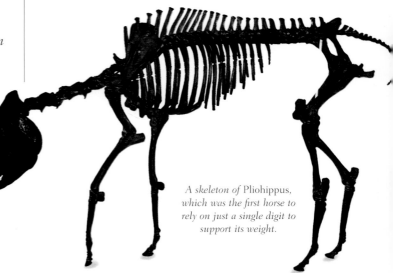

A skeleton of Pliohippus, *which was the first horse to rely on just a single digit to support its weight.*

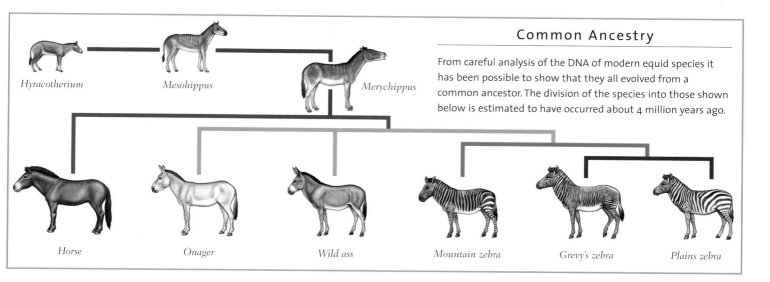

Common Ancestry

From careful analysis of the DNA of modern equid species it has been possible to show that they all evolved from a common ancestor. The division of the species into those shown below is estimated to have occurred about 4 million years ago.

Hyracotherium *Mesohippus* *Merychippus*

Horse   Onager   Wild ass   Mountain zebra   Grevy's zebra   Plains zebra

been found in grassland areas of Nebraska. The premolar teeth, located in front of the molars, also now had broader surfaces for grinding, and the jaw had become correspondingly heavier to accommodate them: it resembled that of a contemporary horse for the first time. In addition, the neck of *Merychippus* was longer, to facilitate its grazing lifestyle, allowing it to reach the ground easily. Changes in the foot structure also start to become apparent (see below). Only the central toe was now used for weight-bearing; the two side toes were smaller and were raised off the ground.

The development of the modern horse

Pliohippus was the first horse to have a foot structure like that of a modern horse, having just a single toe on each leg. This lineage continued to *Equus caballus*, which is considered to be the direct ancestor all today's equids. Its oldest remains, dating back over a million years, have been found in North America. At some point, earlier horse types had crossed the Bering land bridge back into Asia from North America, successfully colonizing this new land, and *Equus* too followed this route.

Members of the horse family also went westwards and southwards into Europe and Africa, but in North America itself, wild horses became extinct. No-one knows the reasons for certain, but the most likely explanation seems to be that an epidemic of a disease of some kind wiped them out. European colonists reintroduced horses to North America about 500 years ago.

The Evolution of the Hoof

The alterations in the structure of the horse's foot occurred partly as a result of changes in the environment. Having four toes like *Eohippus* was beneficial when living in marshy areas because it gave greater agility. Since then, the number of digits has dramatically reduced. But it is still possible to make out a trace of the horse's first digit, equivalent to our big toe, as the horny area above the knee and on the lower part of the hock joint, often known as the chestnut. The ergot, marking the fusion of the second and fourth digits, can be located at the back of the fetlock joints.

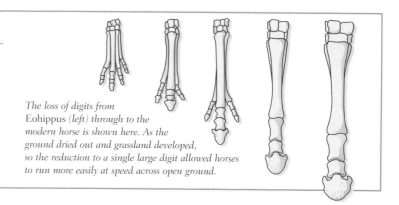

The loss of digits from Eohippus (left) through to the modern horse is shown here. As the ground dried out and grassland developed, so the reduction to a single large digit allowed horses to run more easily at speed across open ground.

zebras
and asses

There are now just six species of wild equid living in the world, with the distribution of the family being centred in Africa. This continent is home to the three species of zebra, as well as the African ass.

Grevy's zebra

Grevy's zebra lives in herds in arid areas in the far east of the African continent, in parts of Ethiopia, Somalia, and Kenya. Weighing about 405kg (900lb), it is the heaviest of all the wild horses.

The social structure in herds of Grevy's zebra, as well as those of wild asses, is very different to modern horses, with the bonds between members being much looser. This may be related in part to the fairly harsh habitat in which they live, since there is often not sufficient grazing to support large groups. Mature stallions establish fairly large territories, which can be up to 10 square kilometres (3.9 sq miles), marking the borders with dung to confirm their presence to others, and mating with mares that enter the region.

Plains zebra and mountain zebra

The lifestyle of the plains and mountain zebras differs from that of Grevy's, being more akin to that of true horses. These two species live in relatively stable herds, or harems, which consist of a stallion and several mares, and they occupy an established territory, known as their home range, which may be shared with neighbouring harems. The plains zebra is found in grassland and savanna of East Africa, while the mountain zebra occurs at the other end of the continent, in the mountain grassland of the south-west.

Quagga

The Quagga was a very distinctive wild equid with a dark rump and stripes. Although originally considered to be a separate species, recent research suggests that it was a subspecies of the plains zebra, with stripes on just the head and upper part of the body. It was hunted to extinction in the late 1800s, but a breeding programme is now underway to re-create this distinctive form.

Zebra Markings

The feature that sets zebras apart from the other members of this group is the striped patterning on their bodies. Grevy's zebra (*Equus grevyi*) has narrow black and white stripes that extend vertically up the sides of its body. The belly is white. Grevy's zebra also has a large, erect mane and unmistakeable rounded ears. The plains or common zebra (*E. burchelli*) can be distinguished from Grevy's zebra by its much broader stripes, the lines curving to become more horizontal over the haunches. The mountain zebra (*E. zebra*) has stripes that are narrower and do not continue under the belly, which is white.

The presence of the distinctive stripes provides what is known as disruptive camouflage, helping to break up the outline of the zebra's body. This is especially beneficial when the zebras are close to each other in a herd, as it makes it harder for a would-be predator to pick out an individual.

Grevy's zebras: Amazing as it may seem, each zebra has an individual patterning.

Recent genetic research suggests that Przewalski's horse is not the direct ancestor of the domestic horse.

Tibet. Asiatic asses have much more rounded hooves, and they more closely resemble horses in terms of their overall appearance.

Przewalski's horse

The only wild horse in the world also occurs in Asia, being found further north than the Asiatic ass, in Mongolia. Przewalski's horse (*E. przewalskii*) inhabits open plains and semi-desert areas in the vicinity of the Altai Mountains. This species first became known to western scientists in 1881. By the 1940s, it was considered to have become extinct in its native habitat, largely because of human pressures. But these tough and distinctive little horses have now been reintroduced to areas of their former range, and hopes are high that they will soon be thriving again in these surroundings.

African ass and Asian ass

The African ass (*E. africanus*) lives in the stony desert region of north-eastern Africa, roaming through parts of the Sudan, as well as Ethiopia and Somalia. It is the smallest of all wild equids and has very narrow feet – an adaptation that helps it to walk easily as it is less vulnerable to foot injuries on the stony ground of its natural environment. The African asses' Asiatic counterpart (*E. hemionus*) ranges from Syria through parts of Iran and northern India to

The stripes of plains zebras extend around the underside of the body.

A mountain zebra: These particular zebras are now scarce in the wild.

domestication
of the horse

The ancestors of today's domesticated horses are thought to have originated from the plains of southern Russia, in the area between the Ukraine and Turkestan.

The domestication process is thought to have begun around 4000BC. At first, horses were probably kept for their meat and milk, but it was not long before they were being used to pull loads as well as being ridden. In the military arena, horses were originally kept for pulling chariots, and then they were used for cavalry purposes. For many centuries, they were ridden without stirrups. In fact, the earliest reference to stirrups is 477AD. They were devised in China and subsequently introduced to the west.

The rapid spread of early domestic horses can be traced across Europe, and soon differences in their appearance had arisen. Those kept in northern Europe tended to be small and powerful, not unlike the Exmoor ponies of today, while those in the Middle East were more elegant and larger, perhaps similar to today's Arab horses.

This Egyptian tomb painting reveals the way that horses and their relatives were viewed in ancient times, and the tasks that they were expected to perform.

Donkeys and mules

One of the difficulties in accurately determining the dates of the domestication of horses is that, at this stage, there were no characteristic changes in their bone anatomy. Had there been, this would have enabled us to distinguish early domesticated individuals from their wild relatives. The African ass was probably domesticated by the Egyptians at

A Suitable Nature

The natural behavioural characteristics of the horse meant that it was much more receptive to domestication than other members of the equid family. In the wild, horses live together in groups with a stallion, who usually follows watchfully at the back of the herd. In domestication, the part of the stallion is assumed by the handler or rider. This goes some way to explaining why stallions must be gelded, if they are to fit easily within the domesticated group, otherwise they can be very difficult to manage. Early portrayals of stallions show them reined in with their heads kept high to ensure that they cannot resort to a threat gesture, which entails bending their heads forwards, which in turn would make them more difficult to control.

Horses were important in battle, as shown by this mosaic of a horse with a Roman charioteer.

BELOW: Horses helped to revolutionize human existence in various ways, not least in terms of agriculture.

RIGHT: The strength of horses has meant they can carry and pull loads that are too heavy for people.

about the same time as the horse, and certainly by 4,500 years ago, donkeys were a common sight in Egypt, carrying people and panniers of goods. There is no doubt, too, that later in the Egyptian era, mules were created by the hybridization of donkeys and horses.

In Roman times, mules were being bred on a relatively large scale, helping to carry equipment for the army throughout the Roman Empire. Writers of this era gave detailed advice on how to breed these hybrids successfully, by fostering a young male donkey, known as a jackass, to a lactating mare. The Romans also had a special design of platform which allowed male donkeys to mate easily with taller mares.

Hinnies are the result of a mating of a female donkey and a stallion. They can be distinguished from mules by the shape of their head, which is finer, and by the fact that there is long hair only at the tip of the tail, not all the way down as is found in horses.

Perhaps surprisingly, in view of their social structure (see p.14), neither the mountain nor plains zebras have been widely domesticated, although some have been trained to pull carriages. Zebras have been used even less commonly for riding purposes.

ponies
– tough and versatile

Ponies are small horses; the name derives from the French word *poulenet*, which translates as small, male horse. Their origins can be traced back to the Celtic ponies that had emerged in northern and western parts of Europe by the Iron Age. These ponies were not like the breeds of today. They varied quite widely in size, some standing less than a metre (3ft) high, but were very strong.

Workers and players
Many of today's pony breeds are linked with areas of northern Europe, where they have lived for many centuries. They include the Shetland, which has been bred for more

ABOVE: *Ponies are ideally suited to younger riders, introducing them to both the skills of riding and the excitement of competitive events.*

LEFT: *A young Exmoor foal. Like other ponies, the Exmoor is relatively hardy, growing a dense, weather-resistant coat at the onset of winter.*

than 2,000 years on the bleak islands of this name located off the coast of Scotland. Ancestral links between the pony breeds and the earliest domesticated horses can be seen in the case of the Highland with its characteristic striped legs and dorsal stripe. This pony is the largest of the British pony breeds, standing approximately 14 hands high.

The Exmoor pony, from the south-west of England, is another ancient breed that has adapted over the course of more than 4,000 years of living on the hard terrain after which it is named. For example, it has a distinctive fan of long hair at the base of its tail, which helps to prevent water from running down and freezing on its hind quarters. Neighbouring Dartmoor is also home to a pony breed, once highly valued for carrying tin from the local mines to nearby towns. Many other British pony breeds were used for similar purposes, including the Fells and the Dales, and often displayed remarkable stamina.

Today, many ponies are valued more for their trekking skills than their ability to work, and they have evolved in new environments. The American Shetland, for example, was developed in the USA in the nineteenth century from Shetlands crossed initially with Hackney ponies. The Welsh mountain pony laid the foundation for the Australian pony, also in the nineteenth century.

The names of some of the more modern ponies reflect the purpose for which they were bred, rather than revealing anything about their ancestral home. Polo ponies (see p.25) fit into this category, having originated in Argentina but they have been bred specifically for sport.

What Defines a Pony?

There are physical differences that help to distinguish between horses and ponies. Compared with their body size, ponies have short legs and a more stocky appearance than horses. Their back is often short, with the withers being fairly rounded. They have a broad forehead and a narrow muzzle. The compact shape of ponies means that they are sure-footed and surprisingly strong for their size. In addition, they also prove to be very hardy, thanks to their thick winter coat and profuse mane, which give them good protection from the elements.

Like horses, ponies are measured in terms of their height at the wither, which is the highest point of the shoulders. The traditional unit used to measure height is the hand, which is equivalent to 10cm (4in). Ponies must be under 14.2hh (hands high). However, not all equids under this height limit are called ponies, a few, such as the Falabella, are regarded as miniature horses. The Connemara pony (shown below) is particularly hardy, due to its origins in the wild and rough landscape of Galway in western Ireland.

A relatively small head, with an arched neck are characteristics of the Connemara.

Sloping shoulders, creating a good stride length, reveal that Connemara ponies make good mounts.

The Connemara's long tail is set quite high on the back.

light horses
– supreme riding machines

The anatomy of the horse can have a distinct impact on the comfort, or otherwise, of riding it. Light horses have a back that carries a saddle easily, thanks to the relatively broad, flat structure of their ribs. Their sloping shoulders produce a strong gait, with a long, low movement of the legs. This allows them to cover a lot of ground, with the minimum of effort, at each stride. Coupled with this is a deep chest, which provides for a good lung capacity, enabling these horses to breathe well.

Breeding matters

The origins of many light horses reside in warfare, with some breeds having been developed as cavalry mounts. In addition, a number of horses intended for pulling carriages, such as the Hanoverian (shown right), have now become widely used for riding. There is also a group of breeds that are valued for their speed, with the oldest lineage tracing back in the Arab and related breeds, such as the Barb. The Arab is believed to have descended from the wild horses that roamed the western part of Asia, although the Caspian is thought to be more closely allied to these original equines. Both the Arab and the Caspian are distinguished by their relatively small head, fine-boned build and high-set tail.

The Akhal-Teke

The other horse type that made a major contribution to light horse bloodlines originated from central Asia. The environment that these horses had to survive in was fairly inhospitable, with hot summers and freezing winters. As a result, they were athletic and lean, qualities that are reflected in breeds such as the Akhal-Teke, which is from Turkmenistan. The Akhal-Teke was bred initially for racing over 3,000 years ago, and has also displayed tremendous stamina, virtually unmatched in the equine world. In 1935 members of this breed underwent an arduous journey from Ashkhabad to Moscow. This is a distance of 4,000km (2,500 miles) and the trip included a three-day crossing of a desert, without water.

The way in which the Akhal-Teke has adapted to its landscape can be seen in its physical attibutes. Its shoulders are well-sloped, producing a very soft gait that assists the breed in walking on sand, while its feet are hard and the associated leg tendons are strong.

The athletic nature of horses is a characteristic that has been refined by selective breeding. Some display more stamina rather than pace.

A long, straight back assists the jumping ability of these horses.

A long, fine neck is a characteristic of the Hanoverian, which is a warmblood that is highly valued for show-jumping purposes.

This horse is a Hanovarian and shows the typical characteristics associated with the breed.

A deep, broad chest.

The girth is deep, which conveys strength.

Strong, well-balanced limbs contribute to the height of these horses, which can stand up to 16.2 hands high.

Solid joints and well-formed feet. Foot weakness has been eliminated by careful breeding.

USA and the Morgan

Further development of the domesticated horse has occurred more recently in the Americas. The colonization of North America by Europeans owes much to the horse. If horses had not been available, it is highly unlikely that widespread settlement could have taken place before the advent of mechanized transport. One of the most important breeds to have evolved in the USA is the Morgan, which has played a part in the development of many other well-known modern American breeds, including the Saddlebred and Standardbred.

FIGURE AND JUSTIN MORGAN

The origins of the Morgan can be traced back to a single stallion, originally called Figure. His name was changed when he passed into the care of a man called Justin Morgan. Although standing only 14 hands high, the young stallion displayed remarkable strength and stamina, winning weight-pulling contests regularly and never being defeated in a race throughout his entire life. His fame was reflected in the number of mares that he covered during his lifetime, and the Morgan of today reveals the impact that a single outstanding individual can have in terms of influencing the evolution of a breed.

heavy horses
– *the ultimate workhorse*

Heavy horses, the giants of the horse world, may look intimidating, but in fact they are usually very docile, responsive, and keen to work. Their strength was vital before the age of machines, and even today, in some forested areas, heavy horses are still preferred to vehicles when it comes to dragging out lumber, simply because they can accomplish the task more easily and with less environmental damage.

The largest of heavy horses is the Shire. It can be over 21hh at the withers, and weigh nearly 1,524kg (3,360lb).

Built for strength

As with all horses, good conformation is very important if heavy horses are to be able to work well. Their strength stems from their very powerful, thick neck and broad chest, with their backs being both wide and short. In direct contrast to the light breeds, their stride length is short, with their knees being lifted high, helping them maintain their balance when pulling a load. Pace is of far less

significance. Heavy horses are often described as draught horses, because of their abilities in haulage, whether pulling a plough or a cart.

The origins of this group of horses are unclear, but some members have a very long history, extending back thousands of years, being valued in the Middle Ages as warhorses for carrying knights into battle. The Comtois for example, with its distinctive light flaxen mane and tail offset against its contrasting dark chestnut coat, was being bred in the region of France after which it was named as early as 300AD. Centuries later, the French Emperor Napoleon took them on his ill-fated campaign in Russia. Today, they are still kept for working the land.

There are heavy horse breeds associated with virtually every European country, although it was in China that horses were first kept and worked as teams for ploughing, as the result of the development of a special padded collar for this purpose over 1,500 years ago.

Shire horses ploughing a field. The upright shoulders of such horses allow them to be fitted with the necessary collar.

Draught horses are still used for a variety of tasks today, here providing an eye-catching means of delivering beer.

Breed development

There has been much cross-breeding between heavy and light horses down the years. For example, another French heavy horse, the Percheron, was developed through crossings with Arab stallions in a programme that began around 700AD. This has led to the Percheron having the distinctive concave profile so typical of the Arab. It has also imbued the breed with great stamina, enabling it to cover distances of up to 56km (35 miles) at the trot in a day. In contrast to most heavy horses, it also generally lacks the characteristic longer hair or 'feathering' above the hooves, which can become heavily soiled by mud.

The breed that has the most unusual action among all the heavy horses is, however, the Clydesdale (shown below), which originated in the Clyde Valley of Scotland during the mid-1750s. It evolved from local horses and imported heavy horses, including Flemish stock. Subsequently, Shires, too, made a contribution to the breed's development. Clydesdales still have proportionately longer necks than many similar heavy breeds but are particularly distinctive in their high-stepping gait, which looks quite exaggerated compared with other heavy horses. There is no doubting their strength and pulling power, however, a contributing factor being that their withers are higher than their croup.

Some Heavy Breeds

Ardennais	France
Boulonnais	France
Brabant	Belgium
Breton	France
Clydesdale	Britain
Comtois	France
Døle Gudbrandsdal	Norway
Italian Heavy Draught	Italy
Jutland	Denmark
Muraközi	Hungary
Percheron	France
Russian Heavy Draught	Russia
Shire	Britain
Suffolk Punch	Britain
Vladimir	Russia

Unlike many heavy horses, the Clydesdale has a straight head when viewed in profile.

Longer hair, called feathering, is often present on the feet of heavy horses.

Hock joints lie close together.

The tail is usually decorated with ribbons for shows.

bred for
action

Around the world, particularly in less accessible places, many horses are still kept specifically for work. The breeds used may remain localized, but they are highly valued by those whose livelihoods depend upon them. In remote areas of Tibet, for example, the Tibetan pony has been worked by the local people for centuries. As with so many other breeds, these ponies have evolved to survive very well in their own landscape, having short yet strong legs that enable them to pick their way sure-footedly across stony ground or along mountain tracks. They are versatile as well, being used for draught work and as pack animals, in addition to making excellent mounts. So prized were these ponies in the past that they were often presented to Chinese emperors during the Imperial Age.

Hunters

In the west however, horses have gradually become less necessary for working purposes and are now increasingly used for leisure pursuits. This has led to the creation of horses suitable for particular uses, but not classifiable as a breed.

Although horses will jump instinctively, experience plays a part in ensuring a safe landing for horse and rider.

Hunters, for example, do not share many common characteristics, because the attributes required for a hunter will vary from region to region, based on the local terrain. For example, open ground calls for speed, with the requirement being for a hunter having a relatively high proportion of Thoroughbred in its ancestry. In areas of more difficult going, however, stamina is likely to be more significant than pace alone. In the show ring, of course, there is a greater tendency towards uniformity, and this has led to distinctions, with show hunters being judged in different classes from working hunters.

The hack and riding pony

The hack is another horse of variable ancestry, although the Thoroughbred tends to predominate in its bloodlines, often along with horses of Anglo-Arab stock. Hacks were originally kept simply for riding, with their looks being significant as well. The scaled-down version of the hack is the 'riding pony' of today, in which a strong Arab influence is usually discernible.

Azteca

The processes that lead to the evolution of new breeds are on going, as reflected by the case of the Azteca, which is of Mexican origin. Although its name may suggest that this breed is of ancient lineage, the Azteca did not appear until 1972. It is the result of a carefully planned breeding programme involving crossings between Andalusians, Quarter horses and Mexican Criollos.

A BREED OF QUALITY

Not only does the Azteca have a very attractive appearance, but it has also proved to be very versatile, and it is starting to build up a strong international following. Quite apart from its elegant appearance, part of the reason for its popularity is its temperament, which is calm and intelligent.

Cobs

When it comes to strength and power, the cob is still a popular choice both for hunting and general riding. Such horses usually have some Irish Draught horse in their ancestry, although the Welsh cob may feature in the breeding programme as well. A sturdy, deep-chested appearance and relatively short legs are characteristics of the cob, and serve to distinguish these horses, which are also bred to be good natured and responsive.

Polo ponies

Selective cross-breeding for sporting purposes has also taken place in the case of the polo pony. These are bred specifically to play polo, an ancient game dating back to about 525BC in Persia. Agility is very important for polo ponies, which need to be able to turn in tight circles. Thoroughbred and Quarter horse crosses often underlie the ancestry of modern polo ponies, which are significantly taller than their ancestors, averaging about 15.1hh.

Polo is popular worldwide, and some of today's best polo ponies come from Argentina.

bred for
colour

The basic colour of horses is described as dun – a pale yellow-brown with dark mane and tail. The classic dun is Przewalski's horse, which has a yellowish- to reddish-brown coat, offset against its darker mane and tail. This coloration helps to disguise wild horses in their natural environment, but nowadays horses occur in a very wide variety of colours and patterns, some of which are associated with a particular breed. The Friesian, a member of the heavy horse group, is always jet black, whereas Quarter horses can be any solid colour. There is often confusion over the palomino because this is both a colour recognized in many breeds, and a breed in its own right, members being distinguished by their golden colouration, with contrasting white manes and tails. The Palomino breed was developed in the USA from Spanish stock.

A Palomino, showing its distinctive coloration, which is characteristic of these horses, as well as being a colour that is seen in other breeds.

The Pinto or Paint

Horses with patterned coats, usually white combined with darker markings, are highly valued for their distinctive camouflage, particularly in the USA, where there is a number of such breeds. The Pinto is well known and has

Appaloosa Coat Colours

Leopard – white over all or part of the body with dark spots on the white
Snowflake – white spotting all over the body
Blanket – white or white-spotted over the hips
Marble – mottled white and dark patterning all over the body
Frost – white specks on a dark coat

OTHER CHARACTERISTICS
● Wispy tail and mane
● White surrounding the iris of the eye
● Mottled skin where it is visible – for example, on the muzzle, eyes, and genitals
● Hooves often vertically striped with black and white

This Appaloosa has a very impressive white blanket patterning over its hindquarters.

Spotted patterning is very closely linked with the Appaloosa.

Blotched patterning is always highly individual, with no two horses displaying identical markings of this type. In some cases, white rather than dark areas predominate.

two basic colour forms: the 'ovaro', which usually has white areas in the centre of its body and elsewhere, offset against large blotches of colour, and the 'tobiano', which has white, rather than coloured, patches predominating in the coat. While all such horses are considered Pintos, there are restrictions based on ancestry, which mean that Paints form a sub-group within the broader Pinto category.

Appaloosas and the Nez Percé Indians

The actual origins of part-coloured horses are believed to lie in Europe, where horses with black-and-white coats are described as piebalds. Other colour combinations with white are referred to as skewbalds.

Patterned horses played a significant part in native Indian culture in North America. There the Nez Percé Indian tribe, based in the US state of Oregon, were responsible for the development of the Appaloosa. This particular breed of horse has more discrete spotted markings than the Pinto.

feral
horses

The word 'feral' is used to describe domestic animals that have reverted to living in the wild. Feral horses have a relatively coarse appearance with a large head, and usually display considerable stamina. They generally do not settle well into a domesticated lifestyle, however, proving to be difficult to break for riding.

Perhaps the best known feral horses are the Mustangs of North America. Horses were reintroduced to the Americas in 1519. Gradually, as expeditions took place from Europe and settlers arrived, some of these horses escaped and began to spread across the vast North American continent. It was in the south of what is now the USA that feral horses first became established. The native Indian population of this region, particularly the Comanches

A mustang round-up. Weaned foals have traditionally been caught with lassos and broken for riding.

and Apaches, did not try to domesticate these feral horses. Instead, they attacked European settlements to steal their stock and this added in due course to the number of feral horses, as not all were recaptured.

Increase and decline

Numbers of feral horses probably peaked in the late 1700s, when there may have been as many as five million, covering much of the USA and often in vast herds comprising several thousand individuals. Subsequently, increasing human settlement led to a decline in their numbers, particularly close to developing towns, although it was still not unusual for unwanted domesticated stock to be turned loose, to augment the wild herds, which were left largely unhindered.

The situation changed dramatically as the result of the Boer War in 1899, however, when there was a huge demand for horses to be shipped to southern Africa.

A herd of mustangs. Their name is derived from the Spanish word 'mestena', which means group, although their numbers today are much smaller than in the past.

Australian Brumbies

In Australia the pattern of equine colonization was similar to that which occurred in North America. Horses were introduced to the Australian continent in the late 1800s, and one of the earliest recorded breeders was a Private James Brumby of the New South Wales Corps. When he was transferred to Tasmania, Brumby left his horses behind and they became feral. As a result, feral horses in Australia today are known as Brumbies, with their population reckoned to be between 125,000 and 205,000. Their numbers may plummet during periods of drought however, and they are also hunted.

A NATURAL LIFESTYLE

Brumbies normally live in small groups, consisting of a stallion and up to 12 mares, with young colts being driven out when they are aged between a year and 18 months old. Herds display strong territorial instincts; even during times of drought and scarcity of grazing, they are reluctant to move from their home area, which may be up to 150 sq km (58 sq miles). Brumbies still range quite widely through much of Australia, although they are not found in desert areas, nor close to major centres of human settlement.

The African continent is not a good environment for domestic horses because of their susceptibility to disease spread by the tsetse fly and other biting insects. This resulted in high mortality, and so the demand for horses continued throughout the war, leading to a dramatic reduction in the feral horse population in the USA.

US military commanders soon realized that they had an asset in these feral horses, which became known as Mustangs, and they released a number of stallions in certain areas, with a view to improving the bloodstock. Large numbers of Mustangs were again rounded up for military service during the First World War, but this was to be the last time that they were used to any significant extent in combat, as horses were gradually replaced by mechanized transport. Hunting pressures on herds in the USA increased during the latter years of the twentieth century, to the extent that estimated numbers have now fallen down to as few as 16,000 individuals.

adapted for
survival

As herbivores, equids are potential prey for a number of carnivorous mammals. Living in herds helps to provide them with some protection however, as it makes it harder for a predator to creep up on the group without being detected. In some cases, these herds associate with other animals in order to increase their chances of survival. For example, on the plains of Africa, zebras are often found with giraffes. The long necks and alert nature of the giraffes make them well placed to spot danger from a distance away and raise the alarm. This is of great benefit, as wild horses depend largely on an early warning to outrun a hunter. For example, the cheetah is ideally built for sprinting and can outpace a fleeing zebra over a short distance. However, if the zebra has a sufficient head start, then the cheetah will tire and lose interest in the pursuit. Lions pose much more of a threat in this instance, because they will hunt in prides rather than on their own. The pursuing lion is likely to attempt to drive its prey towards other pride members lying in ambush.

Instinctively cautious

Equids are cautious at all times, not just when grazing, but also when drinking, and with good reason, particularly in Africa. Here, they may face attacks not just from on the land, but also in the water, as crocodiles may lurk just under the surface, lungeing at the unwary and pulling them to their death. For this reason, zebras and other herd animals have developed a particular strategy at watering places. When a herd approaches the water, not all the individuals will drink simultaneously. They take it in turns, with some remaining watchful for possible danger, just as when they are grazing.

Physical defences

Once caught by a predator, a horse has few defences. If cornered, the zebra may lash out with its powerful hindlimbs, which can easily smash a lion's jaw, if they make effective contact, but often it will succumb to the attack. Stallions represent a more significant challenge than other members of the herd, and so potential predators, especially lions, will more usually target a young or obviously weakened individual, because they are likely to be able to outrun and pull it down more easily.

Disputes between horses can be quite violent affairs, as shown by these zebras A kick can result in a broken jaw, leading to a slow death from starvation.

The Horse's Senses

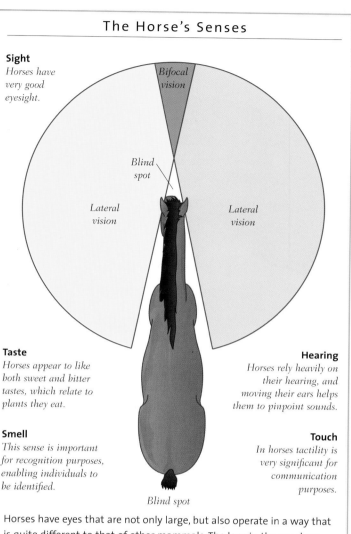

Sight
Horses have very good eyesight.

Bifocal vision

Blind spot

Lateral vision

Lateral vision

Taste
Horses appear to like both sweet and bitter tastes, which relate to plants they eat.

Smell
This sense is important for recognition purposes, enabling individuals to be identified.

Hearing
Horses rely heavily on their hearing, and moving their ears helps them to pinpoint sounds.

Touch
In horses tactility is very significant for communication purposes.

Blind spot

Horses have eyes that are not only large, but also operate in a way that is quite different to that of other mammals. The lens in the eye does not focus by shifting in size – instead the horse moves its head up and down to bring an object into view. This is a further adaptation to the fact that horses spend so long grazing with their heads down.

covers a large area behind them and the other is directly in front. It is not a good idea to approach a horse from behind, because it may not see you and could be spooked.

Acute hearing

Horses have keen hearing. When listening, their ears point forwards, which helps them to locate the sound source accurately. Ear position is also a means of visual communication. By putting its ears back, a horse can indicate that it is fearful, particularly if this is combined with vocal communication such as a snort. Horses rely more on visual than vocal communication.

Brilliant sight

Horses have very acute vision, partly due to the position of their eyes on the sides of the head, which enables them to see almost through 360 degrees. The eyes are also set quite high so that horses are able to drink or graze while still being able to see danger. They have two blind spots – one

Living in open country, horses have evolved particularly acute vision, to warn of danger.

the mechanics
of the horse

The horse is equipped for speed, thanks to its relatively long, powerful legs. It also has a long neck, which allows it to graze easily. The length of the neck comes not from an increase in the number of cervical vertebrae that make up this part of the vertebral column, but rather from an increase in their breadth.

The Thoroughbred is the fastest breed of horse, in terms of its pace. This is primarily due to its long hindlegs and excellent lung capacity.

In total, there are seven cervical vertebrae. The first articulates with the skull and is known as the atlas; the second has a vertical raised area on its upper part for the attachment of muscles and is known as the axis. At the base of the neck the cervical vertebrae connect with the thoracic vertebrae, which mark the start of the ribcage and the chest. The lumbar vertebrae extend above the abdominal area, providing support for the hip joints, along with the sacrum behind. The tail is made up of coccygeal vertebrae, which taper along their length and mark the end of the vertebral column.

The structure of the horse's vertebral column is very significant as it allows the propulsion provided by the hindlimbs to be transmitted to the forequarters. In addition, it needs to be relatively stable and rigid in order to carry the great bulk of the horse's digestive tract as there is relatively little bony support for this under the body.

The hindlimbs

The horse's speed comes from its well-muscled hindlimbs, although there are very obvious differences in conformation, based on the evolution of the breed or the purposes for which it was created. Tall, slender horses, for example, will have less stamina than those with a broad chest and short, powerful limbs.

Where bones meet, they form joints. The structure of the joints is reinforced by the tough, fibrous ligaments, which extend across the joint, attaching to both bones.

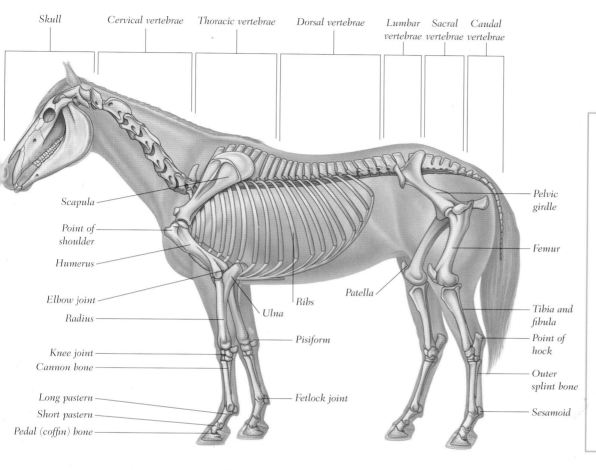

Skull   Cervical vertebrae   Thoracic vertebrae   Dorsal vertebrae   Lumbar vertebrae   Sacral vertebrae   Caudal vertebrae

Scapula

Point of shoulder

Humerus

Elbow joint

Radius

Knee joint

Cannon bone

Long pastern

Short pastern

Pedal (coffin) bone

Ulna

Ribs

Pisiform

Fetlock joint

Pelvic girdle

Femur

Patella

Tibia and fibula

Point of hock

Outer splint bone

Sesamoid

Fact File

● There are 250 bones in a horse's body, although there can be slight differences between breeds.
● The horse's skull alone is comprised of 34 bones in total.
● Typically 40 teeth are present in the jaws of an adult horse.
● The tallest horse was a Shire, which grew to a height of 21.2hh.
● A Palomino horse called Chinook had the largest tail ever recorded, measuring 6.7m (22ft) in length.
● The mane can grow as long as 5.5m (18ft).

Points of a Horse

The points are the external features of the horse, which contribute to its conformation as well as its appearance, although not its coloration. They are basically a series of terms used to describe different external parts of the body. Although the names of the points are standardized, their relative size and angulation can vary significantly between different breeds. This in turn means that there are significant differences in conformation between light and heavy horses, for example. These differences can be related to the primary purpose for which the breed was developed.

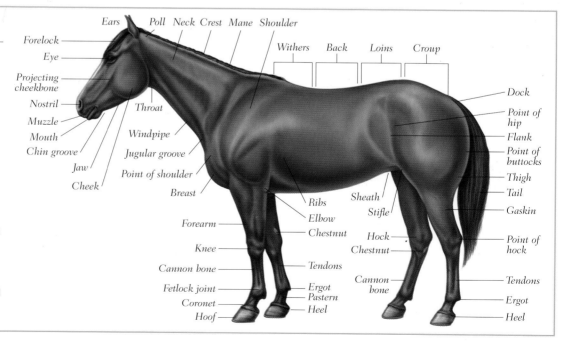

Ears   Poll   Neck   Crest   Mane   Shoulder   Withers   Back   Loins   Croup

Forelock

Eye

Projecting cheekbone

Nostril

Muzzle

Mouth

Chin groove

Jaw

Cheek

Throat

Windpipe

Jugular groove

Point of shoulder

Breast

Forearm

Knee

Cannon bone

Fetlock joint

Coronet

Hoof

Ribs

Elbow

Chestnut

Tendons

Ergot

Pastern

Heel

Sheath

Stifle

Hock

Chestnut

Cannon bone

Dock

Point of hip

Flank

Point of buttocks

Thigh

Tail

Gaskin

Point of hock

Tendons

Ergot

Heel

The elasticity within the ligaments ultimately determines the degree of flexibility at the joint itself. Tendons also attach to the bones, helping to bind the muscles and preventing them from tearing apart.

The pelvic girdle provides the support at the rear of the horse's body, with the head of the femur fitting into the cup to produce the hip joint. The lower end of the femur forms the stifle, the point at which the hind limb becomes clearly defined. In front of the stifle, there is a separate smaller bone, known as the patella, which corresponds to the human kneecap and aids the stifle's movement.

Below the stifle is the tibia and its smaller, thinner companion, the fibula. Together these extend down to the hock joint. This middle part of the leg provides stability, because the muscle groups located here are shared by the hock and the stifle. The horse cannot flex its stifle without flexing the hock at the same time.

The hock joint is complex, consisting of the small tarsal bones bound tightly together by ligaments. Externally, however, it should feel relatively smooth on each side of the leg. Any swelling here could be a sign of abnormalities affecting the joint such as spavins or curbs, which in turn will detract from the soundness of the horse. Below the hock, the cannon bone extends down to the pastern where there is a joint, corresponding to our ankle and called the fetlock. The pastern bones should show a moderate slope, and this part of the leg must be of medium length, if it is to act effectively as the shock-absorber for the foot.

The forelegs

The forelegs do not have a bony attachment to the body; instead, ligaments and muscle bind the upper part of the leg, which includes the flattened scapula, to the sides of the chest. This, too, helps to absorb the stresses of

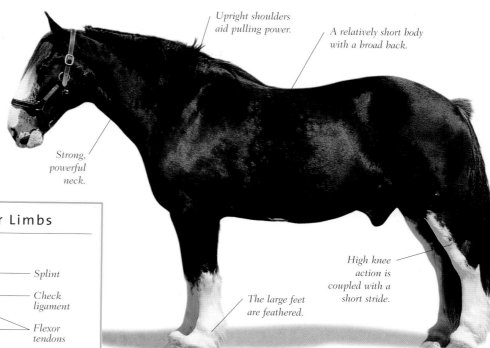

LEFT: *A huge international bloodstock industry has grown up in centres such as Newmarket in the UK.*

RIGHT: *Heavy horses are built for power rather than speed, as displayed by this Shire. Their bodies are heavily muscled, and their legs thick and strong.*

Upright shoulders aid pulling power.

A relatively short body with a broad back.

Strong, powerful neck.

High knee action is coupled with a short stride.

The large feet are feathered.

The Structure of the Lower Limbs

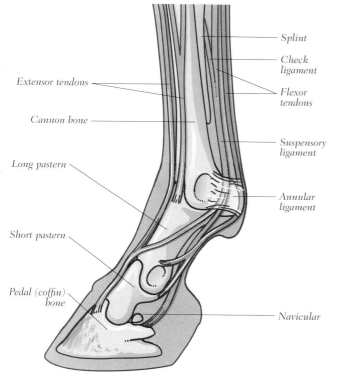

- Splint
- Check ligament
- Flexor tendons
- Extensor tendons
- Cannon bone
- Suspensory ligament
- Long pastern
- Annular ligament
- Short pastern
- Pedal (coffin) bone
- Navicular

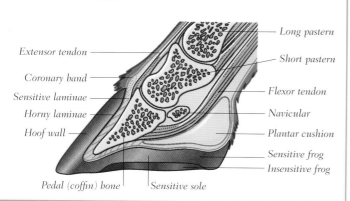

- Extensor tendon
- Coronary band
- Sensitive laminae
- Horny laminae
- Hoof wall
- Long pastern
- Short pastern
- Flexor tendon
- Navicular
- Plantar cushion
- Sensitive frog
- Insensitive frog
- Pedal (coffin) bone
- Sensitive sole

movement at speed. Otherwise, the structure of the foreleg is similar to that of the hindleg, with the knee replacing the hock. Roughened areas on the inside of the leg just above the knees are normal: called chestnuts, they are the remains of a digit lost during evolution. Chestnuts are also found on the hindlegs just below the hock.

The foot

The shape of the horse's foot comes from the pedal bone. Shape varies somewhat according to the type of horse, with the heavy breeds having not just larger but also flatter feet than the lighter breeds. With all breeds, however, it is important that there are no cracks or ridges evident in the hoof. When the foot is lifted up to show the sole, it should be possible to see the distinction between the outer horny wall, into which the shoes are fixed, and the sensitive inner part. Shoeing, which is carried out on most domesticated horses, prevents the hooves being worn down from work on hard surfaces, such as tarmac. Shoes need changing every month to six weeks and must be made specifically to fit the individual horse's feet.

different gaits
different speeds

The word 'gait' is used to describe the way in which the horse is moving, and its pace. Horses generally display four distinct gaits of increasing pace. The first investigations into the way that they move was carried out in Victorian times by the photographer Eadweard Muybridge, who took a series of exposures of horses at different speeds, and so revealed key differences in the sequence in which the legs move during the various gaits.

Pacing

Other gaits have also been created in association with certain breeds. Pacing is typically associated with horses being kept for harness racing and is a two-beat gait, with the legs moving in corresponding pairs, starting on the left side of the body and followed by the right side. Harness racing is especially popular in the USA where it draws large numbers of spectators. The race track is usually 1.6km (1 mile) long and the horses often complete the course in under two minutes.

Harness racing is very popular in the USA. The American Standardbred has been evolved for this sport, which can draw huge crowds.

THE WALK

The slowest of the four gaits is the walk. In the walk, two or sometimes three feet are on the ground simultaneously. The steps are even and so the footfall sounds even. The sequence begins with the left (or 'near') hind, followed by the matching forefoot, then the right (or 'off') hind and the corresponding forefoot. The sequence then continues with the left fore, right hind, right fore and left hind. The Tennessee Walking horse has a very different walking gait. Two distinct walking paces – the flat walk and the running walk – are recognized in this case, both of which are four-beat paces, with the hind feet extending in front of the corresponding front hoof prints.

THE TROT

When the horse starts to move at a faster pace than walking, this is described as trotting. The legs in this case move in diagonal pairs, commencing with the left fore and right hind, which creates the first beat, followed by the right fore and left hind, creating the second. The rider is thrown up a short distance from the saddle in this gait, and then lands back down gently. There are a number of trotting horses with a specialized gait, including the French and Russian Trotters. A long stride length is very important in these horses, allowing them to cover the ground well. Strong, powerful legs also tend to be characteristic of such horses, which are used for racing purposes.

THE CANTER

Faster still is the canter, a three-beat gait, during which, for a brief period of time all the feet are off the ground (suspension). Cantering on the right lead starts with the right foreleg, followed by the left hind, and then the so-called left diagonal movement, involving both the right hind and left fore, and finally the right fore, after which the period of suspension occurs before the sequence is repeated. Horses can also canter on the left lead. In this case, the gait begins with the left fore, followed by the right hind, then the left hind and right fore, with, finally, the left fore. Cantering is the last pace at which it is possible to make out the sequence of the individual hooves falling.

THE GALLOP

Galloping is the horse's fastest pace, during which often only one foot hits the ground at a time, and never more than two. Thoroughbreds are the fastest horses in the world and can reach speeds equivalent to 70kph (43mph). The posture of the rider is altered at gallop. By leaning forward in the saddle, rather than sitting upright, the rider allows the horse to move more freely, with the weight being more evenly distributed along the horse's back. Two distinct sequences can occur during galloping. One starts with the left fore then right fore, followed by the left hind and right hind; the other starts with the right fore, left fore, right hind and left hind.

A horse will normally walk readily, but you need to be alert, because if spooked, it is likely to speed up very quickly.

Trotting is known as a two-beat gait, because of the way in which the legs work in diagonal pairs.

Good balance is an important feature of cantering, and this applies to the rider as well as the horse.

Note the marked extension in the positioning of the forelimbs, which is a feature of galloping.

teeth
and teething problems

The herbivorous diet of the horse has had a major impact on its appearance, particularly its head, since the jaws need to be large and powerful to accommodate the deep-rooted teeth and associated musculature necessary for chewing grass. The incisor teeth are located at the front of the mouth, and used for plucking herbage. Behind them may be canine teeth, known as tushes, although these do not always develop in mares, and there is then a gap known as the diastema. The diastema allows the horse to pluck new vegetation and keep it separate from food already in its mouth that it wants to chew. Further up, towards the back of the jaw, are the premolars, followed by the molars or cheek teeth.

Horses have two sets of teeth through their lives: foals are born with milk (or deciduous) teeth, which are gradually replaced by permanent dentition up to the age of about five years. Adult horses typically have 40 teeth, consisting of 12 incisors, four canines, 12 premolars and 12 molars, although the number and size of the canines (tushes) is variable. Similarly, the first premolar or wolf tooth may only be evident in the upper jaw.

Ageing by teeth

The teeth continue to grow throughout a horse's life. A number of alterations occur in the incisors as the horse becomes older, and these provide a means for ageing an individual. The changes relate to the structure of the crowns, with the different layers in the tooth wearing down at different rates, as well as to the sides of the teeth, which show different characteristics above the gum line as the tooth grows. In young horses, the remains of the 'cup',

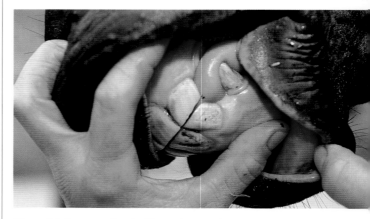

The teeth help to provide valuable insight into a horse's approximate age.

Teeth Development

As the foal starts to switch to a solid diet, it becomes increasingly dependent on its teeth. It sheds the milk teeth, which are replaced by its permanent teeth and will last throughout the remainder of the horse's life. Grass is plucked by the incisor teeth protruding from the front of the mouth, and is then ground up by the premolars and molars, which can suffer heavy wear as a result. This is why the teeth gradually wear down with age.

CONSEQUENCES OF DENTAL WEAR

It is the degree of wear on the teeth that enables a horse to be aged, by the changes apparent here. Ultimately, however, if the horse's teeth wear right down, it can have difficulty in eating, and this affects its life expectancy, particularly in the case of wild horses.

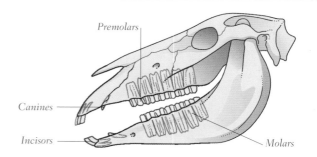

Mature Horse

The jaw of a mature horse has 12 premolars and 12 molars (for grinding) as well as 12 incisors (for biting). By this stage, the roots of the premolar and molar teeth in the jaws greatly exceed the crown above the gum line.

Crib-biting is a vice that causes horses to bite on hard surfaces, such as the stable door. It can lead on to wind-sucking (see p.158).

caused by dental cement, is apparent as a streak on the surface of the incisors, but as the tooth becomes worn down, so a second, more circular, mark becomes apparent behind it. Formed by exposure of the pulp cavity, this is known as the dental star. By the time a horse is about 12 years old, the final vestiges of the cup will have eroded, leaving just the dental star visible. In horses of about nine years old, a groove appears on the outside of the third incisor, being apparent at the margin with the gum at this stage. This is called Galvayne's groove, and it provides a further means of ageing a horse. As the tooth grows because of wear on its surface, the groove gradually extends. When the horse is 15 years old, Galvayne's groove has reached halfway down the tooth, taking a further five years to reach the cutting edge. After this, it starts to wear away, disappearing from the base of the tooth.

The Horse Dentist

Dental care in the domesticated horse is very important as sharp edges occur on the upper molars and lower premolars because the the teeth do not align exactly. This is due to the horse's jaw structure, with the lower jaw being narrower than the upper. The sharp edges have to be removed by rasping every six months or so.

Apart from regular visits, it is also time to call the dentist when:
- Your horse drops partially chewed food from his mouth on a regular basis. Known as quidding, this indicates pain in the mouth.
- He dislikes being touched on the cheeks or pulls away when you stroke the sides of his head.
- When being bridled, he shows reluctance to take the bit in his mouth, or reacts badly to having the noseband fastened.
- On being ridden, he appears resistant to the bit.
- He seems to be losing condition despite being well fed or being in good pasture.

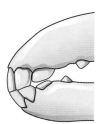 

Flat, oval tables and long, small cups

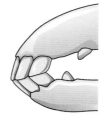 

Round tables and oval cups

 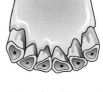

Triangular tables and rounded cups

Five Years
At five years old, the milk teeth have been replaced by permanent incisors and molars, and cup marks appear on the tooth surface, or table.

Twelve Years
At 12 years old, the teeth have begun to slope outwards and cup marks are less distinct; the dental star is still visible.

Old Age
In old age, the outward slope of the teeth is very pronounced and Galvayne's groove has almost entirely disappeared.

the anatomy of
eating

Horses have to spend long periods grazing each day to meet their nutritional needs.

The food a horse eats is generally of low nutritional value, so it has to consume large quantities to meet its needs. As a result, horses spend a great deal of their time eating. In a typical day, they will consume roughly 2 per cent of their body weight, in contrast to carnivores, which may not even eat every day in the wild.

To cope with this huge and constant intake of food, a horse requires not only strong teeth, but also a large digestive tract. The digestive process begins in the mouth, where the teeth break down the herbage and saliva starts chemical digestion. Horses produce large volumes of saliva, typically about 11 litres (24 pints) daily.

The food mix passes into the stomach and through the small intestine, being exposed to further enzymes here. The blind-ending sac, known as the caecum, marks the division between the large and small intestines. It has a key role to play in the digestive process, because it is here that beneficial bacteria and protozoa act to break down the cellulose present in plant matter. Absorption, mainly of vitamins and water, occurs in the large intestine, after which waste matter passes out of the body as faeces.

The problem of laminitis

Unfortunately, as they are so dependent on microbes to assist the digestive process, horses have great difficulty in coping with sudden dietary changes, and any such changes may have an adverse effect. For example, ponies allowed on to lush grass are likely to suffer from the foot condition laminitis, caused by inflammation of the laminae in the hoof (see p.35). Severe cases of laminitis can lead to a shift in position of the pedal bone, with the front feet being most vulnerable. It is intensely painful, and affected animals usually try to stand with the weight shifted as far as possible to the back of their hooves. Inflammation

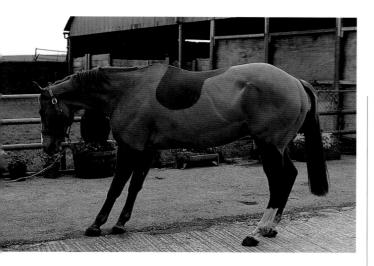

If the grass is too rich, the highly painful condition known as laminitis may strike, causing the horse to be reluctant to walk because of the pain in its feet.

Dear Equine Casebook

I have just had a horse suffer from colic. It was a horrible experience for both of us, and for a while it was touch-and-go whether he survived. How do I ensure that it will never happen again?
kind regards Frank Williams

Colic may prove to be a life-threatening condition, but you can greatly reduce the risks by sensible management. Never be tempted to feed your horse just before or immediately after exercise, and always carry out a regular deworming, based on your veterinarian's advice. Horses have relatively small stomachs, and need to be fed in small amounts throughout the day, with their diets being changed gradually over the course of several days, rather than suddenly. Bulky rations are vital, so if your horse does not have access to grass, it is important that he receives adequate quantities of good quality hay or haylage. Hay needs to be sweet-smelling and slightly green. Never feed excessively dusty or mouldy hay, as this is also likely to harm your horse's health.

causes the feet to feel hot, and the pony will also be reluctant to move. Painkillers and dietary adjustments are needed, and once an animal has suffered from this condition, recurrences are not uncommon.

Coping with colic

Colic, too, is intensely painful, and affects the abdomen. It is often linked with diet, as well as parasitic worms that are present within the intestinal tract. Affected horses are distressed, rolling more than usual and kicking their abdominal area in an attempt to relieve the problem. Sweating and constipation are other signs, along with an increase in the horse's respiratory rate. Veterinary advice needs to be sought without delay in such cases. In some cases of colic the gut will be twisted and surgery is likely to be required.

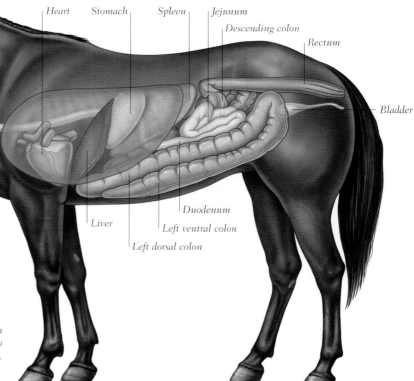

Oesophagus · Heart · Stomach · Spleen · Jejunum · Descending colon · Rectum · Bladder · Duodenum · Left ventral colon · Left dorsal colon · Liver

The horse's high fibre intake requires a correspondingly large digestive system to cope with the amount of bulk.

a close-knit
community

In a number of parts of the world, horses still range freely over areas of open land. In the south-west of England, for example, Exmoor is home to one of the oldest pony breeds in the world, while further east, in the New Forest, ponies have lived continuously in a state of what could be termed 'semi-liberty' since the tenth century.

Mutual grooming

Within these herds, behaviour patterns clearly associated with those of their wild ancestors can often be seen. It is quite easy to recognize individuals that are closely related, since they will often engage in mutual grooming. This is when two horses nuzzle up to each other and then one, or both, gently nibbles at the coat of its companion. Grooming like this can last for several minutes at a time. The areas of the body chosen for grooming are not random; they are associated with parts of the autonomic nervous system, and this type of behaviour appears to have a calming effect on the horses involved, which results in a measurable lowering of their heart rates.

ABOVE: *There are strong bonds that exist within a herd of horses, with herd members being able to recognize their companions without difficulty*

LEFT: *The bond between mare and foal is reinforced by mutual grooming, which consequently has a social as well as a practical function.*

Grooming behaviour may also be seen in horses living in a field, although the bonds between these animals may not be as strong as those between members of a semi-wild herd. Studies have shown that firm bonding can be achieved by removing two horses from a herd and keeping them together, but in isolation from the main group, for a minimum period of two weeks. During this time, they will form a close relationship, which will be retained, even if they are then reintroduced to the larger group.

Homing instinct

If a horse is cut off from from the herd, it can usually rejoin them in much the same way that a domesticated horse can find its way home. This ability depends partly on being in a familiar landscape and also on the fresh trail left by others in the herd. When seeking out its herd, a horse will actually follow in their footprints where possible, as well as using its sense of smell to sniff out the correct path when there are no obvious visual clues.

Scent is very important in horses, helping to maintain the stability within the herd. Stallions living in the wild will defecate in piles, which serve as both visual and olfactory indicators that they are occupying the territory; they also mask the droppings of their mares by urinating and defecating in the same spot, having sniffed the area first.

Vocal communication

It is possible for horses to keep in touch with each other by means of their calls, with some sounds being audible over a much greater distance than others. Vocal communication is not of very great importance to horses, however, since they have evolved to live in grassland, where their large size means they tend to be visible from far off. As far as a herd's well-being is concerned, the most significant sound in their repertoire is undoubtedly the 'blow': this is made by the horse blowing air through its nose and can be audible over 200m (656ft) away. A blow is uttered almost instinctively when a herd member unexpectedly encounters an unfamiliar object or creature, and serves as a rapid alarm call to others nearby, being made within seconds of the sighting.

Tail swishing

Unlike that of a dog, the horse's tail is not significant for communication purposes. However, it does have a very important function, which is particularly obvious during hot weather: it acts as a fly swish, with the horse flicking it to and fro to deter insects from landing on its body. Aside from causing irritation, some flies will bite through the horse's skin, causing inflammation and infection. Horses will often group together under trees and in other more shaded areas when the sun is at its hottest, standing nose to tail, so that the swish of one horse's tail also helps to deter flies from landing on its neighbour's head.

The language of stallions

The natural behaviour of stallions, particularly communication between rivals, is unlikely to be seen in the field environment, simply because they are difficult to manage, and keeping two together is not recommended. In the wild however, the subtle changes that occur as the breeding season approaches can be observed from a safe distance. For example, an established stallion may be challenged by a younger rival. Initially, a ritual of body language will be used and this sends out strong messages that will often resolve the matter, with fighting occurring only as the last resort. In fact, the vast majority of encounters end without

Horses like this Exmoor pony will only lie down when they feel secure, usually with other herd members standing nearby, to warn of approaching danger.

overt physical violence being displayed. Even then, the conflict tends to be brief: the stallions will circle each other and may paw at the ground nervously before one rears up, lungeing out with its front feet, which can inflict a serious blow on a rival. Stallions will also use their teeth. When the weaker individual backs down, he will be chased well away from the mares, although the combat has essentially ended by this stage.

Mares and the herd hierarchy

An order of dominance also exists between the mares in a herd, but this may be less obvious for much of the year. Mares with foals tend to be more protective and thus aggressive, and so move up the social hierarchy, at least on a temporary basis. Unfortunately, when a mare becomes particularly aggressive, this can create problems, not least because the foal itself may end up being inadvertently injured as the mare rushes towards a potential threat. Such behaviour is most commonly seen soon after birth, with most mares becoming less protective as their offspring grow older. The risk of injury to the young horse under these circumstances is obviously lessened outdoors in a paddock rather than within the confines of a stall.

Lying down and rolling

Other natural behaviour in horses includes lying down to doze, and rolling. In spite of their size, horses lie down only when they feel secure in their surroundings. It is much more common for them to sleep standing up, effectively napping for short intervals. This not only allows them to become aware of predators more quickly, but also ensures they are in the best position to escape if danger threatens. If they are caught lying down, they are disadvantaged by the relatively slow process of standing up, as well as the inability to strike out with their hooves. Horses are well-equipped with what is known as the 'stay apparatus' in their legs, which allows them to remain standing for long periods, while minimizing the muscular effort required.

Dear Equine Casebook

Why does my horse keep rolling on her back? When I ride her, I give her a good grooming before turning her out in the field, but she always goes straight for the muddiest patch and rolls until she is filthy dirty.
kind regards Emma Firth

On occasion, horses will roll on the ground. This sort of behaviour is more likely to be seen when a horse has recently been turned out into a field, than among wild or semi-wild herds. Rolling is rather similar to our desire to stretch, and allows your horse to tone up her back muscles after being ridden or standing in a stable for a while. Repeated and agitated rolling is, however, a typical symptom of the intestinal complaint known as colic (see p.41), particularly if the horse attempts to kick its belly with its hooves, and requires veterinary assistance.

courtship
and the reproductive process

Horses mature at a relatively early age, with stallions often attaining sexual maturity at just 18 months, and mares about six months later, although in domestic circumstances they are not normally allowed to breed until they are three or four years old, by which stage they will be fully developed. In the wild, bands of young stallions often do not begin breeding until they are quite a bit older, usually starting to do so when they are strong enough to maintain and defend their own harems.

The breeding season

The breeding period extends from early spring through until late summer, which, in the case of the northern hemisphere, means that mares come into season between February and August; the peak months are April to June. The response is triggered by increasing daylength and rising temperatures. Provision of artificial daylight and increased temperature are used to bring Thoroughbred mares into season in January to make sure that foals are born as close to 1st January as possible – gestation being

Flehmening is a very distinctive gesture, usually carried out by stallions, with the lips being extended forwards rather than drawn back.

approximately 340 days. This is to tie in with the racing calendar, which takes a horse's birthday to be 1st January. (A youngster born soon after the beginning of the year will have a distinct advantage when raced against one born later in the season.)

Normally, the breeding cycle serves to ensure that foals will be produced at a time when there is likely to be plenty of good grazing for them, which in turn will allow them to develop well before the onset of winter.

Flehmening

When a mare is coming into season, she emits pheromones (chemical molecules), which are carried through the air and indicate her reproductive state. A stallion can detect this olfactory cue by a behavioural response, known as flehmening. He curls back his upper lip, effectively sucking air into his mouth, which passes over something called Jacobson's organ. This is located in the roof of the mouth, and connects directly to the olfactory centre in the brain. The stallion may also sniff at a mare's urine in a similar way, as well as her vulva. Flehmening is linked to sexual behaviour and is distinct from smelling, for which the nostrils are used. On occasion, however, particularly when feeding your horse something that it has not encountered before, such as a herbal treat perhaps, it may also curl up its lips in this fashion. Such behaviour may be linked to memory with the horse seeking to identify an unfamiliar scent that it does not immediately recognize.

On stud farms where the stallion is kept separated from the mares, teasing is carried out to see whether a mare is ready to be mated. Otherwise, she could react aggressively, which could injure the stallion.

Where stallions and mares are run in natural herds, there is a period of courtship before mating takes place.

Covering

A mare comes into season and is receptive to a stallion at intervals of approximately three weeks up until the time she falls pregnant. The oestrous period itself lasts five days, and there are behavioural signs that indicate when a mare is ready to mate. She often spends more time associating with other horses, but will not hesitate to rebuff the attentions of a stallion if she is not yet ready. As a result, in domestic situations, mating has to be carefully timed, and often, a so-called 'teaser' stallion is used to determine whether a mare is ready to permit mating, and only then will the chosen stud be brought forward. In the wild, a receptive mare will mate repeatedly, as frequently as once an hour, over the course of the next two or three days.

pregnancy
and the birth

There is usually a slight variance in the length of the pregnancy, which lasts just over 11 months, depending on the gender of the foal, with the gestation period for colts often being a couple of days longer than for fillies. Twin pregnancies are very uncommon in horses, and if conceived, they rarely go to term, simply because the mare is unable to meet the requirements of two foals in her uterus.

During the early stages of her pregnancy, the mare will not increase noticeably in size, since putting on a significant amount of weight at this stage would be a handicap in the wild. Instead, the development of the foal and its body organs occurs during the first eight months or so. The major growth spurt happens in the final three months, when additional food is very important.

Two months after the mare is covered, the gender of the foal is clearly apparent, and the limbs are formed, although it will be another two months before the hooves are obvious. At this stage, the young horse weighs just 1kg (2.2lb). In another four months, its weight will have increased to about

Pregnancy Chart

Month 2 – The body shape of the young foal is already apparent, and it is possible to distinguish its sex at this age.

Month 4 – The hooves are well-defined by this stage, and signs of hair are visible, especially around the muzzle.

Month 6 – By now the young foal is well covered with hair over its entire body, although the mane is not yet developed.

Month 8 – The mane of the foal in the uterus is now beginning to grow, but there is little hair on the tail. The body weight of the foal is increasing.

Month 10 – This is the major growth phase of the foal in the uterus, and its weight increases rapidly from now through to the end of pregnancy.

Month 11 – With birth imminent, the foal's position shifts, so that it can be born head first, with its front legs extended.

19kg (42lb) and it will measure about 71cm (28in) long. Ten months after mating, the foal will be almost fully developed with a full coat and mane and tail evident. The birth weight of a typical foal lies between 38.5 and 48.5kg (85 and 107lb), and its length will be at least 109cm (43in).

Pregnancy

It is usually not possible to tell visually until about eight months after covering occurred that the mare is pregnant because, up to this point, the foal is small in size. This is the stage at which the amount of food offered to the mare will need to be increased to take account of the foal's spurt in growth. Even so, it is important to be aware that covering was successful before this, as it is not a good idea to ride a pregnant mare in the latter half of her pregnancy. Using an ultra-sound scan, pregnancy can be detected as early as 12 days after mating, but generally this technique is used from three weeks on. Blood testing between 45 and 120 days after mating is another alternative.

Four months

Eight months

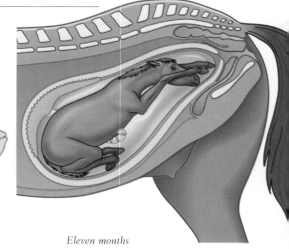

Eleven months

Foals are normally born head first, with the vast majority of mares giving birth lying down rather than standing.

In the wild, it is vital that young horses are up on their feet and able to move as soon as possible after birth.

Birth

Just prior to the start of the birth, the foal's position alters, and the uterine contractions begin. The only external sign that birth is imminent may be a waxy secretion on the mare's mammary glands. The fluid present in the allantoic sac, which enveloped and protected the foal from trauma during pregnancy, will break and pour out of the mare's vulva as the contractions become more intense. The mare becomes increasingly restless, lying down and sweating.

Under normal circumstances, the foal's front feet are the first part of the body to emerge, with the head between them. Once the shoulders have passed through the birth canal, the rest of the body emerges very rapidly. The umbilical attachment, which nourished the foal during pregnancy, is then torn and this separates the young horse from the placenta. The mare will then start to lick her offspring, helping to ensure that its coat dries off. She will also encourage the foal to stand. Within 30 minutes of birth, the foal should begin suckling. The placenta passes out of the mare's body anything up to four hours after the birth. Veterinary assistance must be sought if it does not appear, because it will otherwise cause a serious infection.

development
of the foal

It is vital that the foal starts suckling as soon as possible after birth: any delay could affect its chances of survival. This is because the 'first milk' or colostrum produced by mares contains proteins called immunoglobulins that will give the young foal protection against infections until its own immune system is fully functional. If deprived of this, the foal is likely to be more sickly and its growth may be stunted. The time factor is important, since a foal can only benefit from colostrum for the first 18 hours of its life; after this it cannot absorb the protective proteins. If a foal is unable to feed, then the mare may have to be milked in order to obtain the thick yellowish colostrum, so this can be given directly to her offspring, either from a bottle or through a stomach tube. Subsequently, the foal will feed from its mother around the clock, and the mare will be drinking more water to compensate for the amount of fluid

---

Foal Development

1 Day Old – Foal is standing and suckling without problems.
2 Weeks Old – Already used to the presence of people, the foal is becoming used to a leather foal slip, and being led.
6 Weeks Old – Should be growing well and active. May even start to sample some solid food for the first time.

8 Weeks Old – Foal now eating more concentrates, rather than mother's milk and grazing.
12 Weeks Old – Farrier required to trim the foal's feet for the first time. Becomes used to being loaded into a box with its mother.
26 Weeks Old – Foal will have lost its furry milk hairs and be ready to be weaned from its mother.

---

being used for the production of her milk. Milk output varies depending on the breed, but in the case of Thoroughbreds is typically 4–8 litres (1–2 gal) daily.

When the foal is born, it has faeces in its intestines, and these should be expelled from its body within 12 hours of the birth. The consumption of colostrum helps to trigger this process as it encourages gut activity, but if the so-called meconium has not been produced by this stage, then an enema may be necessary. The meconium differs

A mare will suckle her foal until it is at least six months old in the case of domestic horses, and for as long as 18 months in the wild.

Foals lying asleep, under the protection of their mothers. Even in domestication mares are happiest rearing their foals in groups, rather than on their own.

problems. Results are often better if it is possible to wean foals in batches, rather than individually, and subsequently allowing the youngsters to stay together.

Whinnying

The bond between a mare and her foal is reinforced by whinnying. This is a relatively high-pitched call, audible over some distance, and studies have revealed that mares will respond more frequently to the whinnying of their own offspring than of other foals. Whinnying is also recognized within the structure of herds of feral horses, as a means of identifying group members, with stallions responding to such calls made by foals and their mothers.

ignificantly from normal horse droppings in being black nd harder than usual. When the mare comes into season gain after giving birth, the consistency of her milk hanges during this period, and it can result in the foal uffering from a bout of diarrhoea.

Weaning

rom about six months onwards, the olume of the mare's milk declines, and his marks the start of the weaning rocess. In domesticated animals, weaning s normally carried out between six and eight nonths of age, before the onset of winter. It is mportant that any young colts are removed rom the group before they are a year old, ecause although they will not be sexually nature by this age, they are likely to be howing signs of sexual behaviour, and this an prove disruptive.

Weaning can be a difficult time in a foal's fe and needs to be carried out carefully to ninimize the risk of any long-term

Weaning foals together in groups proves less traumatic than separating one off on its own.

opting for ownership

2

Keeping a horse is an expensive and time-consuming undertaking, and you do not need to own one to be able to ride frequently, either at a riding school or on one that you have borrowed. However, once you decide that you wish to have your own horse, it is important to choose one whose character you like; all horses are individuals and have their own distinct personality. A good bond between horse and rider is most apparent in the field of competition, with close collaboration being vital for success. Of course, fitness is also important, as is the horse's conformation, which can have a significant impact on your chances in a discipline. Equally, understanding the way in which a horse sees the world is necessary to help you get the best performance from it.

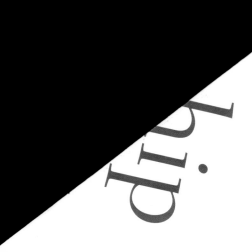

It will...
animal can be ridden...
meet the costs of keeping the horse, ...
matter of feeding costs, either: there will be regular
shoeing, worming, and vaccinations to budget for, as well
as equipment, such as rugs and saddlery.

Having your own horse is a year-round commitment. Bear in mind that, whatever the weather, your horse will require attention every day.

Loans

If you do not want the responsibilities attached to owning a horse or pony, then it is possible to opt for a loan arrangement, which in effect means sharing a mount owned by someone else, in return for a contribution to its maintenance costs. Although this arrangement may seem appealing, it is not without potential friction. For example, problems can arise when one rider wants to go to a show on the same day as the other rider is planning to enter an event elsewhere. Of course, these difficulties can be avoided by having a comprehensive written agreement, which is strongly advisable in any case. Perhaps the most satisfactory type of loan is when a horse is being kept solely for hacking.

Benefits of Buying
- The horse becomes your property.
- You can ride your horse whenever you want.
- You can enter events of your own choice.
- You can breed from your horse if you wish to.

Benefits of Loaning
- You will not have to pay out to buy the horse.
- You can see how you get on, with no long-term commitment.
- You may be able to split costs of caring for the horse.
- You may be able to have a better horse than you could afford to buy.

Where to keep your horse

If, despite the drawbacks, you decide to acquire a horse, the first consideration must be where you will keep it. While you may be in the fortunate position of having your own land, there may still be significant costs involved in making it suitable for a horse. You will need to consider the construction of suitable stabling and safe fencing, not overlooking the cost of supplying water. If you do not have land, you will need to make other arrangements for the care of your horse. For many people, this means finding a suitable livery stables.

If you opt for full livery, the staff at the yard will care for your horse, but this will be expensive compared with a part-livery arrangement.

If you are lucky enough to have learnt to ride in the area and have a riding school that you have been visiting on a regular basis, you will already have met a number of people locally who are involved with horses and you can ask them to recommend a nearby livery yard. It could be that your local riding stable does liveries, which might be ideal. A word of warning – although it may be an appealing way of reducing the cost, think carefully before agreeing to your horse being used for general hacking by those attending the riding school. This could affect its performance with you; it may start to develop unwanted vices or even go lame. Another possibility, when it comes to finding suitable accommodation, is simply to look in the telephone book, and call some of the yards listed. Arrange to visit the premises to see the facilities on offer before reaching a final decision. Clean surroundings, well-maintained buildings, and enthusiastic staff are obviously all good indicators that the yard is suitable.

In terms of costs, there are usually two options available – part and full livery. In the case of a part livery, you have to undertake some of the work yourself, which should be clearly agreed in advance. This is cheaper than a full livery, where the staff will look after all your horse's needs for you. Should you work unpredictable hours or travel regularly, opting for a full livery removes many of the practical worries associated with buying your own horse.

Equipment You Will Need

There is a huge range of equipment available, and this can add considerably to the expense of having a horse. Be selective about what you buy, but do not scrimp on safety. You may be able to buy some items second-hand, but check their condition carefully. Always purchase riding hats new.

- A head collar.
- A suitable saddle that fits your horse properly; safety stirrups are recommended.
- A numnah to fit under the saddle.
- A girth to hold the saddle securely on the horse's body.
- A bridle with a bit and reins.
- Boots and travelling bandages.
- Grooming equipment.
- Rugs and sheets for all-year use.
- A pair of riding boots.
- A riding hat conforming to the latest safety standards.
- A whip and possibly gloves.

what are you looking for?

Once you have decided where you will keep your horse, you can set about choosing one. It is vital to match your size and weight to your mount. It is also important to have a clear idea of which aspects of riding appeal to you as this will have a major influence on the type of animal you require.

Size

Deciding what size of horse to buy is particularly difficult with children, as they grow rapidly and soon become too big to ride a pony. You are then faced with deciding what to do with an animal that has been outgrown by its rider, but is a

Your choice of mount will be influenced by the size of the rider and what they want to do with the horse. Sadly, ponies can soon be outgrown.

treasured friend. It is not fair to allow a child to continue riding an outgrown pony, because this may well cause lasting injury to the animal. To avoid having to pay for the upkeep of both the old pony and the new horse, you may want to defer any purchase until your child is older.

When choosing a pony for a child, those under 12.2hh will be suitable for children under 12 years old, ponies with a height between 12.2 and 13.2hh are recommended for riders aged between 12 and 14, while those up to a hand taller will suffice for most young riders over the course of the next two years. It is always better to obtain a slightly larger pony than you require; obviously, this is particularly recommended in the case of a child who is above average size.

Although the height of the horse is important when assessing its suitability for an adult, build is also a factor, with cobs, for example, being relatively strong for their size. The size of the mount is affected by the weight as well as the height of an adult, particularly as the weight of adults of the same size can vary quite widely. In general terms, a height from 15.2hh upwards is suitable for most women, whereas for men, a horse above 16hh is likely to be required.

Breed

Those with a particular interest in breeding are most likely to seek out pure-bred mares. Many of the horses offered for normal riding purposes are not of pure-bred stock, but are the result of a mating between a pure-bred stallion and a cross-bred mare. This type of mixed breeding is preferred, since the stallion has a greater impact on the progeny under these circumstances, influencing aspects such as stamina and size. By changing the breed of stallion, a cross-bred mare can be used to produce different types of

foals. Larger breeds, such as Hanoverians, will inevitably result in stockier offspring than, for example, Thoroughbreds, which are bred for their pace.

The horse's immediate ancestry can also affect its relative hardiness and, therefore, requirements for winter care. Those originating from warmer parts of the world, such as stock of Arab descent, are less hardy than breeds that evolved in more temperate climates – cross-bred ponies, for example. In any case, ponies are generally hardier than horses. Pure pony breeds are usually very well-suited to living outside for most of the year, and so rarely need stabling. This applies particularly to those, such as Shetlands or Welsh Mountain stock, that have adapted to survive in fairly harsh natural conditions.

Gender

Many people prefer mares, partly because if they are very successful in a discipline or have to be retired prematurely, there is the possibility of breeding from them. Some owners also consider mares are more amenable than

Cob is a description that is applied to a general type of horse, as well as to specific breeds, such as the Welsh cob. Cobs are steady and dependable by nature.

geldings. They may undergo slight shifts in temperament when they come into season, although this is only likely to be a problem during the spring and summer.

Buying a stallion is not a practical proposition for most people. They are usually kept only for stud purposes. A gelding is a male horse that has been neutered. Neutering makes the horse much more manageable, although, of course, there is no possibility of breeding with a gelding.

Age

The age of the horse will affect its price and its abilities. An unproven youngster is likely to be significantly cheaper than a horse that has won competitions. If you are considering buying a horse that is claimed to be a prize winner, it is worth checking its performance in show reports in equine magazines or with the relevant organization concerned, such as your national show jumping association. There can be advantages to buying a foal, but this is a serious undertaking as it will need to be taught everything from scratch (see pp.68–69 and 150–151).

The best type of horse for a novice is described as a schoolmaster. This is a horse of around eight years old, with experience in the discipline that interests you. A schoolmaster can be especially valuable if you are looking for a horse that jumps well. This is a skill that needs refining, so choosing a horse that is used to jumping should give you confidence as well.

A schoolmaster is often to be recommended when you are seeking your first horse.

what do you want to do?

One of the major factors influencing your choice of horse will be if and how you intend to compete. Bear this in mind at the outset, as some horses are more suitable for certain tasks than others. Lipizzaner horses, for example, have a particular talent for dressage, whereas in showing classes, conformation of the horse is especially significant. Select carefully as any basic deficiencies will be impossible to correct.

Showing

Showing is a popular pastime, with judges concentrating on the appearance or 'type' of the entrants in each class, those corresponding most closely to the ideal being judged the winners. Horses or ponies are suitable for showing classes, with good behaviour and conformation being two of the most important characteristics. If you are keen on showing, it is best to opt for a particular breed or type, which can then be entered in classes aimed specifically for it.

Show jumping

Show jumping is very popular, with classes at various levels, from local shows to national competitions. At the top levels, it requires excellent training and a high degree of skill, as well as corresponding fitness.

Successful show jumping entails competing against the clock, without incurring penalties.

Dressage

Dressage is less flamboyant, but exceptional understanding is required between horse and rider to be successful at this discipline, and training is a slow process. It takes at least four years of intensive training for a horse to approach Olympic standard, for example.

Eventing

Dressage and show jumping are two components that feature as part of eventing competitions. The third component is the cross-country section, in which horses jump a course that uses the natural terrain of the countryside. Steeplechasing and roadwork may also be included. Eventing, therefore, represents probably the most demanding challenge for horse and rider alike.

Western riding began and remains very popular in North America. It has its own design of tack and riders often wear the traditional stetson.

Endurance

Endurance riding is not for the faint-hearted, being probably the ultimate test of both the horse and rider's fitness, with courses being up to 161km (100 miles) long. It has a very strong following in North America.

Sidesaddle

It used to be considered inappropriate for women to ride astride a horse, and so they rode in this fashion, using a

TOP LEFT: Dressage competitions are based on the ability of horse and rider to work together, carrying out a precise series of movements on which they are judged.

LEFT: Regular veterinary and farriery checks are carried out at stages when horses are participating in endurance races, to safeguard their welfare. Endurance horses may have log books, setting out their past history.

BELOW: Gymkhanas test the abilities and agility of young riders, and can encourage them to participate in other disciplines in due course, once they have mastered the basics of riding.

special saddle devised over 700 years ago. Riding sidesaddle is still popular today, with the fitting of the saddle being critical to prevent any spinal injury to the horse.

Western riding

There are a number of different styles of western riding, based on the western saddle (see p.123). The saddle's large and comfortable design derives from that of the Spanish saddles introduced to North America with horses in the 1500s, and its most noticeable feature is the raised pommel.

Riding Clubs

When they are starting to ride, many young people join the Pony Club. Established in the UK in 1929, this has grown into an international organization with branches in many countries, including the USA and Canada, as well as Australia and New Zealand. One of the most popular Pony Club activities is the gymkhana (derived from the Hindustani *gend-khana* – sports ground). A gymkhana offers a wide range of competitions that often involve racing against the clock. Ponies are better suited to this type of activity than horses, because they are more agile, even when they have only a moderate level of fitness.

finding
a horse

Once you have decided on the type of horse you are seeking and you have set yourself a realistic budget, you can begin looking. Start by reading specialist equestrian magazines, many of which carry advertisements offering horses for sale. This will give you an idea of the horses on offer and, perhaps more importantly, an indication of their price. Always be particularly suspicious of horses that appear to be priced cheaply – they could have either chronic health or behavioural problems, or both. Never rush into a purchase on these grounds, as it is likely to be a costly undertaking.

Why is the horse being sold?

Try to establish whether the person offering the horse has a genuine reason for wanting to sell it, as this will suggest that it is not being sold because of some unpleasant vice. It might be a child's pony that has been outgrown, for example, or perhaps a change in job means the current owner no longer has time to spend with the horse. It helps if someone in your locality has an animal they want to sell, since you may be able to find out about its background more easily. If it has been a regular participant at shows or other events, you may even have friends who recollect seeing it in action.

Dear Equine Casebook

I recently visited an auction, where there were quite a few nice-looking horses being sold very cheaply. Is this a good way to buy a horse?
regards Jeremy Barton

If you are looking for your first horse, it is not wise to buy it at an auction. You really do need to have considerable experience before making a safe purchase at such sales. Even with experience, it is still possible to make a bad choice, partly because it is difficult to check up on the horse's background, whether it has chronic health problems or tendon injuries, for example. At auctions, horses are sold basically as seen, with no reliable safeguards.

Veterinary Inspection

When you think you have found your ideal horse, under normal circumstances and prior to completing the purchase, you should ask the vendor if they have any objection to a veterinary inspection being carried out. This is a routine practice, so if they refuse, you should abandon your interest in that particular horse. Vetting entails the horse being given a standard examination by your vet, with any problems being noted in the resulting report. This process should detect any signs of lameness, past injuries, or underlying illness, such as respiratory disease, which could affect a horse's performance and may not be immediately obvious, particularly to a novice. It is clearly not possible for a vet to detect an illness that may not be showing obvious symptoms at the time of inspection, but it is certainly worth paying for vetting to be carried out. Otherwise, you could end up later not just with large veterinary bills, but also with an unsuitable horse.

One of the first things that needs to be checked is the horse's age. This can be assessed by an examination of its teeth (see p.38). It is also worth noting how readily the horse co-operates in letting the vet inspect its mouth.

Dealers

When you contact a vendor in response to an advertisement, try to find out as much as possible about the horse. Unfortunately, it is not unknown for some unscrupulous dealers to advertise as private individuals. There is an easy way to find out whether this is the case. When you first get in contact, say you are interested in the horse being advertised. If the seller has to ask you which one, then you know they have more than one available and thus could be a dealer. Since this fact has not been made obvious at the outset, proceed with great caution.

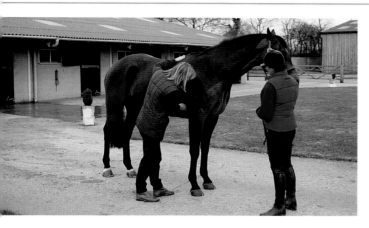

Using a stethoscope enables the vet to listen not just to the horse's heart, to detect any abnormalities there, but also to the lungs. Any damage to these will seriously compromise its performance.

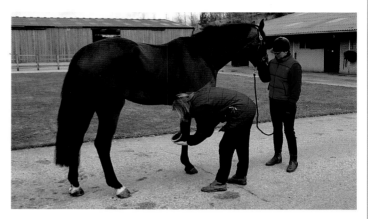

Soundness is obviously vital, and a close inspection of the lower limbs and feet forms a very important part of a veterinary inspection. It will be possible to detect signs of diseases such as laminitis (see p.40) as a result.

The way in which a horse moves can also help to reveal problems associated with its gait, and by trotting it vigorously your vet will then be able to listen to the airways again, comparing the results with those taken when the horse was at rest.

Flexion of the joints is a routine part of an inspection, but if there is a particular joint worry, then an X-ray examination may be needed, using portable equipment, to ascertain the full extent of the problem.

There are, however, reputable professional dealers who buy and sell horses on a regular basis. Placing your trust in someone like this is not necessarily a bad idea, because they depend on satisfied customers to stay in business and will have built up a network of reliable contacts. If you do decide to buy through a dealer, for added insurance, seek out someone who has been established for a long time and has built up a reputation, and make sure that you prepare a detailed list of all your requirements before they start to look for an animal for you. When they do find you a horse, try it out carefully, and do not feel that you have to buy.

Insurance

You will need to think about insuring your horse after you have acquired it, and it is useful to have taken the time to investigate the various options beforehand. You can then take out the policy at soon as you have completed the purchase. Third-party insurance, to protect you in the event of your horse causing an accident, is essential for all horse owners. As far as the horse's health is concerned, bear in mind that in strange surroundings, with a new rider, this is the time when the horse is most likely to fall ill or injure itself (see p.74).

conformation

Being able to assess a horse's conformation, basically its proportions, is very important when it comes to deciding on its suitability for particular tasks and can also indicate likely problems, such as a tendency to stumble. You may blame the horse because it proves to be a clumsy jumper, but this could be more a fault of its conformation, which causes it to drag its feet, than any reflection of its character. The different breeds each have a distinctive build and the shape of a horse's body can also change with age. Old horses are often described as hollow-backed, thanks to the dip that develops in this part of the body as they age.

Head

The shape of a horse's head is popularly supposed to provide an insight into its temperament. Those with small eyes in comparison with their head are reputedly ill-natured, while a horse that puts its ears back when approached is thought to be bad-tempered and difficult to deal with. Horses with quite broad heads are considered to have a better disposition than those with a more elegant shape.

Neck

The size and shape of the neck may have a distinct impact on the ease with which a horse can be ridden. Concavity along the top of the neckline, known as 'ewe' neck, is considered a weakness. Here, the underside of the neck is more heavily muscled and protrudes, which can make riding difficult in extreme cases, simply because the bridle will not fit well and the saddle may tend to slip forwards.

The Perfectly Proportioned Horse

There is no such thing as a standard conformation in the case of horses, because the shape of their bodies – or conformation – is directly influenced by the purpose for which they are bred. The relative proportions of the body are significant, with a heavy, thick-set frame revealing a horse bred for power and strength.

A horse bred for speed has a lighter body and longer legs. It is the way in which the proportions come together that influences the conformation. The proportions of the body in various respects are of common length, in cases of good conformation, as shown in the accompanying diagram (middle right).

Good conformation enables the horse to carry out its work effectively.

LEFT: The conformation of the head varies between individuals. Some have a straight head, while those of Arab descent have a noticeably dished profile.

Chest and front legs

The chest should be broad and deep, to provide good lung capacity. If it is very narrow, then the horse may have to wear a breast plate, to prevent the saddle from slipping. In extreme cases, the inner faces of the front legs will be very close together, which will affect the horse's movement. The conformation of the front legs is very important. Ideally, there should be a straight line extending down from the shoulder passing through the centre of the knee and both the fetlock and foot. Recognized deviations include pigeon-toes, caused by the fetlocks being turned in and putting strain on these joints.

Hindlimbs

Poor conformation is more common in the hindlimbs, but here the effects are less serious. Ideally, the end of the buttock muscle should form part of a straight line that extends down through the centre of the hock, the fetlock and foot, when the horse is viewed from behind. The conformation of the hock joint is especially important,

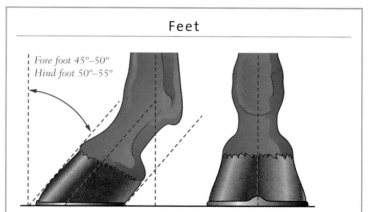

Feet

Fore foot 45°–50°
Hind foot 50°–55°

The conformation of the feet must not be overlooked, with the ideal being shown above. It is particularly important that the feet point forwards in their pairs, and show no signs of deviation. If they turn out, this is likely to cause brushing, which is when the feet come into contact with each other as the horse moves. Feet that turn inwards from the midline can cause injury to the fetlock. The relationship between the hoof and pastern is especially significant as the horse moves. Long toes increase the likelihood of navicular disease.

because it is responsible for absorbing the concussive effect arising from movement. Horses with markedly angular hocks are at greater risk of suffering from a sprain of the plantar ligament, which runs down the back of the joint. Such an injury is known as a curb.

The green lines are the same length, indicating the best relationship between seat bone, stifle, and point of hip.

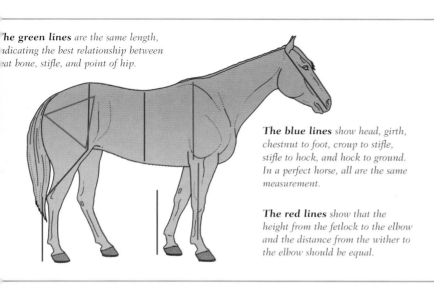

The blue lines show head, girth, chestnut to foot, croup to stifle, stifle to hock, and hock to ground. In a perfect horse, all are the same measurement.

The red lines show that the height from the fetlock to the elbow and the distance from the wither to the elbow should be equal.

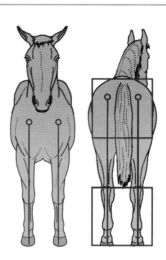

The purple lines reveal the perfect relationship between the parts of a horse from the back and the front. On the left, the point of shoulder, knee, fetlock, and hoof should all be aligned. On the right, the seat bone lines up with the point of hock and the centre of the fetlock and hoof. The measurement of each side of the two squares indicated should be exactly the same as that of the length of the head.

considering **character**

When choosing a horse that is suitable for the work you want it to undertake, you should also take into consideration its temperament and breeding. Do not be guided simply by liking the appearance of a horse. Just because it has a good conformation, there are no guarantees that you will bond well together. Breeding, background and health all have an effect on the temperament of a horse.

Breeding

There are distinctive differences in temperament, reflected by the breed background of an individual. Heavy horses are generally very phlegmatic characters, with patient natures, as are cobs. On the other hand, Arabs and Thoroughbreds tend to be highly strung, as befits their athletic natures. It can be very difficult to find suitable homes for racehorses after retirement simply because their highly strung temperaments require specialist management.

Experiences

Aside from breeding, much also depends on the horse's previous experiences, such as the way in which it has been treated and

Although many horses will often become excited when first turned out, a horse that rears repeatedly in this way in a field is likely to prove very difficult to control, and will not be a good choice.

Vices and Behavioural Disorders

Spend time looking at the horse that you are thinking of acquiring, before even approaching it. You should then be able to gain some insight into its character, whether it is stabled or out in a field. Unfortunately, however, it can be quite difficult to detect certain vices on the basis of just a brief encounter of this type. You are less likely to be able to detect signs of crib-sucking, for example, when the horse is out in a field, compared with when it is stabled. If you note anything that concerns you, ask the vendor and draw it to the attention of the vet who is carrying out an inspection for you. While advertisements may give some reassurance regarding a horse's temperament, these are not warranties and should not be relied upon.

Stable vices (see pp.156–159) will not necessarily be obvious when you are simply viewing a horse.

Always seek the opportunity to ride the horse yourself. You need to be sure that a horse will be biddable, being willing to follow your instructions, such as riding across a stream if required.

rained. Very few horses are actually born with a nasty temperament, but they will acquire unpleasant traits from ad handling. This is why it is so important to check out he background of a horse prior to purchase, so you can be ure, as far as possible, that it has no bad vices (the box on .64 gives some tips on how to spot these).

If you are used to a riding school mount, be prepared for difference when assessing the temperament of a horse hat has been kept privately. Riding school horses can ecome rather bored with following the same routine, and his often leads to them seeming very placid. However, the ame horse, given a change of scenery, will often prove to e much more lively.

Health

he physical condition of a horse can have an effect on its emperament. One that is in a poor state, perhaps suffering om a heavy burden of parasites, is likely to be far less vely than if it was in good health. Similarly, a horse that as been stabled, with little opportunity for exercise, may ecome very excitable when allowed out and ridden. Bear his in mind if you are thinking of buying a horse whose resent owner is having to sell through lack of time.

Dear Equine Casebook

I fell in love with a horse that seemed quiet and affectionate, but now I have got him home, he tries to bite me when I tack him up.
best wishes Lucy Walker

Do not despair. Your horse is still adjusting to a new home. With a little time and patience, it is possible to win the trust of even the most nervous individual, and in so doing, increase its capabilities. It is worth considering whether he is in pain – not necessarily from something that is physically wrong, but simply because of ill-fitting tack, such as a saddle or bridle. Do not assume that the tack he came with fits properly. Particularly suspect this type of problem if your horse appears to be co-operative in other ways. If you are in any doubt about his health, get him checked by a vet, and it is worth calling in your saddler to ensure that his tack is not the problem.

going through
the paces

If you find a horse that seems suitable, it is advisable to see it go through its regular routine, as this should highlight potential problems, such as whether it is reluctant to be caught in a field or is difficult to persuade into a horsebox. A horse that is well-schooled is likely to be a more reliable prospect than a badly-trained animal, especially for the novice owner. It is also very useful to see the tack in which the horse is usually ridden, as this may reveal much about possible problems associated with riding it. A standing martingale, for example, suggests that the horse may naturally attempt to keep its head too high.

The bridle and the bit, which fits into the horse's mouth, assist the rider in controlling the horse's movements. It is important to choose the right combination for an individual horse.

Trying Out the Horse

It is vital to ride any horse you are thinking of buying, both in the school and out on a hack, if possible, as this will tell you a lot about it and whether you like the way it feels. Do not be surprised if it seems less responsive to you than it is with its regular rider; this need not be a cause for concern. But there are occasions when horses display a particular dislike for people of a certain gender, usually men, and the reason for this reaction probably resides in repeated mistreatment in the past, which it has not forgotten. This form of fear is very difficult to counter in many cases, especially as it can resurface when, for example, the farrier visits or a judge approaches in the show ring.

At walk

Watch the horse as it walks, from both front and back. Its movement should be smooth, with the joints being flexed as appropriate, to create an even gait. Should the horse be reluctant to flex its legs properly, it will tend to stumble, as well as covering only a relatively short distance at each stride. Pay particular attention to the feet because, even if the horse is not lame, conformation faults can be revealed through their action. In some cases, such faults can also be indicated by the wear on the shoes. If it is uneven, this may be due to a peculiarity in the gait. If there is heavy wear on the outer edge, for example, then the horse may have an undesirable paddling gait, with the toe tending to move inwards, towards the midline and then outwards again, rather than progressing directly forwards. The reverse of this problem, described as 'dishing' or 'winging', is caused by the toe being directed outwards, and the wear in this case is on the inner side of the shoe.

Carry Out a Thorough Examination

When you find a horse that you like, do not be afraid to ask the vendor to demonstate as many of its purported abilities as you want to see. It is vital that you are happy with a horse's behaviour when it is being led, as well as its performance when it is being ridden. Watch, too, as it is being tacked up, to see whether there is any sign of resistance at any stage. For example, check if it seems to be reluctant to pick its feet up, if it pulls faces when it is being groomed, if it is unhappy about approaching a mounting block, or if it moves around restlessly once mounted. All these can be indicators of underlying problems, although they can also be caused by inexperience and so, with time and patience, may not be insurmountable.

When assessing a horse's soundness, you should see it being put through its paces, when any weakness is likely to show up. A smooth rhythm is obviously essential throughout the exercise.

As the horse passes you, you will have the benefit of seeing it trotting from different angles. If you are concerned about its gait, ask for the horse to be trotted back past you in the other direction.

You may be able to pick up other indicators regarding its temperament as well. A nervous individual may be reluctant to continue trotting once it is expected to move out from the confines of the yard.

Ask any questions you need to. Depending on the circumstances, some of the horse's tack may be for sale, so make suitable enquiries and inspections to ascertain condition and fit.

Watching the horse being ridden is essential, and riding it yourself is also to be recommended, to help you to pick up any behavioural quirks. Remember the horse may not be used to being ridden by a stranger.

Watch out for just how biddable a horse is. It should be quite easy to persuade it to progress from a trot to a canter. You will be able to feel any problems with the gait when you ride the horse yourself.

t trot

ou are more likely to spot signs of lameness when the orse is being trotted. This is because it will be harder for he horse to conceal the sensitivity of the foot, or the roblem affecting its leg, at a faster speed. Your vet will so be able to assess the overall level of fitness, having hecked the horse over when it was at rest, by examining it gain after a period of exercise.

At canter

Encouraging the horse to canter in a circle will clearly show how well it lifts its legs, and this movement has the added advantage of determining the degree of suppleness in the horse's back. Persuading it to move in an ever tighter circle, both clockwise and anti-clockwise, serves to ensure that it can cross its hind legs without difficulty. Watch again for any sign of unsoundness.

buying
a foal

Although there can be advantages to buying a foal, not the least of which is that it should not have developed serious vices at a young age, there are drawbacks as well, particularly if you have little experience. You will need to train the young horse to be ridden and then teach it the discipline you are interested in. All this will take a great deal of time, although if you are fortunate enough to have experienced advice to guide you, it can be immensely rewarding.

You will also have to be patient, as young horses may not be broken until they are four years old. In addition, there are no guarantees about the ability of the horse, even if it is bred from a good bloodline. This is made abundantly clear by the racing industry, where promising youngsters frequently fail to make the grade. Foals are naturally quite playful and high-spirited, so it is important that the young horse is used to walking on a headcollar (see p.131), otherwise it will be very difficult to handle. You will obviously not be able to determine its suitability for riding at this stage, but it is important to pay particular attention to its conformation for this reason.

Settling it in

The first difficulty you are likely to face on bringing your foal home is being able to settle it down in the absence of its mother. Horses tend not to thrive when they are kept on their own, and this certainly applies to youngsters. It may be advantageous to obtain a much older

To prevent weaning difficulties, a foal must not only be kept out of sight but also out of sound of its mother when they are first separated.

Reasons Not to Buy a Foal

Buying a foal is a serious, long-term commitment, and you should be prepared to consider all the disadvantages beforehand. Long before you can ride your youngster, the costs will continue to mount up in terms of food and bedding, farriery, and routine health care, with colts having to be gelded as yearlings. The youngster's feet will need to be checked and trimmed back as necessary, roughly every six weeks on average, and certainly in the early days it will be important to keep a check on the weight of the foal by weighing it regularly. As the young horse develops, there is always the risk that it will not meet your requirements, and deficiencies in its conformation may become apparent. Bear in mind that foals do not grow evenly, but in spurts, so that it can be quite difficult to spot the true potential of an individual, especially if you do not have much experience of judging young horses.

is very important that a foal learns to be led from an early age, partly because a ...ung horse is relatively easy to manage at this stage, thanks to its size.

...nimal on loan as a companion, but you need to agree in ...riting what you are liable for should the horse fall ill in ...our care. Never be tempted to keep a donkey as a ...ompanion, because they carry lungworms and there is the ...isk that your horse will become infested.

If you buy a foal that has just been weaned, find out the ...iet it has been receiving and stick to this as closely as ...ossible to minimize the risk of any digestive upset. You ...ill need to be prepared to keep the foal boxed for at least ... fortnight, so you can keep a check on its wellbeing. ...hen, assuming the weather is good, you can allow it out ...nto a secure paddock during the day, bringing it back in ...gain at night. At first it may be rather nervous, which is ...here an older companion can be of assistance. During the ...ummer, it should then be possible to allow the foal to stay ...ut permanently. It may be able to remain in its field over ...he following winter, provided that it has a suitable shelter.

You must be prepared to lead the foal every day using a ...alter, so that you continue to be able to control it as it ...natures into a larger adult.

Making Early Progress

Once your foal is two or three years old, it may benefit from some light work to get it used to being handled and to build up its muscles. Do not overdo this activity, however, as it is easy to make a youngster stale.

Lungeing a youngster will teach obedience to the aids (see p.139) and begins work towards an acceptance of the saddle and bridle, as well as being ridden, in due course. The horse will also establish a bond with you through this regular exercise.

You may find that when being lunged, your horse will at first try to pull away or may slow down rather than progressing at the pace you want. Gentle encouragement from a lungeing whip is sometimes required.

You will be able to assess your horse's gait by lungeing it regularly. Do not be afraid to use your voice as a way to communicate with your horse at this stage, as this is a useful training tool that you will use when riding.

Exercise is important to keep a young horse not just physically fit, but also mentally alert. Try to vary the routine to an extent so that your horse does not become bored. A bored horse is more likely to play up.

getting your
horse home

It is very important that your horse will travel without difficulty in a box or trailer, because not only do you have to have it brought home, but there will inevitably be other times when it needs to be moved, not least to events. The vendor may be prepared to deliver the horse to you or, for an appropriate fee based on the distance, you may be able to arrange for someone with a lorry to pick it up for you.

Travelling equipment

You will need to buy or borrow the necessary equipment to ensure that your horse travels safely. Leg protectors are vital to protect against possible injury to the limbs, should the horse slip on its journey. Either use the leg guards made specifically for the purpose or wrap travelling bandages around the lower part of the legs, extending from beneath the knees and hocks down to the coronet. Knee and hock boots are also to be recommended, while extra

Travelling

Even if you do not intend to compete with your horse regularly, it is vital that it is trained to be easily transported. Otherwise, it can not only be inconvenient and embarrassing, but also dangerous.

It is important that a horse is properly equipped for travelling so as to minimize the risk of injury. Always allow yourself adequate time to get your horse kitted out with boots and other equipment before it is due to be moved.

Dear Equine Casebook

I recently bought a young horse and it took us five hours to get it into the horsebox to bring it home. I am now worried that the next time I need to take it anywhere I will have the same problem, which could be embarrassing, particularly at a showground.
yours sincerely Margaret Short

A young horse that is unfamiliar with a box will be difficult to transport. This is why it is important to train youngsters to load as a matter of course, before you need to move them anywhere. In this way, they can get used to the procedure. Don't worry. With a little patience, you can overcome most loading problems. Horses can often be reluctant to enter such a confined space at first, so use plenty of words of encouragement and consider feeding a tidbit. Park the box in a safe location and then lead the horse up the ramp, using a bridle to give a greater degree of control if it appears to be reluctant. Always try to encourage it to enter the box voluntarily rather than trying to force it. Should the horse walk a short distance up the ramp and then stop, you may be able to persuade it to advance by lifting each foreleg in turn, placing these progressively further up the ramp. Alternatively, keep walking the horse up and down the ramp so that ultimately, it becomes possible to lead it into the box itself. Provide a haynet inside, and leave the horse tied up there for short periods. When used around the hindquarters, lungeing reins can sometimes be successful in persuading the horse to enter.

A side-opening horsebox is just one variation on horse transport. The horse should be happy to follow you up the ramp without rushing. This one looks somewhat tense about entering. It could do with some time and practice.

As you reach the ramp top, steady the horse to enter the box. Be careful that it does not try to back off again. Ideally, there should be longer side gates here, as a panicking horse might get its legs caught between these and the ramp.

protection in the form of coronet boots may be advisable for longer journeys. A tail bandage is also important, particularly when a horse is being moved in a trailer, since it will tend to lean back against the tailgate, and an uprotected tail will get rubbed and damaged as a result.

Do not forget to put on a travelling rug to ensure that your horse does not get too cold, or that if it gets hot, it does not chill on cooling down.

Comfort

Providing a haynet often encourages a horse to settle down. If the journey is likely to last for more than a few hours, be prepared to stop and allow it an opportunity to drink. Since horses are unable to vomit, because of the structure of their palate, and appear to be immune to travel sickness, there is no need to worry that horses will

be taken ill, but they often get hot in the confines of the box, and so ventilation is very important. Finally, remember to tie the horse up once it is securely confined.

American trailers are designed so that the box is very low to the ground and there is no ramp. Horses are taught to step up into the box and seem happy to do so.

settling in
to a new home

When moving a horse to new stables, be sure that everything is prepared well in advance, before your arrival, so that your horse can be transferred to its new quarters at once. Here a straw bed is being made ready.

Prepare your new horse's stable before you set out to bring it home. Then, when you arrive, you can simply unload it and lead it directly into its new quarters. Bear in mind that the change in environment will be a very stressful period for the horse and it should be allowed to settle down for a day or so in its new surroundings. This is a good time to organize such things as a visit from the farrier and the equine dentist, and getting vaccinations done.

Once your horse has made itself at home, you can start working together to build up a bond. Spend time each day just observing it, whether it is in a stable or out at grass, so you can become familiar with its behaviour. This will have the advantage of alerting you at an early stage if it falls ill or starts to display signs of lameness.

Unloading your Horse

Although it can be difficult to persuade a horse to enter a horsebox up a ramp, it is equally important that a horse will walk safely out of a box down the ramp when it arrives at its destination. Some may instead rear up or rush out quickly from the confinement of the box. If possible, have a few practices with your horse before you finally collect it to bring it back. Bear in mind, however, that after the unfamiliar sensations of the journey, your horse is likely to be rather stressed and may not behave as well as during its previous training sessions.

Getting your priorities right

Unless you were handed the vaccination certificates by the horse's previous owner, there is no guarantee that the important immunizations against tetanus and influenza are up-to-date. These should be arranged as a priority, because such illnesses are serious. Should a horse become ill, it may not recover, and if it does its performance may be compromised in any case. If you have not taken out an insurance policy on your horse prior to bringing it home, now is the time to do so.

Both you and your horse will need to get used to the stable routine at a new yard. Horses invariably take an interest in what is going on around them, watching what is happening even though they may not be involved.

Tetanus

Horses are very susceptible to the effects of the toxin produced by the bacterium known as *Clostridium tetani*. The clostridial bacteria responsible are found in soil, and can be introduced to the body through wounds, particularly deep puncture wounds, where they thrive, releasing a deadly nerve toxin. Stiffness of the muscles involved in

Dear Equine Casebook

What is equine influenza and how important is it that I protect my horse against it? Friends say that it's not always necessary to inject, but I want to be sure that I do the right thing for my new horse.
kind regards John Peterson

There are two main strains of equine influenza, and the illness is passed on very rapidly between unvaccinated individuals, being spread by sneezing and by contact with nasal discharges. The incubation period is very short, typically between one and three days, and so an epidemic can develop very quickly in a stables. In mild cases, horses take two or three weeks to recover, but often the period is much longer and can extend over six months, during which time there is always the risk of complications, such as secondary bacterial infections leading to pneumonia. Although equine 'flu is usually not fatal, it can cause lasting damage to the respiratory system.

All horses need to be protected against equine influenza by vaccination, since there is no effective treatment for this viral disease, and although this will not offer complete protection, if your horse contracts the virus the resulting illness should be shorter and less severe. Two doses need to be given initially, separated by a gap of about six weeks, with a third dose being required after six months. Annual boosters to maintain immunity are then necessary, although if there is an outbreak in the area, an earlier booster may be advised by your vet. The immunization programme in foals can begin as soon as they are three months old.

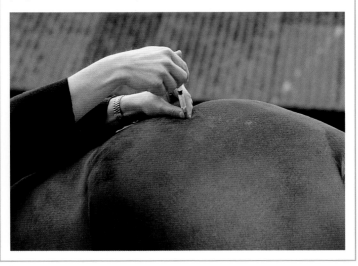

chewing is typical, which is why the disease is also known as lockjaw. Other symptoms include the appearance of the so-called third eyelid at the corner of each eye, muscular spasms of the neck and back, and a stiff, extended tail.

Two vaccines, given six weeks apart, followed by an annual booster will safeguard your horse against the effects of tetanus, which are frequently fatal. Once symptoms develop, treatment is difficult and, even if the horse survives, it will almost certainly be vulnerable to tetanus in the future if it is not vaccinated.

Tetanus is especially common in some areas of the world, and vaccination of pregnant mares in the last six weeks of pregnancy is one means of providing some protection for their foals after birth.

Insurance

Your insurance policy needs to cover your horse – against illness, loss and theft – and yourself. First, compare as many different policies as possible to be sure that you select the one most suitable for your circumstances. Note particularly the amount of veterinary cover that is provided as surgery on horses, for colic for example, can prove to be very expensive. If you buy a young horse that starts to win prizes and so increases in value, do not forget to tell the insurance company and increase the premiums accordingly, as payments are otherwise likely to be scaled down in the event of a claim.

Many policies also provide ancillary protection against the theft of tack or your trailer. This is well worth considering. All horse owners must have cover for public liability, which you will need in the event of an accident occurring between you and your horse and a third party. Personal accident insurance is advisable – you will be thankful for it if you are injured in a fall from your horse.

The other risks that you should insure against are theft and straying. The latter can happen, especially if your horse is kept at grass. Although such cover cannot replace your horse, it does mean that you can acquire another, which might not otherwise be a financial possibility.

Identification

Even if your horse is fully insured, you obviously do not want to go through the upsetting experience of having it stolen. There are a number of steps you can take to safeguard it from becoming the target of thieves. The most notable of these is to get a freeze brand, which is very obvious and cannot be easily obscured (see box, right).

Most horses have unique markings on their coats, which can also be used for identification purposes, particularly if there is a dispute over ownership. These include facial markings, such as white blazes or stars, and leg markings, such as socks or white stripes on the feet. Other distinctive features are whorls of hair on various parts of the body and any nicks or scars. These may have been noted down during your horse's vetting (see pp.60–61), but it is a good idea also to photograph or video your horse to show these features, as well as recording them clearly on a chart.

Other methods of identification, such as hoof branding can be helpful, but they are not permanent, with hoof branding typically lasting just six months. Also, such methods may not be sufficiently visible to act as a deterrent for a thief. Microchipping is not visible, but does enable the owner of a stolen horse to be traced. This technique entails the injection of a small microchip in the neck. The microchip has a unique code, logged on a central database at the time of the implant. It can be read by a special scanner passed over it. This hiddens means of identification can be vital if your horse is recovered.

Freeze-branding

The technique, which is painless, entails freezing a code on a pigmented area of the coat (the branding iron is chilled to minus 293°C in liquid nitrogen). This kills the pigment cells, so that the hair turns white, highlighting the code, which will remain permanently visible for the rest of the horse's life.

Usually the area just behind the shoulder is used for branding, although the shoulder itself is sometimes branded. It is important that your horse stands still during this process so a clear impression can be created.

Freeze-branding results in a permanent mark, which is recorded in a central database. This then acts as a discouragement to thieves who may be hoping to steal your horse to sell it.

introducing
horses to each other

After a move, your horse is likely to be stabled alongside other horses that it has not met before, and it may be turned out in the field with some of them. Although horses are sociable by nature, a group will have established hierarchies; introducing a newcomer can cause a breakdown of these and may lead to displays of aggression. By being careful about how you make introductions, however, it is possible to minimize the risk of conflict. It helps if your new horse has an opportunity to see and meet some of the others individually, without any group pressure, away from the stables, on a hack for example.

When turning a horse out in a field for the first time, it is not a good idea simply to put it in with the others. Instead, start by placing the new arrival with a horse that is known to be placid. Put these two in a paddock that adjoins the one with the main group, so that all the horses can see and make contact with each other over the fence. When the two horses are settled, you can begin to move

Horses display strong herd instincts and individuals in a group can form close bonds.

Dear Equine Casebook

I have a lovely horse that I have owned for about ten years. He is nearing retirement so I recently bought a youngster to ride. My old horse has always been good natured and gentle, but he seems to have taken against the new one and drives her away everytime I go into the field to catch her. He has also become difficult at mealtimes, lunging and biting at my youngster. Can you help?
worried owner Annabel Andrews

It is possible for a horse to become jealous of a new companion, and this problem is often created when, as you describe, an owner acquires a second horse to be kept at grass with their established mount. Although the initial introduction may be fine, friction is generated by the fact that, in an attempt to settle the newcomer and to win its confidence, the owner spends more time with this horse, excluding the first horse. This horse then reacts aggressively to what is perceived as a challenge to its relationship with its owner. You can prevent this problem arising very easily, simply by giving more attention to the first horse, so that the new arrival accepts a subservient role from the outset. You may be able to correct a conflict of this type by acknowledging the dominant individual first.

Pair-bonding

If two horses have a strong bond, there can be difficulties when one is removed for a while then reintroduced. There is unlikely to be any problem after a short separation, but a separation over several weeks or more may be more problematic. The risk will be reduced if the horses are in a herd rather than a pair, as there is less potential for constant bullying.

Always keep a close watch when introducing horses to each other. It is much better to turn them both out together at the same time, rather than bringing a new horse into a field that already has a resident.

other docile horses into their field. Each time, allow things to settle down again, keeping a close watch on any adverse reactions. It is important that there is plenty of space in the field and that the grazing is good as both these factors will lessen the pressure. Horses can be very territorial if food is scarce, and so if there is little grazing the established herd members will be more inclined to drive the newcomer away, rather than accept it into their midst.

There is unlikely to be instant harmony, but there should be no major signs of disagreement – any serious display of aggression could leave one or more of the group badly injured. It is much better to progress slowly, rather than be faced with a full-scale conflict where the combatants need to be separated and there is a much reduced likelihood of being able to reintroduce successfully in the future. Once

a bond has been formed, there is unlikely to be discord when the group is reunited after separation – if one member is taken out for a day to go to a show, for example. On the other hand, once two horses have taken a dislike to each other, there is little that can be done to reconcile the differences between them.

getting your horse
fit for work

When you acquire a new horse, you may need to work on its fitness, just as you would have to do if you had an animal recuperating after an injury or illness. You must also always allow plenty of time to prepare for a particular competition or event. Expecting too much of your horse, too soon, can easily lead to it breaking down and suffering a long lay-off. Avoid rushing through any fitness programme and do not forget to increase the horse's food intake in accordance with its work rate. While you are exercising it, keep a watch on your horse's breathing rate. If it becomes noticeably out of breath, and this does not return to normal soon after the exercise has stopped, you are pushing it too hard.

Beginnings

Start off by walking your horse on a hard surface on a regular basis. Roadwork is often recommended, but this depends on how busy the roads are and how your horse reacts to traffic. Keep a check on its shoes, as these will be more susceptible to wear during roadwork. It is also advisable to use knee boots, particularly with inexperienced horses.

Exposure to firm ground is very important in toning up the ligaments and tendons, as well as the muscles. Provided that you ensure your horse moves at a reasonable pace, then there will be cardiovascular benefits, too. It can take three weeks of such exercise, starting off at about 30 minutes daily, and increasing to 90 minutes, to build up the fitness of a hunter, while racehorses may need six weeks to get into shape.

Building up

The next stage is to introduce short periods of trotting, allowing the horse to trot for roughly a minute, about four times during the course of its 90-minute exercise regime. You can then extend the length of the trotting periods, and make them harder by going up short and then longer hills. At this stage, it is a good idea to switch to firm ground, where there are no ruts, because a tarmac surface can become too hard on the joints.

Moving on

Three weeks of fairly disciplined trotting should result in a noticeable improvement in your horse's fitness. The next stage is to start cantering, taking care to warm up properly beforehand to minimize the risk of injury.

Depending on progress, you can then take the horse up gradually through its paces from a walk to a gallop and slow it down again. Schooling exercises may be introduced, too. The actual length of the training sessions is still about 90 minutes or so, but their intensity will have increased noticeably.

Fitness is something that is built up gradually, and should not be rushed lest this increases the risk of injury. At the outset, ascertaining the amount of work to which a new horse has been accustomed can be helpful.

Swimming as Therapy

Horses are able to swim surprisingly well, with their powerful legs enabling them to swim quite strongly when in deep water. This enables them to ford rivers and has also at times allowed them to escape from flooded pastures.

Over recent years the therapeutic advantages of swimming have become appreciated, and there are now a number of centres where horses – especially valuable competition horses such as racehorses – are encouraged to swim in special pools under supervision. This helps them to retain their fitness when recuperating from an injury, particularly one that restricts the ability of their limbs to take their weight. Most horses react well to being introduced to swimming facilities of this type, especially under the guidance of an experienced handler. Equine health insurance may cover the costs involved if your vet feels that your horse could benefit from this type of therapy.

ABOVE: *Gentle roadwork of this type can be a valuable way of increasing a horse's level of fitness after a lay off, but choose your location carefully so that there will be minimal passing traffic and good visibility.*

BELOW: *Horses often become excited when they are first turned out in a field, and this opportunity for exercise will increase their level of activity and thus their fitness. It is vital to check first that the fencing is secure.*

Rest days

Throughout this fitness training, always allow the horse to rest for one day of the week. On its day off, it should be let out of its stable for a lengthy period of grazing if at all possible. This will prevent any stiffness developing, as horses move around more in a field than when confined.

establishing a partnership

3

By evolving a stimulating routine for your horse, you will establish a good relationship with it and reduce the likelihood of behavioural difficulties. It is vital that you learn to recognize when your horse is off-colour, as this will enable you to seek veterinary advice at an early stage, which, in turn, will enable the problem to be resolved without it becoming major or even life-threatening. Remember that horses can never be entirely predictable and always allow for the unexpected when you introduce yours to something new: clipping it for the first time, for example. If you encounter abnormal behaviour in your horse, try to resolve it as soon as possible. Never be afraid to ask for help. In larger yards, you may even find someone who has had a similar experience.

looking after your
horse's feet

The care of a horse's feet is a very important aspect of its daily management. From the outset you will need to be able to pick up each foot in turn. Always choose a quiet spot in your yard or field to do this, so that your horse will not be upset by any disturbance. Initially, it may help to have someone hold your horse while you pick its feet up, but once a routine is established, you should be able to pick them up while it is tied up.

The procedure

Never be tempted to bend down and lift the foot without warning, especially with a newly acquired horse. Instead, approach slowly and run your hand gently down its leg, speaking softly to reassure it if it appears to be nervous. Once you reach the foot, lean gently against the horse, which should make it shift its weight on to the other side of its body. This will allow you to lift its leg more easily. Take particular care with the hind legs, being careful not to stand behind the horse, where you could be kicked, and do not forget the horse's blind spot (see p.31) around its rump when approaching from the side.

The underside of the feet need to be cleaned regularly using a hoof pick. Always work in a downward movement, from the heel to the toe, to avoid damaging the heel and frog at the back of the hoof (see p.85). The frog is especially important, because it makes initial contact with the ground and serves to prevent the horse from slipping, as well as helping to absorb the force of movement. If the underside, or sole, of the hoof suffers any damage, it can extend to other structures deeper within the foot, which may lead to lameness or other complications.

Trimming and shoeing

Even if its shoes are not very worn, your horse is likely to need a visit from the farrier every month or so to have its feet trimmed; the horn covering at the front of the hoof is usually particularly in need of attention. Horses at grass and not being ridden also require attention from the farrier. Even ponies, which are less commonly shod, even when working, need to have their feet trimmed regularly.

Having removed the old shoe, the farrier will pare back the horn. He will then prepare a new shoe, if required, fitting it carefully to the hoof while it is still hot, before cooling it in water and then nailing it in place. Special nails are used for this purpose, and should keep the shoe firmly fixed as it wears down. Protruding clips at the front of the shoe – usually one on each of the front shoes and two on the hinds – provide further support.

Horses need their feet attending regularly to prevent lameness. Cleaning the feet is very important, while shoeing serves to protect the hooves from damage during work.

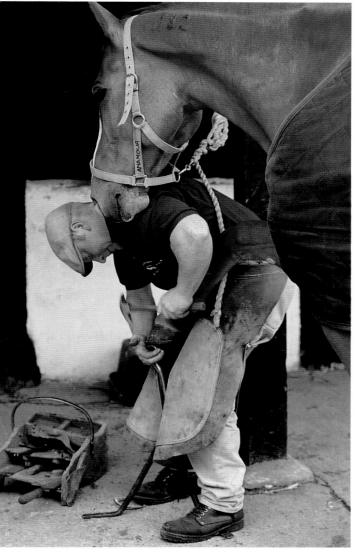

Regular visits from the farrier are vital to a horse's wellbeing, and the shoes will be made individually to conform to the needs of your horse.

Types of shoe

There are various types of shoe, such as those intended to give hunters extra grip, and your farrier will chose the sort that is most suitable for the work your horse is currently doing. There are also surgical shoes (see box), which can help to compensate for deformities in the foot or faults in the horse's action. Studs may be recommended, if, for example, your horse is doing a lot of road work.

Remedial Shoes

In some cases, particularly when a horse may have a faulty action or is suffering from a weakness of the hoof, remedial shoes may be advised by the farrier. In order to reduce the risk of injuries caused by brushing, for example, when one leg is hit by its neighbour, either a feather-edged shoe or a three-quarters shoe may be recommended. Shoes with rolled toes will prevent overreaching injuries, when the hindlegs come into contact with the forelegs. Shoes may also be devised to help rest an injury. The Patten shoe has a raised heel and a bar and is used for tendon injuries.

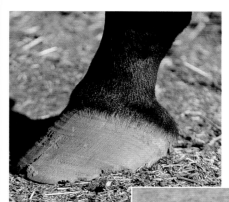

LEFT: *If horses' hooves are neglected they are likely to grow in an increasingly deformed way and it will take time to get them sound again.*

BELOW: *This horse's neglected hoof has been partially rebuilt with plastic to protect it, until it starts to grow again properly.*

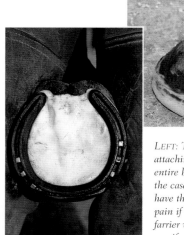

LEFT: *The shoe can also serve as a means of attaching a protective covering over the entire base of the foot, as shown here, in the case of a sole injury. It is also possible to have the heel set so that it avoids causing pain if there is a corn for example. Your farrier will be in the best position to advise you if your horse would benefit from having one or more special shoes.*

grooming
your horse

If you do not have one already, you will need to invest in a grooming kit, which is usually kept in a special carrying box (shown below). Your kit should include a body brush, which is used for general grooming, its soft bristles helping to remove dust. It is cleaned using a curry comb. A dandy brush is required to remove dried mud. Dandy brushes have hard bristles and must not be used on the mane or tail, because they will damage the longer hair, nor after clipping, or if the horse has very sensitive skin. Plastic or rubber curry combs are alternatives to the dandy brush. They also stimulate the skin and can help to improve the natural gloss on the coat. A similar effect can be obtained using a cactus cloth, especially if it is dampened slightly prior to use. This is basically a piece of sackcloth, and it can be used over the entire body.

A mane comb is useful as its deep teeth enable the long mane and tail hair to be groomed easily. For plaiting purposes (see p.90), a short comb is required.

You will also need a couple of water brushes: one is to clean the feet, if they become very muddy; the other is dampened and used to remove dust from the coat. It is also useful for grooming the mane.

Wisps and stable rubbers
Many horses enjoy being groomed with a wisp or leather massage pad, both of which can be used in conjunction with a stable rubber to improve the muscle tone. The wisp is made from plaited lengths of hay, and should be dampened with a little water. The wisp or pad is applied firmly over the muscular areas of the horse's body, such as the hindquarters, causing it to tense its muscles, which are then relaxed with the stable rubber.

Sponges and sweat scrapers
Two sponges, preferably of different colours, are needed. One is for wiping around the eyes, the nose, and the muzzle – do not use this sponge on another horse, as this could result in the spread of respiratory infections. The other sponge is for wiping the dock area, around the tail.

Grooming Essentials

Body brush – short bristles, soft in the centre, harder at the edge

Stable rubber – this is a bit like a drying up cloth

Plastic curry comb – with rows of short, tough plastic teeth

Sponges – in different colours or sizes for different jobs

Rubber curry comb – with short, flexible teeth in circles

Tail bandage – similar to a crepe bandage; store this neatly rolled

Hoof pick – a hoof pick with a brush does two jobs in one

Dandy brush – this has long, comparatively hard bristles

Water brush – with long, soft water-retentive bristles

Metal curry comb – with rows of metal teeth

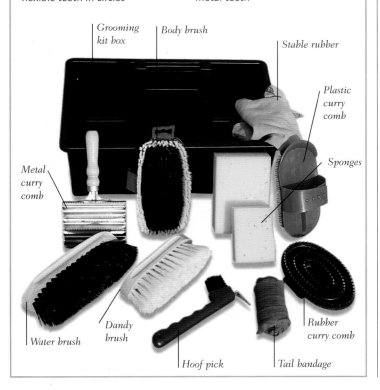

Grooming kit box

Body brush

Stable rubber

Plastic curry comb

Sponges

Metal curry comb

Water brush

Dandy brush

Hoof pick

Tail bandage

Rubber curry comb

EYE WIPING

This should be carried out using a clean sponge dipped in tepid water and wrung out to prevent water running down the face. It prevents tear-staining, and will also clean this area of the face. Wipe away from the eye itself.

NOSE AND MUZZLE CLEANING

Carefully wiping these areas will remove any trace of food or hay deposited here. This is also vital in the case of any nasal infections, but always reserve a sponge for each horse to prevent a possible spread of infection.

DOCK HYGIENE

A separate sponge should be used for this area. Any soiling here is especially serious, because faecal deposits will attract flies to lay their eggs, with the resulting maggots producing toxins that enter the horse's blood stream.

After a horse has been washed down (see pp.88–89), a sweat scraper is useful in forcing water out from the coat. Use the rubber side over more sensitive or bony parts, with the metal edge being applied over the rest of the body. The coat can then be given a final polish with a stable rubber.

Hoof pick

A hoof pick is essential to keep the feet clean, and should be brightly coloured, so that if it is dropped accidentally, it can be retrieved easily on the bedding – its sharp end might, otherwise, cause injury. Hoof oil will also be required, with a small paintbrush to apply it. Each hoof should be painted with water and then oil, which not only makes it look more attractive, but also aids recovery in cases where the hoof may be brittle or damaged.

Picking out Hooves

This is an essential task, helping to keep your horse sound as well as minimizing the risk of any infection developing on the underside of the foot. As a result, it is very important to train your horse to allow you to pick up, inspect, and clean its hooves without difficulty.

The hooves should be checked regularly, and cleaned out as required. If dried mud has accumulated in this area, it will need to be brushed out.

Picking out the hooves needs to be carried out carefully, to prevent accidental injury, so work downwards from the heel to the toe.

The grooming process

A horse requires daily grooming, the extent of which is influenced by the way in which it is being kept and the work it is doing. Full grooming, known as strapping, can take as long as 45 minutes, and is normally carried out after a period of exercise. In some large stables, automatic grooming machines are available. These can assist the process, but their noise may be upsetting to horses that are not used to them. If you use such a machine, it is vital to bandage up the tail first, and a circuit breaker must always be incorporated into the electrical supply.

Preparation

Grooming is normally carried out with the horse tied up and any rug either removed or folded back, depending on the weather and whether you are outside in the yard or

Precautions to Take

Take care not to upset your horse when you are grooming its hindquarters, being particularly wary if it raises a foot off the ground, as this could indicate that it is about to lash out. As always, standing behind your horse is not recommended, as you are more vulnerable to being kicked. Although young horses especially can sometimes prove rather excitable when being groomed, if you always follow a distinct routine, starting at the head and working backwards, your horse will soon come to recognize that it has nothing to fear. Temperament can be significant, with heavy horses generally proving more amenable to being groomed than Arabs or Thoroughbreds, for example, thanks to their more placid natures.

Grooming

Start grooming your horse at the top of his neck, and work downwards. A muddy horse will need cleaning off with a dandy brush or curry comb to start off with, and you can then tidy up with a body brush. Next, concentrate on the mane. First, brush it onto the wrong side of the neck and groom the underlying hair, before starting to comb the longer hair in strands. The tail will also need some attention, although regular brushing of the long hair is not recommended as it will cause damage. This should be enough for going out on a hack. For more special occasions, add a final polish with a stable rubber.

Most horses enjoy bein[g] groomed and will stand still [or] even doze while they are bein[g] brushed and cleaned u[p]

warm and dry in a stable. It is usual to start by picking out the hooves into a skep, adding this to the muck heap in due course. Hoof cleaning needs to be done twice daily, and particularly when your horse is being brought into its stable from the field. If its lower limbs are very muddy, you may need to wash them – try not to use more water than necessary – and then dry them off with an old towel. The basic grooming process is described below.

Finishing off

If you are not riding, once you have finished with the body brush, you may like to use a wisp or massage pad on your horse's muscles. Most horses really appreciate this attention and will be happy to doze for as long as you want to continue grooming. On most occasions, you should also wipe the eyes and nose with a damp sponge (see p.85). You also need to clean the dock and sheath on a regular basis.

Use a rubber curry comb to remove any dried mud from the horse's body. Start at the top of its head, between the ears, and work systematically down towards the extremities. Do not forget the legs, but be careful not to be rough or to tickle.

Now you can go over the horse with the body brush. Start on the neck, brushing the coat in short, circular strokes, and using a curry comb to clean the brush as you go. Stabled horses need only a quick brush over with the body brush.

You can use a dandy brush instead of the curry comb, if your horse is not too dirty. Once you have removed or broken up the worst of the mud clumps with a curry comb, get the rest out with the dandy brush.

When you are happy that your horse is clean and tidy, use a stable rubber to give the finishing touches and to make its coat shine. If you are planning to go to a show, you are now ready to start plaiting the mane and tail (see pp.90–91).

giving your horse
a bath

It is normally not recommended that you wash the horse's entire body, because this is likely to strip out the oils in the coat. In wet weather, these oils help to insulate the horse by ensuring rain runs off the hair, leaving a warm layer of air trapped close to the skin. In addition, they are responsible for the glossy sheen on the coat, which is associated with good health. On the rare occasions when a horse may have to be washed, it is important to dry it off properly so that it cannot develop a chill.

Should a horse become saturated, by being trapped in a river for example, then its coat must be dried off thoroughly as soon as possible, and it is advisable to keep it rugged up for at least a week afterwards, to prevent it from becoming chilled. With ponies and horses that are kept outdoors throughout the year, it is important to be careful during grooming not to remove too much grease from the coat. For this reason, the body brush should not be used to any great extent on the body; a dandy brush is preferable as this only strips out sweat and mud.

Thanks to their pale coloration, grey horses can be more vulnerable than other horses to showing areas of dirt in their coats, and so will benefit from more frequent and thorough grooming.

Most stains on your horse's coat should be removable through brushing, especially once the mud or dung has dried, but if you do need to carry out localized washing, minimize the area that is made wet. First wash the dirt off using some soapy, lukewarm water, remove excess water with a sweat scraper, and then dry the area with a towel. Always be particularly careful washing around the face, and do not use soap or shampoo, since they will cause discomfort if they get into the eyes.

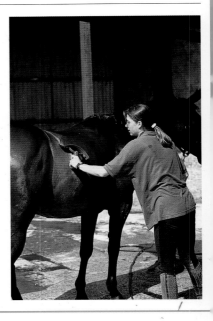

Dear Equine Casebook

My horse's tail is looking dreadful, with dried mud and other bits in it and lots of scurf and loose hair. I have heard that it is a good idea to wash the tail once in a while, but I am unsure about how to go about it. Can you advise me?
kind regards Martin Cochrane

Washing the tail is generally a fairly straightforward procedure, especially if your horse is co-operative. It is simply a matter of partially filling a plastic bucket with lukewarm water and immersing the tail in this, before working in a mild shampoo. Use a water brush or sponge to wet the top of the tail area. Rinse the shampoo out thoroughly, shake out as much water as possible, and brush the tail along its length, using a body brush and concentrating on a few strands at a time. Finally, wrap it up in a tail bandage until it has dried.

Dear Equine Casebook

Recently, my very naughty pony got into a field that had had cows in it, and she managed to roll in some cow dung. After lots of brushing, I've managed to get it off most of her coat but it is still stuck in her hair and along her neck, and it stinks! Please help.
yours sincerely Millie Fisher

The mane and surrounding area may need to be washed occasionally, and it sounds like this is one such time. Choose a day when the weather is reasonably warm and use a sponge and a mild shampoo, taking care that none of the water can run into your horse's eyes. A sweat scraper will be helpful to mop up water elsewhere as it runs out of the coat, after which the hair and neck should be dried with a towel.

Removing dried-on dirt may require some thorough washing. This should only be attempted on a warm day when you have plenty of time to dry off your horse afterwards.

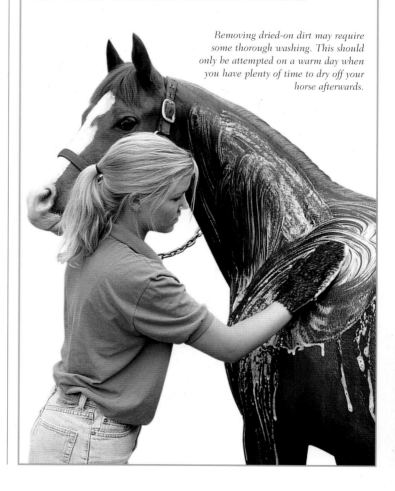

plaiting
mains and tales

A horse that is being shown or is taking part in competition should look its best, so it will need additional grooming and, except in the case of some pony breeds, this usually includes plaiting the mane, and sometimes also the tail. Normally, the mane is allowed to lie naturally, but plaiting helps to highlight the crest and the outline of the neck, which makes the horse look neater and more attractive. For plaiting, you will need a blunt-ended needle and some thread that matches the colour of your horse's mane. It is worth practising mane pulling and plaiting before the day of the show, so that you can do them neatly and quickly.

Pulling the mane

Before plaiting, the mane must be pulled. This must be carried out carefully and over the course of several days, to prevent the area becoming sore. Pulling is a process whereby the longer, more straggling, hairs are removed to produce a level mane that lies in a neat line along the neck. It has to be done by hand with the hairs not being cut at all. It is easier on a hot day or following exercise, when the pores are open, and it often helps to watch

PULLING A MANE

Before plaiting, you need to pull any long or straggling hairs from the mane. Push most of the hair up out of the way with a comb and remove the long strands a few at a time along the neck. Repeat until you have a neat, straight mane.

PLAITING THE MANE

Once you are ready to start plaiting, divide up the hair into rough clumps. Thread your blunt-ended needle before beginning plaiting. Make three main strands from each clump and plait them together as you would any hair.

ROLLING THE PLAITS

When you reach the end of each plait, tie the thread around the tip and then fold the plait up and stitch it to itself, refold and stitch. Do this as many times as necessary to complete the plait so that you have a neat top-knot shape.

LEFT: A gypsy plait is a distinctive style whose origins can be traced back to the Romany community.

ABOVE: Certain plaits, such as the Arab plait, are linked to particular horse types, complementing their appearance.

someone carry out this task before attempting it yourself. It is important only to pull the long hair from the underside of the mane, rather than the top hairs; those left at the top will otherwise stand up, forming a ridge and unsightly tufts will form when the pulled ones regrow.

How to plait a mane

Once it has been thinned and shortened as necessary, the mane should be damped down with a brush, and then you can plan where the plaits will fall. Each bunch of hair should be about as wide as a mane comb, allowing for a forelock plait and an uneven number of plaits running down the neck itself (see far left).

How to plait a tail

The tail may also occasionally need to be plaited, but it is not always advisable to pull it as many horses resent this. It is important to assess at the outset whether the tail can be plaited successfully – long hairs must be evident at the sides of the dock. Before you begin plaiting, brush the tail and dampen the hair as you would for plaiting a mane.

Putting Up

If there is a risk that the tail could become very muddy or get in the way during work – such as on the polo field or across country – a modified form of plaiting, called 'putting up', is used. The plait is continued to the end of the tail and then rolled back up to the dock, where it is doubled up and held in place with stitches or tape, ensuring that it lies flat, at the level of the tail vertebrae.

How to Plait a Tail

Although it looks quite complicated, tail-plaiting is quite easy to do, so long as you take your time and make the plait as tight as possible. There are a number of variations on the theme (see below right), but the one shown here is probably the most popular and straightforward.

Divide part of the tail into three small bunches, one on either side and one top. Work in bunches of hair from each side of the tail, as you plait downwards. After completing about three-quarters of the length of

the dock, stop taking in new hair and continue until what you have in your hands is finished. Once you reach the end, tie the plait with thread, loop it up, and tuck it behind itself. Then sew it in place.

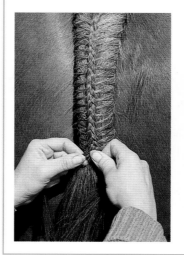

clipping
a winter coat

A horse's coat becomes significantly thicker for the winter. This means that vigorous exercise during this period can lead to excessive sweating and then chilling. Making the coat shorter through clipping avoids this problem, although the horse will then need to be warmly rugged up, particularly if it is turned out. In the northern hemisphere, a first clip is usually carried out in October, with further clipping being done on roughly a monthly basis through to January. Clipping at a later stage will affect the spring coat.

Preparing to clip

The noise of the clippers and the unfamiliar sensations may upset a horse that has never been clipped before. If you are also inexperienced, ask someone who has clipped a

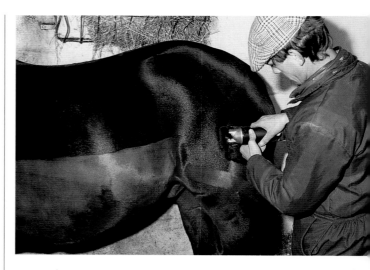

Clipping is a straightforward procedure, but it can be upsetting for nervous horses, s approach the task cautiously. Be sure that the clippers are sharp before starting.

Types of Clip

There are a number of different types of clip. A full clip is when all the hair is removed from the body. A variation on this is the hunter clip, which leaves a saddle patch and longer hair on the legs, affording some protection against cuts when out hunting. In the blanket clip an area of long hair in the shape of a blanket on the body is left. Blanket clips offer more protection against the cold, although rugs will still be required. Trace clips in various styles leave the horse with shorter hair on the lower neck and body, and are often recommended for horses spending the winter out at grass.

A gullet clip extends from under the lower jaw to the belly. It is commonly used on ponies.

The hunter clip leaves longer hair on the legs, as well as a distinctive saddle patch.

The blanket clip creates a blanket-like layer of longer hair on the body, and sometimes on the head.

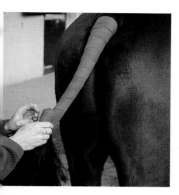

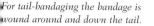

For tail-bandaging the bandage is wound around and down the tail.

The bandage is held in place by being tied in a knot as shown here.

horse to do the first clip, rather than attempting to do it yourself. In any case, do not attempt to clip on your own, but ask someone to assist by holding the horse. Wear old clothes and rubber-soled boots; a dust mask may also be advisable, particularly if you are sensitive to animal hair.

The clippers must be well-maintained, with the blades being sharpened after each full clip. They will need oiling and possibly tightening as well, prior to use. The clip may take more than 45 minutes to complete, and the clippers can become very hot, so you will need to pause at intervals to apply a special coolant.

Clipping needs to be done where there is adequate space to move easily around the horse, and good light, but it should not be done outdoors. The floor must be level and not slippery, while a power supply must be easily accessible. A circuit breaker is vital. It is much safer to have the electric lead threaded on hooks in the ceiling, to be pulled down as necessary, rather than dragging on the floor.

Starting a clip

Depending on the type of clip (see box, left), the process usually begins on the shoulders and goes against the direction of the hair. Always bandage the tail before starting out. Where the skin is not flat, clip with particular care – stretching the skin with your hand can help to prevent nicks. Potentially difficult areas, such as the groin, should

Rugs and Their Uses

There are many different types of rug available, most designed with a particular purpose in mind.

OUTDOOR RUGS

Outdoor rugs are usually made of ripstop, light and quick-drying materials and can be made warmer by putting a liner underneath. They generally give good protection against the elements, but must fit well to prevent them slipping. Exercise rugs (right) keep a horse dry or warm when it is being ridden.

STABLE RUGS

Stable rugs are used to keep stabled horses warm overnight. Those that are easily washable are usually best, although the more traditional jute rugs tend to be more durable. Jute rugs usually require an underblanket. They are fixed with a roller, whereas modern synthetic rugs have surcingles.

OTHER RUGS

Stabled horses may also wear day rugs during the day and for travelling. These are usually made of wool and buckled at the front, with a roller over the back. After vigorous exercise, a sweat or cooler rug (right) can be used to help any sweat evaporate quickly, while still keeping the horse warm.

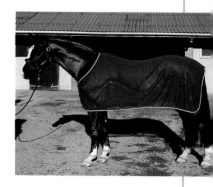

be left until last, to minimize any upset to the horse. Never clip inside the ears. Slightly overlap each stroke to ensure that you do not miss any hair. Use a blanket to keep the horse warm as you proceed, and when you are finished, go over its body with a stable rubber to remove any loose hair.

feeding hay
and other bulk foods

To meet their nutritional needs, horses naturally spend relatively long periods eating each day. Their grazing habits are influenced by the seasons. During the summer, they eat during the day, tending to rest at night. The converse is true in the winter: they will graze at night, which is when the weather is coldest, their movements helping to keep them warm. They then rest during the relative warmth of the day. It is not, therefore, a cause for concern that your horse appears to be grazing less when you see it during the hours of daylight in the winter months.

Hay and haylage

Horses require bulk and roughage in their diet, and if this cannot come from grazing grass, then it must be supplied in the form of hay or haylage. Good quality meadow hay, comprising a variety of grasses, including rye grass and other components, such as clover, is often used. Care should be taken that it does not contain poisonous plants. This is unlikely to be the case with seed hay, which is grown specially for making hay, rather than being cut from an established paddock (see box, right). Other types of hay such as lucerne can be of higher nutritional value, and you will probably need to adjust the amount of concentrates in the horse's diet as a consequence. Another richer food is haylage, which needs to be introduced in small quantities.

Horses feed naturally by grazing, consuming both grass and herbage.

Dear Equine Casebook

Recently, my horse has been diagnosed as suffering from COPD. He's been treated by the vet, and I've been told that he will never fully recover. I understand that dust from hay will make the condition worse and wonder if you can give me any ideas on feeding to avoid this?
kind regards Penny Aldridge

When a horse is suffering from COPD, it can help to soak his hay for about 12 hours before feeding it to him. This is most easily accomplished by putting a full haynet in a container of clean water. Allow it to drain afterwards, otherwise it will be very heavy to lift. If you can find a decent supplier, you might consider feeding haylage. Another alternative is to buy semi-wilted grass, which is vacuum-packed and free from dust. Once the pack is opened, it must be used rapidly, before the contents deteriorate; damaged packs should never be fed to horses. This type of grass contains more protein than hay, and so can be fed in smaller quantities.

Hay must always be stored in a dry place, such as a barn. The disadvantage of this barn is that it will be very dusty.

Hay

Seed hay or meadow hay are common choices for feeding horses. If you choose to feed meadow hay, be sure that it comes from a reliable source so that you do not need to worry about it containing poisonous plants, particularly the very dangerous ragwort (see p.109).

Seed hay (far right) is paler than meadow hay (right) and has a higher nutritional value. Beware of hay that looks brownish or very dark yellow, as this indicates that it is old and its nutritional value will have declined.

Although it is now generally recommended that hay is fed on the floor as it is a more natural way for a grazing animal to eat, haynets are still popular as they keep the hay in one place and make the horse eat more slowly. They must be tied up carefully.

Quality

It pays to be fussy over the quality of your hay. Old hay, for example, not only has relatively little nutritional value, but will also be heavily contaminated by dust and mould spores. These are likely to be harmful to your horse, being the cause of the condition known as chronic obstructive pulmonary disease (COPD) or heaves – this latter name due to the way in which the horse's breathing becomes laboured. The damage to the lungs is irreversible, and the horse will appear worse at different times, especially during hot weather. COPD also usually causes a long-standing cough, and often a discharge from the nostrils. Although it is difficult to assess the quality of hay, unless it is obviously very dusty, it should have a sweet smell and appear light greenish-brown; old hay is a decidedly yellowish or brown shade.

Ageing hay

Hay must not be fed as soon as it is made as it will be difficult to digest. It needs to be at least six months old, and preferably nearer to a year, to reduce the risk of colic. As a further precaution to protect the horse's health, mix the old hay with the new, when your stocks are running out. Haylage must also be allowed to age for about six to eight weeks before being fed.

giving your horse
concentrated foods

When a horse is working hard, it is unable to meet all its nutritional requirements solely from hay and grass, which is why its diet needs to be supplemented with concentrates. These provide additional energy and protein, as well as vitamins and minerals.

Formulated feeds

There are many different types of cubes (or nuts) and coarse mixes, each with carefully formulated ingredients to meet the nutritional needs of horses undertaking a variety of tasks. They are commercial preparations, generally available from equestrian outlets and agricultural merchants. As they are quick and easy to feed, not requiring any preparation, many people choose to use these mixes, rather than the individual grains or cereals. However, it is vital to match the type of feed to your horse's requirements. These are usually described on the packaging, but if you have any doubts, ask the retailer for advice before buying. It is important to check the expiry date for the vitamins; this will be stamped on the packaging. Do not be tempted to buy a large sack that will go out of date before its contents can be consumed by your horse – coarse mixes tend to deteriorate more rapidly than cubes. Store feed sacks in a dry place out of the reach of rodents. Metal dustbins are useful for this.

How much to feed

Cubes or coarse mixes can constitute your horse's or pony's entire concentrate ration. A little water should be used to dampen the food – too much will make cubes break up. The quantity to feed is given on the packaging, and should not be exceeded. It is advisable to add some chaff (well chopped hay or straw) to cubes or coarse mixes to prevent them from being eaten too fast. If your horse persists in trying to eat rapidly, try placing a brick in its food bowl. The effort of eating around the brick will slow it down.

Traditional feeds

Oats, barley, chaff, bran, linseed, and sugar beet are traditional horse feeds, and they are normally given as a mixture to provide a balanced diet (see pp.97–99 for detailed preparation instructions).

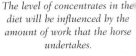

The level of concentrates in the diet will be influenced by the amount of work that the horse undertakes.

Types of Feed

There are a number of different foodstuffs that are used as concentrates for horses. These include oats, barley, bran, alfalfa, linseed, and sugar beet. It is important to remember that, unlike cubes and similar foods, however, these are not supplemented with additional vitamins and minerals, and therefore cannot be considered as balanced foods. They may need to be mixed before use.

Alfalfa chaff is prepared by use of a chaff cutter, which cuts the stems into suitably small pieces. You can mix the alfalfa chaff with molasses.

Bran provides bulk in a horse's diet and can help to correct loose droppings if fed in a dry state. More commonly however, it is fed as a wet mash.

Be sure to match the formulated nuts and coarse mix to your horse's needs, and feed in accordance with the instructions.

Rolled barley increases the choice of feeding options. It is also sometimes used in a crushed form, as an alternative to oats.

Rolled oats are the most widely used of the cereals fed to horses, with rolling helping to increase their digestibility.

Dried sugar beet pulp is sold in the form of cubes, which must be soaked prior to use. Buy in small quantities as these turn mouldy quite quickly.

It is important that horse food is kept dry and in clean surroundings to deter rodents. Use the bags in strict rotation so the food content does not deteriorate.

Oats

Oats need to be given in moderation, particularly to ponies, because they can cause excitability, making the animal more lively than usual. Whole oats cannot be digested easily, so they are usually fed crushed or rolled. Their nutritional value declines in this state, however, so do not stock up with more than three weeks' supply at a time.

Dear Equine Casebook

I have been feeding my horse with a good-quality coarse mix to which I add some chaff and, occasionally, sugar beet. Although he seems generally very healthy, his grazing is restricted and I want to be sure that he is getting all the vitamins and other nutrients that he needs.
yours sincerely Alan Johnstone

If you are using any one of the many good-quality formulated mixes, there is little need to worry over vitamin and mineral intake, although it is still a good idea to provide a salt lick, which your horse will rasp with its tongue, and gnaw. In fact, it is not usually recommended to provide any other vitamin and mineral supplement, for fear of overdosing, which can be potentially harmful in the long term.

Barley

Barley, which is prepared in a similar way to oats, provides another feeding option. It should never be given whole unless it has been boiled. Flaked barley is popular and it can be used as a substitute for some of the oats in a ration, being less likely to trigger hyper-excitability.

Chaff and bran

If your horse rushes its food without chewing it properly before swallowing, then consider adding some chaff. Bran, too, can be beneficial in slowing down a fast eater. It should not be fed in large quantities on a regular basis though, because it interferes with calcium absorption from the intestines. If offered dry, bran can help to firm up the droppings if necessary; as a mash it can act as a laxative. A mash is made with about 1kg (2lb) of bran, adding sufficient boiling water to give it a moist consistency. Stir the mixture well and leave to cool before feeding. If your horse is unused to eating bran, the addition of some linseed jelly should make it more palatable.

This type of food bowl greatly simplifies the task of feeding a large number of stabled horses. Each bowl can be filled without having to enter the stable.

Linseed

Linseed itself is especially favoured for creating a healthy gloss on the coat, although it is poisonous until cooked. The jelly is made by soaking the linseed in water for 24 hours before bringing it to the boil and simmering it for several hours. It is allowed to cool and then added to the evening feed. Half a kilo (1lb), covered with about 10cm (4in) of water, will produce enough for one feed. It all needs to be used within a further 24 hours. Sometimes, linseed is prepared alongside boiled barley.

Sugar beet

Sugar beet pulp also needs to be prepared carefully. It must be very well soaked, because otherwise it can cause choking or may swell up in the horse's digestive system. Use cold water for soaking, adding no more than 0.5kg (1lb) of sugar beet pulp to half a bucket of water, and leave to stand for 12 hours. The soaked sugar beet must be fed immediately, because it starts to ferment – a process speeded up by hot water. If you buy sugar beet cubes, these need to be soaked until they have disintegrated.

Carrots and other fresh foods

Although horses should ideally be allowed to graze daily, this is not always possible. Especially during the winter months, you may need to supplement their diet with other fresh foods, such as carrots. They should be cleaned before being sliced lengthwise. Never make small, circular pieces, as these may cause choking. The same applies with apples.

Fact File

FEEDING REGIMEN

While hay can be almost constantly available, the daily concentrate ration is normally divided into three feeds, which are offered at regular times throughout the day. Stabled horses should not be fed just prior to exercise, and so the day should start with a relatively small feed, and a restricted quantity of hay. Exercise can safely begin about 90 minutes later. A larger meal should be given afterwards, with the haynet being filled, and then a third meal towards the end of the afternoon.

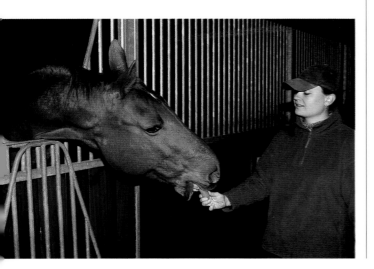

Horses will enjoy the attention of being fed tidbits, but be sure this type of food is safely prepared first and beware that you do not get bitten. This can happen quite easily, especially if the horse is impatient for its treat.

stabling
and the stable yard

Although it is sometimes possible to use an outhouse or other building for stabling your horse, some conversion work may be necessary first. For example, insulation may need to be added to brick-built buildings, not just in the roof but to the walls as well. This will keep the temperature more even in hot summers and cold winters. Above all, draughts must be excluded. Even so, ventilation is very important to the horse's wellbeing, to minimize the risk of respiratory infections, and the interior needs to have good natural lighting.

The ideal stable

For a horse, the ideal stable needs to have a floor area of at least 4.5 x 3.5m (14 x 12ft). Any smaller and the horse may be unable to stand up again if it slips over for any reason.

The ceiling needs to be approximately 3m (10ft) above ground level. The stable door opening should be a minimum of 1.5m (4ft) wide and about 2.5m (8ft) high. This will allow the horse to go through it easily, without risk of injury.

Traditional stable doors are hinged in two parts: the upper section opens on its own to provide ventilation, while the lower section is normally kept closed when the stable is occupied. The lower section should be high enough that a horse or pony cannot climb out, but low enough that the same animal can see over it and watch what is going on in the vicinity, which will help to prevent boredom. For security, there should be a draw bolt on the upper door; the lower door should be fitted with a draw bolt at the top and a kick bolt, which can be operated

ABOVE: *A typical row of stables, with good access at the front to enable the horses to be led in and out easily. They afford plenty of ventilation.*

LEFT: *High-tech, purpose-built American barn stabling. Note the wide access doors and external covered areas.*

easily with a boot, close to the bottom (see box on p.102). All the bolts and hinges in a stable must be kept well-oiled to prevent them from sticking or rusting.

Ventilation

Additional ventilation can be provided by windows, which are best built facing south to avoid cold winds. As a further precaution against draughts, they need to be relatively high up and should be louvred to open inwards. On the inside, the window needs to be protected by bars, particularly if it is glass. This will prevent the horse from breaking the glass, which should in any case be reinforced with mesh.

Tidiness and Safety

Tidiness in the stable yard is very important, not just for the sake of appearances but also for the horse's safety, as well as your own. The yard should be swept regularly and any tools stored away after they have been used. Pitchforks especially can be very dangerous if left lying around because of their sharp prongs. The same applies to hosepipes, as they can cause both people and horses to stumble. In cold weather, it is very important to ensure that the hard surface outside the stables remains free of ice. Otherwise, it can become an additional hazard.

Bolts and Hinges

The perfect stable is fitted with a variety of bolts to keep the horse safely inside when required. They must also be easy to open in the case of an emergency. For example, with practice, it is quicker to kick open the lower bolt than bend down and slip it open. Cabin hooks should also be fitted to make sure the doors stay safely open when required.

A kick bolt at the bottom of the door provides added security against the horse learning to open the door, or kicking it open or catching its hoof.

Draw bolts on both the upper and lower door of a stable. The eyes above and below are for cabin hooks, another vital piece of stable furniture.

Roofing

The interior of the stable needs to be dry, whatever the weather, so the roof should be sloped and should overhang slightly at the front of the stable. Guttering should be fitted to convey rain water away. This also makes it easier to attend to the horse's needs when it is raining hard.

Fittings

Inside the stable a tie-ring needs to be fixed to the wall approximately 1.5m (5ft) off the floor. Never tie your horse to a tie-ring. Instead tie a piece of string to the tie-ring and fasten your horse's lead rope to this. The string serves as a safety device. If your horse spooks in its stable when tied up, it will break to prevent the horse being injured by its head collar. When not required for tying up, the ring can be used for the haynet, which needs to be fixed up at the horse's eye-level. It should not be any higher, otherwise

The Ideal Stable

● The floor surface must be durable and textured so that it is not slippery.
● Include a very gentle slope to allow for drainage.
● Gullies need to run outside, and must be kept clear of bedding.
● Options other than concrete may be worth considering.
● Do not site a drain under the haynet as it will become easily blocked.

Well-ventilated and light internal stables where the horses can see what is going on around them.

small pieces of hay may fall into the horse's eyes. Some people prefer to feed hay on the floor in any case. Feed concentrates in a corner manger or in a tub on the floor. Water must be provided in a separate bucket, which should have a capacity of at least 9 litres (2 imperial gallons).

Stalls

Although many horses are kept in individual stables, in some establishments they may be housed in stalls in a larger building. Stalls, as their name suggests, are partitioned areas and horses are kept in them with a head collar and lead rope. To prevent the lead rope becoming entangled, it is threaded through the tie-ring and a weight is

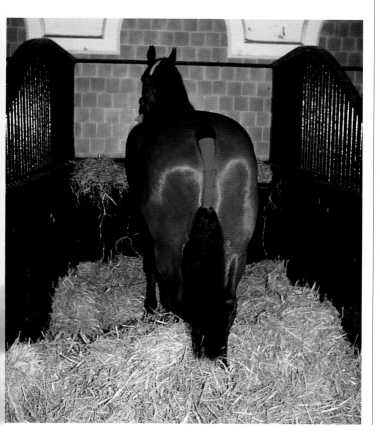

Safe Electrical Supply

Having an electrical supply to stables is vital on winter evenings and for carrying out clipping and similar tasks. Safety is a very important consideration from the outset. Any electrical work should be undertaken by a professional electrician who will fit equipment designed for use outside, such as waterproof switches and sockets. If you do not wish to go to the expense of installing an electrical supply, then reliable battery-operated lights are obtainable. The stable lights should be located right up in the roof, where they will give off a good light with little shadow. A switch should be positioned outside the stable door, out of the horse's reach, so that you can turn the light on before entering the box.

attached to the loose end. As the horse approaches the ring, the weight falls towards the ground, taking the slack with it so there is no loose rope. Most stalls are also fitted with a conventional tie-ring at approximately 1.5m (5ft) high.

Ventilation can be a problem when it comes to housing a number of horses in a single unit. It is made worse by the fact that such an environment inevitably has a larger accumulation of muck and associated ammonia levels. Ammonia can damage the horse's respiratory tract, making it more susceptible to infection, and where ventilation is poor, infections will spread more rapidly through a group. A horse in a stable on its own is likely to enjoy better ventilation and also be less vulnerable to contagious infections.

Horses are more likely to become bored when housed in stalls rather than stables. Entry to the stall is from a central passageway.

bedding
— which sort is best?

There are four main types of bedding available for covering the stable floor: straw, shavings, paper, and rubber matting, and a number of other variations, such as hemp and flax.

Straw

Thanks to its low cost, straw is still very commonly used for bedding, in spite of newer options. There are three types of straw: wheat, barley, and oats. Wheat straw is often favoured, partly because it is less likely to be eaten by the horse. It is also relatively tough and so drains well, rather than becoming saturated when wet, which tends to

LEFT: You will need to remove all the droppings in the stable and also the wet bedding each day.

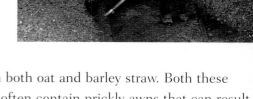

RIGHT: Shavings are an alternative to straw, but watch out for any odd sharp pieces of wood.

be the case with both oat and barley straw. Both these latter types also often contain prickly awns that can result in skin irritation in humans and horses.

Straw bedding is quite easy to manage. Take out the droppings and soiled straw each day, adding extra bedding as necessary. The stable should be cleaned out completely each week. When you add new bedding always break up the bales thoroughly. If your horse starts to eat the straw, try placing old straw on top of the new as a deterrent.

Shavings and paper

If your horse suffers from respiratory problems, then shavings or paper are a better choice than straw, as they are relatively free from dust. Shavings are supplied in large polythene bales, which can be stored easily in the dry until required. Paper bedding in various forms has become more popular over recent years. Although based on recycled products, it is still relatively costly. It has good absorbency,

Mucking out Tools

A variety of tools will be useful for mucking out purposes, and these are widely available from tack shops and similar outlets. Shovels are needed for clearing up droppings, while forks are essential for moving straw and organizing the muck heap. A stout brush is required for sweeping up.

Shovel   Short fork   Yard brush

Long fork   Pitchfork   Pitchfork   Shavings fork

Clean the stable thoroughly every week, removing all the bedding, and washing and disinfecting the floor. A sturdy,, good-sized wheelbarrow will simplify this task.

Muck Heap

Management of the muck heap is important, especially in a large yard, where the volume of material to be disposed of will be significant. The heap itself should be located some distance from the stables because it will tend to smell, especially in warmer weather, and looks unsightly. Over a period of time the bedding will rot down, providing valuable garden manure. It helps if the muck heap can be divided into sections so that each can be filled in turn, rather than simply adding to one existing pile, as this allows manure to be removed more easily.

out this can be a drawback when mucking out, as it is very heavy when damp. Another disadvantage is that the inks in the paper could cause an allergic skin reaction.

As with straw, shavings or paper bedding must be spot-cleaned daily, and the surface raked to prevent it becoming compacted. Drains can be blocked by paper and may need covering when you are cleaning out the stable.

Rubber matting

One of the most hygienic forms of bedding available is rubber matting. This was originally devised for use in horseboxes and trailers, but is now available for fitting over the floor of a stables. It is reasonably warm, and can be supplemented as necessary with just a thin layer of more conventional bedding, such as straw, on top, lessening the

problem of waste disposal. If used on its own, it can be hosed down very easily, and also provides a surface on which horses are unlikely to slip.

Deep littering

Rather than a weekly clean out, some horse owners operate what is known as a deep-litter system. This not only saves time but also uses less bedding material. However, it is vital that the droppings are removed daily and fresh bedding added. It is also important to keep a close check on the horse's feet, to ensure infections do not develop.

keeping your horse
at grass

To have plenty of space and food, each horse needs 0.6–0.8 hectares (1.5–2 acres) of grass. It is not a good idea to keep a horse in a field on its own, because it is unlikely to settle well in isolation, so you will need to multiply these figures by the number of horses that you will be keeping to arrive at the amount of land required.

Fencing

The perimeter of the field must be securely fenced. A hedge with a post-and-rail fence makes the best boundary, the hedge providing protection from the worst of the elements. Where this combination is not possible, then a post-and-rail fence, three rails high, is recommended. Provided that it is at least 1.5m (4ft) high, most horses will not attempt to jump out.

Wire can be used instead of the rails, but never barbed wire as it can be very dangerous if the horses panic in the field and get caught up on it. The sharp projections are also likely to tear rugs when the horse brushes against

them. Broad-mesh sheep fencing is also potentially dangerous, if a horse puts one of its feet through the mesh.

To ensure a long life and security, all the timber should be treated with a non-toxic wood preservative and the posts must be set 0.6m (2ft) into the ground. Rotting wood or shallowly set posts can fall down, allowing the horses to escape from the field.

Gates

Entry to the paddock should be through a gate of the same height as the fence and at least 3m (10ft) wide. If possible the gate should be sited on well-drained or high ground, because the horses will often congregate around it, awaiting their meals, so if it is in a low, damp corner it will soon become a morass of mud in wet weather.

Be sure that gates are kept securely closed at all times.

Fencing and Boundaries

A number of different types of fencing may be employed around a field, sometimes combined with a natural hedge, giving horses somewhere to shelter when the weather is bad. Hedges offer more protection against the elements than a fence alone, though they take years to become established, and a young hedge will present no effective barrier to a horse. It is also important to check that there are no poisonous plants within the hedge. Fencing needs to be well maintained to ensure that it, too, is both sturdy and safe for horses.

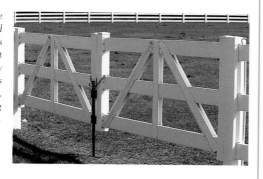

Field gates must be easy to open and close, as well as being of sufficient width to give easy access. Keep fitments well-maintained, with regular oiling of hinges.

Post-and-rail fences are traditionally made of wood, and are a relatively expensive way of enclosing a field. A similar but rot-free plastic alternative is available.

The presence of trees here behind post-and-rail fencing offers good protection against the elements, especially when this barrier is north-facing. Look for windbreaks of this type when choosing a field for horses.

A horse on its own in a field is less likely to become bored and look for ways out, if it is provided with toys that it can use to amuse itself.

Water

Since horses may drink about 36 litres (8 imperial gallons) each day, providing water in the field is very important. If there is no mains supply available, you will have to bring this in each day, which is a laborious task. In this case it helps if the water trough is located close to the fence, as you can fill it up more easily. It may be worthwhile considering having a supply put in, the location being influenced by the cost of extending from the nearest source.

A field shelter

A field shelter may also be required, particularly for horses that are living outside throughout the year. Not only does this provide them with somwhere to escape the worst of the elements, but also ensures that their food can remain dry when the weather is bad. It will need to be slightly larger than a stable (see pp.100–103), and should have a solid floor of concrete or well-compacted earth. Two doors or one large entrance may be preferable, so that no single horse can monopolize the shelter.

maintaining a
healthy paddock

Always ensure that there is plenty of space, and grass, for each horse in the paddock (see p.106). Never be tempted to overcrowd a field, since this will leave the horses more exposed to the risk of parasitic infestations – especially worms, which can cause colic – as well as a loss of condition. The first animals to suffer are foals, and their growth may be permanently stunted as a result. The other effect of having too many horses in an enclosure is that the overgrazed grass will quickly get into a poor state. In

ABOVE: The grass in this paddock represents good grazing for horses, but do not overlook parasite control, which is important in terms of their health.

RIGHT: A rather overgrazed meadow, which needs time to recover. An adequate area for grazing is vital to prevent one field being completely stripped of grass.

Poisonous Plants

Before turning the horses out in a paddock that has been rested, it pays to check it over for harmful plants. Cut back branches of yew, laburnum, and any other poisonous trees. Privet hedges can be equally dangerous. Although oak trees are not a problem themselves, horses can become ill from eating the acorns as they fall off the tree in late summer. You should, therefore, be prepared to rake these up regularly if there is a mature oak tree in your paddock.

RAGWORT AND OTHER PROBLEMS

One of the most common hazards in poorly maintained, overgrazed paddocks is ragwort, which has distinctive yellow flowers. Paddocks should be inspected in the spring for signs of young plants, which will need to be dug out, to prevent horses from eating them and suffering liver damage. Other plants that are potentially dangerous include deadly nightshade, which often grows in hedgerows, and bracken. It pays to learn to recognize which poisonous plants grow in your area, so you can identify them easily.

PHOTOSENSITIVITY

Even plants that are not directly poisonous can cause problems, such as photosensitivity. St. John's wort (*Hypericum*) is one of the best-known examples in this category. It contains a chemical that makes the skin react badly to sunlight, particularly relatively unpigmented areas of the coat. These areas then become badly inflamed and may slough off. Treatment involves keeping the horse in its stable, out of sunlight for a period, and removing the plants that are causing the problem.

Ragwort

Yew

Privet

Some common poisonous plants

- **Yew** Trees often grow in church-yards, but can easily overhang fields or may be growing in hedges.
- **Laburnum** Yellow bracts of flowers and long seed pods characterize this ornamental but deadly tree.
- **Ragwort** A common weed, with yellow flowers in late summer. Invades paddocks and must be dug out.
- **Deadly nightshade** This plant with tomato-like flowers followed by berries is often found in shade.
- **Bracken** This will be eaten by horses especially if other greenery is in short supply. Can be in hay as well.
- **St John's wort** Small yellow flowers characterize this plant, which is often present in meadows.
- **Privet** Tough, hardy green or variegated shrub used for hedging. May be present around fields.
- **Ivy** Grows widely in shade, normally as a climber.

addition, if the horses have insufficient food, they may resort to eating other plants in the vicinity, some of which may be poisonous (see box above).

Grass management

Along with a regular deworming programme, frequent clearing-up of the horses's droppings in the field minimizes the risk of parasites becoming established. In some cases, resting and fertilizing the paddock may be sufficient to restore the condition of the grass. Harrowing can be beneficial, but be careful with weedkillers, as these may have harmful effects, particularly if not used in accordance with their instructions. If you need to re-seed a paddock, then be sure to choose a suitable mix for horses. It should include perennial rye grass.

a year in the life of
a field

The way in which horses and ponies at grass need to be looked after will vary through the year, and may also differ from year to year, depending on the weather conditions.

Spring

In the early spring, hay and concentrates still need to figure prominently in the diet. When the grass starts to grow well, the level of concentrates can be reduced and hay can cease to be fed. At this time great care needs to be taken with ponies, particularly those that have been kept inside over the winter. They are liable to succumb to laminitis (see p.48) through gorging themselves on new grass. Laminitis is more likely if they are allowed become overweight, so it is a good idea to limit their access to grass, perhaps by keeping them in a paddock where there is less grazing available.

Summer

In the summer, the grazing is likely to be at its best, and as the temperature rises, so the horses will be drinking more.

The water trough will need to be emptied and refilled regularly, before the water turns green because of algal growth – especially as some forms of algae are toxic.

The warm weather also brings out flies. These can be particularly irritating to horses, congregating around the head and tail, which they flick repeatedly to deter the flies from settling. Flies do, however, have the benefit of encouraging a horse to keep moving, so that it will take more exercise. Even so, offer some relief by using a suitable insect repellent.

As summer progresses, the grass will die back if the weather is very hot and dry, making good grazing harder for the horses to find. This is when they are at the greatest risk of eating toxic plants, which they would otherwise ignore. If there is little grass left in your fields, you will need to consider supplementing the

The quality of grazing in a field will alter significantly through the year, being at its most lush in spring.

orses' diet with hay or other forage. You need to take
articular care in areas where the soil is sandy, because if
e horse ingests any sand while browsing on very sparse
ass, it can cause intestinal irritation, manifested as colic.

utumn and winter

here may be a lesser secondary flush of grass in the
tumn, and horses will often seek out ripening fruit, such
blackberries, in the hedgerows, undeterred by the
orns. Once winter descends, horses living outdoors will
ed to be rugged up, as appropriate, against the cold.
creasing quantities of hay must be added to the diet to
aintain condition, along with concentrates.

Offer the hay in well-spaced piles on the ground, rather
an relying on a haynet in a field shelter. This allows all the
orses to feed with minimal risk of disagreements. When it
ows, horses will have great difficulty in grazing and will be
most totally dependent on hay and concentrates.

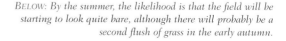

ABOVE: During the winter, the field may be very muddy, and grazing will be difficult, especially during periods when there is snow on the ground.

BELOW: By the summer, the likelihood is that the field will be starting to look quite bare, although there will probably be a second flush of grass in the early autumn.

basic first aid
for horses

Horses often acquire minor cuts, either as the result of injuries out working or in their home environment. These will usually stop bleeding quite readily, particularly if you can apply pressure to the site of the injury, either with your hand or a clean handkerchief. Bear in mind that if your horse suffered a fall immediately before an injury, it is likely to be rather distressed, and you will probably need to concentrate on calming it down before dealing with the wound.

Tears of any kind are frequently the result of the horse being frightened and subsequently injuring itself on a sharp object. In a paddock, repeated minor injuries of this kind may be associated with bullying. Should the wound appear deep, however, it could have been caused by a projection such as a loose fencing nail; cuts from glass or cans usually have cleaner edges. If either of these injury types have occurred in a paddock, it is important to try to find the cause, so that they will not happen again.

Minor wounds

Where the horse's tetanus vaccination is up to date and the wound is not huge, you may be able to treat it yourself and then leave it

A horse's incisor teeth are sharp, and a bite from them can easily puncture the skin, causing injury.

Basic Equipment

Essentials for the stable yard are antiseptic and wound powders for less serious injuries. A selection of dressings is also recommended, particularly to keep flies off minor wounds, plus a round-ended pair of scissors to cut dressings. A thermometer is useful. Prepare a portable first-aid kit for travelling.

CLEANING A WOUND

It is important to clean a wound thoroughly to minimize the risk of infection, especially on the lower limbs, where it can easily become contaminated with mud. Careful cleaning also enables you to check the extent of th e wound, to assess any other injury and ensure no splinter or other foriegn body is lodged in the area. Anything like this will have to be removed.

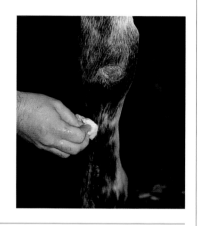

STITCHING

Your vet will stitch the wound in just the same way as if you had a bad cut. Stitching helps to draw the ends of skin together, facilitating the healing process, and also reduces the likelihood of contamiation of the wound. The stitches can be removed painlessly after about seven to ten days, once the wound has healed well.

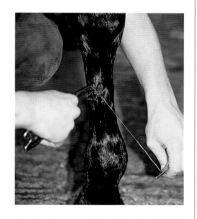

WIRE SCARRING

Although stitching a small area usually results in no very obvious scar, the risk of permanent disfiguation is likely where the injury is much more extensive, as here, where the wound was caused by this horse having been caught up round its neck in barbed wire. Barbed wire should never be used to ence a field housing horses, because it is so dangerous.

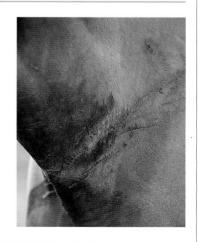

to heal on its own. To assist the healing process, clean the area thoroughly. Use blunt-tipped scissors to cut back the surrounding hair so it does not become incorporated into the scab. Bathe the wound as necessary, applying an antiseptic ointment afterwards. During the summer, wounds often attract flies, so it is advisable to use a cream that incorporates an insecticide, to prevent maggots attacking the area. If you suspect that the wound is becoming septic, seek veterinary advice, as further treatment, including antibiotics may be necessary.

Major wounds

More extensive wounds will need not just cleaning, but also suturing. While minor wounds will heal without a blemish, those that have to be stitched are more likely to show residual scarring. Urgent veterinary is needed in cases where blood is pumping out in large volumes, as this indicates that an artery has been severed. In this instance, while waiting for the vet to arrive, you should bind up the wound and apply pressure to restrict blood loss and, therefore, increase the horse's chances of survival. Try to calm your horse as much as possible, as this too should help to prevent blood loss.

Joint injuries

On occasions, a horse can be unlucky enough to sustain an injury that penetrates into a joint, rather than being confined to the muscle tissue. Joint injuries are potentially very serious. A heavy fall while jumping a hedge out hunting, for example, may cause a fracture as well as bleeding. If your horse has obvious difficulty in walking after a fall or other accident, veterinary advice will need to be sought. However, the most important thing initially is to catch the horse and try to calm it down, to minimize any risk of worsening its injuries.

lameness
and the foot

Horses suffer from lameness for a variety of reasons. When you are riding, you will notice almost immediately if your horse becomes lame, because its foot fall will be uneven. However, it may not immediately be obvious which leg is affected. This can be determined by having someone walk your horse up and down, allowing you to view it from the side. If the lameness is in the front, when the affected leg makes contact with the ground, the horse will try to lessen the pain by lifting its head up, putting it down when the

Diagnosis

You need to be able to pick up your horse's feel easily to examine them in a case of lameness. It may be an acute condition, which comes on suddenly, suggesting an injury to the underside of the foot, or it could be a long-standing condition, which flares up on occasions. Stones in the feet are a common cause of sudden lameness, and can usually be removed easily.

Cleaning off the hoof may give a clearer indication of the cause; take care as the foot could be more sensitive than usual.

Start by checking the foot when a horse goes lame, as the cause may be obvious.

sound leg takes over. Where the lameness is in a hindleg, there is a similar scenario, with the hock and hip being kept higher off the ground than normal when the painful leg comes down, resulting in a shorter stride. Short stride is also a feature when both forelegs are affected by lameness, as the horse is reluctant to put more of its body weight on them than necessary.

Finding the cause

When faced with a horse that has suddenly gone lame in one leg, start by examining the foot. It may well be that a stone has lodged under the shoe, causing bruising of the sole. This is why it is so important to act as soon as any hint of lameness emerges, as action taken at this stage can prevent a much more serious injury and a longer lay off. Lameness caused by bruising is worse when the horse is on uneven ground, where there is more variable contact with the surface, and on wet ground.

Treading on a sharp object, such as broken glass, may cause deep cuts in the underside of the foot. As well as lameness, cuts like this can also lead to serious infection, so veterinary advice must be sought rapidly.

oof testers can be used to locate a ainful spot on the foot, indicating that is is the affected area.

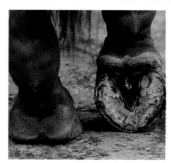

There is clear bruising of the sole in this case, which will need to be poulticed to assist its recovery.

f lameness emerges soon after shoeing, it is possible that a ail has damaged the sensitive laminae of the foot. Once he shoe is removed, the horse should soon become sound gain, so do check with the farrier in this case.

ecurrent lameness

ome causes of lameness, such as corns, may become hronic, with regular recurrences. Corns can be related to oorly fitted shoes and inadequate hoof care, and their reatment may require special surgical shoes.

Laminitis is another typically recurrent reason for ameness, being commonly encountered in obese ponies. diet based on meadow hay, rather than grass, is usually ecommended in the case of an outbreak, which also auses distinctive rings to appear over the wall of the hoof.

Navicular disease is another chronic cause of lameness, rising from a poorly formed hoof, which damages the avicular bone at the back of junction between the pedal one and short pastern (see p.35). Its rough surface then auses pain, affecting the flexor tendons, which is worse /hen the horse first starts working. There is relatively little hat can be done for this arthritic problem.

Dear Equine Casebook

My horse went very lame recently. I called the vet who found that there was an abscess in the hoof. She cut a small hole in the hoof and some pus came out. She then advised me to poultice the hoof for a couple of days until no more pus comes out. I have been poulticing, but have had trouble getting the bandages to stay on. Can you help?
yours sincerely Vincent Humphreys

It is easier to keep a poultice on if you stable your horse for the few days that the poultice is needed. Follow the simple steps below to make sure that the bandage is firm and the dressing is in the right place. After you have stopped poulticing, it is a good idea to clean out the hole on a regular basis and, if possible, put a small piece of antiseptic-soaked cotton wool in it until it begins to heal up and grow over.

Step 1 Ensure the poultice is at the correct temperature by pressing it on to the back of your hand. If it is painfully hot, it needs to be allowed to cool before being applied on gauze, with a suitable dressing on top.

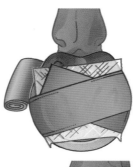

Step 2 You can then start to bandage up the hoof, so that the poultice remains in place, using a crepe bandage for this purpose. Applying petroleum jelly over the heel at the outset will help with the later removal of the poultice.

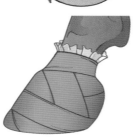

Step 3 The poultice is now secured in place with the bandage. If possible, fit a poultice boot to keep the bandage clean. Alternatively, you can use a stout plastic bag, with a pad at the front to stop it being torn.

lameness
and the leg

The cause of lameness may be in the leg. This is where the advice of an experienced equine veterinarian can be invaluable in rapid identification of the source of the problem and advice on the best course of action, which is likely to involve rest. Initially, however, you can carry out an examination that may help to find the affected area.

Finding the source

Start by simply running your hands gently down the horse's limb, comparing it with the other one of the pair as necessary. Watch out for any indication of heat on the skin. This indicates underlying inflammation, and there could also be a growing swelling at the site. Be careful when examining the suspected site of lameness, because this may be painful, and your horse might lash out.

Many horses become lame as a result of strain injuries to the soft tissues of the limbs, such as the muscles, tendons or ligaments. Reducing the risk of lameness is partly why it is essential to allow them the opportunity to warm up before undertaking exercise. Soft tissue injuries are most likely to occur when the horse is undertaking strenuous exercise, such as galloping or jumping.

Treatment

Never be tempted to work a horse with strain injuries. This sort of damage may take a year or even longer to repair. Seek advice from your vet, who will be well-placed to determine the

Brushing boots can be useful especially when there is a conformational weakne where injuries can result from a foot brushing against one of the other legs.

Dear Equine Casebook

My vet has recently diagnosed my horse as having splints. Please can you tell me how he got them and whether they will affect his performance in the future? Also can you tell me the difference between splints, spavins and ringbone?
regards Laurence Smith-Parker

Splints are small, bony projections associated with the splint and cannon bones (see p.33). They often develop as the result of injuries, and initially resulting in lameness, although this usually disappears once they have formed. Bone spavins, affecting the hock, and ringbones, on the pasterns, are similar. Bone spavins can lead to permanent lameness, inhibiting full flexion of the hock so the horse drags its foot. Ringbone is a bony swelling of the pastern and again reduces movement of this joint. A curb is associated with the hock joint, causing transient lameness and often linked with bad conformation. In this case though, it is the ligament, rather than the bone, that becomes enlarged.

Stable Bandages

These bandages can be very beneficial, not just in terms of offering protection to the limbs, but also for improving the circulation. Stable bandages are usually fitted to all four legs, helping to warm them up. It is very important that they are applied correctly, otherwise they can cause injury, especially to the tendons. Seek expert advice before using them for the first time if you are in any doubt. Padding must be wrapped around the leg first, before the bandage itself is applied on top.

xtent of the injury by using ultra-sound equipment. Hosing he affected area with cold water can help to reduce the nflammation in the initial stages, with both legs of the pair eing wrapped in stable bandages.

oint damage

oint damage can also result in lameness, causing swelling f the sacs known as bursae, which contain the synovial uid responsible for lubricating the joints themselves. Bursae are also found in association with tendons and ulnerable bony projections, such as the point of the hock n the hindlimb (see p.33), and they, too, can be subject to nlargement. If this occurs at the front of the hock, they re called bog spavins, while in the vicinity of the point of he hock, they are described as thoroughpins. On the etlock, such swellings are referred to as windgalls. The orse needs to be rested. Cold hosing and massaging the ffected area should resolve the problem.

Preventing Injury

There are a number of steps you can take to safeguard your horse from injury when you are out riding. There is a range of special equipment available for this purpose, but care needs to be taken that it is always fitted correctly. Knee-caps can be helpful, both for travelling and for when out on the road. The top strap has to be fitted to hold the boot in in place, while the lower strap is to ensure the boot cannot flap about. It must not be too tight because this would interfere with the joint movement.

Overreach boots safeguard the heels. They are made of rubber and extend around the lower pastern.

Knee-caps, also known as knee-boots, are traditionally made of thick felt, to provide protection, and leather.

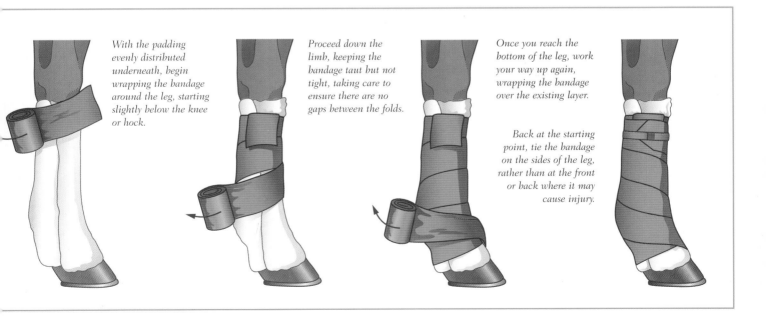

With the padding evenly distributed underneath, begin wrapping the bandage around the leg, starting slightly below the knee or hock.

Proceed down the limb, keeping the bandage taut but not tight, taking care to ensure there are no gaps between the folds.

Once you reach the bottom of the leg, work your way up again, wrapping the bandage over the existing layer.

Back at the starting point, tie the bandage on the sides of the leg, rather than at the front or back where it may cause injury.

recognising
signs of illness

By spending time with your horse, you will become aware of its normal character and will notice very quickly if it becomes ill, because of changes in its appearance and behaviour. Although much depends on the illness, there are a number of significant general signs. Any discharge from the eyes or nostrils, for example, should be treated suspiciously, particularly if coupled with coughing or other signs of respiratory distress. Excessive sweating and a taut

Problems with the Eyes and Nose

Discharges from the eyes or nose are always a cause for concern as they can indicate underlying disease. Although there may be a less worrying explanation, such as fly irritation, you should always be prepared to consult a vet when your horse has either of these symptoms.

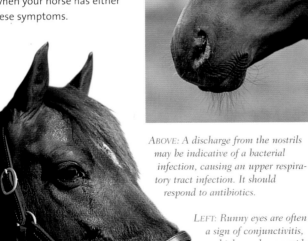

ABOVE: *A discharge from the nostrils may be indicative of a bacterial infection, causing an upper respiratory tract infection. It should respond to antibiotics.*

LEFT: *Runny eyes are often a sign of conjunctivitis, which can have a wide range of causes, with one or sometimes both eyes being affected.*

When you are familiar with your horse, you can quickly spot if it is feeling unwell.

skin are causes for concern, as is a loss of appetite and lack of thirst. A change in the colour of the horse's urine, to a brown or reddish shade, for example, or alterations in the consistency of the droppings may require veterinary investigation. Difficulty in walking or any other signs of unusual behaviour, such as pacing or attempting to kick at the underparts, must not be ignored.

An old horse is likely to be thinner and more bony, than a young one, so you need to be extra vigilant to see any signs of weight loss as they occur.

Taking a temperature

When you contact your vet, it can be helpful to relay information about the horse's temperature, which can be taken quite easily with an ordinary thermometer and a helper. Shake the thermometer down first, then dip it in a small quantity of petroleum jelly or a similar lubricant. Get your helper to hold the horse at the headcollar, before lifting its tail and sliding the bulb of the thermometer into its rectum so that it lies against the rectum wall. Take care not to push it too far in, otherwise it is likely to be drawn inside. Keep a firm grip on the thermometer throughout the minute that it is left in place. Remove it from the rectum, wipe it clean, and note the reading. A horse's normal temperature is approximately 38°C (100.5–101°F), and any increase of more than 0.5°C (1°F) indicates that it is raised.

Respiratory rate and pulse

When your horse is at rest, you can take its respiratory rate by measuring its chest movements over a minute. The figure should fall between 8 and 12 in total. Taking the pulse is slightly more difficult, and again the reading needs to be timed. It should work out at between 35 and 42 beats per minute in the resting horse. You may be able to locate the pulse from the artery running on the inside of

---

Indicators of Disease or Discomfort

If you suspect that your horse is off-colour or ill, contact your vet. A horse's condition can deteriorate rapidly, and this will extend the recovery period if it does not receive prompt attention.

Appetite – If your horse is grazing in a field, it can be difficult to check on how much it is eating. Should you suspect something is wrong, check the mouth first as there could be a dental problem.

Behaviour – A horse that is in pain may start to behave strangely, and even aggressively if a sensitive part of its body is touched.

Bumps or swellings – It is important to determine the cause of a problem of this type, which could range from an insect bite to a tumour or injury.

Coat – Some parasites such as lice can localize here; the condition of the coat also provides insight into the horse's overall state of health.

Discharges – These are often linked with an infection and antibiotics may be required to overcome the bacteria responsible.

Dung and urine – The consistency of the dung and the colour of the urine can both be indicators of the horse's state of health.

Eyes – Injuries to the eyes are not uncommon in horses, and they can even suffer from eyeworms (*thelaziasis*) on occasions.

Pulse – This provides an indication of the horse's overall state of fitness, and it can vary as the result of certain infections.

Respiration – The respiratory rate, depth of breathing, and whether any abnormalities can be heard when the chest is listened to with a stethoscope are all significant.

Temperature – The body temperature is typically raised in association with a febrile illness, and should be taken seriously.

---

the lower jaw, but do not press too hard, as this makes it more difficult to find. Some people prefer to take the pulse from the artery that extends across the inner face of the foreleg, at the elbow. Practice taking the pulse when your horse is well, so you can locate it easily if the need arises.

When the horse has a raised respiratory rate or pulse, veterinary advice should be sought without delay. It is also a good idea to keep it away as far as possible from its fellows, to minimize the possible risk of spread of infection. Thanks to antibiotics however, many diseases that might have been fatal in the past can now be treated with great success.

being a good equestrian

4

Many riders often fail to appreciate just how observant and sensitive horses can be in terms of the world around them. Horses can recognize a change in routine at an early stage, indicating an outing to a show for example, or respond to the slightest shift in muscular pressure from you when out riding. This does not equate directly with intelligence, however, in spite of the fact that horses have large brains relative to their body size, but is really a manifestation of a survival instinct. Failing to detect a slight movement in the grass, for example, could spell the end for an unobservant equid in the wild, faced with a waiting predator. Awareness is their key to survival and, as a rider, you will need to be responsive and appreciate your horse's sensitivity.

choosing a
saddle

There are a number of types of saddle, designed for different purposes. All have evolved from early saddles, which were initially like modified blankets and simply kept the rider's weight off the most sensitive parts of the horse's back. One of most specialized saddles of today, the sidesaddle, is based on a 700-year old design. Riding sidesaddle was the style favoured by ladies of nobility. It demands a saddle that fits perfectly, as any deviation is likely to result in injury to the horse's spine.

General-purpose saddles, which are widely used by everyday riders, evolved from the jumping saddle. The modern jumping saddle is based on the design of Count Toptani, a Spanish nobleman, and reflects the ideas of Frederico Caprilli, a cavalry officer from Italy. Caprilli advocated that riders should sit forward and shorten their stirrup leathers for the gallop and, when jumping, be in balance with the horse (see box, right).

Construction

The saddle is constructed around a frame called a tree. The tree is usually made mostly of

Different saddles have been designed for specific purposes, such as jumping, as shown here.

wood, but those used for flat racing are made of fibreglass to reduce the weight of the saddle – racing saddles weigh no more than 0.2kg (8oz). The bulk of the saddle is traditionally made of leather, although synthetic substitutes are now commonly available.

Saddle fitting

A saddle must be the correct width and length for your horse, to ensure a comfortable fit. Never use a numnah (see p.125) when fitting a saddle.

A saddle's length is measured across the centre, from the pommel to the cantle, and is usually given in inches. The most common lengths are 16in, 17in 17^{1}/2in, and 18in. Widths are usually called narrow, medium, wide, and extra

Saddle Types and Fitting

Jumping saddles have forward-cut flaps with large knee rolls, and the stirrup bars are also sited in a forward position, allowing for shorter stirrup leathers. The general-purpose saddle has larger saddle flaps and a larger waist, so that the rider's weight is more evenly distributed over the horse's back. The dressage saddle has a much deeper seat with straight flaps. This enables a rider to have longer stirrup leathers and, thus, a deeper seat.

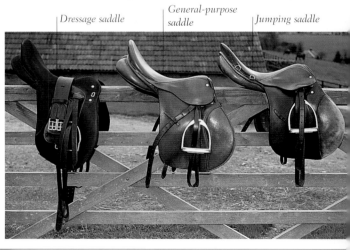

Dressage saddle   *General-purpose saddle*   *Jumping saddle*

Western Saddle

Fork or swell
Horn
Seat
Cantle
Gullet
Seat jockey
Back jockey
Latigo holder
Latigo
Front rigging dee
Skirt
Saddle strings
Fender
Hobble strap
Rear rigging dee
Stirrup leather
Billet
Back cinch
Stirrup
Stirrup head
Front cinch
Cinch connecting strap

The origins of the western saddle lie in North America, where cowhands spent most of the day riding over large areas attending to their herds of cattle. First and foremost, it needed to have a comfortable design. This was achieved by ensuring that the seat of the saddle was well padded, and by having the stirrups long, so there was no need for the rider to crouch up on the mount. The horn at the front could be used to wrap around a rope, to make it easier to move along a lassoed steer for example. Such saddles are often heavily ornamented with ornate designs carved into the leather.

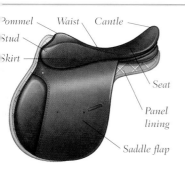

Pommel
Waist
Cantle
Stud
Skirt
Seat
Panel lining
Saddle flap

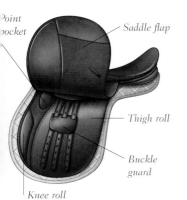

Point pocket
Saddle flap
Thigh roll
Buckle guard
Knee roll

A saddle must be neither too wide, exerting undue pressure on the spine and withers, nor too narrow, pinching these areas of the body. The correct length is also important. The degree of stuffing is significant too because, if it needs restuffing, it may well slope down on one side of the body.

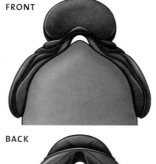

FRONT

BACK

wide, based on the tree. Your saddler should visit your horse to check on the size required. If you are buying a saddle without the help of a saddle fitter, find the width your horse needs by making a template, or wither pattern. This is done by moulding a length of reasonably stout wire or a 'flexi-curve' over his withers and transferring the resulting shape on to a piece of card. Cut this out and use it to check the front arch of the saddle. A suitable saddle will have a front arch of the same width and shape.

If the saddle is too wide, it will press down on the withers and spine, whereas if it is too narrow, it will pinch this part of the body. Looking at the saddle from behind when it is on the horse, you must be able to see a clear area running centrally beneath it, and it should be level from front to back, when viewed from the side (see box, left). If the stuffing on the panel causes it to slope more on one side than the other, this can be easily corrected by having the saddle reflocked. This needs to be carried out regularly in any event, even if you purchase a new saddle.

girths
and other saddle accessories

The girth keeps the saddle on the horse's back. Girths are available in various materials in a range of lengths and designs. All girths should be inspected regularly, to ensure the stitching holding them together has not deteriorated. Particularly check the stitching around the buckle.

Leather is the traditional material for a girth; it must be kept clean and supple to prevent it rubbing and causing soreness (girth galls). The three main designs of leather girth are the three-fold, the Atherstone and the Balding. Nylon girths made from lengths of cord knotted together with string should be tightened with care as they may also cause chaffing. Webbing girths are not particularly popular as they are not very durable and need to be worn in pairs. All these types of girth must be washed on a regular basis to maintain their flexibility.

Surcingles and breast plates

Where the risk of a girth breaking is high – for example where your horse is taking part in a cross-country event – a surcingle, or overgirth, may also be fitted. This runs over the

---

Girths

Girths are traditionally made of leather, although cotton, nylon, and polyeurethane are also used. The girths shown below are mostly leather in various designs. When fitted correctly, the buckles on standard girths are sandwiched between the saddle flap and the panel. Here, they cannot pinch the horse's body and are not felt by the rider. Dressage girths are shorter than standard girths as the girth straps on the dressage saddle are very long. This design lowers the position of the girth buckles so that they do not interfere with the very subtle leg aids given to the horse by the dressage rider.

Types of girth from left to right: Atherstone, with and without webbing, three-fold, and Balding.

Two designs of dressage girth. An extra tongue of leather protects the horse's body from the buckles.

A breast plate serves to prevent the saddle slipping backwards, and comes in the form of a leather strap.

*Safety stirrups are very important
to prevent your feet from being
trapped if you have the misfor-
tune to fall off.*

top of the saddle and the girth, and is fixed with a buckle.
Breast plates are used to stop the saddle from slipping
backwards. They are attached to the front of the saddle by
a system of thin straps.

Numnahs

A numnah is a pad, often shaped like the saddle, that is
fitted under the saddle to provide extra comfort for the
horse or to temporarily improve the fit of a saddle. Lying
directly on the horse's back, it will absorb sweat and so
must be washed regularly to prevent any risk of soreness.
The centre of the numnah fits into the gullet of the saddle,
to avoid pressure on the horse's spine.

Stirrups

The stirrup irons are the rider's foot rests. They are usually
made of stainless steel, which is very durable, and some
can have rubber treads fitted, which give a better grip.
Safety stirrups are recommended for younger riders, to
avoid the possibility of them being dragged by the horse in
the event of a fall. They incorporate a thick rubber band on
the outside edge. This will break easily in an emergency,
freeing the foot from the stirrup. Check the band at regular
intervals, to ensure the rubber has not perished.

It is vital to ensure that you have the correct size of
stirrup for your feet, to avoid them getting stuck or slipping

The Tack Room

Tack is costly so it is important to look after it properly in a secure tack
room. Here, there are individual saddle racks fitted on the walls, as well as
bridle hooks. The room also has sufficient space to clean your tack.
Although cleaning is important before a show, it should be carried out on a
regular basis, to prolong the life of your tack. Leather, for example, will crack
if it is allowed to dry out and the natural oil is not replaced by use of saddle
soap. Some tack, such as numnahs, may be cleaned in a washing machine.

With theft of tack being relatively commonplace, you need to mark your
tack so that you can identify it easily should it be stolen and then recovered
– although in reality relatively little stolen tack is retrieved, and it is more
likely that you will need to claim for this on an insurance policy. Most
equine policies offer cover for tack, but there are frequently quite strict
stipulations about how it should be kept, and if these conditions are not
met any claim is likely to be turned down.

through, either of which is potentially catastrophic.
Wearing your usual riding shoes, put your foot into the
stirrup. If the stirrup fits properly there will be a gap of
approximately 12mm ($^1/_2$in) between your foot and the side
of the stirrup on each side.

bridles
and how to fit them

The bridle gives control over the horse's head and, via the bit, enables the rider to steer and brake. Most commonly made of leather, it consists of a number of different components, held together with buckles and hooked billets. The names of the pieces give a good indication of where they fit on the horse. The headpiece loops over the top of the head, behind the ears, with the cheekpieces running down each side of the face and providing the point of attachment for the bit at the lower end. The browband slips onto the headpiece and crosses the face just below the ears. It prevents the bridle moving backwards. Looped around the back of the cheeks, the throatlash stops the bridle slipping off forwards. The noseband runs over the top of the horse's head and is held in place by the browband loops. There are various types of noseband (see box, right); the simplest is the cavesson, which can be used on its own or as an attachment for a standing martingale.

Fitting the bridle

For the horse's comfort and the most efficient rider control the bridle must fit well. There are three basic sizes: pony, cob, and full. These come in various designs with straps of

---

Types of Bridle

WESTERN BRIDLE

The bridle shown below is one of several that Western riders might use. It is a one-eared rolled bridle with a fixed-cheek curb. The bit looks severe, but it is only used to give the lightest of commands to highly obedient horses.

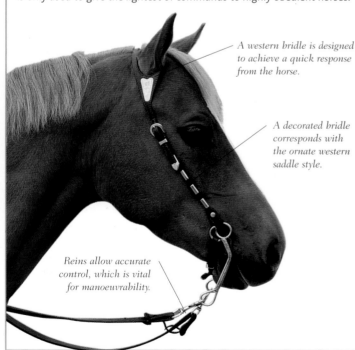

A western bridle is designed to achieve a quick response from the horse.

A decorated bridle corresponds with the ornate western saddle style.

Reins allow accurate control, which is vital for manoeuvrability.

ENGLISH, OR CLASSICAL, BRIDLE

The snaffle bridle is probably the most commonly used of all bridles. It is designed to be very adjustable so it can be altered to fit an individual horse. It is also safe and is not easily pulled or slipped off.

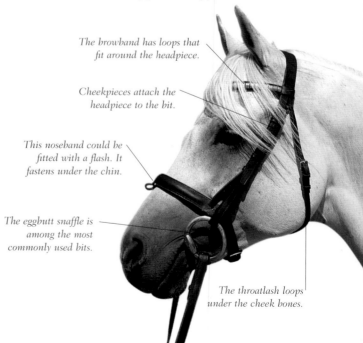

The browband has loops that fit around the headpiece.

Cheekpieces attach the headpiece to the bit.

This noseband could be fitted with a flash. It fastens under the chin.

The eggbutt snaffle is among the most commonly used bits.

The throatlash loops under the cheek bones.

This pony has a flash noseband, which closely resembles the cavesson but has an extra lower strap above the nostrils, fastening below the bit.

Nosebands

Although the cavesson is more for appearance than function, other nosebands assist the rider in controlling a difficult horse. The drop noseband (below centre) is a typical example. It prevents the horse from opening its mouth and crossing its jaws, thereby evading the bit.

The bosal is traditionally part of the bitless bridle used in western riding. The nosepiece, which is the part generally described as the bosal in this case, is made from plaited rawhide and lies about 10cm (4in) above the nose. Both its weight and that of the heel knot under the jaw become lighter as the horse learns to respond to this control.

A drop noseband must be properly fitted to avoid restricting the horse's breathing. When fastened, it rests approximately 10cm (4in) above the nostrils, and is buckled under the chin, in the chin groove. In this position, it keeps the bit in the centre of the mouth and exerts pressure on the nose, encouraging the horse to keep its head down.

The grakle works in a similar way to the drop noseband, but has an upper strap so restricts the jaw more. The kineton (not shown) does not inhibit movement of the jaw, since there is no backstrap. It is operated by the reins and, when correctly adjusted, exerts pressure on the front of the nose. It can be effective in controlling a horse that pulls.

ifferent widths and with plain or decorated nosebands nd browbands. The cavesson and the throatlash are usually undone to fit the bridle, which is slipped over the ead, the bit being gently eased into the horse's mouth. The throatlash and cavesson can now be fastened. The avesson is buckled so that you can fit two fingers between t and the horse's cheekbone. There needs to be roughly a and's width between the throatlash and the cheeks. If this s the first time the horse has worn the bridle, check the fit f the browband – it must not pull the headpiece forwards s this will cause chaffing on the ears – and the lie of the it in the mouth. (More details about how to put on a ridle are given on p.134.)

bits
and their uses

The bit fits into the horse's mouth, and should rest over the tongue. It is very important that it is the right type for your horse, and that it is the correct size. If the bit is too wide for the horse's mouth, it will protrude and the action will be affected. Obviously, if it is too narrow, it will pinch the lips at the corners of the mouth. A thin bit will apply pressure to a restricted area of the tongue, so is considered harsher than a thick one. But a very thick bit may make the horse gag. Check that the tongue fits easily under the bit and that there is plenty of space in the mouth for it: a horse with a narrow nose will need a thinner bit than one with a more generous muzzle.

Choosing a suitable bit, such as this loose-ring snaffle, depends partly on the horse's individual conformation.

Dear Equine Casebook

About six months ago I bought a 14.2hh, part-bred Arab of about seven years old. I am quite pleased with him, except when we go out for long hacks, when he can become very difficult, pulling and shaking his head, and generally snatching at the bit. I have tried many different types of bit, but none of them seem to make any difference to his behaviour. A friend suggested I try a bitless bridle, but I don't know much about them.
yours sincerely Josie Jones

First of all, you must get your horse's mouth and back checked. It could be that he is in pain and trying to evade the bit to ease the discomfort. If these areas turn out to be fine, you might, indeed, find that a bitless bridle will help. Bitless bridles are commonly used in endurance riding because they are less tiring on the horse's mouth but also give a greater degree of control over an excited animal. Arabs and part-Arabs seem to have particularly sensitive mouths and often benefit from this type of bridle. The most sensitive parts of the mouth are the tongue and bars.

There is a very wide variety of bits available, and all work by applying pressure to different parts of the horse's mouth and lips, and in some cases to the head. Most are made of stainless steel, which is very easy to clean, but other options include rubber and nylon, and these are not as hard or as cold in the mouth.

The most common bit is the snaffle. It acts primarily on the lips, tongue, and bars of the mouth, although the precise actions differ slightly, depending on the design. The mildest form is the unjointed snaffle, which acts on the ridges on the roof of the mouth. Other common bits include the pelham, which has a curb chain and a bridoon mouthpiece. It was developed as a substitute for the double bridle (see box, right).

Snaffle Bits and How to Fit Them

The choice of a suitable bit is very important. The mildest versions of the snaffle bit are straight and thick, and these are usually recommended for young horses. Most single-jointed bits will have a squeezing action in the mouth. The bit needs to fit so that once it is straight in the horse's mouth, it extends out about a further 5mm (¼in) on each side. It must not lie so tightly in the corners of the mouth that it causes a distortion here.

When selecting a new bit, it is vital to ensure that it fits correctly in the horse's mouth.

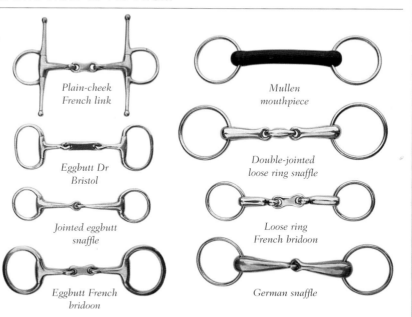

Plain-cheek French link

Mullen mouthpiece

Eggbutt Dr Bristol

Double-jointed loose ring snaffle

Jointed eggbutt snaffle

Loose ring French bridoon

Eggbutt French bridoon

German snaffle

Bitting problems

There are several reasons why a horse might object to the bit. In youngsters, lack of experience is most likely to be the cause. However, with suitable training and patience, most horses will learn how to respond. Care must be taken to prevent lasting damage to the mouth during the learning process. If the horse is being backed, it will need to adjust to the weight of a rider, and this, too, may affect its ability to cope with a bit.

Ill fitting bits and dental problems are other causes of resistance in the mouth, as are conformational problems and discomfort in the back.

The pelham is a combination of the bridoon and the curb, positioned lower in the mouth.

Double Bridle

The double bridle is used for more advanced schooling and showing, where precise control and response are very important. As its name suggests, the double bridle incorporates two bits in the form of a bridoon (snaffle) bit, working in combination with a curb bit. The bridoon has its own headpiece and cheekpiece, and lies above the curb bit.

When a horse keeps its head low, in an approximate vertical plain, the bridoon exerts an effect on the bars in the mouth.

Once the horse raises its head, this bit works further back, towards the molar teeth. This has the effect of stiffening the horse's back area, restricting forward movement from the quarters.

catching
your horse

Horses, with their instinctive curiosity and alertness, soon recognize when you come to their field, often because it means that you are bringing them food. You can build on this when it comes to catching your horse. Make a routine of approaching and patting the horse whenever you enter its field, so that it becomes used to being handled when loose. You can even reward it with treats and groom it.

Catching problems

With a youngster, you should establish your routine from an early age. However, a newly acquired older horse might not respond immediately to you, as it is in new surroundings and you are a stranger. Over time, the bond between you will grow, and it will learn to trust you. In the meantime, however, the worse thing that you can do is to run after the

Dear Equine Casebook

My pony is very naughty about being caught. He waits until I get close to him with the headcollar and then trots off, just out of reach. This is very frustrating and I can't think of how to stop him. Please help.

best wishes Betty Harris

When a horse is reluctant to be caught, it will often move off as you approach, responding to your movements and remaining just out of reach, rather than disappearing off across to the

other side of the field. It is important not to allow him to do this as it will become a habit that is hard to break. You could try getting someone else to help you usher him into the corner of the field, so at least he has not got so much space to run away. Alternatively, try following him gently but persistently, so that he cannot graze. It may take some time, but eventually he may decide to take a step towards you. At this point, walk off. Hopefully, he will start to follow you and, at least on this occasion, the problem will have been overcome.

LEFT: Approach your horse slowly so that you do not spook it. Don't flap the headcollar around.

BELOW: Slip the headcollar quickly and smoothly over your horse's head. A well-trained horse will stand still for this.

horse in an attempt to catch it. Not only will it be able to outrun you, but it may see the running as a game or even a threat. As a precautionary measure, before you let a horse out in the field for the first time, consider putting a headcollar on it to make it easier to catch. It is sometimes recommended to attach a short rope – 30cm (1ft) or less – to the headcollar. Should you feel that this is necessary, use a length of leather, which will break if caught. The headcollar should also be leather, or designed to break easily.

Dear Equine Casebook

I have a very well-mannered gelding of about ten years old. I have owned him for about six months and he has always been very happy to be caught and ridden. However, recently I went to get him in from the field and he ran away as if he was scared of me. It took me ages to catch him. What have I done?

kind regards Martin Stevens

When a horse that is normally very willing to be caught proves difficult, it may indicate that something has happened to upset it. For example, dogs or even other people wandering through the field could have affected its confidence. It could also be that there was a storm brewing. Horses seem to be able to sense a storm before it starts, and this can affect their behaviour. When they are out in a field, horses often find thunderstorms at night upsetting.

Most horses can be caught quite easily by means of bribing them with tidbits, but try to avoid falling into this trap if possible. Train your horse to either stand or come to you.

leading
your horse

Being able to lead a horse comfortably and safely is such an important part of its management that this aspect of training must never be neglected. It can make the difference between enjoying the company of the horse and suffering a long catalogue of embarrassing and possibly dangerous incidents, whether in the yard or at a show.

Teaching a foal to lead

One of the earliest lessons a domesticated foal has to learn is how to walk on a halter. From birth, a young horse will instinctively follow its mother, and it is this instinct that we make use of when

teaching it to be lead. This should be done while the foal is still comparatively small, rather than when it is a larger and more unruly youngster. A soft foal slip (smooth headcollar) is used. Unlike a halter, it exerts no pressure on the head, which might be actively resented by the young horse.

Start by wrapping a towel around the foal's neck, and then encourage the mare to walk forward, with the youngster following. You can push from behind, if necessary, at this stage. Before long, the foal should be accustomed to moving with the towel, which can be used increasingly for directing its movements, and you can eventually replace the towel with a lead rope. When the foal is moving as you wish, keep the lead rope just slack so there is no pressure on it. If the foal pulls away, the halter will tighten unpleasantly, so it will soon learn not to do this. This is a very important lesson. Encourage the foal when it responds correctly, but do not allow it to come so close to you that it steps on your feet or makes you stumble. It is vital that its head is level with you at all times – in this position, you will be well away from its feet, whereas if you walk parallel with its shoulder, the horse will be in front and more inclined to pull ahead.

Leading problems

Unfortunately, once the initial stages have been mastered, some owners do not continue with the training, and as a result, especially once the horse is significantly bigger, it may become very difficult to lead. Do not feel intimidated by this. Should the horse start to pull

Horses that are obedient and trustworthy on the lead rope can be enjoyed, safely, by everyone.

An animal that responds well in hand (left) will usually also be a pleasure to ride (below).

ahead, stop and make it back up, assuming the correct position, before setting off again. Be prepared to admonish it, if it fails to respond as required.

In the case of a strong individual, a chain lead is a safer option than a bridle, which might injure the horse's mouth if it misbehaves. With the lead held between your thumb and first finger, pull on it briefly when the horse starts to tug away from you, and then immediately allow it to slacken off again. The horse should soon realize what is expected of it and its behaviour should improve accordingly.

getting ready to
go riding

Before you begin tacking up, make sure that you have all the necessary equipment and that it is in good order. Include in this your hat, gloves, riding boots and any other items you need for riding. Make sure that your horse is properly groomed (see pp.84–87) and that its feet have been picked out.

Putting on the saddle

Start tacking up by putting on the saddle. Before you put it on, you should be sure that it is clean, so it will not make the horse's back sore, and that it is in good condition – a worn girth strap is potentially very dangerous. Lift it over the horse's back, and ensure that the numnah is properly positioned underneath, without creases under the saddle. Loosely buckle up the girth so that the saddle cannot slip.

Putting on the bridle

Once the saddle is secure, you can fit the bridle. Again, you must be sure that all the buckles and billet hooks are safe and particularly check that the bit is clean.

Holding the bridle over your left arm, undo the lead rope and place the reins over the horse's head. Remove the headcollar, using the reins to provide control if necessary.

Preparing to mount

Before mounting, check the girth to ensure that it is tight, but not pinching the skin. Check that your riding hat is firmly in place, so that it will not slip off when you mount the horse and that you have the whip held securely in your left hand. It is probably better to wait until you are mounted before carrying out any adjustment to the stirrups.

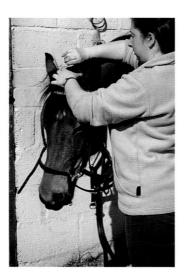

Step 1 – To fit the bridle you must first slip the bit into the horse's mouth using your left hand. A reluctant horse can usually be encouraged to open its mouth by pressing with the thumb just behind the curve of the lips.

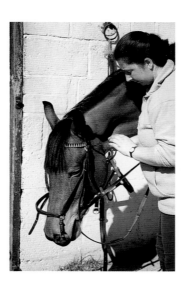

Step 2 – Now, with your right hand, slide the headpiece over the horse's head, using your left hand to pull its ears gently through. Ease the forelock over the browband, and ensure that the mane lies flat under the headpiece.

Step 3 – Do up the throatlash, ensuring that you can slip four fingers between it and the horse's cheekbones, then check that all the parts of the bridle are correctly positioned and not twisted. This could otherwise be painful for the horse.

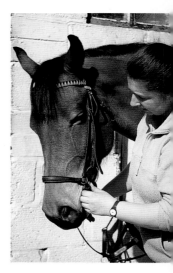

Step 4 – Finally, fit and adjust the noseband. This is a drop noseband so it should be fitted as described on p.127, so that it does not restrict the horse's breathing. Any badly fitted tack may cause even a good-natured horse to play up.

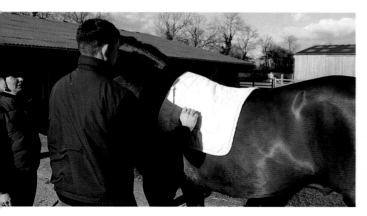

Step 1 – Position the numnah on the horse's back, ensuring that there are no creases and that there is the same amount on both sides of the backbone. Always use a clean numnah, otherwise you risk making your horse sore.

Step 2 – Lift the saddle over the numnah. Pull the numnah up into the gullet of the saddle so that it does not pull down on the horse's backbone. Never drop the saddle down hard as you risk causing long-term problems.

Step 3 – Go to the offside to buckle the girth. Leave it hanging down while you return to the nearside where you can reach under the horse's belly to bring it up on the nearside of the saddle and fasten it loosely.

Step 4 – Before tightening the girth fully, check that there are no wrinkles in the numnah or the horse's skin, particularly near the elbow. Do not tighten it fully until you are ready to mount.

Riding Kit

When riding or working with horses, it is very important to be correctly dressed, for the sake of safety as well as comfort. A riding hat that conforms to the latest safety standards is absolutely essential. It must fit you properly and will need replacing if you fall off. Special riding boots will help you keep a secure grip in the stirrups. Breeches or jodphurs are not vital, but are much more comfortable to ride in than jeans. For jumping, particularly across country, you should wear a body protector. It is important to keep warm and not become soaked if it rains while you are out riding. If the weather looks bad therefore, you may decide to wear lightweight waterproof clothing. Gloves are also important, especially when lungeing your horse. Should you be taking part in a competition, then you will need to dress according to the context of the event. You will also need to wear a number for identification purposes while competing.

first steps
to riding

Mounting a horse should always take place from the left-hand side (nearside), as distinct from the right-hand side (offside). Hold the reins and whip in your left hand, keeping the reins short so that the horse does not attempt to move forwards. Use your right hand to position the stirrup, so you can place your foot easily into it.

Mounting should be done in a gentle and flowing movement. Place your right hand on the farside of the saddle at the waist, your left one on the mane. Put your left foot in the nearside stirrup and hop up, removing your right hand from the saddle as you swing your right leg over the horse's back and down into the offside stirrup. It is helpful to use a mounting block, which raises your position before you start to mount. Alternatively, get someone to give you a 'leg-up' – push your bent left knee up, allowing you to mount without using the nearside stirrup.

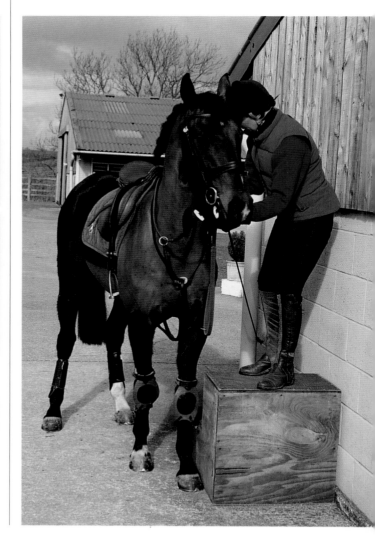

ABOVE: *To mount from the ground, use the stirrup for your left leg, placing your left hand on the saddle, which will allow you to swing your right leg and body over the horse's back.*

RIGHT: *A mounting block can make it easier to get yourself up into the saddle and is less uncomfortable for the horse. Follow the same routine as mounting from the ground.*

The hands help to communicate with the horse through the reins, and so must be responsive.

The rider needs to remain alert. With the head up any problems ahead should be spotted at an early stage.

Adopting correct posture in the saddle improves balance and so makes a fall less likely.

It is important to be comfortable in the saddle, and this can be achieved in part by good posture. Exercises too can be helpful, to improve the general suppleness of the body.

The lower legs can be used to encourage the horse to move faster if required, as well as helping to control the horse's direction.

The feet can also be used to encourage a reluctant horse to pick up its pace.

BELOW: The two reins should be held as shown, with a gap of about 10cm (4in) between the hands.

Dismounting

When you dismount, take both feet out of the stirrups, taking the reins and whip in the left hand. Place your right hand on the front of the saddle, lean forwards, and swing your right leg over the horse's back, so that you dismount on the nearside. Take care not to inadvertently hit the horse while moving your leg across.

Sitting on the horse

Correct posture is vital for all riders. By sitting properly you allow the horse to perform to the best of its ability, as well as being much more secure in the saddle yourself. When riding normally, sit straight in the saddle, with your

Practice sitting in the saddle to improve your posture. There are also various stretching exercises you can undertake in this position.

closed and facing inwards (see p.137). As the horse walks, its head moves; you should move your arms with the motion of the head, keeping your elbow and hand in a straight line with the rein and the bit.

When you need to hold both reins in one hand, the right rein is usually transferred across to the left hand, where it is held between the second and third fingers, also being restrained by the thumb on top of the index finger.

Communication from the saddle

Riders communicate with their mounts in a number of ways. The movements of your body are very important, as are those of your hands and legs.

To persuade your horse to turn as required, the position of your hands will need to alter. When turning to the left, slacken off on the right rein somewhat, and increase the pressure with your left leg on the girth to institute the turn.

weight evenly divided on both sides of the horse. Keep your legs relaxed, as any tension will immediately be transmitted to the horse. The feet should be flat on the stirrup bars, the heels slightly down and the toes pointing almost directly forward.

Picking up the reins

The rein comes from the bit, slots between the last two fingers, crosses the palm, is folded across the side of the index finger, and is held in place with the thumb. The thumbs are always uppermost, with the palms slightly

Your legs should be in constant contact with the sides of the horse's body. You can encourage the horse to increase its speed by nudging him with them. They can also be used to direct the horse's hindquarters, by increasing the pressure on one side or the other.

Leg movements are generally combined with the hand signals, via the reins, to communicate what is required. For example, in a well-schooled horse, squeezing the left rein more than the right, while putting more leg pressure on the left side of the body, will result in a turn to the left. Equally, if you sit up in the saddle and give a very slight but even pressure on both reins, a responsive horse will come to a halt, or drop from a trot to a walk.

The voice

Vocal communication plays a part in instructing a horse, with the tone often giving encouragement as well. For example, saying 'walk on' will give the horse confidence if it appears slightly unsure of itself. Remember to show appreciation when your horse has responded as you wish, both by patting it on the side of the neck and speaking to it.

Artificial Aids

The voice, legs, hands, and body are called natural aids. Riders may also require artificial aids to encourage a horse to perform. Spurs fit into this category, being worn on the back of the riding boots. They reinforce your leg signals, indicating more determinedly to the horse that it must move forwards. The aim is not to cause injury.

WHIPS AND SPURS

The whip is more widely used than spurs, and again it serves to reinforce leg commands. There are a number of different types with the standard length being about 0.74m (2^1/$_2$ft). The whip is always held at the top and directed downwards. The purpose of the whip is not to scare the horse, but to encourage it to behave as required. When it fails to respond to a leg command, repeat the instruction and give a sharp tap at the same time on the area just behind your leg. When out in the countryside, a whip can also be useful for shutting gates behind you, without having to dismount.

TRANSFERRING THE WHIP BETWEEN HANDS

One of the skills that the rider needs to master is transferring the whip from one hand to the other, without alarming the horse by waving it around its eyes. Take both reins into the hand that is holding the whip. Now, with your free hand, pull the whip through the palm and then resume your hold on the reins. A longer whip is passed from one hand to the other by making a semi-circle in front of you over the withers.

Whips and spurs are artificial aids that can assist the rider. They should not be used spitefully to punish a horse.

getting to grips with
trot and canter

It helps to be relatively fit for riding, otherwise you will feel rather stiff afterwards, particularly if you ride only occasionally. A supple body is also helpful in communicating successfully with your horse. The upper parts of your body, from the shoulders down through your arms to your hands, are especially important for being in control from the outset. You should also be sitting deep in the saddle as you set off together. Try to relax in your mind and body. Horses are very sensitive, and will recognize if you are feeling nervous, particularly as this is likely to be transferred through your hands to the reins.

Trot

The need to be in harmony with the horse's movements becomes even more evident once you start to trot. At first, it can be difficult to pick up the rhythm of the rising trot – partly because this is a diagonal pace – but it is largely a matter of getting the timing right. At trot, concentrate on keeping your hands level and remaining upright and balanced in the saddle, rather than crouching, as the pace becomes faster. Stay alert as well: it is vital to be aware of what is in front of you, in case you need to change direction suddenly. It is important to get into the habit, even while you are learning to trot in a school environment, then, if you meet hazards when you are out hacking, you will be able to cope with them.

Dear Equine Casebook

I have been riding for several months now, and can trot and canter quite well. I am interested in learning how to gallop and would appreciate it if you could tell me a bit about what I should do at this pace.

best wishes Lily Gordon

A change of posture is required once you start to gallop. In fact, the stirrup leathers are often shortened for gallop which makes it easier to lean forwards, while still maintaining your balance. By adopting the forward position, you shift your centre of gravity back over the horse's centre of gravity. Lifting your weight off its back will ensure that you do not restrict its movement. Keep your head up and remain alert when galloping because this is a very fast pace and obstacles can come up very quickly. If you encounter something unexpected ahead, you will have less time to react to it. Be careful where you choose to gallop. Make sure the route is clear, with plenty of space to slow down at the end. Gently ease into gallop from a canter so that your horse does not become excited, which may make stopping difficult.

The working trot has two beats to each stride and, at first, it may be helpful to count these beats so you can become familiar with the rhythm. Should this be too slow, it is known as elevated or swimming; if it is too fast, it is called running.

At the canter, you will be able to count three beats. When both the leading fore and hindlegs are on the same side of the body, the canter is described as being either united or true, and this is the most comfortable for riding purposes.

If you are exercising in a school, it becomes quite easy to learn how you need to move, which is by picking up the trotting motion from the horse's forelegs. When the outside front leg (the one closest to the side of the wall or arena) comes forwards, you should rise in the saddle, lowering your body down again gently into the saddle when the horse moves this leg back under the body.

Canter

As the pace picks up to a canter, it is important to retain your balance. Avoid tipping forwards as this is unbalancing for both you and the horse. On the other hand, you do not want to get 'behind the movement', as this means you are tilting backwards, behind the horse's centre of gravity. The canter rhythm should be gentle, so avoid bumping up and down in the saddle. In trot, the horse's head is still so your hands should be still, but in canter, its head will rock with the beat, so allow your hands to follow this motion.

Four clear footfalls characterize a stride in the case of the gallop, with the horse's stride lengthening as its speed increases. This is the fastest pace, with all four feet momentarily being off the ground.

riding
on the road

With more vehicles than ever on the roads, and many drivers being less ready to slow down for horses, the need for training both your mount and yourself for roadwork has never been greater (see p.148). There will probably be a number of occasions, particularly when you are out hacking, that you will need to ride across or along roads with passing traffic, so it is important to ensure that your mount is as steady as possible in these surroundings. It is also sensible to avoid riding on a road when the weather is very foggy or after dark, since this is when accidents are most likely. Despite an extensive range of equipment (see right), accidents involving horses are on the increase, emphasizing the need for public liability insurance cover (see p.74).

Dress to be seen

When you are planning to ride on a road, especially for any distance, you need to equip your horse with kneeboots, just in case of a stumble, which can easily happen, especially on minor roads that are not well-maintained. It is also important that you are properly dressed to alert motorists to your presence.

Brightly coloured retro-reflective equestrian clothing is now widely available, and works by reflecting back the lights from a vehicle. The range includes lightweight polyester tabards embossed with warnings, gloves, which are especially useful for hand signalling if there is a vehicle behind you, and cap covers. Retro-reflective strips around the stirrup irons emphasize the width of the horse and rider, and there are similar leg bands and tail covers for the horse, all held in place with velcro fastenings. As an additional precaution, stirrup reflectors can be used, showing red at the back and white in front. Small, high-visibility safety lights are also available from tack stores.

If you are out riding on a dull day, particularly near traffic, wear high visibility clothing to alert motorists to your presence.

Dressed for road riding, this horse has kneeboots with reflective strips and the rider is wearing bright gear. A reflective vest would be a useful addition.

Consider other road users

It is important to show consideration for drivers. For example, if the lane is too narrow for a vehicle to pass you and your horse, do not continue down the road apparently oblivious to the car behind, otherwise, the driver may use the horn in an atttempt to alert you to his presence. Although you should have accustomed your horse to this during training, horns can sound different, depending on the vehicle, and this might distress him. Do not be tempted to speed up if a driver gets too close behind you, particularly since there could be another vehicle coming the other way.

This horse seems very sensible, calmly putting up with all sorts of distractions, but this is a busy road and the rider should have made herself more visible to be on the safe side.

> ### Fact File
>
> **Do:**
> • Wear reflective clothing.
> • Put kneeboots on young horses.
> • Ride on the correct side of the road.
> • Make clear signals of your intentions.
> • Wave a thank you at courteous drivers.
>
> **Don't:**
> • Hog the road – ride to one side.
> • Ride two or more abreast.
> • Ride along chatting and not paying careful attention to other road users.
> • Assume that all drivers understand horses.
> • Speed up if a car comes up behind you.

When a driver overtakes you, you may want to check your horse's pace, but ultimately it should be sufficiently confident to be able to carry on walking. Finally, remember to take time to thank a thoughtful driver with a wave. It may seem a rather old-fashioned courtesy, but it is always appreciated and emphasizes that slowing down for a horse is a necessary manoeuvre.

how horses
jump

Horses jump instinctively, but in the wild they will normally do so only if they are being pursued by a predator. Jumping is potentially more dangerous than riding on the flat, and it is not something that should be undertaken until you are confident about remaining in the saddle. Wearing a body protector and getting proper instruction are highly recommended. Balance is the key to jumping, and it is not uncommon for novice riders to become unseated as the horse takes off.

Five stages in jumping

There are five recognized stages in jumping (see right). The approach is especially important since, if this is wrong, the horse is unlikely to clear the obstacle. The take-off follows, with the horse using its strength to leap into the air. There will be a period when it is suspended off the ground as it clears the obstacle, before landing and then getting back into its stride during the final stage, known as the recovery.

Stage 1 - *The first stage in jumping is the approach, which must be right for the horse to clear the obstacle easily. The best approach is a straight line towards the centre of the jump. If the pace is too fast, then the horse will have difficulty in timing the jump, and may get to too close to clear it. Do not to pull on the reins in the last few strides, as this will distract the horse and put it off its stride.*

Dear Equine Casebook

I have been riding for about two years and am quite competent, except for jumping. My horse regularly refuses at fences. I have fallen off him a few times because of this, and I am beginning to loose my nerve. In fact, when I approach a fence, I expect my horse to refuse, which he then does. How can I get him out of the habit?
yours sincerely Barry Barlow

It is not uncommon for horses to refuse when they feel that the rider is less than certain of the jump. I recommend that you have a few lessons with a good instructor and she or he will soon be able to tell if the refusal problem is yours or your horse's. If your horse has lost confidence, then a few schooling sessions over smaller fences will help to rebuild this. However, if your horse has had a long show-jumping season and is simply stale, it might be best to avoid jumping for a while and concentrate on hacking and fun activities. A horse can become bored simply repeating the same tasks, and it may start to play up as a result.

Stage 2 - *The second stage is the take-off, when you become airborne. With the hindlimbs tucked up under its body to provide the propulsive power to leap forwards, the horse pulls back its neck and lifts its head. The rider adopts a jumping position at the point when the horse's forelegs are lifted. A serious riding fault is to be behind the movement at the take-off, which will hinder the horse's ability to get over the jump.*

Stage 3 - *When in the air – stage three – the horse stretches forwards with its head and neck, which point downwards in preparation for landing. Its back is rounded and first the forelegs then the hindlegs are tucked up under the body. At this stage, the rider should be looking up rather than down, remaining still in the saddle. If the horse does not lower its head and neck, it may have difficulty clearing the obstacle.*

Stage 4 - *Just prior to landing – stage four – the horse stretches out its forelegs, in preparation for impact. Its forelegs touch down first, one slightly before the other, followed by its hindlegs. At the same time, its head and neck move upwards to maintain its balance, while the rider needs to be moving to a more upright position, but still without puting any weight on the horse's back.*

Stage 5 - *The fifth and final phase of the jumping sequence is the recovery or get away, and in some cases by this stage, horse and rider will be very close to the next jump, so there is little margin for error. Once its hindlegs have touched down, therefore, the horse needs to get back into its stride and rhythm without delay. At this point, the rider's control is very important in lining up the horse on its approach to the next obstacle.*

learning some
advanced techniques

There are a number of variants that can be developed once walk, trot, and canter have been thoroughly mastered. It is most important that you do not attempt to force your horse to learn the more advanced paces outlined here until both of you have a full grasp of the basic paces. Bear in mind that some horses learn at a faster rate than others and be prepared to be sensitive to the way your mount responds to schooling and adjust your methods accordingly. While it may be tempting to blame your horse for not doing everything correctly, it may be that you are expecting it to learn too fast.

Collected and extended walk

In advanced schooling, walk is refined into various sub-categories. The collected walk is a slower, more deliberate pace than the medium and free walk. In collected walk, the horse's legs are lifted further off the ground but the

strides are shorter, so less ground is covered. This is quite a difficult pace to achieve, since horses are often reluctant to shorten their stride.

On the other hand, one of the characteristics of the extended walk is an increase in pace, with the strides themselves also being lengthened. In extended walk, the hind feet will land beyond the hoof prints made by the

In the case of the medium trot, a horse takes longer steps than during the working trot and moves at an increased speed.

During the extended walk, a horse covers as much ground as possible.

The extended trot is the fastest of the trotting paces, with the feet reaching consistently forwards, without then being drawn back.

front feet. The aim in this pace is to increase speed through extending the stride, not, as happens with many horses, just to move faster.

Changing paces in the trot and canter

Equivalent changes in stride length can also be taught for in trot and canter. In addition, however, there is also a medium pace, which lies between the usual working pace and the extended one. In medium trot, for example, the horse should have a longer stride length, thus covering more ground, but the rhythm, as well as the tempo, must not differ from that of the basic trot. Until the horse has mastered these movements, loss of balance can be a problem in achieving the correct rhythm.

Lateral Movements

Lateral, or sideways, movements increase the horse's responses to the rider, as well as improving its balance and suppleness. Teaching lateral movements can begin very simply in the yard or stable while you are on the ground. Simply lean on the horse's body, in the area of the girth, to persuade it to step sideways. Once it has learnt to do this with the minimum of pressure, the next stage is to teach it to turn on the forehand. This is when the back legs step a semi-circle around the inner front leg, by repeatedly crossing over each other. This movement is very useful when out hacking as it allows you to position the horse easily for opening and shutting gates without dismounting. Start training for this manoeuvre in front of an obstacle, then there is no risk of the horse attempting to move forwards unexpectedly.

The ability of horses to master these more complex movements depends partly on the individual. The most highly schooled horses in dressage can make a full pirouette, through 360 degrees, at the canter.

Shoulder in often features in dressage tests. During this action, the horse moves forwards at an angle.

Haunches in to the centre of the school indicates the movement known as travers, carried out at the trot.

Half pass entails crossing of the outside legs in front of the inside legs, usually at a trotting pace.

teaching a young horse
about traffic

Teaching a horse that traffic poses no significant danger is a long-term process, and it helps to accustom even a relatively young foal to the sights and sounds of cars and other vehicles in the yard, perhaps by leading it past with its mother. You may also be able to turn a youngster out in a field adjoining a road, with a mature companion, where it will have the opportunity to become accustomed to the noise of traffic. Once the horse is broken, ride through puddles occasionally, so that water splashes its legs, like a passing car will do on wet days.

When you venture out on a quiet road for the first time, lead the youngster on the side of the road, as you would if riding it (the left-hand side in Britain). Take a light schooling whip and use this to keep it straight, flicking at its hindquarters if necessary. If your horse proves very nervous, take a steady companion along and get this horse to walk on the outside, nearest the traffic. Do not allow your horse to become over-reliant on having company,

Dear Equine Casebook

I have been working with a youngster for the past few months and have recently backed her with no problems at all. She is quite bold in the school and also fairly relaxed. We have begun short rides on the road and she is relatively good with traffic, but she seems to be afraid of tractors. Please could you tell me how I can persuade her that they are not going to hurt?
regards John Tucker

This is an awkward situation because, although the driver is likely to be more sympathetic to your predicament than many motorists, many horses do dislike tractors, partly because they see relatively few of them and partly because they are noisier and wider and so may need to pass closer. On the next few occasions that you meet a tractor, pull in at a convenient spot and allow the tractor to come by, so your horse can see it more clearly, before riding on. In this sort of situation, it is very important not to send the wrong message to your horse by keeping the reins short, which will suggest that there could be a problem ahead, but equally, be sure to have firm control of the right side of its body, to ensure that it continues to walk in a straight line alongside the verge.

It is well worth teaching a foal at an early age that horseboxes are not a threat, encouraging it to walk up the ramp readily. This is partly because it is much easier to overcome a young horse's reluctance at this age, as it can be persuaded to enter the vehicle more easily than an adult horse, especially with its mother nearby. Repeat this training regularly until the foal will enter on its own.

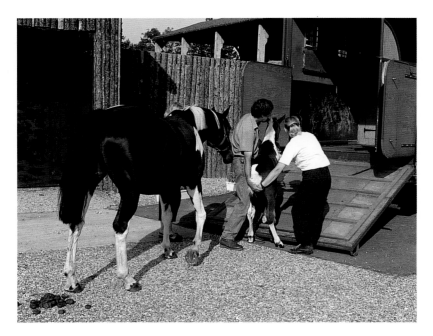

Road Sense

Horses do not instinctively have any road sense, but they can be taught to overcome their fear of traffic. This is an important skill to teach your horse even if you do not intend to ride on the road, because horses do sometimes escape or they may be deliberately released from fields, and they can then run amok among traffic, which will be very dangerous for all concerned. Do not neglect to take out at least third-party insurance, just in case your horse does become involved in an accident.

however, since ultimately it will need to gain the confidence to walk alone. When signalling to traffic, be careful to use the hand without the whip. Otherwise, this is likely to upset your horse and could even catch it in the eye.

The first ride

When you start to ride your horse on a road for the first time, choose the location and time carefully. Although proper riding equipment must be worn at all times, a secure helmet and back protector are especially important when taking an untried horse on the road, to protect you from injury – if you are thrown off, you are almost certain to land on a hard surface.

Follow the route that your horse has become accustomed to walking, as this will give it confidence, and aim to go only a short distance. Setting off early on a summer's morning, when you are unlikely to encounter a lot of traffic, is a good idea.

Fact File

- Tell someone where you are going and when you expect to be back.
- Ideally put protective and reflective gear on your horse and yourself (see pp.142–143).
- Aim to go for a short distance without too many challenges.
- Take a companion, if it's the youngster's first trip.
- Take a schooling whip to guide the horse's movements.
- Consider taking a mobile phone, but if you think you will have trouble, spend more time schooling before you venture out.

t helps if you can train your horse at first with the assistance of a friend, who will drive past as shown, allowing you to develop your horse's road sense. However, not all drivers will be sympathetic and pass slowly.

Always acknowledge a driver's patience by thanking them with a wave. You should also ensure that your horse is properly equipped to be out on the road, unlike the horse in the box above.

riding
a young horse

It may seem ideal to start with a young horse that you break and school yourself, in this way ensuring that it is free from vices and other behavioural problems. However, this is rarely the best route to take unless you have plenty of experience with a variety of horses: it is definitely not to be recommended if you are a relative newcomer to riding. Not only are there many potential pitfalls along the way, but bringing on a youngster is also a fairly lengthy process, meaning that it could be months before you are able to ride on a regular basis and years before it is able to do all that you require. There is also the cost to consider, especially if you keep the animal at a livery yard.

Dear Equine Casebook

How does a foal become used to actually being ridden ?
yours sincerely Eliza Dunn

The breaking process, known as backing, starts with the rider simply lying across the saddle. The horse is led up and down slowly several times, so that it becomes used to the rider's weight. After several days of this, the rider can mount cautiously, without placing their feet in the stirrups, while the young horse is still on a lead rein. Subsequently, it is a matter of walking normally, although the horse should still be led. Recently backed horses are more likely to be nervous than experienced mounts, and they need to be ridden with care.

What You will Need

A lunge rein is an essential piece of equipment for backing purposes. It should be at least 6m (20ft) in length, and attaches to a lungeing cavesson, which is basically a head collar with a noseband. The horse will also need to become accustomed to wearing a mouthing bit at this stage, for some time each day. Before long, it will learn to associate the movements of the cavesson with those of the bit. To accustom the horse to the feel of the girth, a breaking roller is used. This needs to be padded and must fit correctly, so that it will not slip if the horse tries to buck it off. The breaking roller is usually held in place with a breastplate, which can be removed once the horse allows the roller to be tightened without bucking. In due course, the horse can be introduced to the saddle and is then lunged with the saddle on (see box, right).

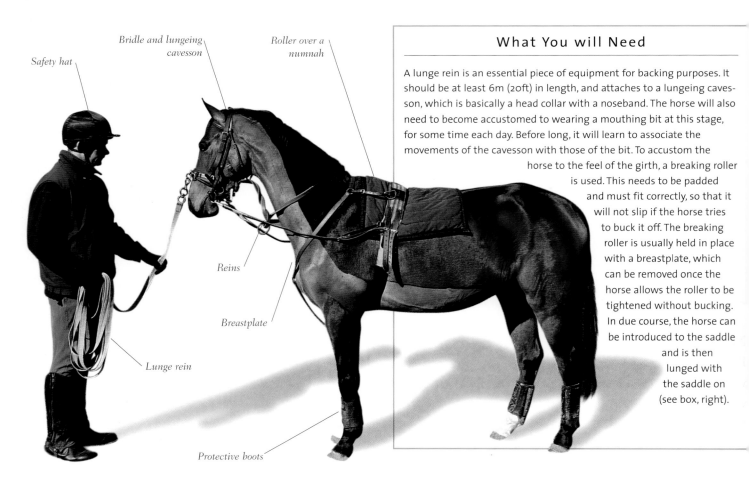

Safety hat

Bridle and lungeing cavesson

Roller over a numnah

Reins

Breastplate

Lunge rein

Protective boots

Starting a Young Horse

Horses learn at different rates, but it is important to carry out regular training sessions lasting relatively short periods, so that you can maintain your horse's concentration. Avoid over-working, as this can lead to health problems, with lungeing for example placing stress on a horse's body. Ensure that all tack fits properly, making adjustments as required, since this can otherwise cause discomfort or even injury to a growing horse.

Step 1 – *Lungeing is a starting point for a young horse being schooled, so that it can grow used to the feel of the saddle on its back. At first, it is likely to kick and buck, but this phase will pass quite quickly.*

Step 3 – *When the horse is going well, you can mount fully. Ride around gently with someone holding on to the lead rope. This gives the young horse no opportunity to take off and start bucking, and provides closer control than lungeing.*

Step 2 – *The next step is to increase the weight on the horse's back, rather than trying to mount up into the saddle. By leaning across the saddle in this way, you can escape danger easily if the horse starts to behave badly.*

Step 4 – *Once the horse has accepted being ridden, and is used to the weight and feel of a rider on its back, you can then start lungeing again, this time with the rider in the saddle.*

Making a start

If you are determined to obtain a youngster, find someone with experience who can guide you. Alternatively, you may want to send the foal away to someone who is used to training young horses for the saddle. Before your horse is ready to be ridden, it is very important to get it used to being caught and handled (see pp.130–31). Horses mature at different rates. For example, if you have a Thoroughbred, you might begin breaking in and schooling at just a year old, whereas another breed may need to be left until it is three. Arabs are notoriously late developers, often not being ready until they are five or even six.

behavioural problems

5

Behavioural problems, varying from aggression towards people to stable vices, are not uncommon in horses. However, it is often possible to overcome them successfully, sometimes simply by making changes in the horse's routine and environment. Remedial training can also be helpful. Luckily, today, there is plenty of help and advice available for dealing with a variety of difficulties. Just as with most physical illnesses, it is best to seek assistance as soon as possible. Ignoring the problem will not make it go away, and may give it time to become habitual. It is worth remembering that it will be far quicker and, therefore, cheaper to treat a problem if it is caught early, than if it has become an ingrained habit.

head-shy and
nervous horses

Horses are instinctively nervous by nature. In some individuals, this nervousness is manifested in such a way that it creates great difficulties in day-to-day management. Take the example of a head-shy horse. Virtually every routine procedure, including grooming, tying up and riding, will be a challenge, with the horse constantly moving its head away from you.

Again considering a head-shy horse, the reasons for its actions may be that it has not had sufficient contact with people to get used to being touched, or it could be that it has been deliberately hit around the head in the past, making it very wary of any new approach. Before you start working on the head-shyness, it is well worth consulting a vet, particularly if the horse has only recently started

Horses may only misbehave under certain circumstances, as here, when the owner is trying to administer a dewormer. Holding the head down will assist in this case.

Dear Equine Casebook

I have a Thoroughbred-cross who is five years old and he is generally going very well. He behaves impeccably in the school and is now beginning to show a real talent for jumping. Unfortunately, when we go hacking he gets very nervous and leaps at the slightest thing, especially plastic bags, so I can't relax and enjoy myself at all.
please help Arthur McCartney

Flapping objects, such as bags caught in hedgerows, can be very upsetting to a nervy horse. Don't worry though, there are ways to increase your horse's confidence.

DESENSITIZATION
Get hold of a large sheet of plastic to desensitize him with. First, wrap it around your hand and then gently rub it over his body. Do this slowly and repeatedly so that he becomes used to the sight and sound of plastic. Remember to give him plenty of encouragement. Now, open the sheet out and shake it slightly, not too far away from his head, before folding it up again. Should he show any signs of distress during this stage, do not carry on unfolding, but stop and repeat the first stage again. Always proceed slowly and with patience. A number of short sessions of this type should soon overcome this problem.

behaving in this way. Many apparent behavioural problems have an underlying medical cause. A painful neck, soreness in the mouth, or a painful tooth can all lead to a dislike of being touched around the head. If something amiss is discovered, veterinary treatment should resolve the problem without further worry.

Once you are sure that head-shyness is the true cause, you should deal with this directly. Do not be put off by the horse constantly pulling away. Start by offering it a treat in your hand (keeping this flat as always), and then slide your hand up around the horse's face, patting it gently and talking to it calmly. Repeat this several times as necessary to built up your horse's confidence.

If all else fails, the use of a pressure halter may be necessary (see box, right). This will encourage your horse to move on your command, rather than hanging back or pulling away.

Pressure Halter

A pressure halter is a means of encouraging a horse to go forwards. It consists of a rope halter attached to a lead rope. The horse is persuaded to go forwards by the lead rope. If it is reluctant to do so, this causes the halter to tighten over the horse's poll, creating pressure. Although effective, a pressure halter must be used carefully. Keep constant pressure on the lead rope when the horse refuses to go forwards, and release the pressure as soon as it moves as required, giving words of encouragement. It is useful for young horses, but also for older ones that do not respond well to a halter.

If your horse is head-shy and rears away from you, start by encouraging it to lower its head by offering tidbits from your hand while you stroke the side of its face.

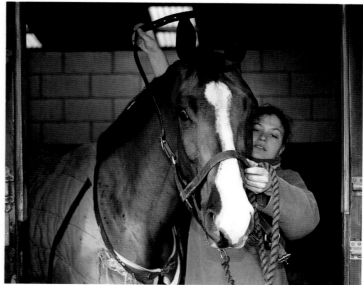

This should then enable you to be able to put on a head collar without your horse trying to escape your hands by pulling its head away.

what are
stable vices?

A stable is an unnatural environment for a horse, so it is not surprising that being kept in one can lead to medical and behavioural problems. Stable vices are common, with affected horses showing what are known as stereotypic patterns of behaviour, which are constantly repeated. Although they are called vices, there is no ill-intent on the horse's part, and this sort of problem has been likened to the compulsive-obsessive disorders that can afflict people.

What causes the problem?

Equine behaviourists often classify vices into distinct categories – for example, oral problems, such as chewing, and abnormal movements, such as weaving – but recent studies have revealed a common link, reflected by changes in blood chemistry. Affected horses have raised levels of endorphins. These are opiates, produced naturally in the body, and they make the animal feel good. It is believed that horses become addicted to endorphins, and so continue their abnormal behaviour, which may initially have been triggered by a physical cause. A dramatic illustration of the part played by endorphins was shown when a group of seven horses were treated with drugs that blocked the actions of this narcotic. Crib-biting ceased in all cases within 20 minutes – previously some of the horses had been biting their stable doors up to 15 times per minute. In some cases, the effects of this treatment lasted for days.

By watching your horse regularly, you should detect signs of behaviour that may develop into vices, such as chewing a chain on the stable door. Rapid action should be taken to prevent this becoming an habitual problem.

An anti-weaving grille lessens the accessible area over the stable door, and so restricts the horse's ability to move its head, but it will not actually resolve this abnormal behaviour.

Boredom can be a contributory cause to the development of stable vices, and it is therefore a good idea to offer your horse a suitable stable toy to play with if it has got to be confined for long periods.

Horses are naturally curious and their playful natures mean that they will soon start to play with toys provided for them.

Avoiding vices

Boredom plays a part in stable vices, but the underlying cause is often more closely related to the management of the horse. It is important to keep horses outside whenever possible, suitably protected against the cold as necessary. This not only allows them to graze, but also allows for their natural social interactions. While they are stabled, it is possible to ease or avoid vices by using one of the range of toys designed for this purpose.

Coping with vices

Like all addictions, vices are very difficult to treat successfully. Although its repetitive behaviour can be very irritating, there is absolutely no point in punishing the horse for doing it. In fact, punishment may even make the situation worse, by triggering the release of more endorphins, which also serve as natural pain-killers.

Alterations to the horse's environment, such as fitting an anti-weaving grille to the stable door, may make it harder for a horse to engage in behaviour of this type, but they will not offer any long-term cure. The use of certain drugs, notably tranquillizers and anti-depressants, may offer some relief, and giving a supplement of the amino acid l-tryptophan, which is important in brain chemistry, has proved beneficial in certain instances. Complementary treatments, notably acupuncture (see p.159), may also help in treating some stable vices. Your vet will be able to refer you to a specialist in this area if necessary.

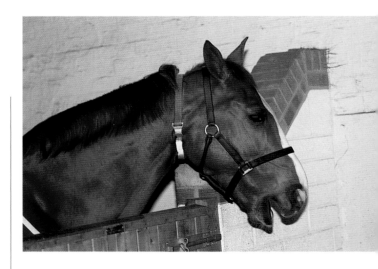

Wind-sucking horses can be fitted with special collars, as shown here, to try to restrict their habit of gulping air.

Crib biting and wind sucking

Some horses could be more susceptible to behavioural problems, notably those with naturally low levels of endorphins. These are usually released during activities such as grooming, but if the level of release is low or the receptors are less responsive than normal, then the horse may try to find ways to increase the effect, and this could lead to stable vices, which, as described above, are addictive.

Investigations in this area have also challenged other established thinking. Crib-biting is where the horse bites a piece of wood, such as its stable door; it is called wind-sucking when the horse grips the wood and then appears to suck in air. It used to be thought that this behaviour gave rise to colic, because of the swallowed air. Studies have shown that this is incorrect, as no air actually reaches the stomach. Instead, it only travels a short distance down the gullet. The characteristic noise that accompanies wind-sucking is caused by air entering the gullet. It seems that

this behaviour simply prevents the horse from eating properly, and it is this that causes the colic. There are other health problems associated with crib-biting and wind-sucking, notably the wear imposed on the incisor teeth at the front of the mouth. This can be so excessive that the horse finds it difficult to graze. Worse still is the fact that, by this stage, turning the horse out in a field may no longer provide a solution. It may simply carry on crib-biting or wind-sucking, choosing a new site, such as a gate

Allowing a horse as much time out of its stable, turned out into a field, is recommended as a general way of helping to counteract stable vices.

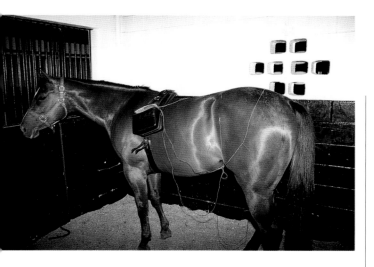

Acupuncture is giving good results in some cases, in terms of correcting vices. Veterinarians interested in complementary medicine are best placed to advise on the likely value of this treatment.

Domestic Problem

Vices have not been observed in wild equids in their natural habitats. However, when Przewalski's horses are stabled, a high proportion of them will suffer, exceeding the typical figure of around 15 percent seen in their domestic counterparts. Studies on wild herds have confirmed just how active wild horses can be, with Przewalski's themselves typically grazing for more than half a day, being actively on the move for about 2½ hours during this period. In contrast, if a domestic horse spends barely an hour daily out of its stables, it is not really surprising that, when problems do arise, they are most likely to be encountered in this environment.

or a fence post. Some horses can progress to wind-sucking through simply arching their necks, without having to grip an object. A special collar, which makes arching the neck difficult, can help to alleviate this problem.

The list of possible abnormal behaviours that can be seen in the stabled horse is large. Some, such as licking the lips, are not immediately indicative of a vice developing, whereas others, such as self-mutilation, where the horse starts to bite itself, are obviously problematic.

RIGHT: The teeth of crib-biters will be worn unevenly and need regular attention from an equine dentist.

problems with
the farrier

A horse that is difficult to shoe or dislikes having its feet touched is very frustrating. Shoeing is a routine necessity for most horses, and even if you decide to keep your horse without shoes, it will still need regular foot care. If you have a youngster, concentrate on teaching it to pick up its feet from a very early age, rather than waiting until later in its life, when it will find learning much more difficult. If you have acquired a horse that is nervous of the farrier, it may simply never have become accustomed to having its feet picked up. On the other hand, it could be that it has had a bad experience in the past. Unfortunately, unless you can speak with its farrier before buying, you will not usually be aware of this until it is too late. Whatever the cause, you will have to try to overcome it.

Correcting behaviour at the farrier

Although most farriers are sympathetic, they do not have infinite time to wait to carry out their work. If your horse plays up very badly on the first visit, therefore, it is best to abandon the attempt. Book another appointment and arrange for your vet to sedate the horse, which should make shoeing easier. Sedation may also help the horse to

RIGHT: Work on getting your horse to pick up its feet as a matter of course. This will not only make it much easier for you, but also should mean less difficulty when your horse needs its feet attended to by a farrier.

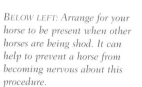

BELOW LEFT: Arrange for your horse to be present when other horses are being shod. It can help to prevent a horse from becoming nervous about this procedure.

Twitching

Twitching should not be used as a routine method of persuading a horse to be shod, but it might help in the early stages when you are trying to get it to accept having its feet handled. In other circumstances where a more positive restraint is needed, a twitch can be useful. The twitch is wrapped around the nose where it causes pain, resulting in the release of natural painkillers, called endorphins. It seems that these reduce the horse's desire to lash out. The maximum time that a horse should be twitched is between 10 and 15 minutes, after which it may show signs of aggression, particularly when released from the twitch. This is probably because the endorphins start to lose their effect. If the horse is twitched for no longer than this period, it should not resent the process in the future, but otherwise it is likely to react badly if a further attempt is made to apply the twitch.

overcome its fear, although it is obviously not a long-term solution. You could try other ways of soothing your horse in preparation for the farrier. For example, use a calming feed supplement – there are many on the market – or try complementary treatments, such as Bach's Rescue Remedy.

If you know that your horse is likely to be difficult with the farrier, book an appointment at a time when you will not have to rush off if it overruns. Hurrying creates a tension that is likely to be transmitted to the horse, worsening the situation. Also consider booking a longer session than usual, and when the farrier comes, stay with the horse to emphasize that there is nothing to fear. In between visits from the farrier, work on encouraging your horse to pick up its feet. You may also be able to arrange for it to witness a co-operative individual being shod, as this too could help to allay its fears.

Change your farrier

If you make no progress, consider trying another farrier, possibly one of the opposite sex. It might be that your current farrier reminds your horse of someone to whom it took a dislike, for whatever reason, earlier in its life.

dealing with
aggressive horses

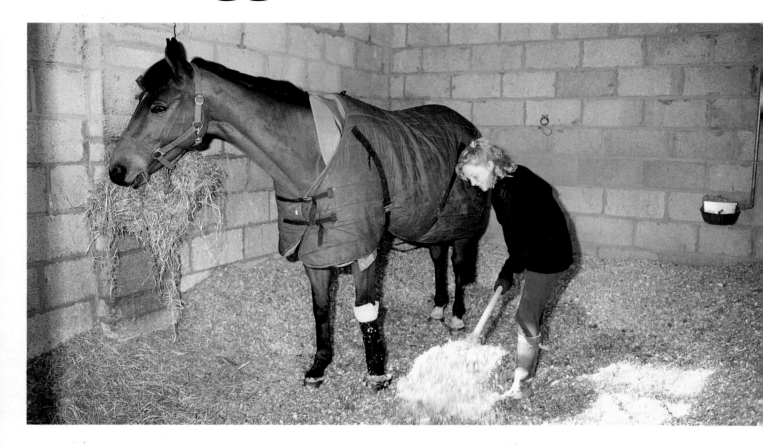

Horses can sometimes be aggressive towards people, which, in view of their size and strength, is potentially very serious. Temperament can be significant in this respect, with Thoroughbreds, for example, being much more likely to lash out than the generally easy-going cobs. It is important to get to know your horse, so that you are aware of what is likely to upset it and what it is not worried about. There are certain obvious precautions you can take from the start. For example, take care when grooming a sensitive area, because if you accidentally hurt your horse, this might lead to an aggressive response. Similarly, never approach your horse from behind, where its blind spot is. This could frighten it, which might be dangerous.

Stable precautions

Take care when entering a confined space, such as a stable, because your horse is more likely to react badly when there is no means of escape. Particular care is needed when you are entering a foaling box. Bear in mind that even normally docile mares can become very combative if they feel that their youngster is in danger, and avoid moving between the foal and its mother.

At all times, move slowly and deliberately around the stable, keeping within your horse's field of vision. It can help to establish an organized routine when working with a horse in its box. This will enable it to learn what you are going to do next, which will give it confidence and make it

LEFT: A haynet can serve as a distraction for a horse when you have to attend to its needs in a stable.

RIGHT: Stabled horses that nip when you pass are attention-seeking and may have been fed too many tidbits.

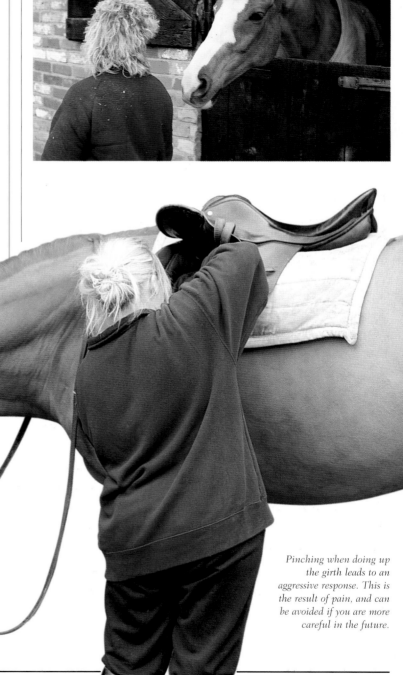

Dear Equine Casebook

The other day a friend asked me to muck out his horse and see to its feed. I was happy to do this, until I got into the stable. His normally friendly mare pulled horrible faces at me and put her ears back. She also kicked out at the back wall of the stable. I was quite scared, but managed to get out safely. How can I prevent this happening again?
regards Susannah Mapleson

If you find yourself trapped in a stable in a potentially difficult situation, you may be able to make the horse back down by behaving in a dominant way, mimicking the sort of body language that is common in herd power plays, where an established herd member might bully a newcomer, for example. Stand tall and hold your arms out away from your body, which will make you look bigger. Maintain eye contact with the horse and step slightly in its direction, rather than backing off. Speaking in a loud voice can also help. If all else fails, give the horse a sharp tap on the nose – this area is very sensitive in horses. Avoid being caught in this way again by ensuring that the horse is out of the stable in the future if possible.

feel relaxed. Should you need to provide a diversion, then offering a haynet can be useful.

If you notice a decided change in temperament, with the horse being more excitable than normal, consider a dietary cause, with crushed oats in particular having gained a reputation for having this behavioural effect.

Pinching when doing up the girth leads to an aggressive response. This is the result of pain, and can be avoided if you are more careful in the future.

how to cope with
bucking

One of the most common fears among novice riders is that their mount will buck and they will fall off. Bucking is a natural part of a horse's behaviour, and may occur when it is excited or scared; it is also a feature of rodeo events, where an unbroken horse is actually encouraged to buck and throw the rider off its back. Really vigorous bucking of this sort is more common among inexperienced youngsters and, once a horse has got used to being ridden, it will tend to be far less dramatic. Nevertheless, novice riders are at greatest risk of being thrown, simply because they do not have sufficient riding experience to cope.

Staying on a Bucking Horse

Since bucking is rarely related to misbehaviour on the part of the horse, seeking to punish the animal when it bucks is unlikely to be effective. Even so, it is important to be able to cope with a bucking horse when you are in the saddle. If you suspect that your mount is going to buck, sit up and use the reins to keep its head up – it will only be able to buck successfully if it can bend its neck downwards. With a confirmed bucker, plan your hacks so that you go up hill first. Horses cannot position themselves to buck when going up a slope. By the time you return from your ride, your mount should feel sufficiently exercised not to try to unseat you on the way home. Some behaviourists, such as Monty Roberts, can offer help in curing confirmed buckers.

Bucking can often be the result of high spirits, especially in the case of a competition horse, which senses the excitement in the arena.

If your horse is not normally a bucker, it could be bucking because it is in pain. Get its teeth and back checked over.

Pain as the cause

Even a relatively placid horse may buck when it is in pain, which is why it is always important to double-check that its tack is properly fitted before mounting. Something as simple as a crumpled numnah can cause discomfort and is easily remedied. More difficult is an ill-fitting saddle. Never ride with a badly fitted saddle as this can cause saddle sores and other injuries, which again could be a cause of bucking. If there is no obvious problem, it could be that there is localized pain in other parts of the body, such as the neck, back, or even teeth. If a horse that has rarely bucked before starts to do so, this is one of the most likely causes and needs to be investigated by your vet.

Too little exercise

Poor management may also be a reason for bucking. A horse that is not receiving enough exercise may buck when taken out riding. Lungeing before riding may be helpful in taking the edge off its high spirits. It is also worth turning it out into a paddock for longer periods during the day. Its diet may also need reviewing – a ration that is too high in concentrates, especially crushed oats, can cause problems.

Rearing

Rearing is much more dangerous than bucking as the horse can fall over backwards on to its rider. Even experienced riders find it very difficult to cure a confirmed rearer. Never consider buying a horse that is known to rear. Again, rearing can be caused by pain, so if your horse starts rearing for no apparent reason, do have its teeth and back checked. If your horse is apparently healthy, however, and yet continues to rear in this way, you will need to take effective action. Always start by slackening off your grip on the reins, because you cannot balance with these, and pulling back could easily cause you to fall, dragging the horse down on top of you. One suggestion, if someone is close-by in the arena, is to slap the vulnerable underside of the horse's body with a damp towel, to bring it down rapidly to the ground.

preventing *bolting*

When your horse starts to bolt, pulling hard on both reins together is not likely to be effective, because the horse's strength will be much greater than yours.

Dear Equine Casebook

A friend of mine nearly had a nasty accident recently when his horse took fright and bolted as he was bringing it in from the field. Luckily, she stopped by her stable and no harm was done, but could you tell us how to cope with this in future?
yours sincerely Mark Morgan

In this situation, the horse's strength means that you will lose the tug of war and have to relinquish your grip. Try to steer it into a safe area first, so that it cannot run out across a busy road, for example. By doing some groundwork, such as getting the horse to react instantly to preassure on its headcollar, you may be able to prevent a recurrence in the future.

Some riders worry that their horse will run off out of control, taking them with it. Within a herd of horses, bolting, or at least running off, is a common defensive mechanism, allowing the group to escape from danger. Thankfully, however, it is quite unusual when a horse is being ridden, although certain types of horse may be more prone than others. For example, Arabs and other horses bred and kept for racing can run great distances at speed.

Running off in youngsters

The risk of bolting behaviour coming to the surface in domestic stock is greatest in young horses. Their inexperience of the world, means that they are likely to panic more quickly than older ones. When taking a youngster out on a

A rider needs to stay in the saddle to regain control of a bolting horse, otherwise, the situation can become very dangerous for all involved.

hack, you need to be alert and watchful, even a large dog with which the horse is unfamiliar can provoke this type of reaction. Bolting is more likely if you are already travelling at speed, so you need to recognize any potential danger spots and be prepared to act swiftly to avoid problems.

Draw your body back, sitting up in the saddle, if you suspect that the horse is going to bolt. Do not crouch forwards in the saddle, as this is likely to worsen the situation. Try to steer the horse away from whatever has frightened it, and head for open ground, avoiding fences, ditches or other obstructions that increase the likelihood of you falling off. If you manage to stay aboard, your horse will soon tire and will want to slow down – at this stage, show you are in control by urging it to continue galloping for a period.

Confirmed bolters

Should the horse have a reputation for taking off, you may have prior warning through the reins. Be alert to this, and if you feel that it is about to go pull sharply and repeatedly on one rein. This makes the horse flex its neck and makes it slow down. It also unbalances it, which also makes it slow down. Careful schooling and dietary changes can help to cure confirmed bolters. In some cases, however, it is the inexperience of the rider that enables the horse to accelerate out of control.

A bolting horse can be slowed down by being forced to turn in a circle, pulling on just one of the reins.

where and how to
get help

With growing interest in the field of equine behaviour, it is becoming increasingly easy to get expert advice on a wide variety of problems. However, it is still a good idea to start with an experienced vet, who will check your horse for signs of illness or pain, which can underlie a number of problems. Your vet should also be able to advise you on the best person to contact in your area, if you do need to consult a behaviourist. If your vet refers you to a behaviourist, the basic costs of the consultation may be covered by your equine insurance. Check the small print in your policy to find out the best way to proceed.

Do not delay in seeking assistance if you think that your horse could have a behavioural abnormality. It is very much easier to deal with this type of problem in its initial stages, before it develops into a chronic habit, after which it will be harder to treat successfully. One thing you can almost guarantee is that the problem will not go away of its accord. It may even worsen without help, and you will be putting your horse through unnecessary trauma.

Keeping records

One of the key elements for a vet or behaviourist is to know the full history of the animal. Before a consultation, spend some time making notes covering such details as when, where, and how you acquired the horse, its feeding and management, and its age. Also write down exactly when you first noticed the signs you are concerned about, and whether any alterations in the horse's environment occurred at the same time. Include any other factors you think may have been involved in its change in character.

LEFT: It is often easier to keep control of a horse indoors in a riding school, partly because there will be fewer distractions here. Seek advice at an early stage if you encounter a problem.

ABOVE: Outdoors, horses are more likely to be exposed to unexpected noises, such as vehicle horns or thunder, which may upset them. Try to identify possible causes if your horse behaves badly.

In spite of everything, most horses give their owners many years of both companionship and enjoyment, with few worries along the way.

Next steps

Under most circumstances, the vet or behaviourist will need to visit the horse to see it in its usual surroundings and get a full understanding of the problem. If you have a video camera, it is well-worth trying to film your horse as it exhibits the unusual behaviour, just in case it fails to replicate this when the vet or behaviourist is with you. Your horse may be treated then and there or the therapist will come up with a series of exercises for you to follow. It may sound obvious, but once you have been advised on a particular course of action, do not become faint-hearted and stop too soon. A large percentage of owners do just this and, not surprisingly, the problem persists. However, there is obviously no guarantee that even if you do follow the instructions to the letter, your horse will return to normal.

Monty Roberts and Joined-up Thinking

One man more than any other has had a major influence internationally on our understanding of horse behaviour, as well as aspects of equine communication. Monty Roberts worked for many years as a rodeo rider in the United States, being faced regularly with particularly difficult rides throughout his career. This led him to investigate the possibility of using the horse's natural behaviour as a means of allowing him to communicate with his mount, and ultimately resulted in the development of what has since become known as the join-up technique. This technique places the rider firmly in control, as the dominant partner in the relationship, with the horse gradually learning to appreciate the benefit of co-operating with its rider. The method relies heavily on the rider's keen observation of the horse's body language, and a high level of confidence on the part of the rider concerned.

Although Monty Roberts has achieved remarkable results at public demonstrations, often 'starting' a horse in under 30 minutes, join-up almost always requires longer to achieve permanent results. It has proved to be especially valuable to use with difficult horses, as well as those being started for riding.

glossary

Action The movement of the horse. The action in some cases may be characteristic of the breed, as for example in the Orlov trotter.

Aids Ways in which a rider can communicate with a horse, which includes the use of certain *tack*.

Backing This describes the process of teaching a young horse to accept a rider. It involves getting the youngster accustomed to the *tack* and to listening to the *aids*.

Bars These are toothless areas in the horse's mouth, between the *incisors* at the front and the *molars* at the back. The *bit* rests on the bars of the lower jaw when it is fitted correctly.

Bit The metal, rubber, or plastic device on the bridle. This fits into the horse's mouth, over the tongue, and is used as a method of control during riding.

Breed A group of horses with distinctive, recognizable standard characteristics that will emerge in their offspring, leading to the description 'pure-bred'.

Cast When a horse is cast in its stable, it has slipped over, or laid down, and cannot get up. Cast horses can do themselves a lot of damage, and may be dangerous to try to help as they tend to thrash their legs about in an attempt to get up. When a shoe is cast, it has come off accidentally, rather than by the actions of the *farrier*.

Concentrates Formulated foodstuffs that help to provide much of the horse's nutritional requirements in a concentrated form.

Conformation The overall appearance of the horse, based on its relative proportions. These will differ, depending on the *breed*, but individuals may also display poor conformation, which will affect their ability to work.

Cover The mating of a filly or a mare by a *stallion*, usually arranged where the stallion is being kept.

Crib-biting A vice that results in a horse biting its stable door, or a fence pole outdoors. It may lead on to *wind-sucking* if not corrected.

Dish face This is a feature particularly associated with Arab horses, which are known for their concave profile. It is a characteristic that they may pass on to half-bred offspring.

Dishing A conformational fault in which the horse throws either one or both front legs outwards in a circle as it moves forward.

Draught horse A heavy horse used for pulling carts or other loads rather than for riding purposes.

Farrier A qualified professional who works with horses' feet, keeping them trimmed and shod.

Feral Horses Horses and their descendants, that have reverted to living wild after having originally been domesticated.

Flehmening This describes the way that stallions curl their upper lips to sniff the air when a mare is coming into season, with the scent molecules registering via Jacobsen's organ in the roof of the mouth.

Gait The way in which a horse moves, as well as the sequence of the movement of the feet. The common gaits are the walk, trot, canter, and gallop, but others are recognized as well.

Hack To ride out of the yard to exercise the horse and for the enjoyment of the rider, as opposed to schooling, which is usually done in a manège.

Hand The traditional method of measuring a horse, which is taken at the withers. One hand corresponds to 4in (10cm), the width of a human hand. For example, 14.3hh describes a horse that is 59 inches high (14 x 4 + 3) at the withers; 'hh' means 'hands high'.

Incisors The teeth at the front of the horse's mouth, used primarily for plucking herbage and grooming.

Lungeing Exercising in a school or paddock, with the horse moving in a circle around the handler. Aside from the long rein, the handler may also have a lungeing whip.

Molars The teeth at the rear of the mouth that are used for grinding up food before it is swallowed.

Nappy A horse that objects to going in the direction required, sometimes rearing or spinning around when obliged to do so.

Numnah The cloth that fits under the saddle to increase the horse's comfort and keep the underside of the saddle clean. It may be padded to reduce rubbing, however, a well-fitted saddle should not require a numnah.

Pony A group of horses mainly distinguished by the fact that they measure less than 14.2hh when fully grown. They also have a relatively distinctive *conformation*.

Stallion An adult male horse that has not been castrated. Usually hard to manage, stallions are normally only kept for breeding purposes.

Strike off This refers to the first step of canter, e.g. the horse strikes off on the offside fore when cantering on a right lead.

Tack The equipment that is necessary for riding a horse, such as the saddle and bridle.

Twitch A loop of cord attached to a stick and used to restrain a horse. The loop fits over the muzzle and causes the release of endorphins, which seem to relax the horse.

Vice A behavioural problem that can range from a minor individual quirk to a serious flaw which can make the horse difficult to manage or ride.

Wind-sucking This is when the horse stands and sucks air directly into its lungs. It is often linked with *crib-biting*.

Wolf teeth The name given to small premolar teeth in the upper jaw. They are not always present, but will need to be removed to prevent difficulty fitting a bit into the horse's mouth.

useful **addresses**

Association of British Riding Schools,
Queens Chambers, 38–40 Queen Street, Penzance, Cornwall
TR18 4BH. Tel. 01736 369440.

Bransby Home of Rest for Horses,
Bransby, Saxilby, Lincoln LN1 2PH. Tel. 01427 788464.

British Dressage,
National Agricultural Centre, Stoneleigh Park, Kenilworth,
Warwickshire CV8 2RJ. Tel. 024 7669 8830.

British Driving Society,
27 Dugard Place, Barford, near Warwick, CV35 8DX.
Tel. 01926 624420.

British Endurance Riding Association,
National Agricultural Centre, Stoneleigh Park, Kenilworth,
Warwickshire CV8 2RP. Tel. 024 7669 8863.

British Equestrian Federation,
National Agricultural Centre, Stoneleigh Park, Kenilworth,
Warwickshire CV8 2RH. Tel. 024 7669 8871.

British Equine Veterinary Association,
5 Finlay Street, London SW6 6HE. Tel. 020 7610 6080.

British Horse Database Ltd.,
52-60 Sanders Road, Wellingborough, Northamptonshire
NN8 4BX. Tel. 01933 274363.

British Horse Driving Trials Association,
National Agricultural Centre, Stoneleigh Park, Kenilworth,
Warwickshire CV8 2RJ. Tel. 024 7669 8856.

British Show Jumping Association,
National Agricultural Centre, Stoneleigh Park, Kenilworth,
Warwickshire CV8 2RJ. Tel. 024 7669 8800.

The Classical Riding Club,
Eden Hall, Kelso, Roxburghshire TD5 7QD.
Tel. 01890 830380.

**Commons, Open Spaces and Foothpaths
Preservation Society,**
25a Bell Street, Henley-on-Thames, Oxfordshire RG9 2BA.
Tel. 01491 573535.

Equine Behaviour Forum,
Grove Cottage, Brinkley, Newmarket, Suffolk.
Tel. 01638 507502.

Riding for the Disabled Association,
Avenue R, National Agricultural Centre, Stoneleigh Park,
Kenilworth, Warwickshire CV8 2RJ. Tel. 024 7669 6510.

Western Equestrian Society,
20 Newlands Close, Yateley, Hampshire GU46 6HE.
Tel. 01252 875896.

Worshipful Company of Farriers,
19 Queen Street, Chipperfield, Kings Langley, Hertfordshire
WD4 9BT. Tel. 01923 260747.

Worshipful Company of Saddlers,
Saddlers' Hall, 40 Gutter Lane, Cheapside, London EC2V 6BR.
Tel. 020 7726 8661.

Breed societies

These are some of the main breed societies; there are many others.

The Arab Horse Society,
Windsor House, The Square, Ramsbury, near Marlborough, Wiltshire SN8 2PE. Tel. 01672 520782.

British Appaloosa Society,
c/o 36 Clusterbolts, Stapleford, Hertforshire SG14 3ND. Tel. 01992 558657.

British Andalusian Society,
High Oaks, The Cwm, Forden, Montgomery, Powys SY21 8NB. Tel. 01938 580192.

British Miniature Horse Association,
Howick Farm, The Haven, Billingshurst, West Sussex, RH14 9BQ. Tel. 01403 822639.

British Mule Society,
Hope Mount Farm, Top of Hope, Alstonfield, Ashbourne, Derbyshire DE6 2FR. Tel. 01335 310353.

The British Palomino Society,
Penrhiwllan, Llandysul, Ceredigion, SA44 5NZ. Tel. 01239 851387.

The British Show Hack, Cob and Riding Horse Association,
Chamberlain House, 88 High Street, Coleshill, West Midlands, B46 3BZ. Tel. 01675 466211.

British Show Pony Society,
124 Green End Road, Sawtry, Huntingdon, Cambridgeshire PE17 5XA. Tel. 01487 831376.

British Warmblood Society,
Moorlands Farm, New Yatt, Witney, Oxforshire OX8 6TE. Tel. 01993 868673.

Caspian Pony Society,
Sparrow Farm, Lanhill, Chippenham, Wiltshire SN14 6LX. Tel. 01249 782246.

Coloured Horse and Pony Society (CHAPS UK),
Newbarn Farm Cottage, Stadhampton, Oxfordshire OX44 7RR. Tel. 01865 400447.

Dartmoor Pony Society,
57 Pykes Down, Ivybridge, Devon, PL21 0BY. Tel. 01752 897053.

Donkey Breed Society,
The Hermitage, Pootings, Edenbridge, Kent TN8 6SD. Tel. 01732 864414.

Exmoor Pony Society,
Glenfern, Waddicombe, Dulverton, Somerset TA22 9RY. Tel. 01398 341490.

Heavy Horse Preservation Society,
Old Rectory, Whitchurch, Shropshire, SY13 1LF. Tel. 01948 663559.

The Icelandic Horse Society,
22 Smiley Knowes Court, North Berwick, East Lothian, EH39 4RG. Tel. 01620 893391.

Welsh Pony and Cob Society,
6 Chalybeate Street, Aberystwyth, Caredigion SY23 1HS. Tel. 01970 617501.

index

Mary Gilliatt's
NEW GUIDE TO
DECORATING

Mary Gilliatt's
NEW GUIDE TO
DECORATING

This edition specially produced for
The Leisure Circle Limited
by Conran Octopus Limited
37 Shelton Street
London WC2H 9HN

Parts 1,2,3 text copyright © Mary Gilliatt 1988
Part 4 text copyright © Conran Octopus Limited 1988

Author of Part 4   Elizabeth Wilhide

Project Editor   Polly Powell
Editor   Paul Barnett
Technical Editors   John McGowan   Roger DuBern
                     Christine Parsons
Editorial Assistant Jane Harcus
Visualizer   Jean Morley

Art Editor   Karen Bowen
Design Assistant   Alison Shackleton
Picture Research   Shona Wood
Production   Michel Blake
Illustrators   Hayward Art Group   Vanessa Luff
                     Cherrill Parris   Maggie Raynor
                     Chris Welch   Roy White

Typeset by Tradespools
Printed and bound in Singapore

CONTENTS

Part 4: *Successful Decorating*

INTRODUCTION

This book is not only a comprehensive and practical guide to decorating, it is also a very personal work. It is personal because it is an updated distillation of my own experiences as an interior designer, experiences which I think have universal application.

As a design writer I am fortunate enough to see not only other people's design and decoration, but also all that is new and interesting in decorating techniques, lighting, furniture, fabrics, and wall and floor coverings. But as an interior decorator who has had to learn the hard way for myself, I have to think how best to use this wealth of merchandise and techniques, and where. On a daily basis I have to cope with the reality of juggling with these elements to create a satisfying whole. I have to deal with the problems that so often occur to upset the best laid plans. I know the compromises one has to make before a room, or an apartment, or a house can be finished to one's satisfaction. I understand the difficulties so many people have in reaching a decision, making choices, and the frustrations this can cause. But equally I know the pure delight of achievement, of seeing ideas and schemes translated into rooms that really do give pleasure and enjoyment. And this is worth a very great deal.

Although I have written other guides to decorating in the past, the fact is that I never stop learning, never stop experiencing. And it is with this ever-increasing number of experiences fresh in my mind that I write now. I hope that this book will help people to recognize the pitfalls that can exist and how to avoid them, offer them formulae that I know work well and guide them through the whole process of decorating a home. Above all, I want people to experience for themselves the very real delight and pleasure that good interior decorating can bring.

The Professional Approach

Good interior design is as much about practicality, comfort and detail as it is about style and aesthetics. Any competent designer asked either to improve a home or to plan one from scratch would first try to find out exactly how the occupants live, how they would like to live if they were sufficiently wealthy, and how much they can actually afford to spend. Starting with the ideal and working backwards towards a realistic budget is as good a way as any of sorting out the genuine priorities.

First Questions The most useful thing that the designer can do at first is to draw people out in order to establish their tastes and the factors in their home that make them feel most at ease. This done, the designer can use the information as a basis for his or her design solutions. Obviously, if you are acting as your own designer, it makes sense to ask yourself the same kind of salient questions, however elementary they might seem, and to take a hard objective look, in the light of the money available for the project, at each room you want to decorate. The most successful decoration is the result of effective elimination. And working slowly within a clearly defined framework gives you more time to think problems through, to experiment and to learn.

The questions that a designer would ask clients generally come under three categories: the *practical*, the *aesthetic* (on questions of taste and style preferences) and the *budgetary*. The following are typical examples of questions a designer would be likely to ask you, and which you should therefore ask yourself.

Practical
- How long do you expect to stay in your present home?
- Are there, or are there likely to be, children in the household?
- What is the maximum number of rooms you think you will need? Can these be found from existing space? Could you, for example, use roof or attic space?
- Do any elderly relatives live with you, or are they frequent house-guests? Do you, for example, need extra lighting or hand-grip rails?
- Are there any pets in the household? (This, of course, affects the types of finishes and surfaces used.)
- Where does the family feel most comfortable eating – in the kitchen, living room, family room or dining room?
- Almost certainly some of your rooms will have multiple uses (for example, the children may do their homework in the dining room); if so, are the needs of the various users likely to conflict?
- How often do you entertain, and how? How many people do you generally entertain at once?
- Where do you entertain? The living room? The dining room? The kitchen?
- Is sleeping accommodation cramped for the family?
- Are the washing/bathing/toilet facilities inconvenient? Are there problems at peak times (for example, in the mornings)?
- Is your overall storage space insufficient? If so, is it capable of being expanded?
- What are the regular leisure-time activities of the members of the household? Watching TV or video, or using a computer?
- Do any of the family have any specialist activities or hobbies, requiring rooms to be set aside as workrooms? Should there be rooms reserved for equipment such as the washing machine and dryer, or the freezer?

Aesthetic
- Would you say you and your partner share similar tastes or do you have decidedly different tastes? Have you agreed to have your own way in different rooms?
- When it comes to colour schemes, do you feel quite sure of what you want? Are you confused and uncertain, or are you open-minded?
- With what particular colours are you happiest? Are there any colours you really dislike?
- Would you say your taste in decorating and furnishing is eclectic? Traditional? Modern? Romantic? Idiosyncratic? Minimalist? Do your views depend on the house or room in question? And what styles do you admire? Country style (from whatever country)? Sophisticated townhouse? Oriental? Indoor–outdoor? American Colonial? Empire? Regency? Victorian? Neoclassical? Post-Modern? Edwardian? Art Nouveau? Art Deco? 1950s retrospective?
- Do you possess any particular painting, fabric, rug or similar item which would make a good starting point for your basic colour scheme?

Budgetary
- What do you feel is the maximum you can spend on your project (bearing in mind that you should always keep a contingency sum in reserve for emergencies)?
- Do you think this budget will be restrictive? Reasonable? More than adequate? Is your opinion on this based on research into current prices for merchandise and services, or is it just guesswork? (If the latter, it is essential that you research all prices *first*. You will find that almost everything is more expensive than you think.)
- If you could list (ignoring costs) the ten luxuries that would make your home seem more attractive to you, what would they be?
- Is any member of the household good with their hands? (This can make a big difference to the overall budget.) Skilful at carpentry? Painting?
- Even if your budgeted plans are reasonably modest, will you have to borrow money from somewhere, such as the bank? Would it make sense, in terms of the value of the house or your desire for a better lifestyle, to be more ambitious in your plans and arrange a large loan?

STRUCTURE AND SERVICES	REMARKS
Roof	Slight dip. Tiles missing. Gutter air brick broken.
External Walls	Rendering cracked, patches missing. Damp patch by front window.
Internal Walls	Crack in hall/kitchen wall. Stain on bathroom wall.
Floors	Stairs creak, handrail loose. Dining room floor needs stripping.
Windows	Living room and bedroom one, windows need replacing. How much?
Insulation	Check insulation in attic. Front windows on main road need double glazing.
Woodwork	Get in specialist to check for woodworm.
Ceilings	Cracks in main bedroom and dining room.
Doors	Front door rattles. Back door needs new lock. Dining room door sticks.
Electricity	Does system need rewiring?
Gas	None – any possibility?
Heating	Check boiler – looks old. Check cost of replacement – wall hung boiler?
Ventilation	Ask about an extractor fan in bathroom. Will landing window open?

Assessing Alterations   Once you have a rough idea of what you need, want and think you can afford, list the rooms you want to reorganize, noting for each of them any repairs needed and any alterations that you would like to make. Ask yourself some more questions:

● How will you treat the walls, woodwork, ceilings and windows? Would it be an improvement to add French doors anywhere?

● How new is the wiring in the house? Is it up to the standard required by the law, and is it adequate for your needs? What sort of lighting will you need and how will you achieve it? Do you have enough sockets (outlets), and are they in the right places?

● If you have air conditioning, are the units unsightly? If so, can they be improved? Could you remove them from the windows and resite them in the walls?

● Is the heating adequate? How old is the system? How much would it cost to have it replaced? If you have unsightly ducts for hot-air heating, how much would it cost to replace the system with hot-water pipes?

● What about means of escape in the event of fire? Are there laws in your area governing such things as fire doors and fire escapes? Should you consult an expert on this?

● What about the plumbing? Can you fit in another bathroom, shower room, or lavatory? And how much would this cost? Do existing fixtures need replacing or can they be resurfaced? How (and how well) do all the toilets flush?

● What about the flooring? Are there handsome floorboards under the existing flooring? Can they be scraped and sanded? Do they need repairing or replacing? If you would like a different kind of floor (for example, quarry tiles or marble), is that feasible and, if so, what is the cost? If the price is too high, what about painting the floor, or doing interesting things with linoleum or vinyl tiles? Where do you need carpeting, and what is that going to cost?

● Do you need to put in burglar, fire and smoke alarms? How much will these cost?

● Is the house fully insulated? If not, is it important to you that it should be? Again, how much will this cost? (If it proves extremely expensive, it may make more financial sense not to insulate – but this is unusual.)

● In what condition is the existing hardware – door handles, locks, fingerplates, window catches, light switches, dimmers and taps (faucets)? Do they need replacing, replating or rebrassing? What will this do to your budget? (These are just the sort of details that can all too easily be forgotten.)

Structure and Services   All the questions noted above might seem elementary, but in the enthusiasm or the confusion of the moment it is easy to forget the basics: far too many people embark on ambitious decorating and furnishing projects before they deal with basic structural matters. Moreover, unless you know the answers to all these questions – and the likely costs in each case – you cannot really form a realistic budget. If you own your home, it is vital that you get the framework into good, solid workable order before you embark on the more glamorous cosmetics, such as wall, window and floor coverings, the furnishings and the other various accessories. It is a waste of time, effort and money to start to decorate before the structure is put in order.

So that you do not miss defects that you will later have to remedy, whatever the cost, it helps to make a preliminary checklist. The two main headings are 'Structure' and 'Services'. By each subheading under these main headings, note the basic state of affairs: if a service is in good working order or if improvements or repairs are needed. A typical example of such a list, with the comments written in, is shown here.

Rented homes are, of course, another matter. It is to be hoped that the landlord will have taken care of any structural faults. Nevertheless it certainly helps to be aware, before you sign the lease, of the external condition of the property and the state of its amenities – heating, air conditioning, wiring, plumbing, windows, drainage, roof, and so on. If they seem not to be in good order and the landlord is unwilling to attend to them, think very seriously before you take on the lease, especially if it is for a reasonable period of time and you want to embark on your own decorating.

Getting the Framework Right

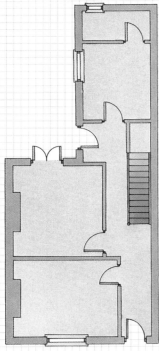

Making the Most of Space

Alterations to the structure and fittings of your home can radically affect internal space – and the way you use it. Some types of building work may cost less than you think, but remember that structural changes will almost certainly cause major disruption.

You could:
1 Unblock fireplaces
2 Knock through an internal arch
3 Install French doors
4 Build a conservatory or back porch
5 Relocate external or internal doors
6 Install larger windows
7 Replace the wall between the kitchen and the dining room with a counter
8 Install an additional washroom

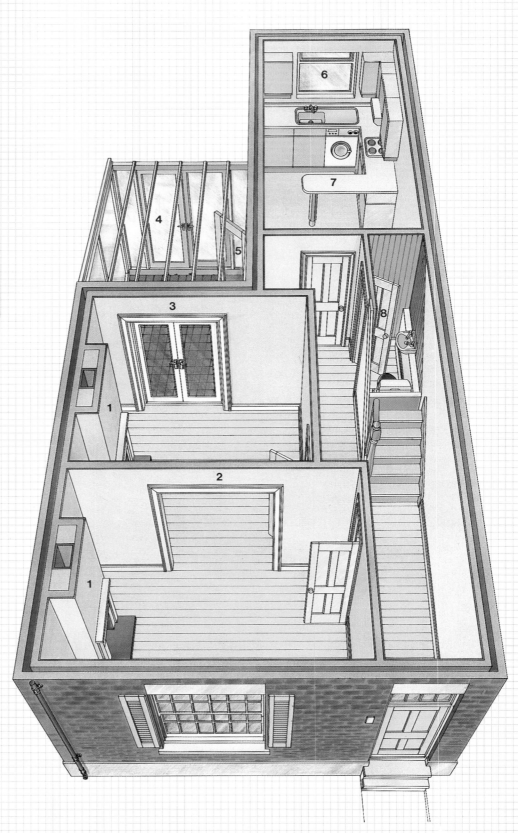

Structural Assessment

Faced with an empty room or rooms which you want to change, what is your first step? Most people are generally so relieved to have found somewhere to live that is reasonably affordable, reasonably convenient and reasonably cheap to heat, cool and light, that they just accept and adapt to whatever space they have, however awkward it might be, without too much question. All too often they start on the basic decoration and furnishing without pausing to consider seriously the shape of the space and how it could be manipulated to its best advantage. Yet rooms can often be rethought, changed around and vastly improved at a surprisingly low cost.

Spatial Solutions Do not be afraid of taking down partition walls. This costs very little by comparison with building new ones, and usually makes a profound difference. However, even if you are certain that you are dealing with a non-load-bearing partition wall, check with an expert before you risk starting to demolish it. You should, of course, be wary of walls that contain water or gas pipes, electrical conduits, and so on. Professional house or apartment plans may show whether things like these are present but, if you have come new to a home and have no means of knowing, common sense and a little detective work reveal their whereabouts. For example, be cautious of walls with electric switches and sockets (outlets), walls below or next door to a bathroom or lavatory or to the sink or appliance wall of a kitchen, and obviously walls with radiators, ducts, vents or air-conditioning units.

Walls can have an archway cut through them, or be cut halfway down or at either side so that they form divisions rather than solid masses. Or, if you have totally removed a partition wall, you can form your own flexible room dividers using bookcases, shelving units, screens or screen-like structures. A particularly graceful effect can be achieved using pillars, or pillars and pilasters; these can be picked up either from places selling architectural remnants and details or from one of the many companies who are now reproducing such architectural merchandise.

Do you need all the hall, gallery or corridor space you have at present? It may well be that you can slice off bits of these to add to your living areas, or to make a kitchen big enough to eat in.

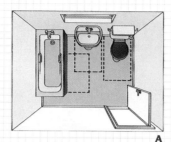

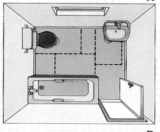

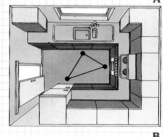

Planning Your Bathroom
An important factor to consider when planning your bathroom is the individual 'activity' space needed around each piece of equipment. Some overlap may be acceptable (A), but ideally each space should be self-contained (B).

Planning Your Kitchen
An L-shaped plan (A) is ideal for kitchens with limited wall space and for combined cooking and dining areas. A U-shaped plan (B) can be used for small spaces, but it can be awkward if more than one person uses the kitchen at the same time.

You might consider making internal 'windows' or openings in a dividing wall to provide more light and airiness. These could be conventionally square or oblong, arched, or in the shape of long slits, like clerestory windows, so that the adjoining space (and its light) shows through and gives more perspective to the room. New doorways, too, can be situated in more convenient positions, and old ones can be closed up in order to provide more wall space. If you find old or antique doors which you would like to work into your scheme you can make the openings to fit them. However, always consult an expert before knocking through a wall; you can never be too cautious when it comes to altering structural elements.

New windows can often be added to rooms. These make an enormous difference to the feeling of light and space, especially if French doors or long windows can be added (or substituted for smaller varieties). There is a large choice of ready-made windows in all shapes and sizes, including storm windows with flyscreens for the summer, and you can have infinitely more varieties made. But it is, of course, important always to think of what the windows will look like from the outside of the building before you enthusiastically cut out new apertures. Moreover, new windows should match existing windows as closely as possible, and should comply with any local building or planning regulations. Putting in new windows is difficult structural work, however, and certainly you should not tackle it without expert advice.

Getting the Framework Right
STRUCTURAL ASSESSMENT

MAKING THE MOST OF SPACE:
Studio Apartment

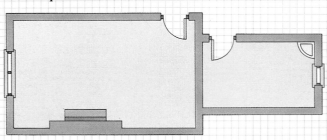

Making the most of a small space demands careful planning and organization. Here two basic rooms have been converted into a studio apartment.

1 *The main dividing wall was removed*
2 *Partition walls were built to create a bathroom, lobby and shower room*
3 *Major plumbing work had to be carried out to install the bathroom and kitchen*
4 *The door into the smaller room was blocked up*
5 *A section of wall was built to enclose the entrance and to support a built-in desk and some storage space*
6 *The kitchen units were extended across the room to act as a space divider and storage area*
7 *The chimney breast and fireplace were removed to make space for a sofa bed*
8 *A cupboard (closet) was constructed for storing clothes*

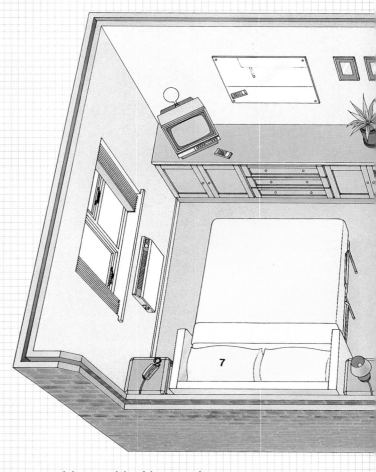

If you definitely need more rooms in your house, think carefully about reorganizing the space you already have. Could you, for example, make a large kitchen–dining room out of the basement in order to free valuable space on the ground or first floor? Or, if the attic is big enough, what about making a pair of bedrooms and another bathroom up there? Again, you could think of converting the attic into a playroom, studio, games room, family room or media room/den. Built-in (integral) garages are often successfully converted into additional rooms. If you are fortunate enough to live in a detached house, you may be able to make more sense and space out of a house simply by reorienting it, so that the main entrance is on another side.

If it is not possible to conjure more rooms from the existing space you will have to think of adding on an extension. This means you will certainly have to hire an architect (see page 24) in order to achieve the best possible blend, but first you must find out the cost of building per square foot in your area and make sure that you can get from any relevant authorities the permission to go ahead and build. Also, look up the costs of adding

on a prefabricated building, such as a conservatory or sun room, before you make a final decision to build an extension from scratch. Remember that, if a prefabricated building contains the kind of space that will suit you, it may be possible to effectively disguise its origins by putting some sort of fence around its foundations, painting it to match the main structure and growing climbing plants up the side. Whatever the alterations you decide to make, remember to first check with your local authorities.

One-Room Living   In a small studio or one-room apartment you can help create the feeling of space by building in multifunctional furniture. For example, you could build a platform big enough to put a mattress on and serve as a desk top with storage space underneath. Other options include a dining-table–desk, built-in bench-seating with lift-up seats and storage underneath, and window seats built along the same lines. Where no window seats exist, or if there is no natural place for them, a little ingenuity can help you out – providing extra seating that does not take up too much space,

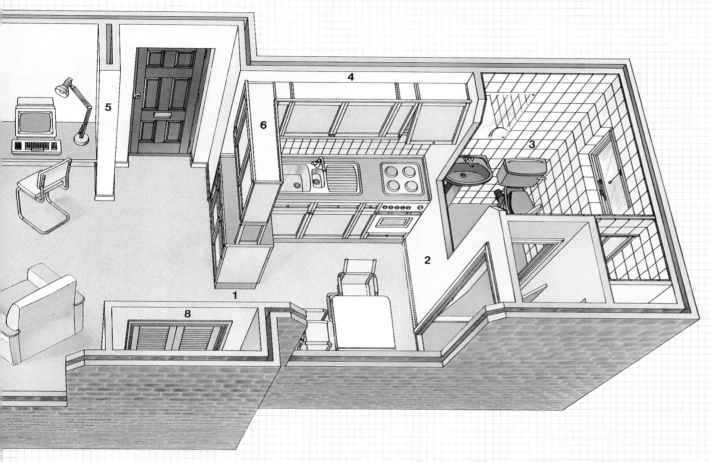

while incidentally helping make a characterless room look much more interesting. You can frame a window down to the floor with lengths of timber (lumber) some 60cm/2ft deep which can be painted in with either the walls or the woodwork. You can then build a ledge across at seat height and make it comfortable with fabric-covered foam and with pillows or cushions at the back. Instead of draperies or curtains, use a shade of some sort which matches the window-seat cover.

Different levels, even if the differences are only very slight, can often segregate the various areas of a single room, whether it is too small and has to serve as both a living and a sleeping room or – as in the case of a loft or a renovated country barn – is too big. In a small studio apartment, differentiating, say, dining–working, sitting and sleeping areas, or even one step up at one end or around the perimeter of the room, can make an extraordinary difference to the way a given space looks and works. This might sound a complicated solution, but in fact it is not as expensive as it sounds. However, such alterations must be considered at the beginning of your decorating schedule.

Storage Ideas

● Hinged window seats provide extra storage space
● Shelving is cheap, easy to install and provides an excellent opportunity for display
● Use hooks and wire grids to hang kitchen utensils, tools and clothing
● Tailor-made beds raised off the floor can incorporate cupboards and drawers
● Simple drapes or curtains can turn a recess into a useful space for hanging clothes
● Brightly coloured stacking systems are ideal for children's rooms – but they are just as useful for storing tools and cleaning equipment
● Old chests and deep wooden boxes – either stripped or painted – make attractive side tables and provide extra storage

Space Savers

● Painting a room in plain, light colours can make it feel more airy and spacious
● Fold-up chairs and tables, which can be stored out of the way, are practical and convenient
● Mirrors, in the form of sheets or tiles, reflect light and can have the effect of doubling the apparent proportions of a room
● See-through furniture is unobtrusive in a room that is short of space
● Choose furniture for flexibility – a piece of furniture that can be moved around a room easily is invaluable
● Buy low-level furniture for small rooms. Towering units and bulky cupboards will overcrowd the space
● Use simple window dressings and keep windows clear of clutter

Drawing Up Plans

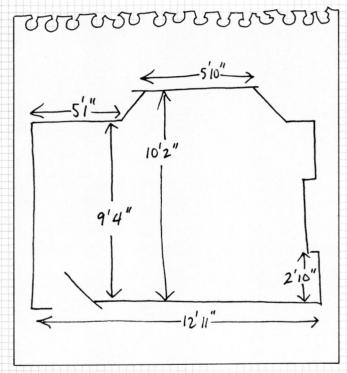

Assuming you own your house or apartment, you can take down internal partition walls, add new ones, block up old doors and make new openings in more convenient places. The visual and practical differences such changes will make are out of all proportion to the comparatively modest expense involved. If none exist already, it is certainly worth making a new set of plans of each room. Quite apart from their usefulness when you are working out any changes, they will also be invaluable for deciding on furniture arrangement later.

To make your preliminary plans you simply measure the room or rooms and draw the area out roughly to scale – not forgetting to add details of windows, doors, fireplaces, odd corners and indentations, fireplaces, supporting pillars and any other permanent fixtures. Then measure accurately the lengths of the walls, the proportions of the doors, windows and any other features, the thickness of partitions, and the distance between fittings. Measure also the positions of electrical sockets (outlets), telephone sockets (jacks), radiators and other permanent heating appliances, and air conditioners. All these should be clearly marked on the sketch. This constitutes your preliminary survey. To draw up an accurate plan you must decide on the scale: a scale of 2cm to 1m (about ¼in to 1ft) is reasonable for general areas, such as living rooms and bedrooms, but a larger scale – perhaps twice this – is better for rooms such as kitchens, bathrooms and laundry rooms which have to take a number of fixtures.

Draw the sketch of the room to your chosen scale using a sharp pencil. It is essential to do this absolutely accurately. It may seem tiresome to keep stressing accuracy, but I have learned from bitter experience how the slightest inaccuracy can spoil an inspired idea. I once had to send back a complete set of kitchen units because the architect's measurements were out by a tiny amount – but just enough to ensure that there was no way in the world the cabinets could be fitted into their assigned niches. Because they had been custom-made I could not reclaim any money, so there was nothing for it but to pay all over again. The only consolation is that the architect is now known to be the most accurate measurer in the world!

Another point to bear in mind is that the correct measurement of windows, doors and staircases (especially at any turns) is particularly important when it comes to moving in furniture. Many a double bed, piano, large armchair or cabinet has had to be returned to the supplier when narrow doors and windows made access to a room impossible. By the same token, do not forget to measure the depth, width and height of elevators.

Once you have a reasonable plan or plans with which to work, you can juggle around the various possibilities for making the most of your space.

Plans also provide an excellent means of working out furniture layout: they can help you to arrange what you already have or to decide what you need to buy. The simplest way to assess the merits of different layouts is to draw the outlines of the furniture on a separate piece of paper, then cut out the shapes and move the pieces about on the plan until you discover the optimum arrangement. Remember that the furniture cut-outs should be constructed to the same scale as the basic room plan.

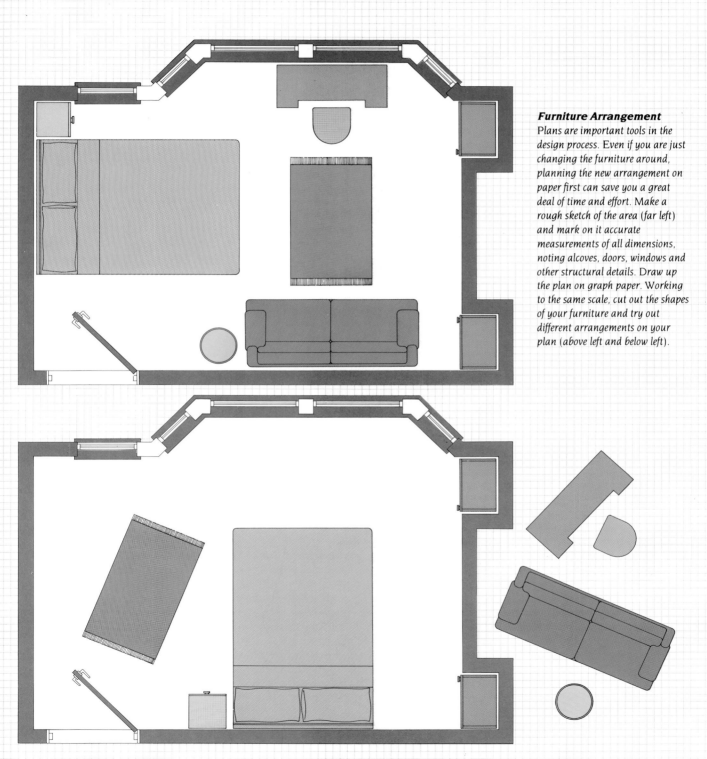

Furniture Arrangement

Plans are important tools in the design process. Even if you are just changing the furniture around, planning the new arrangement on paper first can save you a great deal of time and effort. Make a rough sketch of the area (far left) and mark on it accurate measurements of all dimensions, noting alcoves, doors, windows and other structural details. Draw up the plan on graph paper. Working to the same scale, cut out the shapes of your furniture and try out different arrangements on your plan (above left and below left).

Checking Out the Faults

Dampness, rot or wood infestation should be treated *before* you embark on any decorating. You would not be pleased if your newly painted walls began to crumble because of rot, or your wall treatments began to peel because of damp.

Dampness is a complex problem for which, often, there is no single cause and no single straightforward or cheap remedy. In order to cure a patch of dampness, it is, for example, often necessary to open up sections of walls, floors and so on; doing this can reveal other defects so that the cost of the project rises very rapidly. It is important, therefore, that proper advice is sought right from the beginning of your decorating schedule in order to avoid unnecessary expense.

Dampness is caused by several factors such as:
● excessive condensation
● penetration of water through cracked rendering, poorly constructed exterior cavity walls, bricks or tiles that need repointing
● a defective damp-proof course (vapor barrier), or no damp-proof course at all
● leaking pavements (in the case of town houses with basements)

● badly formed junctions of roofs to chimneys, or leaking or blocked gutters
● badly constructed flat roofs, or missing tiles

All of these factors can cause further defects such as dry rot, wet rot and efflorescence (in which soluble salts in the plaster or mortar, on contact with water, force their way to the surface and spoil decorations).

Applying cosmetic cures is rather like digging holes in wet sand. The only solution is to try to correct the basic constructional fault at the foot of the trouble. In Britain, for example, you can take advantage of certain proprietary systems designed for specific problems. A popular method of putting in a damp-proof course is to inject chemicals into the wall. Another method involves cutting out a course of mortar and putting in a damp-proof membrane. A less common means of eliminating dampness is the use of hygrovents. These are porous earthenware tubes inserted in walls to attract water, which is then evaporated away through them. Finally, waterproof liquids are painted on to prevent penetrating damp; they have to be periodically renewed.

In the United States the problem of dampness is limited largely to basements and there is special damp-

proofing paint available which can be applied to both external walls and the inside basement walls. This paint acts as a water-repellent shield against dampness and resists mildew.

Eliminating Rot   Dry rot starts in moist wood and is usually found in old, damp buildings – although occasionally it is found in new ones – and it can lurk behind walls so that it is not immediately obvious. This type of rot is extremely dangerous because it can spread from wet wood to dry wood by means of airborne spores or through strands of fungal growth. It is essential to eradicate dry rot as quickly as possible after you have spotted the problem. You can detect dry rot by its musty, rotting mushroomy smell, and the excrescences it grows, which are of an orange to deep-brown colour. Affected wood is inclined to crack in squares.

If you find dry rot, your best plan is immediately to contact a firm that specializes in the treatment of dry rot. All defective wood will need to be replaced, and the new wood will have to be treated with preservative. Any adjoining brickwork or plasterwork should also be thoroughly sterilized.

Wet rot occurs only in conditions of constant dampness: if the cause of the dampness is arrested the rot dies. Decayed wood and the surrounding area should nevertheless be treated in the same way as for dry rot, because dry-rot spores may well be present and the drying-out process provides them with the perfect conditions for germinating.

Woodworm and Termites   Ordinary woodworm is caused by the common furniture beetle, which has either flown in through the window or been escorted in, comfortably ensconced in an infected piece of furniture. Young beetles usually emerge in June or July; they lay their eggs in cracks and joints or in the rough backs of furniture. Early summer is thus the time to exterminate them: spray or brush unpainted and unvarnished wood (e.g., beams) with an insecticide, and inject insecticide into every third hole in painted and varnished wood.

Termites are a major problem in the United States and, in many states, a termite inspection report must be done. They should be exterminated as quickly as possible to avoid major damage.

Insulation

Windows, doors, walls, fireplaces, letterboxes, floors and above all the roofs of old houses are all potential heat losers, and money spent on insulation will certainly be saved on fuel bills. Do not, however, make a house so draughtproof that *no* air can get in or out, because rooms will only get muggy, fires will not draw properly, the boiler or furnace (if any) will do less than its best (and become dangerous), and doors will not close. If you are going to the trouble of insulating internal walls, you may want to insulate for sound as well.

Windows   Double glazing, or the addition of storm windows, is not cheap, but it can make an enormous difference to heat loss. It is best installed in a house that is anyway undergoing extensive renovation, since existing windows may have to be removed – a process that will inevitably cause a mess. Another consideration is that the installation of double glazing may add to the value of your house. Remember, however, that you may have to seek permission from the relevant authority before going ahead.

Doors   Gaps under doors can be cured by fixing a draughtproofing strip bought from a hardware store. For outside doors, some manufacturers make bronze strips that are relatively unaffected by rain or damp and are guaranteed to last 10 years. Threshold fittings where one part is fixed to the floor and the other to the bottom so that the two parts are pressed against each other when the door is closed are very efficient, as are the ones that consist of a drop-flap made of rubber or vinyl, which is forced down against the floor when the door is closed to make a draughtproof seal. Small closed porches added to outside doors can make a difference to heat loss.

Roofs   Roofs are fairly easy to insulate. If you have a sloping one and use the space only, if at all, for storage, insulate the floor area with some loose-fill material like vermiculite granules poured between the joists and levelled off. If the area is draughty enough for the granules to be blown around, it would be best to use glassfibre blankets. If you intend to convert the space into an attic room, insulate the sloping rafters with fibreboard or with plasterboard (drywall) or wallboard with glassfibre blankets underneath.

Keeping the Cold Out
Without insulation, heat will escape from your home via windows, doors, walls, the roof, the ground floor – even from fireplaces and letterboxes. Roof insulation, double glazing and draughtproofing will reduce heating bills.

Fireplaces   Always get throat controls fitted to fireplaces – otherwise you will be heating the outside air through the chimney to nobody's benefit except that of the fuel company!

Letterboxes and Pet Doors   These can be protected from howling gales and snow storms by a variety of flaps made of bronze, brass, stainless steel or other metal. Alternatively, you can tack a piece of leather or heavy fabric above a letterbox on the inside. Pet doors can be sealed shut at night.

Floors   Ground-level wood floors can be draughty because of the air flow coming through the air bricks in the house walls. Ventilation is vital to prevent the wood rotting so never block air bricks. Any good floor covering, especially carpet, will eliminate draughts. Before laying the material, seal gaps as described for sanding floors (page 168); lay hardboard (masonite), plywood or underlay – depending on chosen floor covering – and seal gaps below skirtings (baseboards) with beading.

Walls   Cavity walls can be filled with blown glassfibre or other mineral fibre injected by a specialist company. Solid brick walls can be lined with plasterboard (drywall) fixed onto a wood framework with a glassfibre blanket sandwiched in between.

21

Getting the Services in Order

Any alterations or improvements to services or utilities like electricity, gas, plumbing, heating, television, cable, telephone and air conditioning should definitely be done before any decoration is started. Having to add pipes and wires after the walls and floors are finished constitutes a disaster.

Electricity   Anyone buying an old house or apartment should get a surveyor's (engineer's) report on both the structure and services. He or she will give you a reliable indication of what must be done to the building right away and what can wait. However, it is also important to inform the surveyor of any changes you might be planning to make in the electrical supplies (or, for that matter, in the plumbing or heating), since this might make a vital difference to his or her comments on the current adequacy of the service. If, for example, you want to install extra electric appliances – a new stove, perhaps, instead of an old gas one; air conditioning units; a dishwasher, washing machine and dryer; a waste extractor, or a low-voltage circuit to provide special lighting for art and low lighting for the garden – the existing electrical sockets (outlets) might be far from sufficient, especially in an old apartment block. The surveyor can tell you so only if he or she has been informed that this is what you want to do. Ignorant of your plans, the report may state that the electrical services are perfectly adequate.

It will certainly assist any electrician and help you to get an accurate idea of costs if you take a clean copy of your room plans (see page 18) and mark on them exactly where you want to add any new electric sockets and their purpose – for a table lamp, heater, air conditioner, towel heater or whatever. Then mark on the plans where you need any special lighting fixtures, like wallwashers, framing projectors, spots of every description and wall lights, as well as where you want light in every room, and where you want switches and dimmers. If you do not want centre lights you must say so at the outset, and make sure that you specify that you would like the switches for lamps and wall lights to be near the doors, or you will forever be crawling around in the darkness trying to find them.

If you can decide at this stage exactly the fixtures that you would like, it will be an even greater help to your budgetary planning (see page 26). Installing lights – especially sophisticated ones – in a number of rooms can add up to a surprising amount of money: totting up the prices for an ideal lighting scheme can definitely give you an 'electric shock'! Nevertheless, since good lighting more than pays for itself in the long run in terms of looks and comfort – not to mention safety, especially if there are elderly people around – making sure that the lighting scheme you install at least allows you much flexibility as possible for the future.

Gas   Unless the building already has a mains gas supply or you are doing a great deal of renovation, usually it is not worth the trouble of getting it laid on – although 'bottled gas' (or propane gas) appliances can often be an attractive option, particularly if you live in a remote area. That said, if you already have a gas furnace or stove, it should be comparatively easy to run gas pipes to the fireplace for a gas-fuelled imitation coal or log fire: these can be surprisingly realistic.

The ease of installing mains gas supplies varies from country to country. In Britain it is not too terribly expensive and payment can be spread out over a long period. This is not necessarily the case in North America, where you would do best to stick to electrical supplies – unless, as I have noted, gas is already installed. Another factor worth considering, especially if your household contains very old or very young people, is that of safety.

Plumbing and Heating   If you want to add on a new bathroom, shower room, kitchen, cloakroom or lavatory, it is always best to try to plan the addition around existing plumbing, or at least beside an outside wall so that waste pipes can be accommodated. Renovating an existing bathroom to make it more luxurious – even just changing the position of the various fixtures to get more storage space or to make the room seem larger – is a complicated, dusty job which should certainly be finished before any decorative work is started. Equally, remember that items of bathroom equipment like baths, jacuzzis, showers and double basins tend to be bulky, and so should be carefully measured to ensure that you will have no difficulties installing them.

It is likely that the house will already have an adequate heating system but, if not, you should call in

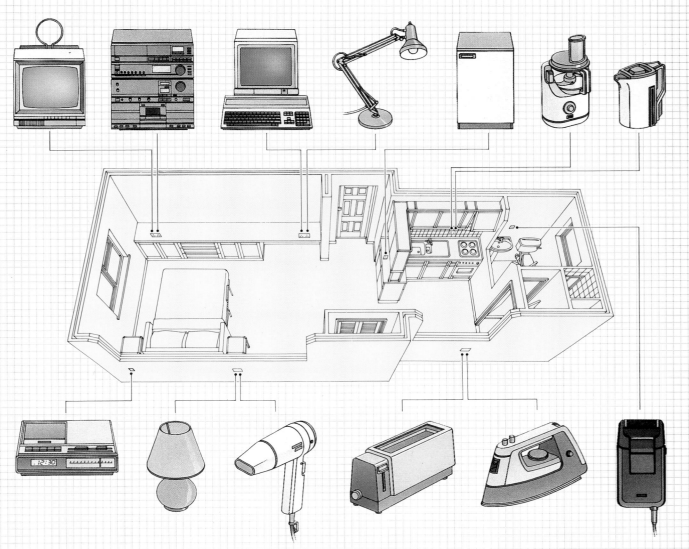

an expert to give you advice and an idea of price. Much will depend on the height of the ceilings and the general age, size and condition of the house. A great many people, however, need or want to change the heating method in their homes – from ducted warm-air heating to small-bore hot-water heating, for example, or from conventional radiators to skirting (baseboard) heating. Consult your chosen contractor on this, or talk to your local oil suppliers and heating engineers. In any event, all this should once again be planned and budgeted for in advance.

Air Conditioning, Telephone and Television Air conditioning, if you want it, is another basic service that must be installed in advance, assuming you want the

Positioning outlets
Before you begin to decorate, it is essential to plan where all electrical appliances and equipment will go

to ensure that there are enough outlets and that they are correctly positioned. Trailing flexes (cords) are both unsightly and hazardous.

units to be fitted into a wall rather than stuck in a window where they will make any sort of window treatment difficult as well as obstruct the view.

Although telephone-service installers are usually tidy and rarely leave behind a tangled mess of cables, it is still a good idea to get them in before you start the final decorations, just as it is important to get the television aerial (antenna), cable equipment, wall-mounted stereo speakers and other fitted equipment installed before your wall decorations are too far advanced.

Finding the Right Help

Architects If your house or apartment is very dilapidated, very inconvenient, too small or too large, you may well find that you need to employ an architect. He or she should be able to make your life a lot easier by suggesting clever ways of getting around spatial problems, by preparing plans and working drawings, by finding out about any local permissions needed or possible legal snags that might obstruct proposed alterations, by estimating how much the structure will cost to renovate, run and maintain, by finding and supervising an appropriate builder or contractor, and generally by coordinating the whole operation to produce a better-looking and easier-to-run home. It is quite possible that the entire renovation, even including the architect's fees, will cost less than if you had gone ahead on your own.

Unless your budget is elastic, it is usually best to use young and local architects for a straightforward renovating job. However, charges may vary: in Britain the Royal Institute of British Architects (RIBA) publishes scales of recommended charges (mostly based on a percentage of the cost of the building work to be done), and most architects should stick to these scales. The American Institute of Architects (AIA) offers a similar service in the United States. Architects generally charge for time and expenses, on top of their normal commission. It is also possible, of course, to persuade an architect to render a 'partial service' which consists of preparing sketch plans (for an agreed set fee) to show how best to realize your home's potential, leaving you to do the rest.

If you do decide to hire an architect, how do you set about getting one? Personal recommendation is probably the best way; asking the advice of an architectural acquaintance is another. Alternatively, you could ask the architecture department of the local college or university, or get a recommendation from your local architectural organization, or write to the relevant national association for suggestions in your area; in Britain, the RIBA has a directory of architects showing which are likely to be suitable for various types of work. The AIA publishes a comprehensive directory of architects working in the United States.

Once you have got together a list of 'possibles', scrutinize some examples of their work. Satisfied clients will rarely mind their houses being looked over, and architects themselves will always be prepared to arrange appointments and provide photographs.

Interior Designers and Decorators The services of a good designer can often, like those of an architect, save money in the long run and should certainly save you time, confusion and strain. A good designer will look at your home with fresh but informed eyes and will suggest ways of making your rooms function more efficiently and schemes that may well cost less, and will definitely look better, than the kind of piecemeal effect which spoils so many homes. A designer will also find fabrics, papers, rugs and carpets that you would be lucky to find in retail establishments — or perhaps he or she might even design these things especially. In addition the designer might get curtains and draperies made up, plan beautiful upholstery and bed treatments, find exactly the right pieces of furniture, recommend and supervise good builders, contractors and crafts people, help you choose accessories, and take all the other time- and nerve-consuming chores off your hands.

Above all, good designers acknowledge that many if not most of their clients have excellent ideas of their own, and need only a good arbitration, editing and translating service — plus the experience and knowledge of resources that a good designer should have — in order to realize those ideas. Finally, a good designer will try very hard to keep to a realistic budget and will always warn you if something is likely to go over budget. In this latter case, the designer should present you with a cheaper option.

There is no cut-and-dried fee structure in the interior-designing profession. Some designers charge an initial consultation fee and, if the client wants to proceed, a full design fee plus a percentage calculated on the cost of all goods purchased. Others charge a consultation fee plus a much larger percentage of the costs of purchases and services. Others still charge an hourly fee for their work — this can really mount up. Whatever the fee structure, most designers take the precaution of asking for 50 per cent of the design fee up front, or a retainer fee based on the overall expense, plus a pool for purchases.

If you do decide to employ an interior designer you should first try to ascertain what kind of firm would suit you best. Obviously word-of-mouth recommendation and asking friends whose homes you admire for details of their designer is one way; as with architects, seeing work in a magazine or in a newspaper's design pages is another way of getting started. Clearly, if your taste is spare and minimalist you should go to someone who specializes in this sort of look and not to someone renowned for their eclecticism, and vice versa.

Builders and Contractors As with architects and designers, the best way to choose a contractor is through a reliable recommendation; seek advice from friends who have recently been pleased with work completed on their homes. Helpful architects in your locality may be prepared to suggest contractors they know to be reliable. And managers of local hardware or paint stores or builders' suppliers, who probably cater for most of the contractors in the area, might be persuaded to give you their opinion on the subject.

When a list of possible contractors has been drawn up and their financial stability checked as far as possible, ask three or four of the firms to inspect your home. Make sure each is given a copy of the general work and decorating schedule so that they can put in a competitive bid or estimate. This might seem a somewhat pedantic way of going about the task, but it could save you a great deal of money, time and worry in the long run since estimates often vary wildly between one contractor and another.

Once you have received all the estimates, study them in detail. First, do any of the bidders guarantee the number of weeks or months they will take? Have any of them given you their time schedule in writing? Do they take into account a similar quantity and quality of paint and the same number of coats? (If you prepared your specification properly all of the bidders certainly should.) And are all the estimates for exactly the same amount of work and materials? Pay attention at this early stage to the uncertain costs in the estimate, such as the materials whose expense the contractors cannot predict exactly because they have yet to be chosen.

Remember to read conditions on the back of the tender and make sure you thoroughly understand them. For example, there might be denials of obligation in the event of the contractor's employees causing damage or of materials going missing from the site.

If the bids are very similar, you should contract the person or firm who guarantees the earliest completion date (to which you can usually add in your mind at least a month or two, unless you are prepared to bully, cajole, and be on the contractor's tail throughout the job); the largest contractor (bigger contractors have less need to subcontract); or the contractor whose personality you like the best – if the firm is large, try to meet the overseer assigned to the job (a key figure, and someone whose personality might well affect your final choice).

Getting the Best Service To ensure that bills are kept to a minimum, specify that all additional costs are quoted for in writing and are attached to the main estimate; otherwise your contractor is given the opportunity to increase the bill in no time at all, giving as an unanswerable excuse the fact that you kept asking for more things.

If the job is of any size (say, the renovation of a house as opposed to that of a few rooms) it is a good idea to fix up a site meeting at least once a week. Remember to take your master checklist (see page 28) and go over the repair work room by room with the contractor (or foreman), the carpenter, the electrician, the plumber – whoever is relevant and can be mustered. Make a note of anything that is discussed and arranged. Date and file these notes, making sure the contractor has two copies, one of which should be initialled and returned to you.

It is advisable to visit the site as often as possible (unless you are already 'camping' in the middle of the mess) just to ensure that the work is progressing and to sort out any problems or misunderstandings. It is wise not to say in advance when you are coming, unless you specifically want to meet with a particular tradesman, and to vary your times a little. You should not expect contractors to undertake any sort of design decisions for you unless you have complete faith in their taste – or no faith in your own.

Getting the Framework Right

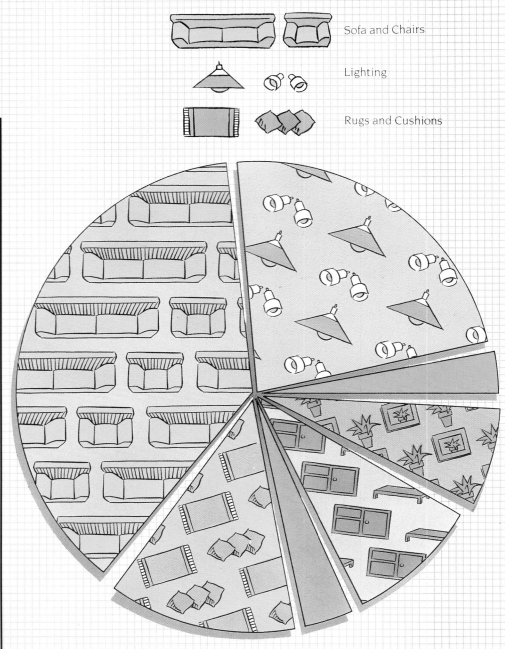

Sofa and Chairs

Lighting

Rugs and Cushions

WORKING OUT THE COSTS

EXAMPLE A: COMPLETE REDECORATION

Structural repairs
Treatment of dry rot and damp
Treatment of infestation
Repair of floorboards, etc.
Contractor's fee

Services
Checking of electrical system
2 sockets (outlets) to be fitted in
    living room
Downlights to be installed in
    dining room
Electrician's fee
Installation of basin in second
    bathroom
Plumber's fee

Decorating
Hire of wallpaper stripper and
    stepladder
Paint and wallpaper
Tiles for bathroom and kitchen
Tools and equipment

Furnishings
Purchase of rug for living room
Hire of carpet cleaner
Fabric for loose covers
Tracks and trimmings
Brass door handles throughout

EXAMPLE B: INSTALLING A NEW LIGHTING SCHEME

Fittings:
    Two recessed downlights
    Picture light over mantelpiece
    New sockets (outlets) in
        alcoves
    Concealed lighting
Building of baffle/pelmet
    (cornice)
Materials
Replastering
Electrician's fee
Contractor's fee

Living Room Budget
This breakdown of a moderate budget for decorating and furnishing a living room demonstrates how money should be allocated, with the major pieces of furniture, such as sofas and armchairs, together with light fittings, accounting for the greater proportion of money spent.

Storage Units and
Occasional Tables

Plants and Prints

Paint

Blinds

26

Successful Budgeting

Having found exactly what *should* be done in a home, what you would like to do in the way of alterations and improvements, what could be done, and what each operation, service and ingredient would actually cost, you will be in a better position to work out a realistic budget. Even if you are hoping to borrow the money for improvements, you will still have to give a summary of these improvements and their various prices to the bank, so it is as well to have your projected expenditure listed in order of priorities.

When you are decorating for the first time, it is difficult to know exactly when to save and when to spend on a home. As a rule of thumb, a large amount of your budget should be spent on items that will get the most wear and tear, and will have to last the longest. The corollary is that savings can be made on less-used furniture and on inessentials where substitutes will do just as well.

As we have seen all structural repairs come in the 'spending' category, as well as any rewiring, pest, damp and rot control, efficient heating, air conditioning if needed, and any insulation. (To this list could be added the matter of precautions against burglary.) These can be followed by necessary appliances and furnishings: kitchen and washing equipment (stove, refrigerator, freezer, washing machine, dryer and dishwasher), beds, at least two good comfortable chairs, the best lighting you can afford, generous closet and storage units, and good flooring. Local or national legislation may have an effect on your budget. It is your responsibility to find out if your plans conform to prescribed safety regulations, if the drainage will be officially regarded as adequate, and so on. The easiest thing to do is to pay an expert to find out all these things for you.

A good deal of furniture can come in the 'saving' category, especially dining tables (which can be cheaper, more adaptable and often a better size when made from a circle of wood fixed to a solid base and covered by a large cloth), conventional window treatments (which can use up vast quantities of expensive fabric), top-quality carpet (when there are all sorts of alternatives), and expensive glass, porcelain, cutlery and linen.

Once you have decided on the sort of budget that you can afford for your home, on how much money, if any, you can realistically borrow, and on what necessities will have to be provided, the plan of action can be drawn up. However, it is important to be realistic about ideas and to cost them carefully. Most important of all, be clear about your designs, needs and ideas of comfort.

Another important point to bear in mind in relation to any improvements is that you do not *over*improve a property in the light of its surroundings. If an area or locality appears to be deteriorating, no amount of apparent luxury will help the resale value of your house. On the other hand, if you are hoping to sell a house within a certain period of time in order to 'trade up' in the property market, there are certain improvements that will be worth their weight in gold, or at least in terms of a quick and profitable sale. Most potential buyers are understandably beguiled by properties which have the sort of sound framework we have been discussing, for this leaves them free to spend their money on decoration that will suit their personal tastes and needs. Good, well fitted kitchens and bathrooms are always a sales plus, as are good entertaining space and a handsome master bedroom, while a well planted terrace or climbers growing up a house can add thousands to the price. You cannot give your house or apartment scenic views out of the window if it is in the middle of a city, or bright summer light if all the windows face in the wrong direction, but you can substitute warmth and cheerfulness for light and particularly interesting colour schemes for a view.

CAN YOU AFFORD IT?

● Have you taken into account all contractors' fees?
● Have you set aside a sum of money for unforeseen expenditure – for example, eliminating rot?
● Do you have a comprehensive insurance policy?
● Have you been over-ambitious in estimating how much work you can take on yourself?
● Have you considered the cost of hiring equipment?
● Will your alterations affect the day-to-day running costs of your home?
● Are your employment prospects and long-term plans stable?
● Will your spending power be restricted or your standard of living affected by the amount of money you intend to spend on redecorating?
● Have you left yourself enough money to buy essential furnishings and fittings?

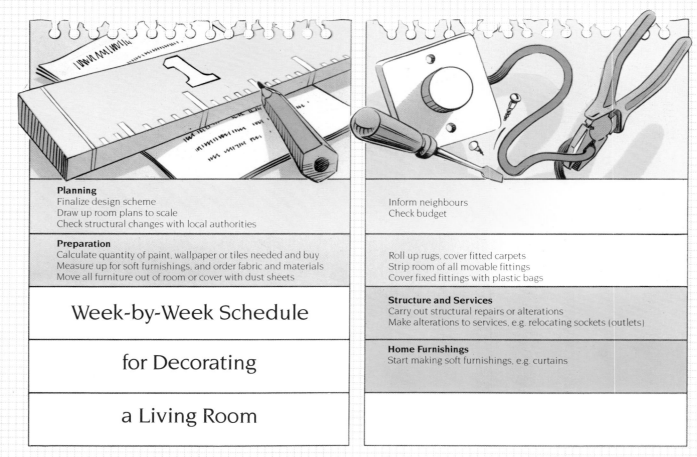

Planning
Finalize design scheme
Draw up room plans to scale
Check structural changes with local authorities

Inform neighbours
Check budget

Preparation
Calculate quantity of paint, wallpaper or tiles needed and buy
Measure up for soft furnishings, and order fabric and materials
Move all furniture out of room or cover with dust sheets

Roll up rugs, cover fitted carpets
Strip room of all movable fittings
Cover fixed fittings with plastic bags

Week-by-Week Schedule

for Decorating

a Living Room

Structure and Services
Carry out structural repairs or alterations
Make alterations to services, e.g. relocating sockets (outlets)

Home Furnishings
Start making soft furnishings, e.g. curtains

Preparing a Master Plan

Once you have worked out whether or not any structural work is required, you can decide upon the decoration and furnishings. Again, rooms must be considered in order of priority: usually the priorities are the kitchen, bathroom(s), master bedroom, living room and hall, followed in due course by the other rooms. This order of priorities is what distinguishes a thought-out scheme from the all-too-usual patchwork process. As with most set plans, you can vary the order so long as you understand that doing so may well increase your costs and take longer. If you are planning to 'camp' in your house or apartment while the work is in progress, it will help to keep your spirits up if right away at least one room can be made comfortable.

To go back to the master plan, when the most important points have been decided (or mostly decided, because fresh thoughts will always be occurring) make another list for every room and include every single thing that you think you will need to install or replace or which could be improved or refurbished. The sample list supplied on page 13 might be useful as a guide; you can add or subtract as necessary. However obvious the items

on the list might seem, so many things are all too easily overlooked in the grand scheme: a lot of minor items generally add up to a major problem — and a major expense. If you read the list you will probably start thinking of other things that ought to be done: note them all. Sensible decisions at the start will prevent much confusion and regret later on.

When it comes to deciding upon the actual decoration, plans should be dictated by the proportions and historical style of a house or apartment, its situation, condition and natural light. This is not to say that all buildings should necessarily be decorated according to their period, but rather that they should be treated with sympathy and that their natural ingredients should be used to best advantage. 'Natural ingredients' are not only doors, windows, view, and staircases, but also the different proportions of rooms, decorative flooring or mouldings (if there are any) and all the architectural details of a house (see pages 82–91).

Normally this sort of 'feeling' for a building can be achieved only after a number of relaxed visits to it while it is empty, or after you have 'camped' in a minimally decorated house for some time. After a period of time it should be possible to absorb the house's shapes, proportions, details and potential so that certain types and colours of furnishings can be visualized in their

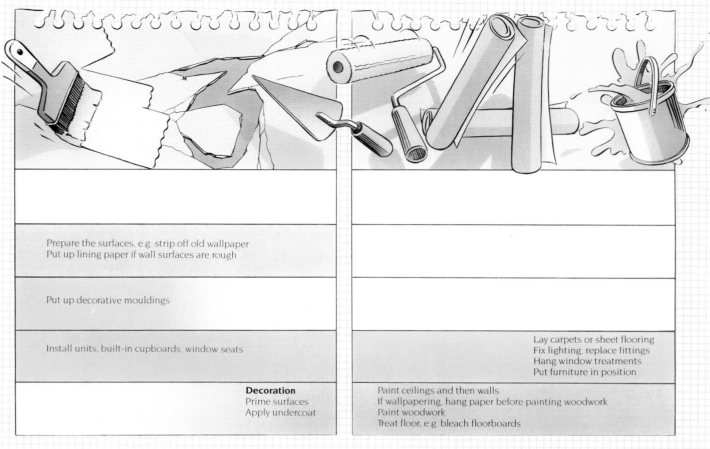

Prepare the surfaces, e.g. strip off old wallpaper Put up lining paper if wall surfaces are rough	
Put up decorative mouldings	
Install units, built-in cupboards, window seats	Lay carpets or sheet flooring Fix lighting, replace fittings Hang window treatments Put furniture in position
Decoration Prime surfaces Apply undercoat	Paint ceilings and then walls If wallpapering, hang paper before painting woodwork Paint woodwork Treat floor, e.g. bleach floorboards

appropriate settings. Also, you should come to recognize those features to emphasize and those to diminish.

If you find it hard to settle on a starting point for a scheme, ruffle through relevant books and magazines looking for congenial arrangements. Investigate local shops, stores and showrooms (or catalogues, if you have a shortage of time) in search of wallpapers, carpets, rugs, hard flooring and fabrics, and collect or send off for samples of anything that accords with your impression of how your home should look. You may want to collect all these samples together in a file or stick them all up on a notice-board. Once you see them all together you should find yourself starting to have some definite ideas – if only on what to discard.

Get into the habit of carrying around a notebook in which you can jot down descriptions or make quick sketches of anything that appeals to you. A ceiling treatment, a particular way of covering a wall or of arranging a group of pictures, a certain juxtaposition of colour – all of these can spark off a train of thought. At the time this may lead nowhere, but you will find that later on many of these ideas will click into place alongside other ones, thereby contributing to your overall scheme. Remember that ideas hardly ever stay in your mind unless you have made some kind of a record of them in writing.

Decorating Schedule
Draw up a plan of the order of work before you begin, even if you are only tackling one room at a time. This will help you to coordinate the services of contractors.

Flexibility   Crucial to your overall scheme is flexibility. A lack of flexibility inevitably leads to frustration. Pieces of furniture or light fittings that you have set your heart on may turn out to be too expensive, or they may have been discontinued. Fixed ideas may prove to be impracticable because of space or time or light or money. If you have lived in the city for years and then move to the country – or to another country, continent or state – your tried, tested and loved belongings may suddenly become unsuitable. All such difficulties may seem insuperable, but they can be overcome if you retain an open mind.

Never be bound by fixed 'rules'. Never think that it is absolutely imperative to have a certain item or a particular colour. Good interior decoration should ultimately be a background, an impression of personality, not an end in itself. It is therefore important to create an environment that is most comfortable for *you*, within the limits of practicability. It is never impossible to substitute what you can get for what you originally conceived – although of course it is important not to make a thoughtless substitution.

Part 2

Setting the Style

What is Style?
Inspiration of the Past
Modern Movements
An Eclectic Taste
Country Style

What is Style?

A sense of style is as intangible and amorphous a thing as having a good eye for colour, a fine sense of scale and proportion or a sensitive ear for music.

Then again, the word 'style' has so many connotations – quite apart from its alliance with that equally nebulous attribute, 'good taste'. When we talk about someone having style or taste we mean that they have a particular and sometimes memorable way of arranging things, of putting things together – whether they be clothes and accessories or furniture and possessions.

There are, of course, the so-called 'national' styles. These have been particularly well documented over the last couple of decades in numerous books with titles such as *English Style, English Country Style, American Country, American South West, French Style, French Country, Italian Style, Caribbean Style* and *Japanese Style*. Then there are 'period' styles, named for a particular age – Renaissance, Restoration, Régence, Directoire, Federal, Empire – or for a monarch or monarchs – Louis XIV, XV, XVI in France, or the Stuarts, William and Mary, Queen Anne, Georgian and Victorian in Britain. Then again there are general terms that conjure up in one's mind particular styles of furniture and decoration: the Baroque, with its elaborate wood carving; the Rococo, with its curves and shells (*rocaille*); the Neoclassic, with its simple classical forms; Art Nouveau, with its sinuous configurations; the Bauhaus, with its stark 'shock of the new'. Finally, there are styles named for particular furniture designers (Chippendale, Hepplewhite and Sheraton), loosely geographical terms (Country Style and Urban Style), and popular turns of phrase (Art Deco, International Style, Eclectic, Hi-Tech and Minimalism).

Finding a Style All in all, the question of what overall style you should choose – or of putting a name to some half-formed mental picture of a room or rooms – can become as intimidating as that of selecting colour schemes to put together for your home. It is easy to say 'Find the style which suits you best and with which you are most comfortable', but putting this into practice is a far more difficult task.

Again, just as in choosing colours, there are certain criteria to follow. As usual, learn to really *look*, take note of what pleases you, and try to analyse *why*. Think about why a particular room gives you pleasure. Look through

books and magazines. Look at room settings in stores and museums. Take more notice of theatre sets and the backgrounds in movies and television programmes. Think about what sort of architecture pleases you most. Old houses in general, or clean modern lines? Quirky, idiosyncratic designs or traditional?

Some people look hard for that indefinable thing, 'charm' – which, while they cannot adequately describe it, they can recognize as soon as they see: it may be something as simple as a good growth of wisteria around a porch, arched stone windows, a fireplace in most if not all rooms, or a general meandering higgledy-piggledy quality that immediately gives them a feeling of genuine pleasure.

In general, unless you are sure of your decorating prowess, if a building already has some distinctive style or 'feel' you should make a point of being sensitive to it. This does not mean that you should furnish it exactly to period: that could look stuffy and lifeless, however beautiful and however much money and knowledge you might have to carry such an exercise through to its best potential. Rather it is that you should try to be sympathetic to the synthesis of architectural coherence

1 Pleasing juxtapositioning in New England of a simple love seat, a complicated Austrian shade, a sophisticated 19th-century side table and an old rustic painted corner cupboard.

2 A decidedly eclectic mix in an old London studio: a kelim on a painted marble floor, crewel upholstery alongside faded brocade, an Indian cloth flung over a white sofa, gilded Queen Anne chairs with assorted over-scale pots, hand-blocked wallpaper sandwiched between a complicated painted ceiling, and a painted dado — not to mention the grandeur of the fireplace.

3 Hand-painted fabric and modern lines in a 19th-century room painted like a grey box.

4 A quietly luxurious all-marbled bathroom in a Parisian apartment. 3

Setting the Style
WHAT IS STYLE?

1 This thoroughly Middle Eastern interior comes as something of a surprise in a London home.

2 A turn-of-the-century Edwardian-style interior in the United States. This was designed for a 1980s US showhouse, and is complete with bamboo occasional furniture, papier-maché and upholstery to match the chintz-lined walls.

3 Rose-on-white toile de Jouy, a white iron bedhead against brick walls, and white-painted boarding feature in this country-style New York bedroom.

4 The Eastern influences on the decor of this Western attic bedroom are all too clear.

5 A hi-tech/minimalist kitchen in familiar black-and-white styling.

and fineness of proportion that define the relevant period. In the case of a Georgian or Federal house – indeed, with any building you live in, whatever its architectural detail – a sense of style is really an attitude of mind, a sympathy with the overall 'feel' of the surroundings and a sensitivity both to what is fitting for those surroundings and to your family's needs. Clearly finance will affect your stylistic choices, as will the furnishings you already possess, whether they are from former homes, gifts or items you have inherited.

Obviously, there are certain commonsense factors to consider as well. For example, country houses look best when they are obviously geared to country living and the outdoor life. Floors, for instance, seem more fittingly rural when they are of wood, brick, stone or quarry tile, or covered with coir or rush matting, than if they have fitted carpets (except perhaps on stairs or in bathrooms and powder rooms). And, although a country look or 'feel' has a certain charm in a town house, a sophisticated urban look is far from appealing in the country.

Again, beach and summer houses do not look appropriate or suitably relaxed when they are too carefully furnished and decorated: they should be casual and slightly shabby, and full of familiar heterogenous objects. This is not, of course, to say that they cannot be pretty. But the whole idea of such houses is to make people feel relaxed, comfortable and carefree.

When you first walk into a new home there is usually a certain 'something' about each room that helps to set the style you will wish to employ. If, for example, a room is heavily beamed and low-ceilinged, you are likely to opt for a comfortable, warm-coloured eclectic ambience rather than a roomful of clean-lined modern furniture – although some people, quite sure of themselves and their tastes, might be tempted to do exactly the opposite to the obvious approach and make the furnishings stark and simple.

Another room might be well proportioned but dark. In such a case you would have the choice of exploiting the lack of light to make the room warm and cosy or resorting to artifice, making the place look much brighter through the use of light but warm colours (apricot, buttery yellow, pale terracotta, old rose, etc.) and plenty of artfully concealed lighting – at the top of windows

under a valance or pelmet (cornice), behind plants and large pieces of upholstery, or even, skilfully, at the top of sun blinds *outside* the windows so that the sun appears to be shining through.

You might have a room with a wall of windows and a marvellous view for you to exploit (use spare furniture and simple lines in order not to distract attention from the view outside) or, conversely, you might be confronted by a room that is boxy and characterless, in which case you can dress up the walls, try to make the windows more interesting, and add various touches of character of your own devising – from mouldings to a cleverly painted floor or exotic furnishings. The point is that, whatever the nature of a room, you should look for any clue that might help you determine the appropriate style of decoration. This clue might lie within the room itself but, if the room says nothing to you, it may be possible to find it among your own possessions.

Putting style into a home is, in fact, much like solving a puzzle in which you have to get the maximum number of words out of a collection of letters. Ultimately, it is all a question of juggling with possibilities.

4

5

INSPIRATION OF THE PAST

Up until the 18th century, style evolved in different countries, sometimes according to the dictates of fashion – for example, seating had to be redesigned to accommodate hoop skirts and crinolines – or as new woods, materials, skills, techniques and domestic articles were introduced. The general interest in Chinoiserie, for example, followed directly from the first appearance in Europe of oriental lacquered goods and silks, and small tables were invented for the new-fangled practices of tea-drinking and card-playing. There was, then, little nostalgic harking back to the past – at least, not deliberately – for the new was always the rage.

Once travel became more general, however, all this changed. The Grand Tour around Europe became *de rigueur* for the young men (and quite often women) of the aristocracy, and a direct result was the Neoclassical movement in Britain during the 1750s. Initially this movement was a product of Inigo Jones's discovery in the 17th century of the work of Palladio. The fashion for Palladianism dominated the 18th century in Britain, thanks largely to Lord Burlington and his protégé William Kent, and it fostered a general admiration for 'the noble simplicity and calm grandeur' of the ancient classical forms, especially the Greek. This was followed by studies of the Italian Renaissance and by the

*A very splendid Art Nouveau bedroom
in an American country house.*

Setting the Style
INSPIRATION OF THE PAST

extravaganzas of the Gothick revival, which spread around Europe and to North America. Late 18th- and 19th-century travellers to the Far East, India, the Middle East and Egypt, not to mention military expeditions and campaigns in those areas, were responsible for the emergence of the exotica of the Regency and for the introduction of ancient Greek and Egyptian influences.

Although the wholesale historical revivalism of the 19th century had more or less burned itself out by the 1900s – Art Nouveau, with its roots in the arts and crafts movement, owed little to other styles – decorative inspiration continued (and continues) to be provided by the styles of many different periods.

'Period styles come and go, and sometimes come again,' remarked Witold Rybczynski blithely in his beautifully written historical survey *Home*. His point would seem proved by such episodes as the rediscovery during the early 1900s of the Rococo, Neoclassical and

1 A richly detailed Victorian restoration, with mahogany mouldings, Victoria plum walls, a modern carpet, and modern stencilling beneath the deep gilt border. All elements add to the feeling of warmth.
2 Painted faux marble bathroom with turn-of-the-century fittings and handsome 19th-century gilded mirror.

3 *Updated Regency in Manhattan: a magnificent round mahogany table, Thomas Hope-inspired chairs, a splendid 19th-century oriental rug, and terracotta scumbled and glazed walls.*

4 *Detail of an early 19th-century mantelpiece.*

5 *A rather Napoleon-III oriented bedroom in Paris, its green marbled dado matching the painted Empire bed, and its mahogany pedestal and handsome polished wood screen used in conjunction with a modern sculpted wool carpet.*

6 *This Parisian apartment revels in 1930s elegance.*

Georgian delights of the 18th century – more often used all together. Another example is the resurgence of Regency ideas in the middle of the 20th century. The further revivals of Victorian, Edwardian, Art Nouveau, Art Deco and early modern styles and the sly allusions to classical motifs in today's Post-Modernism provide further support for Rybczynski's aphorism.

This harking back to the past is rarely a matter of slavish imitation of earlier interiors. Rather, it is the sympathetic use of traditional motifs and forms in conjunction with the best materials of the present to produce what can often be a highly memorable and pleasing result.

At the same time, it means nostalgia, a very salient part of decoration in the late 20th century: nostalgia for what are perceived to have been the 'good old days'; nostalgia, especially in the United States, for 'roots'. Although Modernism is now some 70 years old, the majority of people have been uncomfortable with its tenets, simply because it *is* uncomfortable. By contrast, the nebulous 'past', especially as glamorously recreated by designers such as Ralph Lauren, seems warm, cosy and leisurely, while at the same time distinguished and patrician. People today are therefore looking on the 'past' as a time to be envied – even though we all know it never really happened like that.

Rustic Charm

One of the particular fascinations of the past few decades has been with the country and 'below stairs' furnishing of the preceding generations. These can have harmonious charm – the old pine, yew and elm, cherry, American golden oak and simple English oak; the rustic painted or stained pieces of furniture (cupboards, wardrobes, dressers, dining chairs and side and dining tables); and the wall and floor tiles, rag rugs, bric-a-brac, stoneware, china, prints, engravings and needlework homilies. A fine list, yet nothing on it is at all grand.

The popularity of this type of decoration has been partly a result of the fact that prices were, and still are, comparatively cheap for such generally attractive objects. The main reason, however, has been that the furniture shapes are simple and spare enough, and the objects handsome and interesting enough, for them to be mixed comfortably with modern furnishings. They add a degree of warmth and idiosyncracy to a room, yet are in no way aggressively antique.

1

1 *A comfortable Scandinavian rustic room, the whitewashed boarded ceiling contrasting with the dark boarding just beneath. The highly polished wood shelf running around the room just below the dark boarding is an interesting idea and provides a good display space for a miscellaneous collection. Below this again, the sombre green paint matched to the window blind is a good foil for the blond floor and furniture, the leather seating and the battered old rocking chair.*
2 *Battered painted furniture manages to look appealing against the barn siding wall in this US washroom. Note the geometric precision with which the old blue cotton rugs have been placed side by side. The feeling is good and solid – nicely time-worn. With this old background, even the towels hanging neatly on the wall begin to look like objets trouvés.*

2

3 Brilliant walls, a sculpted fireplace, rustic furniture, an icon and a crucifix adorn this Santa Fe style room.

4 An elaborately-painted 19th-century folk art hutch (dresser), complete with clock, works well in this Swedish country room with its deep green dado and dark wood boarding.

5 Rough plaster walls, deeply inset with a cobalt-painted window frame and a misty Swedish view beyond, make an interesting background for the rather more refined 19th-century furniture and polished blond floor. The contrast between rustic architecture and polished wood is very pleasing.

The 19th Century

In general, we tend to think of the 19th century in terms of the solidity and expansive opulence of High Victoriana. But style during the century was so much more diverse and fragmented than that. At the beginning of the century the exuberance of the Regency, with its exotic oriental and Indian influences, still survived. There were the Egyptian and Greek revivals exemplified by Thomas Hope; *Empire* in France; Empire in the United States; and the fanciful Gothick. In addition there was the anglicized Japanese of the aesthetic movement, the earnestness of William Morris and the arts and crafts movement and (in the United States) the Mission, and the sinuous shapes of Art Nouveau.

Today we appreciate 19th-century furniture, furnishings, art and accessories for much the same reasons as not so long ago we were rejecting them. Now we enjoy the solidity, slavish attention to detail, whimsy and sentimentality of so many of the objects and so much of the art: the fruit and classical figures under glass domes, the framed birds and fish and the bottled ships, the beautifully made brass scientific instruments, spectacle cases, pen boxes, lorgnettes and other collectables. Many of us love the bedsteads, the lamps, the samplers, the richness of the wallpapers, the silks and damasks and velvets, the floral charm of the Victorian chintzes. And there is a distinct harking after the palms and antimacassars, dados and wainscoting, arches, pillars, mouldings and balustrades of the Queen Anne revival and Victoriana in general.

1 Lacy sheer curtains filter the light coming into this Swedish parlour filled with the elegant accoutrements of the 19th century.
2 Mahoganized skirting heating is carefully fitted into the harmonious whole of this restored Victorian room. Note the two pediments of window and closet.
3 Gentle late Victoriana at its bedroom best in a Louisiana house.
4 There is a distinct Victorian feel to this small room.
5 The old pine chest and velvet chair look comfortingly 'old world' against the panelling and velvet.

Art Nouveau and Art Deco

The Art Nouveau style was unusual in having little historical connection; it lasted less than a decade, from 1892 to 1900. It began in Brussels, and spread all over Europe and to the United States, being known by a variety of different names in different countries – *Jügendstil* in Germany, *Liberty* in Britain, *Style Moderne* in France, and so on. Art Nouveau rooms were full of extravagant, sinuous ornament based on forms drawn from nature: this extended throughout fabrics, wallpapers, furniture, rugs, carpets, lighting and ornamental objects to give an amazingly strong stylistic consistency.

Perhaps it was for this reason – that Art Nouveau was so complete in itself, so self-contained – that it had such a short life. Or perhaps it was too connected with the decadence of the Naughty Nineties. In its final form, the Vienna Secession style, it lost much of its floreate style: in the hands of the Austrian architect/designer Josef

1 *A stunning recreation of an Art Nouveau dining room. Look at the structure of the chairs, the sofa under the turn-of-the-century painting, the wall sconces, the fire dogs, the spectacular fireplace and the oil lamp above it. The framework of the room (the fabric-lined walls, the green woodwork and the green-stained floor) has been carefully chosen to enhance the whole.*

2 *An equally stunning bathroom in the same house. Note the handsome bath and basin surrounds, the period lighting and bamboo closet.*

3 *Another detail of the extraordinary Art Nouveau collection in this spectacularly lavish American house. Everything is of the period.*

4 *Art Deco chair and cocktail stand show vivid juxtapositioning of shocking pink and shiny chrome.*

Hoffman – as indeed in the hands of the Scotsman, Charles Rennie Mackintosh – it became somewhat more abstract and geometric, so that, along with Art Deco, it figured as a precursor of Modernism.

Art Deco was primarily concerned with sumptuous surface effects, superb ornamentation, and jazzed-up versions of old forms. Although named after the *Exposition des Arts Décoratifs* in Paris in 1925, it was sparked off by a radical movement in clothing towards sensual and flamboyant lines. Interior design to match this new exoticism followed swiftly. The style was not so much a denial of the past as the past reworked under the influence of new technology.

Art Deco also incorporated African influences (tropical woods for frames and inlays, and zebra and leopard skins) and echoes of the recent archaeological discoveries in Egypt.

5 *This Art Deco bathroom is in total contrast to the Art Nouveau bathroom.*
6 *London hallway in Art Deco: tawny marbled walls, typical stepped-top cabinet and the ubiquitous woven cane chair.*

4

5

6

MODERN MOVEMENTS

At the 1925 international *Exposition des Arts Décoratifs* there were two pavilions which were either scorned or almost unnoticed yet which would have an enormous influence on domestic design over the next several decades. These were the stark, geometric Russian Constructivist pavilion (people joked that it had been made from packing cases) and a little pavilion belonging to an art magazine called *L'Esprit Nouveau* ('New Spirit'), designed by the cousins Charles-Edouard and Pierre Jeanneret; the former was the editor of the magazine, and is better known by his nom de plume, Le Corbusier.

The *L'Esprit Nouveau* pavilion was roughly box-shaped, with a plain white exterior and an equally bare and Spartan interior. On exhibit were no ornamentation, no draperies, curtains or wallpaper, no mantelpiece or small tables on which to display photographs and family treasures, no comfortably panelled study, no polished wood furniture, no rich materials of any kind ... absolutely no vestige, in fact, of familiar home-like things.

Instead, there was starkness. The walls were white, except for one which was painted plain brown. Industrial-type storage cabinets, painted yellow, were used as room dividers and the staircase was made out of steel

A modern interior with Bauhaus-inspired furniture and a marble floor.

Setting the Style
MODERN MOVEMENTS

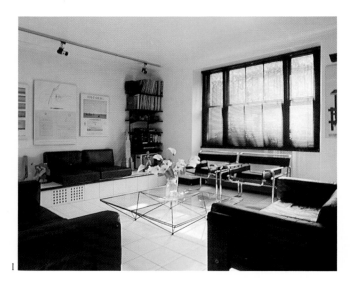

1

1 *Another Bauhaus-inspired living room. This one is furnished with 20th-century classics such as the pair of Marcel Breuer 'Vasily' chairs (made originally in tubular steel and canvas in 1925, and used by the painter Vasily Kandinsky), the ubiquitous black leather and the track lighting.*
2 *The minimalist kitchen here, with its pristine whiteness, is given maximum interest by the Fornisetti plates which are cleverly displayed in a row above the kitchen cabinets.*
3 *A minimalist kitchen in shiny black and glass; another homage to Modernism and sleek technology.*

2

3

pipes. The kitchen was tiny, and the bathroom – almost as large as the living room – had an entire wall made of glass bricks and was intended to double as an exercise room. As for the furniture, there were side tables of the kind usually found in restaurants, tables made of slabs of wood resting on tubular steel frames and some rather nebulous leather armchairs. The whole was meant to show the 'new spirit', the comprehensive rejection of decorative art, and was meant to shock.

However scornful the reaction to this building (one US critic said it exhibited the prosaic literalness of a cold-storage warehouse cube), its architect was actually trying to come to grips with modern living and the advent of the new technologies – to create with his 'machine for living' a style to mark the age. Undeterred by the hostile reaction of the critics, Le Corbusier went on to build a number of villas based on this same austerity. By the 1930s this 'new spirit' architecture was gaining ascendancy.

However, Le Corbusier's pavilion was certainly not the first building to demonstrate conspicuous austerity. As far back as 1908, the Viennese architect Adolf Loos had written a much abused essay called 'Ornament and Crime', in which he advocated the removal of all ornament from architecture and interiors – indeed, from everyday life as a whole. He argued that what had seemed appropriate in the past was no longer appropriate to an industrialized world. Loos had since 1904 been designing villas with plain white plastered walls that lacked any such decoration as cornices (crown moldings) or mouldings. What he despised, however, was not decoration but *ornamentation*, and his otherwise austere rooms were filled with beautiful surfaces. Although he was afterwards to change his mind about austerity, his *cri du coeur* for the elimination of ornament became the basis of a veritable crusade by the German, Dutch and French avant-garde.

The Bauhaus, founded in 1919 in Germany by Walter Gropius, was dedicated to reform. All vestiges of the past were to be removed, and luxury became as much of a crime as ornamentation. This extremism made its mark, for after 1920 there was a decided shift in popular taste: rooms became steadily less cluttered, a tendency which reached its apotheosis with the minimalism and hi-tech of the 1970s.

4 This room is a microcosm of the modernist movement, combining as it does the austerity of the Bauhaus, the Modernism of the 1930s (the two brilliantly curved, white leather, tubular steel chairs and the standing chrome ashtray), and the hi-tech of the 1970s (the industrial carts or trolleys for television and stereo, and the wheeled base for the glass coffee table). Also there is the sleekness of the modern Italian designers as represented by the sharp metal Venetian blinds. In this setting, the tiniest bit of colour 'zings' — the large mauve and white flower arrangement sets off the whole scheme.

4

If dance and clothes influenced the Art Deco style, economics, politics and World War II were the primary factors affecting the acceptance of the modernist style in the 1930s, 1940s and 1950s. With the Crash of 1929 and the Great Depression, Art Deco – which, with its exotic materials and faint air of decadence, had always been the province of the rich – ceased to be a domestic style, although it continued to feature in large buildings, restaurants, movie theatres and ships.

However, Le Corbusier's unglamorous 'cube' style was uniquely suited to post-Depression times, being more adaptable to slim budgets. There was also a political aspect to the style's sudden regaining of popularity during the 1930s: the new totalitarian states, such as Germany, Italy and Spain, were staunchly grandiose and monumental when it came to architecture, and so the new austerity came to represent a rebellion against totalitarianism.

Most of the modernist German architects and designers of the Bauhaus ended up in the United States, where men such as Gropius, Breuer and Mies van der Rohe were fêted and given many commissions. Thanks to this patronage, the new Modernism became regarded as chic, unfettered, an emblem of the 'free world', a refreshing change, and an altogether necessary break

from traditions of the old world. The whole modern movement set new high standards for living. It not only influenced architecture and interior design but also created a general framework for daily living. It advocated a cleaner and more regulated environment and a way of life which would complement the new technological age. Le Corbusier attempted to redefine the home by calling it a 'machine for living'.

Rooms were pure white, uncluttered, glass-walled, and filled at first with the *de rigueur* modern classics of Le Corbusier, Breuer and Mies van der Rohe. Later the marvellous new shapes made possible by airplane-material technology, beautifully reinterpreted by Alvar Aalto, Arne Jacobsen, Charles Eames and Eero Saarinen, joined the works of Le Corbusier and the rest of his generation. Modern abstract and expressionist paintings were hung on the walls, and occasional furniture was made of glass and chrome, plexiglass, perspex or white moulded plastic. Often the only colour to be seen apart from in the paintings was in the leaves of large plants and the tan-and-beige of leather upholstery. Europe's Modernism was glamorized and made sleek and sophisticated. Renamed the International Style, it was for years a favourite of the enlightened rich, filtering down in due course to the enlightened middle classes.

Minimalism

Minimalism – the art of living with the least – uses Mies van der Rohe's dictum that 'less is more' as its creed. At its best, as in traditional Japanese interiors, it is a celebration of space, or of form in space, so that one can revel in the pure sculptural lines of a piece of furniture or architectural element.

Rooms are kept as sparse as possible, with pared-down furniture and no visible clutter. Often there are hi-tech elements: industrial grey carpeting, studded rubber flooring, crisp woven matting, slick tiles and gleaming lacquered or metallic finishes. In good minimalist rooms – as opposed to bad ones which can look merely bleak and uncomfortable – background colours are kept to a minimum, white being prevalent. The shapes of the furniture and all the objects, even the humblest of baskets or a single flower, combine to achieve a special and rewarding significance. In a minimalist environment storage is of course all-important, for the absence of the usual detritus of domestic living is essential to the style. For most of us, minimalism is a difficult style both to live with and to live up to – it is not an easy option. For the enviable and disciplined few, however, who can live without clutter, the visual rewards are great.

1 *Minimalism is not always just a case of black-and-white. In other words, a minimalist design need not be of such stark intensity that any coloured object or plant smites the viewer with all the subtlety of an alarm clock going off. Minimalism can just be very simple, very austere and, as in this instance, very pleasing with its clean-lined soft colours and lack of clutter.*
2 *Much the same feeling of fresh clean elegance is apparent in this small, basically white bedroom. The use of the mirror at the back of the bed is clever, as are the neatly striped and edged comforter and pillows. Colours serve to emphasize its freshness, while the room as a whole makes sensitive obeisance to the craggy green outside.*

3

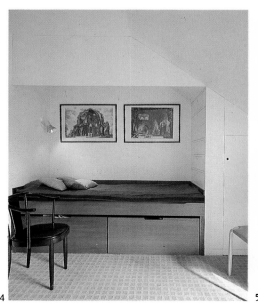

4

5

3 There is great charm in this spare room, all cream, bare wood and neutrality right down to the rooftops and houses outside the bare window wall. Indeed, so neutral is the room and so minimal the creature-comforts, the coarsely woven cane of the three empty baskets stands out — if not like a riveting work of art, at least with some considerable distinction.

4 A study-bedroom of quiet simplicity and concise planning. This time the lines are less crisp, less well defined, but the effect is still disciplined, with that peculiarly Scandinavian calm.

5 Red is used with deliberation in this ordered diner-kitchen to provide a contrast with the quiet beige stripes.

Post-Modernism

Post-Modernism is not so much just another manifestation of Neoclassicism – one of those styles which, like Gothic and Rococo, slips in and out of favour through the centuries – as a somewhat playful style based on allusion or reference to history and the classical order in a movement that is otherwise contemporary.

Pillars, pediments, arches and so on are incorporated on the outsides of buildings and in interiors in a rather dégagé manner – for example, free-standing pillars or pediments and other architectural elements are used as decoration rather than for support or delineation. Post-Modernism makes no attempt to recreate or revive a historical style, but rather it lightheartedly acknowledges the presence and influence of the past on contemporary spaces and elements of design.

The colours used are distinctive – both harmonious and strong. They are pale terracottas, sea greens, lilacs, washed pinks and sky blues – representing land, light, air and sky. In many ways they comprise much the same colour combination as those used in the Neoclassical and Adam rooms of the 18th century.

1

2

1 In this instance, the Post-Modernist influence is more in the colours: the apricots, blues, greens and lilacs. But it is also evident in the somewhat architectural look of the halogen lamp with its blue casing.

2 The Post-Modernist pillared fireplace-surround in this room has the same 'feel' as the 1960s style of the psychedelic colours on the spacey chairs.

3 Post-Modernism works well for this ingenious little bedroom with its interesting ceiling, oeil de boeuf window, wall lights cleverly integrated with the ceiling, closet, drawer and the bookshelf space, not to mention the ladder up to the bed. It is extremely well thought out, even down to the idiosyncratic frieze, with its odd photographs of leaders through the ages.

4 This kitchen door, with its elliptical window and applied decoration, opens onto a Shoji screen window and geometrically painted units – a good strategy for improving a mediocre little space.

Freestyle

One thing the mixture of historical and creative revivals with the modern movement during the last part of this century has done is to create a sense of release, of freedom and experimentation in decoration. This is true especially among the young, the impecunious, the avant-garde and the unconventional.

According to various surveys, the majority of us tend to nostalgia as we grow older, more settled and more solvent, decorating more like our grandparents (or how we would have *liked* our grandparents to have decorated!). But for the more uninhibited minority anything can go, from wonderful (but expensive) experimental furniture by sculptors, painters, architects, craftsmen and designers, through brightly coloured contemporary pieces like the Italian Memphis work and its copies, to ingenious made-up pieces and revitalized junk. All or any of these can be set against a variety of backgrounds and can be rearranged at will.

1 This French dining room has not one but two different kinds of painted finishes.
2 In another French dining-kitchen there is a play on black-and-white checks.
3 The stepped-up 1960s wall and frivolous blues make sense in a narrow space.
4 There is deliberate repetition in this somewhat hi-tech room.

AN ECLECTIC TASTE

When all is said and done, most people – including most professional designers – are happiest or at least more at ease with a rather eclectic look. It is, after all, only natural: you like a bit of this, a little of that, and maybe a touch of something else. One can draw an analogy with cooking: the most interesting dishes are an amalgam of different influences, the alchemy of the various flavours producing a delicious synthesis.

It is precisely this sort of mixing that makes decorating so exciting and varied, and which gives you such scope for your imagination. After all, purist decoration of whatever period by definition has to be fairly predictable. There are only so many early 18th-century styles – or, for that matter, available pieces. The same can be said of any other period. However different the backgrounds, the walls or the window and floor treatments, there cannot be any 'shock of the new' or even 'shock of the different', because, despite any overall beauty of the design or of your collection, the purist approach restricts you to ideas that have been realized a million times before in every combination imaginable.

Eclecticism, on the other hand (and if well done), is a real art. You mix periods and nationalities of furniture,

Aquamarine blue, used on walls, tablecloth and cushions to make a soothing framework for the furnishings in this living room.

Setting the Style
AN ECLECTIC TASTE

1 This mixture of modern upholstery with Victorian needlework cushions, 17th-century Dutch paintings and an early 18th-century bureau bookcase with ancient painted blue doors (echoed in the seats of the painted terracotta chairs) is well framed by the lively yellow walls built up with coat after coat of subtly coloured glazes.

2 At the other end of the same room, two watercolours of Petworth House by Teddy Millington-Drake are juxtaposed with coloured stripes of Italian silk. While the enormous windows allow plentiful daylight into the room, a traditional table light draws attention to the carefully composed corner of this living room.

paintings, sculptures, materials, objects and lighting to create, from all the disparate components, a whole that is completely harmonious. And it is an art of endless permutations. You can mix furnishings of different periods, linking them together with the best of modern background materials: beautiful cottons and wools, matting and tiles and wood. You can use 20th-century furniture in conjunction with classical Roman sculpture, 18th-century gouaches, Expressionist paintings and 19th-century oriental rugs. Other combinations are modern Italian, fifties, and classic Scandinavian furniture with a fine collection of photographs and folk art; abstraction and early oak; or Japanese lacquer, together with matting and Regency.

What you need to be successful when decorating eclectically (and make no mistake: if you are unsuccessful the results can be disastrous) are a sense of form, scale and colour, courage, most definitely a sense of humour and a willingness to experiment. One of the great things about the eclectic style is that it need not be at all costly, for any sensitive eye will be gratified by a judicious choice of colours and thoughtful juxtapositioning of even the most inexpensive of items.

3 The matting underscores the garden theme in this room: the real flowers and greenery are matched by the painted ones – some are even appliquéd on the throw.

4 Here, different shades of cream in the walls, curtains, upholstery, lacquered coffee table and lampshade provide the common denominator. However, the potted plants are an important ingredient in this scheme, adding dashes of green to the basically monochromatic effect of this living and dining area.

5 In this room, on the other hand, the grouping of glass tables, chair and light against the wall has much the same kind of graphic quality as the contemporary framed poster.

3

4

5

Living Rooms

In living rooms almost anything can be used – but there is one proviso: key or anchor pieces, such as sofas and armchairs, should be as comfortable as possible. However idiosyncratic or curious the general assemblage of furniture, paintings and objects, much of the interest and vivacity will be lost if it is impossible to feel physically comfortable in the room.

However different from each other the elements of a room might be, there should be some sort of common denominator – some theme – to unite them all. This is most usually colour – used as a harmonious background on the floor, the walls, or at windows and on some upholstery. For instance, you might have a large old rug whose colours you could lift and repeat here and there in the room – in an armchair and a sofa, on an occasional chair, in some throw pillows or cushions, in the window treatments, the mounts or matts of prints, and so on. Or it might be that you paint the walls in a warm colour or a dark one, such as dark green, blue or red; any of these will act like the lining in a jewel box to

show off your possessions, however disparate those possessions might be.

Another excellent background for a disparate assembly of furnishings is all-over white: white walls, white window treatments (shutters, perhaps) and a white floor (maybe tiles or bleached or painted floorboards). This approach generally makes everything look sculptural and three-dimensional. The use of coir or rush matting has a similar unifying effect, making a mixture of old and new, conventional and bizarre, seem cohesive and right.

1 The uniting factors in this room, with its cheerful red-checked fabric and painted armoire, are the country feeling and the cushions which repeat the terracotta colouring of the panelling.

2 Greeny-grey and greeny-white are the prevailing colours in a room predominantly furnished with different weaves of cane.

3 The extraordinary row of windows topped by equally extraordinary objects can hardly help but distract from the furnishings. However, the mixture is nicely contained within a pale colour scheme.

4 Almost any number of things can be placed with impunity in an off-white room.

Dining Rooms

Interestingly, although rooms devoted exclusively to dining were a fairly late invention, the modern dining room is often the most traditional room in the house, with 'Baronial', late-18th-century, Regency or Victorian table, chairs and sideboard. Yet an eclectically furnished dining room can make for much more interesting eating – as long as it is remembered that the main purpose of a dining room is, of course, to provide a comfortable place in which to enjoy food, drink and conversation, and that any decoration should enhance the meal rather than distract from it. This means that background lighting should be soft and flattering, with specific lighting directed onto serving areas. Chairs, whatever their period, should be comfortable, and walls and floor and window treatments should act as a framework.

1 A Victorian cast-iron fireplace with original stove and grate was stripped, sandblasted and boot-blacked to make a handsome feature in this basement dining-kitchen area of a 19th-century London terraced house. The room is made cheerful and interesting by the use of well-worn bentwood chairs, a 1930s advertisement, synthetic marble tiles, and modern units made to look an indeterminate age with just one coat of eggshell paint.

2 In this kitchen-dining room a polished pine table with Edwardian chairs sits comfortably under a modern Italian light fitting. The pillared 19th-century chest-of-drawers makes a good contrast with the painting.

3 The dining corner of this French kitchen has dark panelled wainscoting, flowered cotton curtains and tablecloth, striped wallpaper and 19th-century cane-backed chairs, all contrasting with the spareness of the green painted kitchen units.

4 In a St Tropez apartment, modern bentwood chairs, a pine refectory table and an adjustable Tizio lamp are mixed with an old pine side table, an old ginger jar and a painting of a window.
5 A painted rustic hutch (dresser) and brick walls in a New York brownstone are in sharp contrast to the mid-18th-century Irish table, the 19th-century elm chairs and the collection of silver. Paisley curtains and shades look good against the distressed blue-and-terracotta walls.

3

4

5

Bedrooms

Since bedrooms are generally the most personal of rooms and are not usually on show to outsiders, they tend to evolve in somewhat haphazard ways. Thus, they are often the most eclectic room in the home. Very often memorabilia, photographs and small collections of 'this and that' jostling for room with books, mineral water, handcreams, make-up, hand mirrors, prints, small paintings, pillows and cushions, can all too easily – albeit charmingly – smother the actual furnishings. And this is nice for, with the best will in the world, it is less difficult to create a beautifully designed room than to keep it that way.

In fact, a precisely and carefully decorated bedroom, however beautiful, can look soulless and uninviting if it does not have its fair share of the detritus of personal life, which is almost by definition eclectic in nature. Be careful, though, not to accumulate too many bits and pieces on dressing tables and bedside tables. They could end up looking like a jumble of possessions and may distract from a well-planned decorative scheme. A judicious clearout once in a while helps to keep your bedroom clutter under control.

4 An elegant four-poster with
sunburst roof. The lively colouring,
repeated in the velvet sofa and
armchair, is balanced by the
oversize lace-edged pillows, the
glazed walls in subtle grades of
apricot, the Victorian needlework
chair and cushions and the
handsome overmantel mirror with
its pale blue and gilt.

5 Coir matting, an old kelim and
palest yellow walls make a
framework for mixtures of different
blue-and-white designs on bed,
cushions, pillows, tablecloth and
window treatment. The blues are
then repeated in the lamp and the
Bristol blue goblets on the
mantelpiece. These are balanced by
the strong dark lines of the oval
mirror, the old cane-sided chair and
the little sewing table.

1 A little vignette of disparate
objects on a lace-covered bedside
table. The books, the gilded skullcap
on a plaster head, the tarnished gilt
palm, silver mirrors and odds and
ends, the old manicure set – all look
good against the smooth greeny-
blue paint.

2 A charming stepped-up sleeping
recess lined with bookshelves and
supported by drawers has been
formed between two closets in this
bedroom. The subtly painted
woodwork matches the ceiling, and
the stencilled border has much the
same feeling as the border on the
flowery black rug.

3 Framed cards surrounding a
green marbled mirror look neat in
this checked and striped room, with
its old polished floor and nice old
oak furniture.

Studies and Other Areas

The time-honoured image of a study — somewhat battered leather armchairs and footstools, a well worn sofa, a flickering fire, a club fender, a capacious desk and shelves crammed with books — stems directly from the average ambience of the library in a typical 18th-century English country house. However, as that century drew to a close, domestic libraries changed: they turned more and more into general family living rooms, and men were forced into smaller versions of their grander libraries — their studies. Today, most studies tend to be somewhat eclectic, if only because, like the grander libraries of the past, they too tend to be family rooms, or casual smaller living rooms containing a desk and bookshelves. Generally speaking, they are comfortable, cluttered, warm and informal, and more often than not they have a sofa that can be converted into a bed for occasional guests. The bookshelves may have a pediment or a Gothic curve, or be modern wall fitments with an integral working surface. The chairs may be of the capacious wing variety, or Charles Eames-style loungers. The rug or rugs could be oriental or calfskin or needlework. Whatever its varied ingredients, if a study is to be successful it must always seem warm and inviting.

1

2

3

4

1 A beautiful arched fanlight over glass doors sets the scene for an equally splendid graphic room with its collection of architectural drawings and bronze objects.

2 A handsomely complicated 17th-century writing table, old leather chair, oriental rug and collection of bronzes are strikingly contrasted in this study with the Tizio lamp, the modern paintings and the hi-tech stereo and projection equipment.

3 Subtle blue-green upholstered walls with matching dragged skirting boards (baseboards) are paired here with a modern carpet, rose-and-green chintz and a collection of 19th-century furniture in mahogany, bamboo and various painted finishes.

5

4 The very different whites and off-whites in this room (the cotton of the chair, the tweed upholstery and the petals of the orchid) are the common denominator binding together disparate furnishings.

5 This hall, made to seem extremely palatial, was in fact created out of a Manhattan apartment gallery. The exotic burled wood is actually painted faux bois, with glazed terracotta panels to match the border of the freshly installed marble floor. The handsome 18th-century mirror and Empire side table, however, are genuine, as are the Chinese pots. Note the dramatic effect of the uplights behind the torchères and the framing projectors set in the ceiling.

COUNTRY
STYLE

The term 'country style' embraces a vast diversity of styles, in that every nation's country style is different in character and easily distinguishable. Nevertheless, whatever their dissimilarities, all of these styles have something in common: they are comfortable, comforting, warm and relaxed. Moreover, they are interestingly different from any other style in that, whatever their nationality, they are equally adaptable to a cramped town apartment, a suburban villa, a rambling house or a small cottage. Endearingly, too, decorating in country style does not require too much money, for the essence of true rurality is simplicity. Here, of course, we are not talking about 'smart country', which is an entirely different kettle of fish: it requires either the passage of many years or the expenditure of a good deal of money to implement. Country style proper has an atmosphere of freshness and prettiness that is redolent more of nature than of sophistication.

English Country is, as the writer and critic John Richardson once put it, principally noted for 'its simultaneous look of relaxed elegance and benign neglect'. Unforced English country is cluttered with slightly bedraggled loose covers of chintz, and typically has worn oriental or

Country kitchens are much the same throughout the western hemisphere: this one is in fact English.

Setting the Style
COUNTRY STYLE

1

needlework rugs on old wood, matting, brick or pamments (large old terracotta tiles). Other typical elements are battered white plaster walls and old pine furniture, great baskets of logs and flowers or leaves and nice old paisley throw spreads. Open fires blaze, dogs stretch luxuriously in front of the hearth, and, at least in summer, French windows open out onto lavender-fringed brick terraces. Grander country houses have delicious Colefax and Fowler prints, swags and festoon blinds, mellow polished mahogany and walls decorated with pictures of horses, dogs and other subjects related to field sports and country life.

French Country vignettes are divided between Provençale and provincial. The former are full of charming little cotton prints, often bordered with rich dark backgrounds (e.g., deep red or intense yellow, green, terracotta or blue). There are old, sun-baked, terracotta-tiled or stone floors, sometimes with straw mats. The furniture is typically old and made of chestnut with cane seats, and has those slightly curved legs so particular to France and Italy. Cupboards and dressers are primitive in style. Provençale interiors look as if they have grown up in the sun and seem set in the knowledge that the sun will always shine – well, almost always.

Rightly or wrongly, one's immediate decorative images of the other parts of France – Normandy, Brittany, Burgundy, the Dordogne and the Pyrenees – are of small red or blue checks, faded *toile de Jouy* on walls and windows and bed alike, lovely old elm or chestnut refectory tables with those practical *tirettes* (extensions that pull out to accommodate yet more children for Sunday lunch), flagstones and terracotta tiles, ceilings with low beams, pewter everywhere and window boxes bustling with bright geraniums.

American Country is all about primitive furniture in faded burnt-out reds or dusty blues, simple bare board, and the lovely spare lines of Shaker furniture. Checks and small all-over print cottons abound in various guises. Other features are stencilled borders and painted floor cloths, rocking chairs and floorboards, rag rugs and four-poster beds with spanking white linen and crisp embroidery. Then again there are the samplers showing tracts and homilies, the wide stone fireplaces with leaping flames. The pervading smell in winter is of woodsmoke and mulled cider, cloves and cinnamon. Summer is typified by old cane and chintz, and rocking chairs on porches for those long still evenings.

American South West is distinct from the general American country style. It features stone and adobe, rough-hewn, solidly-built rustic furniture, faded patched textiles, Navajo rugs, carelessly thrown blankets, Indian sculpture and ceramics, straw matting on terracotta tiling, and great terracotta pots.

Mediterranean Country styles – from Italy, Greece, Turkey, North Africa, Spain, and so on – are something else again. There are cool stone walls and floors, deep window recesses in pink or blue or lemon wash, simple wood and cane chairs, old chests, sun filtering through latticed window screens or elderly shutters, crisp white cotton or linen, and baskets of herbs and flowers, aubergines, peppers and zucchini.

Scandinavian Country style is typified by distressed painted wood, elaborate ceramic and iron wood-burning stoves, bare wood floors, a pervading blue and white, and a clean crispness.

All of these are, of course, nothing more than quick sketches, a kind of shorthand list of ingredients. But you can mix these ingredients in a vast number of recipes to get the kind of look (or looks) you want.

1 Simple wooden shelves over a modern unit and a roller towel holder acting as a mantelshelf on the chimney breast. Both features are contemporary, but do not look out of place in a country kitchen.
2 Grey-painted stairs and woodwork give a pleasant feel to a casual hall with rural pine pieces.
3 A good old English back hall with orderly rows of hats and boots and a chair that has definitely seen better days upstairs.
4 A simple four-poster with an old chest at its foot. The result – a nicely relaxed country bedroom.
5 Painted floorboards are the outstanding feature of this beautiful country bathroom.

Living Rooms

There are two particular points to bear in mind about country living rooms. One is that, however beautiful they might look and whatever their particular country style, unless they are 'loungeable-in' they simply will not work. A country living room must have deep, squashy sensibly covered seating, well placed stools, good light for reading, soft lights for atmosphere, and comfortable pillows or cushions and soft rugs for lazing about on. Other essentials are a capacious fireplace, deep window sills for abundant flower arrangements and windows that open out onto sweet-smelling terraces or gardens – or at least onto the landscape outside.

The second point to remember is that it is more important for country rooms to be easy on the eye than it is for them to be impeccably coordinated. Country rooms are more for relaxing in than to be impressed by, more for peaceful contemplation than aesthetic confrontation. Certainly they should not in any way be 'demanding' rooms.

1 Dark beams and decoy birds in a room packed with geraniums.
2 A Christmas tree, faded-rose fabric and bleached beams in the brick-floored living room of a converted country barn.

3 More beams and an interesting rounded corner fireplace in a room which, despite its cathedral-type ceiling, remains cosy.
4 An interesting horizontally beamed North American room, with a lovely old faded rug, painted mantel and wing chairs upholstered in pale damask. The crewel-covered camel-back sofa and airy whites add freshness.

Setting the Style
COUNTRY STYLE

1 The painted light-brown checks on the floor, exaggerating the checks of the curtains, are matched by greeny-grey wainscoting and mouldings in this quietly decorated dining room.

2 An unusual painted dresser and a collection of Victorian jugs provide the decoration in this simple glass-roofed dining area. Whitewashed brick and coir matting add to the relaxed feeling of casual rurality.

3 The massive family table in this room is balanced by an equally massive dresser packed with china. A collection of old and new family photographs goes surprisingly well with the 19th-century country chairs and the old rise-and-fall pendant lamp.

Dining Rooms

The same feeling of peaceful relaxation and informality should certainly be the chief characteristic of a country dining room. If you are generally a gregarious person or family, it is useful if your table is expandable to cope with guests, or if you have another table nearby that you can bring into service. Likewise, you want to have plenty of spare chairs. Although it can be difficult to achieve, it is well worth trying to design your dining room so that during the summer it is cool and redolent of the outdoors, while during the winter it is warm and snug.

Apart from practical points such as these, there are no real decorational rules to follow. Certainly it is appealing to have country accoutrements – old dressers, sideboards, plates, and collections of antique curios; these latter can be particularly effective if the items have a common theme of eating and/or drinking.

The idea of modern furniture in a country dining room seems like a contradiction in terms, probably because when we think of a country style we are thinking of some imaginary timeless idyll. If, nevertheless, you do wish to incorporate into a scheme items of contemporary furniture, it is felicitous to pair them with more-rustic objects, old or new.

4

5

4 This dining area off a cottage kitchen is furnished with unstudied charm. The tiny space – big enough for four at a squeeze – is crammed full of baskets, plants and hanging shelves for china and other bits and pieces. The interior merges very naturally with the garden outside. It could hardly be called a decorated room, but it definitely seems none the worse for that.

5 A collection of old corkscrews mounted on pine panelling above the jumble of tennis racquets, and mahogany doors panelled with etched glass – these are only a few of the disparate ingredients in this welcoming kitchen-dining room. Differently coloured woods add to the casual charm, as do the extra-tall chairs matching the high table.

Kitchens

The very mention of the words 'country kitchen' is apt to bring to mind comforting thoughts of delicious cooking smells mixed with equally comforting visions of worn chopping blocks, bunches of herbs, garlic and onions, shelves massed with stoneware, crocks, utensils, spices, and esoteric oils and vinegars. De *rigueur* in such a traditional country kitchen would be an old wood table at which one could sit quietly slicing away. The reality of a modern country kitchen is that, instead of the welcoming table, there is likely to be an efficient island in the middle of the room. Nevertheless, all the units should be capacious and made of wood rather than any sort of plastic laminate; the presence of plastics instantly destroys any romantic visions of rurality.

Another practical ingredient for a modern country kitchen is good storage space which might include: glass-fronted cupboards to use for attractive displays; old pine dressers; capacious wooden plate racks; and, perhaps, if you are lucky enough to have the space, a walk-in larder.

1

2

1 An awe-inspiring wire-mesh grid, massed with pots and pans, almost covers the ceiling of this old kitchen. Beautifully made cabinets have what amounts to a frieze of old bottles running along the top shelf. The old apothecary chest in the middle of the room has a practical marble top. The antique fireplace is inset with a stove top. The ovens are set into another brick wall which has the further function of providing hanging space for saucepan lids.
2 Beautiful cabinets, pottery and a nice old table and chairs in this room are softened by the hanging plants and bunches of herbs strung from the ceiling.
3 White glass-fronted units in this room look good against the wooden countertops, floor and old country chairs; the window treatment provides further enhancement.

4 An old fireplace in a kitchen otherwise full of traditional furniture and equipment has been updated with stencilled designs and immaculate white tiles. It now holds the stove as well as providing convenient display space.

5 A very 1980s country kitchen, using all the old traditional ingredients yet in an entirely modern way.

6 This pleasing city room, with its ragged ceiling and walls and its dazzling white tiles, has all the 'feel' of the country.

7 Old cane chairs, a collection of jugs, bunches of herbs and rustic cupboards and shelves turn this kitchen into something much more than just a room for cooking.

4

3

5

6

7

Bedrooms

The general feeling you should aim to achieve when decorating a country or country-style bedroom is one of gentleness. Country-style bedrooms can be overwhelmingly romantic, chastely fresh, demure, simple and folksy, just plain simple or packed with rustic collectables. Whatever their style, though, they do not try to overtly impress — except, possibly, with a sense of complete ease and comfort.

Victorian and Edwardian iron or brass bedsteads, still fairly easy to pick up in antique shops (or junk stores if you are prepared to paint and rehabilitate them), are very useful for country bedrooms. So are sleigh beds and some old wooden beds. Reproductions of these can fit in almost equally well. Old stripped or painted dressers and chests of drawers look good, as do needlework rugs, rag rugs and old patchwork quilts.

If you have sleep problems, or if you dislike the too-early morning, you should use either layers of curtains and blinds or draperies and shades lined with blackout material to mute the bright country dawn and the chorus of waking birds.

3

2

4

1 *Old white-painted boarding and a battered brick wall gives this city bedroom a decidedly rustic character. The mood is compounded by the high Edwardian iron-and-brass bed with its plump feather mattress, pristine white linens and rose and white Roman blind.*
2 *A quite different 'feel' in another room with a boarded ceiling. The graphic quilt, tartan blanket, crisp walls and pine furniture and floor all make for a much more masculine atmosphere.*
3 *A child's room with a decidedly turn-of-the-century air. Cotton-lined walls are adorned with plates and samplers, as are the windows, while the floor is covered with old cotton rugs.*
4 *The blue frill on the pull-up curtain adds a delicate touch to an already pretty room.*

Part 3

The Elements of Design

Architectural Character
Light
Colour
Furnishings
Pattern and Texture
Displays

ARCHITECTURAL CHARACTER

A room's style is generally dictated by its size, proportion and detailing – or lack of these. Clearly, it would be incongruous to furnish a small, low-ceilinged and dark room with massive soaring furniture, or a large high room with delicate spindly pieces. And, although panelled rooms, or rooms with elaborate mouldings, *can* be furnished with entirely contemporary furnishings to interesting and idiosyncratic effect, the treatment needs a sure eye and a good deal of confidence. For most of us it is usually more effective, and certainly a great deal safer, to be sensitive to the general 'feel' of a space, and to design and furnish accordingly.

This does not mean that a poorly proportioned space cannot be altered in any way that seems feasible. Ceilings in cavernous spaces can be lowered at moderate expense, and this might also allow a more flexible lighting plan with a system of downlights, wallwashers and pinpoint spots. (Such light strategies can, of course, also change the look of a space at night quite significantly.) Any existing mouldings should be restored or replaced. If there are none why not think of putting some in? This may be expensive, but the overall effect should be well worth the cost.

Ceilings that seem too low can often be made to seem less oppressive by visual means. For example, you can paint them a much lighter colour than the walls, or you could have them in a slightly darker shade but put in a 30cm/12in stripe around the ceiling's perimeter so that the central space seemed to be raised. Vertically striped wallpaper or fabric will make rooms seem taller, as will uplights judiciously placed in corners so as to splash light onto the ceiling.

Sometimes the simple expedient of blocking up a door and putting in a new one in a different part of the room can make a huge difference to the seeming proportions of a room; additionally, the resiting of a door can make a room a great deal more comfortable and elegant. Also, if there is more than one door in a room and they are of different heights, they can be equalized to make the space seem more harmonious. A room can be made to look considerably more gracious and effectively longer if you replace the built-in shelves and cabinets at one end with a handsome free-standing piece of furniture – for example, a bureau-bookcase with, say, mirrors or paintings on either side and perhaps an accompanying pair of chairs. Alternatively, a small

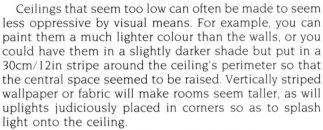

1 *Imaginative use of colour and arrangement, coupled with an eye for balance, helps this awkward space. White paint expands the apparent size while the paintings and photographs between the beams, the objects along the ledge, and the dressing table at the end of the bed make maximum use of the available area.*
2 *Here the lofty shelf helps to lower the ceiling. The arches and the clean lines and colours make the most of natural light and the view of the river beyond.*
3 *This very low attic space is helped by white paint, the oeil de boeuf window (which adds a sense of perspective), the low line of the couch, and the darker colours of the rug which visually 'drop' the floor.*

characterless room can be made infinitely more appealing if you line it with bookshelves, maybe leaving alcoves for sofas.

Mirrored alcoves either side of a chimney breast can add inches to the apparent length and height of a room, quite apart from improving its light. You can get a similar effect by mirroring between a pair of windows.

Lengthening windows – or installing French doors in their stead if a room leads onto a terrace, deck, balcony or garden – invariably has a miraculous effect on the appearance of a room, provided, of course, that such windows do not look incongruous from the outside or spoil a carefully designed facade. In the same way, an additional window or two – assuming once again that they suit the exterior and you have the relevant permission – will vastly improve the sense of light and air in the room.

A final way to disguise poor proportions is to use a wood floor that is either much lighter or much darker; such a tactic makes an immediate statement. If the floorboards are in bad condition they may have to be replaced with new boards and parquet; or they could be bleached, stained or varnished.

4 *An incredibly difficult space has been cleverly disguised using mirror along one wall to double the apparent size, a painted geometric floor and ragged walls to give depth, a large painting to add grandeur, and an interesting mix of furniture and objects.*
5 *Here the walls have been made to look further apart by painting them a darker shade between the pillars, creating the illusion that they are deeply recessed.*
6 *The space in this very high loft area has been effectively 'tamed' through the use of different levels, platforms and stripes.*

The Elements of Design
ARCHITECTURAL CHARACTER

Period Details

All through history, interior architectural detailing – ceiling decorations, mouldings, pillars, columns, arches, chair rails, dados, wainscoting, panelling, door-cases, pediments and so on – has been considered an essential part of a room by those who could afford it. Although the Bauhaus movement in the 1920s resulted in a paring-down of such elements to rely on form and structure for decoration, rather than on embellishments, the more eclectic of the general public have never given up exploring antique shops, country sales, auction rooms, junk shops and demolition yards for decorative elements to incorporate in their homes.

The Post-Modernist movement of the 1970s and 1980s has, of course, put ornament, or an approximation of it, back into the mainstream. Now there is, too, a brisk trade in well detailed fibreglass, plaster and wood columns, mouldings, balustrading, niches, corbels and panelling as people attempt to add character and atmosphere to the plain rooms of new apartment buildings and housing developments. In the same vein, just as it was fashionable in the middle years of the century to rip out or cover up and fill in old beams, mouldings and all too often (alas) old fireplaces, in the course of 'modernizing' old houses it is now equally *de rigueur* to renovate and revive, to try to uncover, open up, and generally restore or replace all the former details.

It is interesting how even the simplest cornice (crown molding) can add elegance to a space and, of course, if a ceiling is sufficiently high, the more elaborate the cornice, the grander the room appears.

If, as in so many rooms built in mid-century and later, the ceiling is not high, it is still possible to add simple slim beading or, as an alternative, one of the many paper borders available; these now include well drawn architectural cornices and dados, as well as the more usual floral and geometric designs. Fabric wallcovering can always be finished off using polished, stained or painted wood beading, decorative braid, or even lengths of picture frame in gilt, silver or polished wood. Stencilled borders (available in kits or made yourself) look decorative on plain painted walls (see page 191).

A good approximation of a dado or chair rail can be effected by simply applying lengths of 4–5cm/1½in–2in moulding to a wall at waist height and either painting or papering the space below in a way that contrasts with

the general wall colour or finish. Painted panelling can be simulated by lengths of moulding applied in rectangles or squares (see page 167). Lengths of moulding in various designs can generally be bought from good hardware or decorating stores.

A final sense of attention to detail will certainly be imparted by the room's hardware: the door handles, fingerplates, window catches, light switches and dimmers. All of these fixtures look handsome in brass, but light switches and sockets (outlets) can alternatively be effectively painted in with the walls to achieve a simple touch of character and style.

4 Simple turned banisters and a dado rail with Lincrusta beneath it are classic turn-of-the-century details in many halls.
5 The addition of an old stained-glass door adds character.
6 Mirrored panels, a graceful fanlight and a gilt strip along the bottom of the moulding give distinction to a small Italian hallway. The new details give it light, space and elegance.
7 The marbled applied pilaster contrasts well with the blue-grey paint and adds character.

1 The applied ceiling mouldings in this room add visual interest.
2 Panelling adds warmth to a small country hallway.
3 Original stained-glass panelled door makes a bold decorative statement as well as defining the space of the hallway.

Fireplaces

A working fireplace – long sacrificed in favour of the assumed higher efficiency of central heating – is once again considered to be one of the best aesthetic assets a room can have. However efficient the heating system, however beautiful the contents of a room, nothing as comforting as flickering flames and sweet-smelling smouldering wood ·or coal has yet been invented – although gas-fired imitations set into a pretty mantel are reasonable runners-up.

Even if a fireplace is not functional, the mantelpiece still provides a natural focal point for a room, and in any case, with some expense and determination, it might well be possible to open up a chimney again or to divert a flue or create a new one. Consider matters carefully before you remove a fireplace or mantelpiece unless it is really hideous. If a building is at all old, the fireplace and its surround may well be original and will almost certainly suit the proportion and 'feel' of the room in a way that no replacement could – unless, perhaps, it is a superior model of the same period and style taken out of another building.

If you are trying to make a room much grander than it already is, you could install a grander fireplace. Some-times, too, the original will have been removed already, in which case the choice is either to find another of the period or suited to the style of the room, whether an original or a good reproduction, or to introduce some other classic fireplace. Old French marble fireplaces, or copies of them, seem to fit in with almost any style of furnishing, and are often used when upgrading a room. You might prefer an old English pine mantel to a marble one, or *vice versa*.

It may be difficult or undesirable to remove an existing fireplace that is undistinguished rather than unattractive. In this case it can always be 'marbleized', *'faux bois'd'* or given some other painted finish – or just painted the same colour as the walls. If the mantel is not bad but the slips (the stone, marble or tiles framing the actual fire-hole) are awful they can (at worst) be replaced – an expensive, messy job. Alternatively, they can be painted; boarded over and then *faux*-finished; tiled over, if they do not stand too proud on top of the old tiles; or even mirrored on top of the old tiles in a room that could benefit from a bit more sparkle.

If a mantelpiece is unattractive and the room has no special architectural characteristics, a comparatively

1 This French fireplace is treated like a painting with a gilt frame around it. The fender and hearth are made out of heatproof glass.
2 Another modern fireplace, this time in Germany. The hood is integrated with the walls, and a continuation of the hearth has been made into seating. Note the space beneath for storing logs.
3 Traditional New England fireplace, untraditionally painted yellow with a painted checkerboard floor for contrast.
4 English between-the-wars mantelpiece and overmantel with a small cast-iron grate filled with dried flowers.

easy solution is to remove the offending mantel, and either install a basket grate in the hole or plan to burn logs directly on the hearth or on fire dogs. Alternatively, once the old mantelpiece has been removed and the recess tidied up, it can be framed.

One technique worth thinking about is – assuming it is feasible – to take down the walls either side of a chimney breast, leaving a central grate between two rooms. The grate can be either knocked right through, so that one fire is shared by the two ends of the enlarged space, or rebuilt so that there is a separate fire on each side; on the whole, the latter is the most satisfactory solution if you want to minimize excess smoke. The exposed chimney breast will usually form a striking shape in the room. There is no reason why the hearth should not be raised a couple of feet above the floor to give extra warmth, and perhaps extended along a wall to form a long brick base that can hold books and magazines as well as providing more seating.

If there is no fireplace at all in an otherwise ideal country house, do not despair. Wood-burning stoves can be added to outside walls provided flues are carefully engineered and the wall is insulated and fireproofed.

4

5 *Marbled pilasters grandly frame this North American fireplace in a painted panelled room. Note the spit left over from earlier days.*

6 *A simple pine surround for a French fireplace makes all the difference.*

7 *Wild flowers and Victorian cast iron, surrounded by unpretentious marble, and a set of variegated 1920s tiles.*

8 *An unusual and sophisticated Swedish fireplace inset into a wall of careful panelling.*

9 *French mantelpiece in an Edwardian house.*

5

8

3

6

9

Doors

Doors, whether internal or external, can make an immediate difference to the feeling and 'stature' of a home. Luckily, it is not very difficult to change them. You can choose from a large range of standard and custom-made designs which can be painted, left natural, stained and/or sealed to suit a particular scheme. There is also a growing choice of insulated French doors and both single and double interior doors with glass panes which, substituted for the solid variety, can totally change the feeling of light and airiness in a room.

You can find old doors in demolition yards, at antique dealers specializing in architectural elements, or at demolition sales. These latter are especially useful if you are carrying out a renovation or conversion where the ceilings are high enough and enough walls are down that you can dictate your own terms as regards door openings. A handsome pair of double doors or a collection of pediments and beautiful door-cases might well dictate the entire style of your conversion.

Existing doors can, of course, be embellished. Mouldings can be superimposed on flat surfaces to give the impression of panelling (see page 167). Conversely, unattractive mouldings can be stripped off and better

1 *This double-sided mirror-panelled door between a study-bedroom and a bathroom is indistinguishable from the mirror-panelled wall when closed.*
2 *Glass-panelled internal doors in a French apartment. These are often found in 1920s buildings in the United States as well as in European apartment blocks.*
3 *Handsome etched glass-panelled doors from France, used here to great effect in a US home.*
4 *Floor-to-ceiling folding doors make a neat space-saver in a very small kitchen area.*
5 *A softly draped doorway leading to a tiny dining room.*
6 *The same draped doorway as in 5, but from the other side, showing the reverse lining.*

7 Graceful panelled double doors in a French room lead to a draped sofa bed with pillows hung from a wooden pole.
8 Extremely ornate archway leading to an Edwardian-inspired ante-room in a US show house.
9 Heavy cotton drapes frame panelled glass French doors.

ones put in their place. Doors can be veneered, stripped or wood-grained (see page 188), or they can have their mouldings picked out in subtle gradations of colour. Undistinguished flush doors can be painted or papered in with the walls – or painted, for example, pastel colours in an otherwise all-white room. Door-cases can be painted in a colour that contrasts with that of the door itself, or left white to frame pine or mahogany panels. In an old house, it is always worth scraping away at a painted door to see what type of wood lies underneath. You may find a series of beautiful old pine doors in a particularly felicitous mellow tone lurking under a shabby coat of white paint.

Good hardware, although often quite shockingly expensive, might well give pleasure long after the shock of the price has worn off. Such hardware can make an enormous difference to the feeling of quality in a home. It is well worth making a careful choice. Alternatively, you might consider sending off old hardware to be cleaned. On modern flush doors, coloured or matt chrome hardware can add a cheering note.

Windows

A window is a lot more than a source of light and air, a base for good window treatments, and a view. Quite apart from how you treat the window – your decision to leave it alone to stand on its own merits, or to put up curtains, shades or shutters – do not forget the decorative potential of the window itself. There is no reason why a pedestrian frame should not be imaginatively treated, as long as it fits in with the general design of the room; after all, window frames are part of the background. Extra trims of wood can be added to make frames seem more substantial. Frames and surrounds can be stained to match the floor, or they can be painted in a contrasting colour and left to stand on their own. A window with an especially pleasing view can be treated like a painting in a frame. Short windows can be made to appear long and graceful by giving them a floor-to-ceiling frame, perhaps with a window seat stretched across, and softening the sides with long, caught-back curtains, or drapes.

Windows, too, can make excellent frames for glass or perspex (plexiglass) shelves which can be used to display glassware or plants. Windowsills are also useful for displaying all kinds of objects, such as china and flower arrangements.

Do not forget that windows are just as visible from the outside as from the inside. Do not decide to alter their structure in any way until you have made sure that the outside view of the building will not be adversely affected and that your new window will not clash with the old ones. In addition, you must remember to obtain permission from any local authorities.

Another important point to be considered is how problematical the windows are. How do they open – inward or outward? How are they set in the wall? Are the windows all the same size and regularly spaced, or of different sizes, asymmetrically spaced? All these points should be thought about *before* you plan any kind of window treatment. How should pivot, French, arched, corner, clerestory and dormer windows be treated, quite apart from those awkward varieties with odd-shaped or sloping tops?

But, just as elegant doors can give an entirely different look to a room, so can more appropriate windows. And remember that well fitting, well insulated windows make a lot of difference to your general comfort.

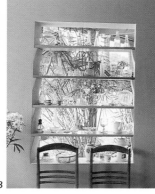

1 A large skylight gives pleasant lighting to this Connecticut hallway.
2 The window behind the basin of this bathroom shows a pretty view of farm buildings. Its sill provides space for a pair of orchids.
3 Wooden shelves stretched across the window of a North American room hold an attractive collection of glass and bibelots, enhanced by the greenery outside.
4 A simple treatment for an attractive arched window. The sill makes a good display area.

5

7

5 Plants are the sole window dressing for this bay window.
6 White Austrian shades against a dense background of greenery, cane furniture and matting.
7 A rod for hanging jugs makes a good-looking display area out of a very simple little window.
8 This large round window in a Scandinavian house is spectacular by day and hidden by an extension of the wall covering at night.
9 Draped sheer cotton looks good in this Italian room.

6

8

9

Stage II (*see page* 112)

Stage III (*see page* 128)

Stage IV (*see page* 144)

Kitchen: Stage I

Room Schemes

In order to show how a room can be built up logically, practically and comfortably – to show a true 'before and after' sequence – this book illustrates the shells of four main spaces: a kitchen, a living room, a bedroom and a one-room studio apartment. These illustrations demonstrate the natural progression of lighting, decorating, furnishing and adding accessories, in that order. The thinking behind the various transitions becomes clear if you read the sections – on lighting, colour, furniture and

fittings, and pattern and texture – which immediately precede each set of illustrations.

By examining the progression of the four different rooms carefully you can analyze exactly how a room can be made to work to fit your particular needs. You can also work backwards – gradually stripping away each layer, as it were – until you are left with an empty shell of a room. If, too, you happen to prefer a less-cluttered look, you can ignore the final stage altogether.

Stage II (*see page* 113)

Stage III (*see page* 129)

Stage IV (*see page* 145)

KITCHEN

The aim here was to build on an extension to a home to make a good-sized kitchen/dining room. The owners desired an efficient and spacious working kitchen, yet at the same time they wanted both rooms to be warm and casual. The most difficult thing to be sorted out was the lighting in the dining area. Since the new space was going to be so much longer, everyone was afraid that

the dining part would be too dark. The architect overcame this problem by stepping down the ceiling in the kitchen extension and adding a row of windows at the junction. However, to avoid too much of a break and to assist the warm 'feel' his clients wanted, he decided to tongue-and-groove both ceilings with pine boarding (see page 205) and to repeat this wood on the skirting boards (baseboards).

LIVING ROOM

This living room in a 1920s apartment block, although spacious, was at the back of the building and thus had very little daylight and a dreary view of rear brick walls. On the other hand, it had nice natural details: a polished hardwood floor, a well proportioned fireplace, high ceilings and good cornices (crown moldings), cased-in radiators under the window and

to the side of the fireplace (with potential, respectively, for a window-seat and extra shelf space) and shutters. It also had a graceful arched doorway with internal windows on either side so that what little natural light there was could filter through to the entrance hall beyond. The main tasks, then, were to get more light and warmth into the room and to take maximum advantage of the good points.

Living Room: Stage I

Room Schemes

Stage II (*see page* 114)

Stage III (*see page* 130)

Stage IV (*see page* 146)

Bedroom: Stage I

Stage II (see page 115)

Stage III (see page 131)

Stage IV (see page 147)

Studio Apartment: Stage I

BEDROOM

During the 1940s and 1950s, in the first flush of enthusiasm for Modernism, many people tore out old architectural details from period buildings. Now, with the new spirit for preservation and restoration, people are seeking to put back the detail – or at least to restore the same sort of feeling. This was the case with this bedroom, which happily still retained its fireplace and handsome window frames and doorcase, although it had, unfortunately, lost its old floorboards and all its former mouldings; also, the room had been made much darker than it needed to be. The decorative aim was to give the room back as much of its former distinction as possible and to make it lighter, yet all this had to be done within the constraints of a fairly restrictive budget.

STUDIO APARTMENT

The main virtues of this studio apartment were, first, that the rent was low and, second, that the unusual dais leading to the kitchen and bathroom areas gave added flexibility and some rationalization to the limited space. The main problems were that, apart from the bathroom fixtures, the apartment was alarmingly empty and that the young owner had a tiny budget and very few possessions (a few family cast-offs, such as a 1930s chest of drawers and an old pair of curtains, as well as generous presents including a stereo system, television, Tizio desk lamp and halogen floor lamp). Nevertheless, this studio-apartment dweller was resourceful and ambitious for his comfort. Also, he had good design sense and, best of all, a willing carpenter friend.

LIGHT

Good light and good lighting – the one natural and the other manmade – are as essential to the success of a room as they are to sight, and yet, curiously, they are often the least planned, the least thought-about, of all decorating ingredients. How often do people fail even to think about the light factor in their rooms, or about how they should control, filter, or enhance light, until long after the decoration is underway?

Natural Light Many people tend to think of artificial light as the counterfeit of daylight, regarding the two as totally separate issues. In fact, an effective lighting system that will provide comfortable light at all times requires you to strike a balance between the two, the one discreetly boosting the other when necessary. To do this successfully, you must understand the limitations of daylight – as well as its qualities. Daylight has, of course, all the advantages of variety: variety in intensity, in the form of almost hourly changes as well as seasonal ones; and variety apparent in colour, from intense blue to overcast grey, from the clear light of early morning to the pale lavenderish dusk of evening.

During each of these phases the interior of a building will look subtly different. That is why small windows should be left as uncluttered as possible to make the best of what light there is; why large windows should have screens, shades, blinds or sheers that can filter any superabundance; and why it is useful to see a room in as many lights as possible before deciding on a colour scheme and furnishings.

However, you should remember that daylight does not actually have great qualities of penetration, although the low angle of the sun in winter gives deeper penetration at certain times of the day than in the summer. In most average rooms, about 1 per cent of the available daylight outside will reach the parts of the space furthest from the windows, as opposed to as much as 10 per cent near the windows. In rooms with windows at both ends, the level of light from outside will fall off towards the middle. For large periods of the year, demanding visual tasks like reading, writing, drawing, painting and sewing can be done in solely natural light only if you are close to a window, and many rooms in buildings with a narrow frontage surrounded by other buildings will have poor lighting at most times of the day, whatever the season. This means that a good many rooms will always need the boost of artificial lighting for some purposes, and that many dark central areas in deep buildings – kitchens, bathrooms, as well as halls and passageways – will need constant artificial light.

This can raise quite a problem. During the day the eye becomes so adapted to the high level of natural light that, in order to remain equally comfortable in darker inner areas, it requires an equally high level of electric light – i.e., a higher level than is usual at night, when the eye will have adapted to the lower overall levels of artificial light. This means that *ideally* you should have either separate lighting systems in perpetually dark rooms – one for day, one for night – or some form of dimmer integrated into the existing system so that the level of lighting can be controlled.

1 *Gauzy white cotton crêpe gently filters and whitens the sunlight pouring through the large windows of this cool-floored country room.*
2 *Skylights can help make the best use of natural light in the middle of the day when the sun is at its height.*
3 *The light entering through the thin glass of this utility room's door is caught and magnified by mirror-backed shelves.*
4 *For bathrooms, where privacy has to be considered, shutters which open at the top keep prying eyes out and allow sunshine in.*
5 *Do not be tempted to think of artificial light as just the poor substitute for natural light. Any daytime lighting scheme must constitute a partnership between the two, in which artificial light is allowed to boost natural light.*
6 *The large square halfway up the stairs lets in a great deal of light.*
7 *Installing glazed doors is an inexpensive way of allowing more natural light to enter your home.*
8 *Three unusually framed and mullioned windows flood this US bathroom with sunlight.*

Lighting a Room

Room lighting can be divided into three distinct types:
- general or background lighting
- task or local lighting
- accent or decorative lighting

Ideally, every room should have a combination – to a greater or lesser degree, depending upon function – of two if not all three of these types. Ideally, too, each form of lighting should meld into the others to form a sometimes dramatic but always harmonious whole.

In order to achieve this kind of lighting harmony it might help to remember that artificial light is, after all, a *substitute* for daylight, which is never static but always shifting and flowing. Think, too, of the three types of light as representing different moods of daylight – the shaft of sun that lights up a particular corner or area; the way a sunbeam highlights a piece of glass or silver or the top of an old polished table – and about how you can use artificial lighting to create similar effects.

Living Rooms   The best effect is achieved if all three types of light are used. Background lighting is more subtle coming from well placed wall lights used on their own or in conjunction with uplights set on the floor and concealed behind plants or furniture or in decorative pots; this set-up will give a soft wash of light as opposed to the bland light that comes from a central ceiling fixture. Another alternative for general lighting is to use a selection of strips of one kind or another so as to bathe the walls with light. These arrangements will, in fact, soften the hard confines of a wall and make a room seem more spacious.

Task (local) lighting is provided by table lamps and floor lamps placed judiciously beside sofas and armchairs for comfortable reading, or by angled wall lamps set just above seating areas if there is not very much floor space. Desk lamps are desirable for writing.

Accent (decorative) lighting comes from eyeballs or spots of various types inset into the ceiling – if at all possible – or in some way angled to highlight paintings, objects, tabletops and so on. Accent lighting can also come from the pools of light cast by table lamps.

One important point to remember if you have the chance to rewire a room for your own convenience is that all of these light fixtures can be controlled and subtly modulated by separate switches and/or dimmer switches set by the door. If you are using uplights positioned on the floor, do remember to ask your electrician to have them switched from the door, for this will save a great deal of irritating stooping and crawling around on the floor to switch them on and off. Alternatively, if the rewiring involved is too difficult, ask your electrician to install kick switches by any floor lamps so that you can control them with your foot.

Dining Rooms and Dining Areas   These look best and certainly more romantic by candlelight, but make sure that candles are either above or below eye level, not flickering directly in the diners' eyes. A combination of candlelight with a discreet downlight or two in the ceiling, controlled by dimmer switches, is better still. Pendant rise-and-fall lights with an opaque shade cast a pleasant light, but again they should have a dimmer switch and be so placed as to avoid uncomfortable dazzle. The serving area should be lit separately, perhaps by a well angled spot or downlight or by concealed overhead lighting in the form of an incandescent strip set behind a cover or pelmet (cornice).

Halls, Corridors and Staircases   Far too many halls and staircases have hopelessly inadequate lighting.

1 A small lamp accents a tiny sculpture whereas a larger, angled lamp provides illumination for typing and writing.

2 A halogen uplight gives a general punch of light in this hallway whereas the recessed spot washes the wall.

3 The pair of table lamps in this bedroom provide both accent and reading light.

4 A chandelier gives general light whereas a series of table lamps provides both accent and decorative light in this living room.

5 A brass lantern supplies general light. Storm lamps illuminate the mirror, the Chinese ginger jars and the botanical prints.

6 The wall lights give background light, the table lamps are for reading, and the fire provides a subtle accent.

7 Spots give both general and accent light.

The Elements of Design
LIGHT

They should be well lit at all times, with light on the floor to show any changes in levels and surfaces and light on the walls to show switches and door handles. When starting a lighting plan from scratch, the ideal is to have a night circuit of low-level lights in those areas, controlled by a dimmer switch so that you can turn them down to the right level at bedtime. Alternatively, you could have a separate circuit of miniaturized lights that could, if desired, be left on the full 24 hours, because this system, although somewhat expensive to install, uses very little electricity and is therefore cheap to run. Both systems have the added advantage of acting as an effective deterrent to burglars and prowlers.

Do not forget to try to light hall closets from the inside, so you do not have to grope frustratedly in the dark for coats. Staircases should be lit to emphasize the distinction between treads and risers. The best way to achieve this is to have a good strong light above the stairs and a softer one below. If lights are on a dimmer switch, they can be turned down to an acceptable level and left on all night with very little waste of power. (You may find, though, that you have to replace bulbs more frequently). This is particularly useful in households where there are small children or elderly relatives. Any paintings and mounted objects – sculpture and so on – can be lit using different varieties of spots, preferably attached to a dimmer.

1 In this beamed dining room, ceiling spots give general light, lamps and candles providing decorative accents.
2 Track lighting gives general illumination and a rise-and-fall lamp lights the table in this spare-lined dining-kitchen.
3 Spots give overall light and the candles and strip light accent. The floor lamp is for reading.
4 Another mixture of general light from the mantelpiece spot and the candles on the wall mirrors.
5 At night goose-neck lamps light the table in this dining room.

3

4

5

6

7

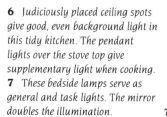

6 *Judiciously placed ceiling spots give good, even background light in this tidy kitchen. The pendant lights over the stove top give supplementary light when cooking.*
7 *These bedside lamps serve as general and task lights. The mirror doubles the illumination.*

Bedroom Lighting   This should be almost as flexible as that in the living room: soft enough to be relaxing and peaceful; bright enough to see to dress and perhaps make-up by; and well placed enough for comfortable reading in bed. Bedside lamps should be high enough to shine directly onto a book. A light above a mirror used for making-up is less helpful than lights placed at either side. Lights positioned to shine outward are much better than lights set to shine onto the mirror itself. The same applies to full-length mirrors: the light should be directed onto the viewer rather than onto the glass.

Children's Rooms   In rooms for small children all sockets (outlets) should be childproofed and lighting fixtures should be kept well out of reach. Wall lights are useful here, for they give a softer general light than central ceiling fixtures. Dimmer switches are useful for children who are afraid of the dark; alternatives are very low-wattage skirting (baseboard) fixtures. Older children will want good light for homework, hobbies and reading in bed, so provide adequate lighting on desks and work tables and above beds, and make sure these fixtures are well positioned.

Bathrooms   Small bathrooms may well need no more than a single ceiling light or a couple of downlights (one set over the bath, with a waterproof bulb). Lights should be fixed either side of any mirror used for both making-up and shaving, or just above if used only for shaving. Unfortunately, all too many bathrooms have wiring for light only above the mirror and often people find it just too much hassle to get the situation changed.

Kitchens   All kitchens should have good general light plus booster light for any precise activity – e.g., reading cookbooks, chopping, assembling ingredients and washing dishes. Well placed general diffusing lights fixed flush to the ceiling, inset spots or a mixture of downlights and angled spots make good background light, supported by strip lights concealed under high-level wall cabinets to shine down on the work surface. Any fluorescent lights should be of the warm white variety, because they make food look more appetizing than do most other fluorescents. Also, try to light the inside of storage cupboards or closets.

Directional Lighting

Task or Local Lighting This is a most important part of any room, providing the right level of illumination for a wide range of activities from reading and writing to cooking, eating, sewing, painting, making-up, shaving and playing cards, as well as creating warm, soft pools of light in the room.

In general living areas task lighting is usually provided by table, desk or floor lamps; in bedrooms it is given by bedside lamps, dressing-table lamps and perhaps 'theatrical' white bulbs set at either side of a mirror. In kitchens and laundry rooms, items such as fluorescent strips or a diffusing ceiling fixture give the sort of bright, even light that is required; this can be locally stepped up by spots angled from the ceiling. In bathrooms, you can obtain task lighting by installing the same sort of 'theatrical' strips suggested for dressing-table lights, as well as appropriately placed downlights.

Often people are beguiled by the shape and look of a table or floor lamp but fail to think very much about what the lamp actually achieves in the way of light output. Lamps should, of course, be as functional as they are good-looking; they should provide both generous light for tasks and reading and add a comfortable feeling to a room.

Other moot questions are the height of lamps and how they should be placed. A good guideline to follow for table lamps is that the total height from the floor to the lower edge of the shade (including table height) should equal eye height from the floor – i.e. 100–110cm/ 40–43in, if you are seated on an easy chair. For reading choose three-way or regular soft white bulbs with a maximum of 150W; this might sound a high wattage, but it is a sensible intensity for close work. Three-way bulbs, if available, are preferable because they can be turned on low when not needed for reading or writing. Alternatively, a table top dimmer can be fitted so that you can vary the level.

The base height of floor lamps should be 100–125cm/ 40–49in to the lower edge of the shade with 150W–200W soft white bulbs, or 50W/150W/200W three-way bulbs – or best of all, a halogen bulb with a dimmer switch. For reading, the lamp should be placed behind your shoulder. This obviously cannot be done if a chair or sofa is against a wall; here you can use something like a swing-arm lamp with a dimmer attachment.

1 *In this sleek kitchen strip lights concealed beneath the cupboards give good light for cooking, food preparation and washing up.*
2 *A flexible angled lamp gives excellent work light as well as providing elegant accent in this Swedish study.*
3 *A brass floor lamp giving reading light.*
4 *An interesting double-angled halogen light shines into the bowl.*

5 Candles and firelight provide warming accents.
6 The table lamp on this desk gives dramatic but mellow accent light to a little study area.
7 Angled spots wash the walls with light and illuminate all the art in this fabric-lined Parisian apartment. Candles on the dining table provide the more mellow accent light. The unified effect is quite dramatic.

The base height of a bedside lamp should be in line with your shoulder when you are in a semi-reclining position, and the lower edge of the shade should be at your eye level. Extended arm wall lamps are particularly good for bedtime reading and are useful too for saving space on overcrowded bedside tables. Bulbs should again be of the three-way variety if possible: if not, the lights should have a dimmer switch so that one partner need not be unduly disturbed if the other has to switch on the light in the middle of the night.

Accent Lighting Accent lighting creates focal points, emphasizes paintings, plants, flower arrangements and ornaments, and can be used to add interesting drama to a room. The sort of fixtures to employ for this sort of highlighting are the various types of spots, wallwashers, pinhole or framing projectors, uplights, and those strips of tiny lights (like Christmas-tree lights) that can also be used below shelves, in bookcases and so on to delineate angles and give sparkle. Not to be forgotten are candles.

For a wall of pictures, prints, wall hangings or other art use recessed wallwashers, or, if this is difficult, surface-mounted strips, which can be bought in any length with any number of sockets to which to attach lights; alternatively, use track lighting with individual housings that are adjustable for spacing and targeting, so that you can illuminate individual paintings or objects as well as wash the whole wall with light.

The ideal for lighting individual paintings and objects is a pinhole or framing projector; note, though, that they are expensive. When their lenses and shutters are adjusted accurately they will focus exactly on the item to be highlighted, with no overspill. They should be recessed into the ceiling 90–110cm/36–43in from the wall. Alternatives are surface-mounted fixtures similar to those specified for track lighting on page 160; these can be used either in conjunction with track or mounted individually on a ceiling or beam.

If you want to highlight a painting over a mantel, for example, but cannot use recessed lighting or surface-mounted lights, you can utilize uplighting provided by very small portable spot fittings, or by halogen lights concealed in a vase or small canister on the mantelpiece. Alternatively, you can use a high-density lamp aimed from below in order to avoid unwanted reflection in picture glass. Should you use a conventional picture light mounted on the picture so as to illuminate from above, it ought to have a rotating reflector and be adjustable to adapt to an extra-thick picture frame.

For plants, floor sculpture and hangings near to floor level use standard uplights or small adjustable floor uplights concealed behind the plants, in corners or just by the object to be lit. These will either bounce light up, or 'graze' the given object with light.

COLOUR

Colour is both the most immediately noticeable and the most malleable element in decorating. Different combinations of colour can make the same room and the same furnishings seem warm or cool, restful or stimulating, harmonious ·or jarring, welcoming or impersonal. In other words, colour is of the utmost importance – and for that reason it is the source of considerable worry to many people.

Inspiration Some rare individuals can carry a colour around in their heads and match it absolutely. They look at a room and know instantly what will or should suit it, and how a single colour will look in this or that colour combination. The majority of us, however, have to work at developing our sense of colour. The easiest and most efficacious way is to get into the habit of *looking hard* at any combination of colours that pleases and appeals to you, and deliberately to analyse the build-up of the colours within that image.

Most visual artists develop the habit of patiently observing colour – of noting all the different shades and nuances that exist in an object or a scene. The Impressionists in particular developed the practice of describing everything they saw in terms of the most detailed breakdown of tones and shades. It is an interesting experiment to take a single item – a rug or a painting, a piece of china or a particular fabric – and to write down the various colours and tones of colours you see in it; not just those that predominate but also all the ancillaries that together make up the whole image. Once you have got used to looking at and analysing colour, you can draw inspiration from almost everything that visually pleases you – particularly, of course, from the natural world.

Think of country or forest or sea or sky colours, or of the build-up of tones in a Mediterranean village or your own garden. Most rural scenes contain innumerable shades of green harmoniously blended with bright flashes of colour from flowers, blossoms, berries or crops. Similarly, looking at an old-fashioned rose garden can tell you how to make successful blends of pinks, yellows, peaches, greens and terracottas, creating a subtle and pleasing scheme of equal tones against a background of the green of trees or the rose-terracotta of an old brick wall.

Another way to build up ideas for a scheme is to observe your own and other people's emotional responses. People often have extraordinarily violent reactions to different colours for no logical reason. 'I loathe green,' they say, or 'I just can't tolerate anything pink.' It is difficult to see how people can possibly object when these colours are used well and with the right balance of contrasts but, whatever the logic of these responses, you can use them positively. Take your favourite colour and think about it in depth. Think, for example, of yellow, and remember everything floral and yellow from the palest creamy yellow of honeysuckle or freesia to the thick

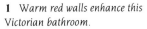

1 *Warm red walls enhance this Victorian bathroom.*
2 *Scarlet walls make a dramatic foil for antiques.*
3 *Sunshine yellow drenches a living room in light.*
4 *A palette of light tones promotes a sense of airiness.*
5 *Adding a sense of depth to a predominantly white room, loose covers on the sofa are palest blue.*
6 *The rich malachite green of the festoon is echoed in the wall colour.*
7 *A dresser painted cobalt blue makes a perfect background.*
8 *A combination of different blues gives a look of serenity.*
9 *Deep blue walls in the dining room of Charleston House.*

creamy velvet of rose petals, through narcissi to daffodils and marigolds. Think of other colours in the same kind of depth and it should be easy to translate all these subtleties and variations of tone into interesting monochromatic colour schemes, especially when the colours are translated into textures to make up a room: wood and wool, cottons and velvet and tweed, paint and paper; all of these and many more can be used to give differing depths and surfaces.

If you are not sure what style of decoration you want to use and are still uncertain about the colours that you find comfortable to live with, there is a useful trick. Buy

The Elements of Design
COLOUR

as many decorating books and magazines as you can. Mark the pages showing pictures of rooms that particularly appeal to you, put the books and magazines aside for a few days, and then look at all your favoured photographs at once. You will notice almost certainly that there is a common style and balance of colours between them.

Matching Colours to Style   Although certain colours and colour combinations are definitely connected with particular periods (dark plums, reds and greens for late-19th-century style; stripes and apricot for the Regency period; perhaps orange, green and cream for the 1930s) and indeed are sometimes called after a period, style or culture – as in, say, 'Pompeiian red' and 'Adam green' – there is no need to feel you are rigorously bound by such traditional conventions.

A comforting example can be found in the recolouring of the William Morris designs by Liberty: these look good today, yet they do not in any way sacrifice William Morris's original style. Or again think of the extraordinarily pretty chintzes revamped from old designs by Colefax & Fowler, Scalamandré, Sandersons and others. It is all a question of balance and proportion.

As far as rooms are concerned, the degree of your success will depend on the way you *personally* manipulate style and 'feeling' to your own best comfort.

1 *Aggressive colour is subdued by the delicate furniture to create a strong design statement in this 1950s kitchen.*
2 *Yellow walls provide a good background for antiques.*
3 *The classic kitchen colours, blue and white, give a look of freshness to this contemporary design. Pale grey tiles provide a softening link between the two colours.*
4 *This streamlined kitchen displays a colour combination evocative of the 1930s: buttermilk counters and units banded in bright chrome and duck-egg blue, set off with bright red.*

5 The shiny black and white of this slick modern kitchen is counterpointed by the dramatic injection of lipstick-red details.

6 The restrained elegance of the soft cream colour scheme suits the curved shapes and warm tones of the 1940s-style furniture.

7 Crisp white with dark wood is the perfect combination for suggesting a cool African interior.

8 Pink candy-stripe wallpaper makes a feature of the unusual angles and corners in an attic bedroom.

9 An authentic 'retro' look is achieved by the use of classic Art Deco colours.

10 There are echoes of Tissot in this languid Victorian-style garden room, with its moss-green festoon blinds and painted furniture.

11 A classical treatment for a Georgian dining room: powder blue walls set off with cream woodwork.

Putting Schemes Together

1

Thinking up colour combinations for a particular style of room is one thing. Achieving the right balance is another. Preparing schemes for an entire home is the most intricate exercise of all.

There are several types of permutation you can use to achieve an interesting balance. One way is to keep most of the room in shades and variations of a single colour but to have a number of items in a harmonious secondary colour, while using objects of quite different colours for the purposes of accent. For example, you could use a warm but pale cream for walls, window shades and carpet, mix it with rose for the upholstery and curtains and add, as accent colours, white (chairs and frames), green (plants and a stencilled design on the walls) and burnt umber (a dried flower bouquet).

Another effective permutation is to keep walls, curtains, floor and furniture all in one colour, perhaps white, the interest being provided by the varying textures. Alternatively, to the same basically white room you could add green-and-white cushions or pillows as well as groups of plants.

Again, you could use a soft blue for walls, a slightly darker shade for dados or wainscoting, paint woodwork a crisp white, and have touches of pale lilac. Another variation on the same theme would be to have the colours as above but with the addition of chairs or even the carpet in olive green.

Planning the colour scheme for a whole house or apartment depends very much on its overall size. If a home or apartment is very large you can afford to have, if you wish, quite different schemes in every room, as long as you remember to pay attention to the meeting points of floor and wall finishes, and to make sure that differing colours, textures and patterns work well together between corridors and the rooms that they adjoin. If the space is small, however, then it is sensible to create a harmonious whole – to think up an overall palette of colours that can be used in differing proportions and combinations in the various rooms. For example, suppose you were particularly happy with apricot, dark blue, burnt umber and green. In one room you could have apricot walls combined with white shutters, a dark polished wood floor, a golden Afghan floor rug, and upholstery in dark blue, cream and plain white, accented with green plants and old needlework cushions or pillows in shades of yellow and apricot and with blue paisley fabric at the windows and on chair seats. Another room could have apricot and off-white wallpaper used with plain deep blue upholstery, and a third room could be basically off-white with an apricot-and-blue border or stencilling, polished floorboards with a blue-and-apricot dhurrie rug, off-white shades with a double border of apricot-and-dark-blue grosgrain, and a mixture of blue, off-white and apricot upholstery, or blue or apricot bedspreads.

Each room would seem entirely different, but each would meld with the others to create an overall impression of harmony.

Manipulating Space and Colour   It can be seen from the above that in a small apartment or house the space can be made to seem much larger if more or less the same colours are used throughout, but in different juxtapositions – especially if they are rooted to the same general floor covering (or perhaps a polished wooden floor). Strong or warm colours like red and burnt orange will make walls appear to close in and the space seem smaller. Cool colours will appear to stretch space, to push the walls out, particularly if the floor, walls and ceiling all relate to each other. A long corridor will seem less so if the end wall is painted or covered in a warm colour, just as a small space will seem larger if all the

2

3

4

6

5

1 The Empire look, in rich cream and purple.
2 A sugar-pink kitchen, carefully coordinated (right down to the teapot), is set off with a jolt of green.
3 Subtle, muted shades of pale terracotta, pale leaf green and light blue blend beautifully.
4 Plastered walls washed in light green create an atmosphere of contemplation.
5 A 1950s 'retro' look, with a splash of paintbox colours.
6 The graphic lines of the modern furniture are softened by light spilling through translucent curtains.

surfaces are painted the same white colour and the walls are washed with light.

A high ceiling will seem less so if it is painted a darker colour than the walls. Another way of making a high ceiling look lower is to add a false wainscot at waist level around all the walls, painting it a darker shade than the walls above. A low ceiling will seem higher if it is painted a lighter shade than the walls, and higher still if you fix moulding around the perimeter of the ceiling and paint it a darker colour than the ceiling.

Colour, of course, has an immediate effect on the 'feel' of a room. Rooms painted in deep warm colours such as rust red seem warm and comfortable; such a scheme would be appropriate, for a home in a northern city, with long winter months. The same room painted white or pale yellow would seem light and airy in a hot climate, especially if it was filled with white wicker furniture.

A rather dark, rich room can be brightened by using accents of more intense colour and lightened by painting the woodwork white. A light, somewhat bland room can be given much more interest and character if you stain the floorboards a deep, very dark brown and add large plants in oversized baskets or terracotta pots. Large pieces of furniture will look smaller if their covering is the same colour as that of the walls; a smaller piece of furniture covered in an accent colour can then be used to balance the effect.

Mixing Colours

When you are on the verge of finalizing a colour scheme it helps to take samples of all the ingredients you plan to use in a room (flooring, curtains, window shades, wallcovering, paint, tablecloths, bedspreads, valances or ruffles, trims, tie-backs and so on) and put them on a table, if possible in the room itself. Then you should give them, as it were, a good squint with narrowed eyes. This is what Emily Malino, the US designer, suggested in her excellent book, *Super Living Rooms*. I have often followed her advice, for it works very well. By squinting at all those assembled colours and textures you can see which really works with the others, and in what proportion; what stands out too harshly; and what patterns and textures contribute to the most harmonious whole.

That, of course, is to assume you have already selected your colours. Sometimes you may have in mind a colour for walls or a piece of furniture that you cannot find in any paint shop – and, indeed, cannot yourself precisely visualize. The best thing to do in such a situation is to browse through magazines (including the advertisements) and look at samples of coloured wrappings, bits of dress fabric and so on. As soon as you see the colour you desire – and if you do this you almost inevitably will – you have something to show what it is that you want. Take your 'sample' along to a paint shop to get the colour mixed, or show it to a painter, who might, if he or she is good, be able to achieve exactly the same subtle effect by tinting a glaze and overpainting a wall, by painting on different layers and rubbing the paint off until the desired effect is achieved, or by some other means.

Then again, you might find exactly the right colour for a curtain in a dress-fabric department. The fabric will be of a narrower width, and you may have more trouble working with repeats, yardage and seams, but it could all be well worth it to get the exact shade you want. Do not forget about antique textiles – and, indeed, old fabrics in general. Dyes vary over the generations, not to mention the centuries, and it is often possible to find beautiful old draperies and tablecloths in thrift stores as well as antique shops.

Finally, do not neglect chance or happy accidents, or think that once a room is done to your satisfaction it is finished. You might suddenly see a new (or old) fabric that seems to go perfectly with, if not match, an old rug. All you have to do is cover a cushion or pillow with the fabric, or use it to make an overcloth for a table, and again the room has a new dimension.

1

2

3

4

1, 2 Here two connecting rooms with different schemes are given unity by the repetition of colours. In the blue dining room, red needlepoint seat cushions and a red lacquered lamp-base tie into the glimpse of red wall through the doorway. In the scarlet living room, blue-and-white china on the mantelpiece and a blue covered footstool link to the dining-room colour scheme.

3 A Mondrian-style painted table-base acts as a colour code for the decorative scheme.

6

5

7

How Many Colours Can You Put Together? This is a point that often worries people. Major areas (walls, floors, window treatments) should generally be restricted to three colours at most, but there is no real limit to the number of accent colours that can be used with pillows, mouldings, accessories, flowers and so on. For example, in a room with glazed yellow walls, the carpet could have a yellow-cream ground with odd touches of various blues and rosy terracotta. The curtains could be yellow-and-white stripes with the undercurtains in creamy white. One sofa and an armchair could be cream, another sofa yellow, and a second armchair could pick up the blue in the carpet. Two other occasional chairs could have frames painted in soft terracotta and faded blue-green seats – again to pick up the carpet's colour. A final colour could be provided by the greens of plants.

The main point is that you do not have to stick to matching colours exactly. After all, in nature colours are never perfectly matched.

4 A strict two-colour scheme can give coherence to an area such as a kitchen where there are many different types of surface.

5 The consistency of the red, black and white scheme is carried right through.

6 The turquoise background of the patterned fabric on the chair, stool and screen is used to draw together different areas of the room.

7 A black-and-white background is a sympathetic frame for pretty floral chintz, plants and ferns.

111

Room Schemes

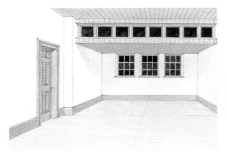

Stage I (*see page* 92)

Stage III (*see page* 128)

Stage IV (*see page* 144)

Kitchen: Stage II

Stage I (*see page* 93)

Stage III (*see page* 129)

Stage IV (*see page* 145)

Living Room: Stage II

KITCHEN

The next step was to install the lighting and tiles. To make a deliberate distinction in atmosphere between the kitchen and the dining area, a chandelier was put in above where the dining table would go. Recessed ceiling lights were set in the kitchen (see page 158), there being ample recess between boards and roof. Sockets (outlets) were installed above the counters to allow both for further lights and for appliances. Large Mexican tiles were chosen for the floor in both the kitchen and the dining area to provide continuity; smaller quarry tiles were set into the wall above the sink and the counters (see page 200). The walls were all painted in white eggshell, and the ceiling boards were lightened with a white stain to raise the apparent height. This also helped the overall lightness.

LIVING ROOM

The first thing to be done was to boost the natural daylight while avoiding having to have artificial lamps switched on all through the day. The best way was to use a system that had enough flexibility to give bright light by day and interestingly subtle light by night (see page 150–161). To this end, 'warm white' fluorescent strips were slipped behind the wood pelmets (cornices) above the window to simulate sunlight filtering down through the shutters. Uplights were placed in the corners, a picture light was installed over the fireplace, downlights were recessed in the internal windows, and a halogen floor lamp was installed on the premise that it really looked like sculpture. Walls were ragged (see page 184), in warm apricot and the woodwork was painted white to add to the lightening effect.

Room Schemes

Stage I (*see page* 94)

Stage III (*see page* 130)

Stage IV (*see page* 146)

Bedroom: Stage II

Stage I (see page 95)

Stage III (see page 131)

Stage IV (see page 147)

Studio Apartment: Stage II

BEDROOM

Although restoring or adding mouldings can be reasonably inexpensive, in this case the cost still went over the budget. It was therefore decided to use a small floral wallpaper with a coordinating border, and to paint all the woodwork white (see page 181), so that lightness was restored as well as character. However, before the decoration was done, heating panels were installed along the skirting (baseboards), as well as wall sconces to enhance the period feel. The less than distinguished 1940s floor was improved by first sanding it down (see page 169) and then staining it in a darker, richer colour; finally the floor was given a couple of coats of polyurethane and a waxing. This at least made it a better-looking background for the collection of cotton rugs.

STUDIO APARTMENT

Clearly the first priority was getting the framework right, followed by obtaining good kitchen equipment. There was no money to add new electric sockets (outlets), but ceiling fixtures were found on sale in a lighting store and a job lot of old spotlights in the local charity store. Although the original intention had been to paint everything white, the scheme was changed to yellow walls with grey woodwork once the major decision had been made to splash out on close-fitting grey industrial carpeting (laid everywhere except in the kitchen), the aim being to give a substantial improvement to the overall appearance of space and comfort (see page 224). Black and white vinyl kitchen tiles were found in a nearby store; they were stuck down with adhesive.

FURNISHINGS

It is quite possible, if you have the money and the time, to plan the furnishings of a room from scratch and, within a few weeks or months, have the room exactly as you originally envisaged it. The result, however, may have all the impersonality of a hotel room or a store advertisement. It may be comfortable, workable and well designed – even lush – but it will have nothing of your own particular character and individuality.

If you have considerable experience of decorating, either because you are a professional or because you have moved frequently, you can get round this problem, but on the whole the most interesting, idiosyncratic and memorable rooms *evolve*. People change their minds. It may be that they have to change them through lack of funds or simply because they cannot find what they originally conceived. Alternatively, though, some different arrangement or juxtaposition might suddenly present itself through a chance happening – perhaps someone gives you a good piece of furniture or a painting, the inclusion of which will affect the design of your room. For whatever reason, half the fun of decorating is living through the gradual changes – the interesting evolution – of a room.

This is by no means to say that you cannot or should not plan the furnishing of a room from the beginning, or have any idea for its eventual style based on your particular needs and preferences as well as the overall 'feeling' you wish to create. It is important to get the framework – the bare bones – right from the start, and to go about the arrangement of a room in such a way that at every stage it *looks* finished, even if it has yet to reach the ideal you envisage for it in the long term. Doing this is not difficult if you make a practice of always buying compromise 'fill-in' furniture, with an eye to recycling it to other rooms as and when you can afford what you really want. For example, inexpensive canvas, cane or wicker chairs can be used in the living room in the meantime and then later they can be moved to a bedroom or a porch.

It has to be repeated emphatically that you should be prepared to change your mind if necessary – to add here and subtract there. Above all you must be flexible, because your tastes and ideas may change, as may your financial status (or lack of it). Happily, even if money is at a premium, imagination need not be.

1 A warm, neutral colour scheme and the natural textures of the coir and the slatted wooden blinds together make an appropriate setting for a collection of wooden furniture.

2 The country pine table and chairs are the focal point in this dining room, blending with the floral festoon and modern print.

3 Living rooms often need to accommodate different activities. Here the right angle made by the pair of long sofas echoes the angled laminate worktop.

4

3

5

6

4 A traditional living-room arrangement: a pair of facing sofas on either side of the fireplace, flanked by occasional tables.

5 In this spare Swedish bedroom, an iron bed, Victorian dining chair and modern leather recliner are set around the perimeter of the space, as if they were objects on display.

6 A truly eclectic mix: canvas director chairs ranged around an antique table, and a simple wooden stool used as a plant stand.

The Elements of Design
FURNISHINGS

Choosing Furniture

It helps when planning furniture for various rooms to think in terms of 'rooted' and 'peripheral' or 'floating' pieces. Sofas, beds, pianos, bookcases, dining tables and storage walls are definitely rooted pieces, as are armchairs and any sort of storage. In the peripheral or floating category come occasional chairs and side and coffee tables; these contribute to the overall effect of contrast – solidity and lightness, permanence and fluidity. Clearly, you will have to buy first the large, comfortable root items. Once these are installed you can adjust your ideas about the floaters, perhaps even improvising them – for example, you could make your own coffee table using a sheet of thick glass set on a cube-shaped base.

Make lists of (a) what you already have that can be used 'as is', (b) what needs to be re-covered, revarnished, relacquered, repainted, stripped and waxed or otherwise titivated, and (c) what needs to be bought; list (c) should also include notes as to when you are likely to be able to afford the various items.

Since, if you are planning ahead for any length of time, you will need to keep colour in mind, it is probably best to start with a neutral palette, arranging your contrasts by means of textural differences and subtle gradations: you can always add the colours as you go along. Remember that dark walls will always make a room look more 'furnished' and richer than in fact it is. Dark greens, Pompeiian or Victorian reds, terracottas, deep blues and chestnutty browns are all extremely helpful colours to use if your budget is restricted.

When you purchase a piece of upholstered furniture – a sofa, armchair or chaise – opt for the very highest quality you can afford: you really do 'get what you pay for' when buying such pieces. A good combination for chair and sofa seats is a foam core surrounded by down; this gives you both softness and firmness.

However beguiled you might be by light colours – the luxurious look of creams and whites, soft rose and blue – do not even think of buying such fabrics if you have children or pets or do a lot of entertaining. While there have been quite radical improvements in fabric treatments, it is best not to test providence too hard. Reupholstering is expensive, so if you act on your preference for light colours you may have to forfeit or put off other elements of your ideal room.

1

2

118

3

4

5

1 There is an interesting juxtaposition here between the soft simplicity of the love seat and the crisp geometric lines of the large side table.

2 Black cane chairs and sofa look elegant in this simply decorated living room.

3 The pale wood table, chairs and stools look clean-lined against the brick floor and darkish units.

4 The cantilevered chairs of tubular steel and rough canvas, and the wicker armchair go well texturally with the somewhat off-beat table and the units.

5 This sofa is very much anchored by the storage units which are placed on either side of it.

6 Good advantage is taken of the deep window recess in this airy North American work room. The specially created window seat works well with the seating arrangement grouped around the desk.

6

Arrangement

Most rooms in a home arrange themselves, in the sense that there are only so many places that you can put the bed, storage units, the dining table or whatever. Living rooms, however, are a different kettle of fish: it is the living room that almost invariably exercises our imagination and flexibility the most. In the first place, this is the room that is most on view to other people; in the second place, a living room always requires at least one focal point and this is always difficult in one of our modern box-like apartment rooms without any fireplace or particular view.

Obviously the shape of the room – long and narrow, square or irregular – will dictate arrangement as much as the various activities that will go on in the room: general relaxation, conversation, reading, music-making, watching television, and so on. Also, you must allow for easy movement to and from the door and around pieces of furniture. About 90cm/3ft is the optimum space to allow for a passageway. There should be about 45cm/18in between a coffee table and a sofa or chair, and about 75–90cm/30–36in should be allowed at the back

2

3

1

1 A relaxed seating group in a smallish room is supplemented by patterned floor pillows. The room is made to appear considerably larger by the use of white for the walls and the floor.
2 A comfortable right-angled seating unit makes the maximum use of this quite small but pleasant attic space.
3 Comfortable armchairs and an upholstered stool nicely angled for conversation in a book-lined study.
4 In this US living room the white-covered day bed with its comfortable squashy cushions sits perfectly under the window without crowding the main seating group.
5 A well arranged area in an old house in New York State. It combines a bar, wine storage, general storage and stereo, not to mention the collection of sticks.

4

6 *The abstract rug defines the seating area and the rise-and-fall lamps give height to this room.*
7 *Black-and-white gives a graphic quality to a French dining area.*
8 *Airy open bamboo furniture keeps a small room looking light, uncluttered and fresh.*

of dining chairs around a table, whether that table is in the living room or in a separate dining room.

A good plan is to think of seating first, the other furniture afterwards. The optimally comfortable arrangement for good conversation and general relaxation is a large sofa and a small sofa or love seat at right angles, faced by two comfortable armchairs and supplemented, if there is room, by occasional chairs and ottomans. This provides the classic conversation group. Occasional chairs can then be pulled up to the main seating group or used to form small groups of their own, by the side of a small round table, for example. A small, narrow room might take only one sofa and a couple of armchairs, or a pair of sofas opposite each other with a couple of occasional chairs. In other small rooms there will be space only for an L-shaped arrangement – modular seating, say, flanking a large coffee table. Again, a small room can be milked of every inch of space if you build bookshelves or storage units all around it leaving two recesses on right-angled walls to take a pair of small sofas. Other ways of getting in extra seating without taking up too much actual floor space include the use of benches around the fireplace and window seats.

The Elements of Design
FURNISHINGS

A foolproof way of tackling any sort of room arrangement is to make a scale plan of the room (see page 18) and to cut the shapes of your items of furniture out of thin coloured cardboard. These you can move around until you think you have found the best solution. Obviously, every seat should have good light as well as some sort of small table nearby on which to put books, drinks, sewing and so on. Again, depending on the room's size and shape and your spending power, you may need bookshelves or some form of wall storage for things like your stereo, VCR tapes, records, drinks and games, as well as side tables, a coffee table and perhaps some sort of round table with a cloth on it to add softness as well as an extra display surface.

It is important to remember that a room is made interesting as much by the differences in scale of the various pieces as by the pieces themselves. This is not so much a matter of aesthetics as of variations in the sizes – especially the heights – of the various items, for a good sense of balance in a space is as visually necessary as a contrast in texture and colour. A room will look boring, however beautiful the furniture, if everything is much the same height. The usual problem is that everything is around or below waist-level. This can be remedied by adding a tall secretary desk, if you can afford one, or a tall bookcase or storage wall, or a screen, or, of course, tall plants and lamps (especially the sculptural halogen variety). Even the most modern and minimal of rooms will benefit from the addition of some larger taller piece.

Another way of obtaining the same effect is simply to position a large picture – or a block of smaller prints or paintings – over a side table, sofa or chest. Paradoxically, in a low-ceilinged room tall objects will actually deceive the eye in such a way that the ceiling appears higher, just as tall objects placed at the end of a corridor or hallway will give the space good perspective.

Making a Focal Point   If you have no fireplace and no other particular focal point around which to arrange the room, do not despair: it is quite possible to create a focal point if you are prepared to use a little ingenuity. If, for example, there is no particular view and the windows themselves are undistinguished, you can still convert

1 *The curved pine-lined cooking island with its multicoloured tile top makes a good focal point in this spacious kitchen-dining room.*
2 *Kitchen window sills provide extra storage space in this attractive Swedish kitchen, whose odd shape required the design to be meticulously planned.*

2

4

5

3

6

7

3 This crisply tiled German kitchen fits into the narrow space available. An added attraction is the slatted upper shelf massed with plants echoing the garden.

4 A well designed unit combining a black-glassed double oven and marbled counter with ample shelf and drawer storage to hold a multitude of kitchen accessories.

5 Eclectic storage is well arranged here, with the books and stereo equipment stashed on natural wood shelving next door to the kitchen.

6 Space for everything, and everything in its proper place, in a Swedish storage wall.

7 This geometric kitchen has crisp sharp lines, a good work space and good storage.

The Elements of Design
FURNISHINGS

them into an attractive feature by framing them with a lambrequin (a valance that goes over three sides of the window) made of painted or covered wood or of stiffened fabric (lined, perhaps, with buckram). Alternatively you can frame a window from floor to ceiling using 3cm × 15cm/1¼in × 6in planks of wood cut to order by your local supplier, applying the thin edge to the walls so as to give added length. If you do this you can even add a window seat by stretching a shelf across the two sides at sill level (or whatever is the best seat-height) and putting on it a piece of foam slip covered to match or contrast with the window treatment. Windows can also be edged by full-length folding screens or by shutters, which might be louvred, painted, lacquered or covered with fabric.

Other focal points around the perimeter of a room can give it added character: a generous wall of books or storage set neatly with stereo components or a collection of memorabilia; or a dresser or hutch, commode or console (old or modern) with a mirror over it.

In a bedroom, the natural focal point of the room will be the bed itself, particularly if it is a brass antique. To emphasise an unspectacular bed, you could position it diagonally in the room or create a dramatic drapery headboard (see pages 206–207) using fabric which matches or coordinates with your other soft furnishings. To attract attention away from a bed, decorate the window with an elaborate treatment.

1 A clever arrangement for a child's room. Bed, storage, and the work and play areas are all encompassed by the gaily painted tubular steel units.
2 Cottage-style curtains and rose walls in a room that is really all bed – albeit a handsome Edwardian example.
3 The window of this ordered London study-bedroom is framed

5 An angled bed can make the most of the space in a smallish bedroom.

6 Bathroom and bedroom cleverly divided by a bedhead wall.

7 Grey-and-white walls, a white-painted floor and white-draped furniture make a tranquil bedroom. The only flashes of colour are in the patterned bedhead and the objects.

8 Walk-in hanging storage off a London bedroom, thoughtfully arranged to take both partners' clothing and personal possessions. A little dressing-table unit has been skilfully tucked in at one end.

9 Grey tiles in the open bathroom area off this bedroom match the bedspread and the Austrian shade. Clothes are kept behind the space-and-light-enhancing mirrored doors.

with bookshelves. The panelled screen behind the slightly angled writing table contrives to make the work area both definite and elegant, and disguises the slightly awkward corner.

4 An intelligently thought-out sleeping and storage area in a corridor-like space at one end of a child's room. The rest is left free and unencumbered for playing.

The Right Balance

It is very difficult to be a purist about furniture unless you have enough money to buy only the most ravishing pieces. Even then, with the best taste and intentions in the world, the result can look sadly disappointing and museum-like – perhaps even downright cold. That sense of *balance*, always important in decoration, applies as much to the 'feeling' of a room as do physical proportions. It is so much more interesting to mix a bit of flamboyance with simplicity, humour with very serious pieces, and flippancy with solidity.

In an otherwise modern room, at least one or two old things, even if they are only accessories (a painting, some old prints or an antique shawl or rug), will make all the difference to the room's warmth – and will, indeed, show off the spare clean lines of good 20th-century furniture all the better. And 19th-century furniture – especially japanned and turned bamboo, chesterfields and bentwood rocking chairs – goes well with today's contemporary furniture, with its light woods, lacquered cubes, glass and natural textures.

Of course, mixing requires a certain amount of nerve. Many people have a fixed idea in their heads about what goes with what, and tend to be overly careful. Moreover,

1 *Deep-seated old cane chairs in a comfortable room are mixed with Kentia palms and other plants to create a conservatory atmosphere.*
2 *Coir matting makes a good uniting background for this Gallic living room with its old chaise, country pine, 19th-century furniture and modern sofas.*
3 *Late 19th- and early 20th-century chaises in a quite different French room.*

4 *Spare lines and a lack of clutter in a Japanese-inspired bedroom.*
5 *An asymmetrically arranged day bed, floor pillows and a 19th-century chair are balanced by the screen, the urn on its pyramidal plinth, and the mirrored fireplace wall in this New York City apartment. Louvred blinds shield the radiators as well as the windows. The checks echo the colours of the rug.*
6 *Amazing pink upholstery in an Art Deco room, its exuberance tempered by the basically grey framework of the room.*

to experiment in mixing several styles demands a sureness of taste and a degree of experience.

A unifying background certainly helps in such experiments. Coir matting, for example, is a perhaps unexpected unifier of different styles, and is much better than wall-to-wall carpeting or a varnished wood floor with rugs. Another good way of unifying a room is to have an all-white background: white walls, floor and windows and window treatments.

5

Balance and Harmony The balance of furnishings and accessories is an important consideration. A large sofa, for example, should be balanced by a sofa-table, desk or work table. A large plant in one corner can be balanced by, say, an étagère or a bank of bookshelves in another. Balance the mass of an armoire or a bureau bookcase with a large painting or group of paintings on the wall opposite – but be careful not to hang a large painting over a piece of smaller furniture: the whole set-up will look hopelessly top-heavy. Similarly, too small a painting or print on a large wall will look just as unfortunate and lost.

The same points about balance apply to colour. Repeat the same colour here and there in a home. The colour of a pillow or cushion at one end of the room can be echoed in a painting or the mount or mat of a print at the opposite end. The tones of a rug can be repeated in upholstery, and flowers can be used to reflect the colour of a throw. All of these may seem quite small details, but they are all the sort of touches that give an agreeable sense of harmony to a home, and harmony, after all, is what most decoration is all about.

6

Room Schemes

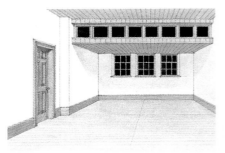

Stage I (*see page* 92)

Stage II (*see page* 112)

Stage IV (*see page* 144)

Kitchen: Stage III

Stage I (see page 93)

Stage II (see page 113)

Stage IV (see page 145)

Living Room: Stage III

KITCHEN

Once the shell was all sorted out, the kitchen units were installed and the lights were fixed under the run of cupboards to illuminate the counters and the stove. A butchers' chopping block was bought and placed in the centre of the kitchen area. A long pine refectory table was found for the dining room; the oriental rug on which it stood served as yet another distinction in 'feel' between the two areas. Old pine country chairs were brought in for seating. Further to enhance the difference in 'feel' between the two rooms, the owners added a capacious old pine settle along the door wall. This had the added advantage of making the dining wall look half panelled, while at the same time balancing the solidity and bulk of the kitchen units which might have looked too modern on their own.

LIVING ROOM

Once the appearance of lightness had been enhanced and two reading lamps had been added, the next step was to emphasize this new 'feel' using furnishings that, clearly, had to be as fresh- and light-looking as possible. We associate white wicker with sun, just as we associate window-seats with light and a view. So a Victorian chaise was bought, its cushions covered in warm light rose, matched by the checked cotton of the seat cushions above the radiator casing. A Portuguese rag rug in rose, apricot and cream was chosen to balance the rose and apricot. The rocking chair was cushioned in blue, a colour repeated in an armchair, stool and a tablecloth. The glass coffee table and side tables take up little visual space. The sofa was covered in cream fabric.

129

Room Schemes

Stage I (*see page* 94)

Stage II (*see page* 114)

Stage IV (*see page* 146)

Bedroom: Stage III

Stage I (see page 95)

Stage II (see page 115)

Stage IV (see page 147)

Studio Apartment: Stage III

BEDROOM

To preserve both the period look and the feeling of light engendered by the pale paper and woodwork, the windows were framed with the sort of ruffled treatment common in Colonial houses; roller blinds (shades) in the same fabric were concealed underneath for night-time use. The patterned cotton tablecloth matches the walls and has an overcloth to repeat both valance (bedfrill) and chair. Good balance was achieved through the solidity of the mahogany military chest, the bedside table, and the stools, counteracting the elegance of the slim-lined four-poster bed (which again preserves the room's new lightness). Tall skinny bedside lamps repeat the vertical lines of the bedposts, further contrast being supplied by the horizontal stripes of the rugs and the large rounded basket by the fireplace.

STUDIO APARTMENT

Kitchen units and equipment took up a sizeable portion of the rest of the budget. The main window treatment was taken care of by hand-me-down curtains hung from an unpainted wood pole and rings. A matchstick blind was sprayed coral for the kitchen window at negligible cost. But how should the room be furnished? The occupant already owned the old chest, which was positioned on the dais between kitchen and bathroom, but what about the rest? The young owner decided to kill several birds with one stone by getting his carpenter friend to make up a wide bed unit, which could also double as a sofa; at one end would be a table, and beneath the bed there would be storage space. Industrial shelving was fitted and the remainder of the furniture was second-hand.

PATTERN AND TEXTURE

As we have seen, the effects of colours are radically changed by differences in texture and pattern, so that a nearly or totally monochromatic room can be as lively and memorable through its subtleties of texture as a room with vividly contrasting colours. The thicker or stronger the texture, the softer or more diminished a colour seems. Flat, smooth glossy surfaces project a much brighter image than soft ones: a painted surface in a particular colour will be very much 'sharper' than the same colour in carpet or felt or velvet.

The Effects of Soft and Hard Surfaces Just as rooms need balance in colour to keep them harmonious and comfortable, so they also need a good balance of textures – matt with gloss, soft with hard. Gaining the knowledge of what contrasting textures go best together is really a matter of experience. You must experiment and develop your taste and a good eye for such things.

To get into the habit of thinking in textural terms, it helps to make lists of all kinds of different surfaces and

materials and to conjure them up in your mind's eye, appropriately distributing them around walls, floors, ceilings, windows and furniture. Such a list might be rather like the one shown overleaf.

There are, of course, certain conventions, and there is no doubt that some textures contrast with each other better than others. For example, brick walls or floors look better with quite strong textures such as linen, hessian (burlap) and cotton than with velvet or silk – although there is no reason why, if you like it, you should not contrast brick and silk.

Comfort is, of course, very much connected in one's mind with softness (even though firmness is often better for the spine), so the softer-looking the covering on a sofa or armchair, the more comfortable and inviting it will seem. Inside the sofa, as we have seen, you can combine both firmness and softness by having a foam core enveloped in down, but if you cover this filling in silk velvet, linen velvet, glove suede or buffalo hide it will look as deeply luxurious as it is harshly expensive. A less

1 *Handmade blue-and-white Mexican tiles on the chimney breast, blue-and-white Dutch ceramics and the charming antique quilts blend pattern and texture beautifully.*
2 *Contrasting marble tiles give a sharp definition to this bathroom. The naturally mottled and flecked surfaces provide a sense of depth.*

3 Wood is inherently textural. Slatted wooden blinds, polished floorboards and wooden bath panelling combine with lush plants to promote a tropical atmosphere.
4 A restrained colour scheme is enlivened by the use of contrasting textures: coir matting, leather upholstery, glass-topped tables, old beams and a lacquered cabinet.
5 The rhythmic pattern of free strokes makes a textural finish.
6 Unpainted plaster has a softness and subtlety that can be very attractive. New plaster can simply be sealed with matt varnish or rubbed with layers of wax; here layers of paint were stripped to leave a mellow surface displaying traces of old distemper.

133

The Elements of Design
PATTERN AND TEXTURE

expensive cotton, linen or chintz covering, while not so luxurious-looking, can be made to *seem* softer if you juxtapose it with, say, a wood or tiled floor of some kind and use scatter-rugs rather than a carpet.

Sofas, armchairs and beds can be made to look more deeply inviting if you heap them with throw pillows or cushions, and more interesting by varying the textures of these cushions. For example, a linen sofa could be piled with cushions made of old velvet, *gros* and *petit point* and silk. A bed covered in a simple quilted cotton will look luxurious if it is piled with white lace and broderie-anglaise pillows. A harder chair – say, a tight-covered or buttoned occasional chair – can have a shawl or throw tossed across its back or an arm.

MATERIALS OF DIFFERENT TEXTURES

Hard	Soft
floorboards	plain cotton
barn siding	chintz
brick	linen
flagstone	satin
marble	silk
slate	ottoman
parquet	corduroy
travertine	velvet
plaster	silk velvet
vinyl	linen velvet
glass	tweed
perspex or plexiglass	wool
brass	cashmere
steel	leather
chrome	felt
lacquer	quilting
ceramic tiles	velvet Wilton carpet
terracotta tiles	shag
cork	low-pile textured carpet
cane	kelims
wicker	dhurrie rugs
mahogany	silk orientals
oak	oriental rug
pine	coir matting
walnut	sisal
teak	hessian (burlap)

The contrast of softness and hardness can also be exhibited on floors. Whether you put a rug on a wood floor, a sheepskin on brick or old tiles, or an oriental on coir matting, you are making use of their differing textures. And think of the feeling of comfort you experience when you see large, soft fluffy towels against the tiles of a bathroom, or the sybaritic effect of a soft warm carpet contrasted with bathroom fixtures.

This same juxtaposition of hard and soft can be carried through by the use of contrasting accessories and possessions. You can offset a piece of sculpture with an interesting plant, or you can line a china or glass display cabinet with velvet – or at least paint a background so that the cabinet looks soft and deep.

5

6

1 A living-room corner rich in detail includes a damask cushion, quilted sofa upholstery, inlaid table and needlepoint rug.
2 Striped cotton ticking curtains and soft furnishings make a simple but effective textural contrast with the rough-hewn stone walls.
3 Old and new: the smooth white walls and wooden mantel make a foil for the mellow old bricks, antique carved clock, spinning wheel and old metal toy train.
4 The sense of warmth and enclosure provided by knotty pine panelling is emphasized by the pretty floral cotton of the bedcover and at the window.
5 A light summery mood is created through the use of cane and basketwork, together with plain white calico upholstery and white cord carpeting.
6 A comfortable country blend of traditional trellis and chintz patterns is set off by plain coir matting and enlivened by the bright-red cane table.

Pattern as a Feature

In many modern buildings, rooms tend to be somewhat featureless: they have no fireplace, no strong architectural elements like mouldings, and not much in the way of a view unless you actually stand on tiptoe to peer out of the window. Yet even the most uninspiring box-like room can be enormously cheered by the clever use of pattern. Obviously you can use beautiful additions – for example, paintings and wallhangings – but an interestingly designed or a subtly coloured needlework carpet or an exquisite rug will immediately distract the eye from any architectural mediocrity, as will a well-chosen patterned wallcovering or a stunning upholstery fabric.

Patterned paper, or stencilled border running around a room just below the ceiling and perhaps down corners and above skirting boards (baseboards), makes an excellent and colourful substitute for mouldings and a cornice (crown molding). And dull rooms can be made to look mysterious and beautiful if you resort to comparatively inexpensive 'disguisers'; for example, you could first paint the walls a strong colour and then shirr them with cheesecloth or a light cotton (see page 206). You can achieve this effect by stretching a generous amount of fabric between two sets of rods, one fixed just below the ceiling and one just above the skirting boards.

When you have no natural focal point in a room you can create one by hanging a good rug on a wall, or even by framing a beautiful piece of fabric or an old paisley shawl and hanging it up. It does not really matter if your windows have no view and are less than graceful, because you can dress them up with attractively patterned fabrics – particularly, you can contrast framing or dress curtains or draperies with inner curtains or with roller, Roman, festoon or ballroom shades or blinds, and add yet more contrast using edges or fringes, trims and tie-backs. A trick you can use with dull windows is to frame them from just below the ceiling, cornice or moulding to the floor using fabric-covered two-by-fours or pieces of plywood. The windows can then have either contrast curtains or a shade within the frame.

Another way of creating an interesting focal point in a monochromatic room is to have a single piece of seating – a large armchair or a sofa – upholstered in an interesting pattern. Or you could set two contrasting tablecloths – one over and one under – on a round table, with perhaps a fringe trailing to the floor.

1 *This room, entirely lined in flowered chintz with chairs to match, has considerable pattern underfoot as well. Note the interesting window treatment.*
2 *A brilliantly coloured quilt flung over some corner seating immediately draws the eye, but the massed Picture Post covers challenge for attention.*
3 *Walls, floors and windows share one pattern and the chairs another in this French room: roses are almost everywhere.*

4

6

5

7

8

4 The interestingly combed painted floor – with its large diamonds of natural wood and arresting malachite-green border – makes the statement here.
5 Mondrian-like tile design makes effective use of the limited space in this dramatic bathroom.

6 Only the carpet, the underside of the canopy and the door frame escape the ubiquitous pattern.
7 In this North American bedroom, the dhurrie rug – although stronger in colour – picks up the design of the fabric.
8 Rose chintz offset by linen.

137

Combining and Coordinating

A very great deal of the pattern in a room is effected by objects and possessions, furnishings, plants, lights and light itself, with its play of shadows, as well as by the varying textures of so-called 'plain' fabrics, carpets and matting and their juxtaposition with each other. There is pattern in the way paintings are hung on the walls. There is pattern in shelved books, with their diverse jacket designs and the gradations and contrasts of their colours – there is even pattern in the arrangement of the shelves. There is pattern in vases of flowers, in the jagged edges of leaves set against a wall or window, and in the way an uplight can shine through the foliage at night to cast shadows on the walls and ceiling. There is pattern in the arrangement of furniture, and in the display of accessories and collections.

If you think about the way all these things form a pattern in their own right, you can see how you should not worry too much about mixing patterns in fabrics. With all the other things that are going on, one fabric more or less will hardly make a difference so long as the scale, tone, proportion and colour are right. Nevertheless, many people remain very nervous about mixing patterns. To counter this lack of confidence, fabric and wallpaper manufacturers often get together to produce coordinating prints and plains, using perhaps a large floral design together with a small, more open pattern having similar but scaled-down elements; these in turn can be combined with a geometric pattern or basket weave or some similar all-over design in matching colours. In this way one design can be used for curtains, another for shades, and yet others for different pieces of upholstery, combined perhaps with some plains. One of the designs can also be used for wallpaper, or at least for a border. This sort of coordination has proved very popular. Manufacturers have also expended a good deal of effort to find other complementary designs in their ranges. Their catalogues are usually filled with photographs of room settings to show you how well different designs can look together.

However, suppose you have the requisite confidence and want to be a little more idiosyncratic in juxtaposing designs, to do your own mixing and matching. What is the best way to go about it?

As we have seen, scale, tone and proportion are of prime importance, and to this list you might add

1 *Collier Campbell updated designs in a superb combination.*
2 *Grey-blue and roses combined in different permutations of colour and texture.*
3 *The same colours used to good effect in a quite different way.*
4 *Wall, sofa, cushions and rug merge into each other, but all retain their own intensely floral identities.*
5 *A host of different designs given an overall harmony by the common denominator of colour.*

4

5

similarity as well as overall suitability. Always bring home as large a sample as you can get so that you can see what the design will look like *in situ*, with your sort of light and in the context of your other possessions. Unless you possess a very good sense of scale, larger patterns that you thought eye-catching in the store may look fairly dire once you have brought the materials home and set them up in your own private setting. Likewise, the colours may clash if the room is otherwise gentle. Conversely, very small, detailed patterns can often blur so that they give the impression of a single colour when actually used for curtains. On the other hand, small-scale repeats in upholstery or soft furnishings of a larger pattern on the walls, curtains or shades can give an interesting sense of perspective. It is worth experimenting to see what looks good.

You can often use together materials of the same pattern but in two different colour schemes, or you might opt for the same pattern reversed or in negative – for example, a predominance of terracotta on cream for some items and a predominance of cream on terracotta for others.

Patterns that are fairly but not exactly similar – that is, patterns from the same 'family', like a large rose print with a smaller rosebud print, a floral abstract or a single colour on white like a *toile de Jouy* – will look good together. To the combination suggested here you could alternatively add a damask in one of the deeper colours, or a stripe, check or small geometric in the same

colouring as the leaves of one of the flowers. Very often, as we have noted, an old fabric or textile thrown across a sofa, chair or table will add an interesting dimension.

The best thing is always to experiment. Get together all the samples of fabric that you like and look at them simultaneously – and look at them, too, in conjunction with your chosen rugs and/or carpets. It should quickly become obvious as to which fabrics enhance each other and which detract from each other.

Another good way to learn about mixing patterns is to look at a collection of Indian fabrics and dhurrie rugs. The various designs look effortlessly harmonious, their patterns all being of much the same size and in good proportion with each other. Once you have studied the way their colours repeat and intermingle with one another, and the way in which colours are balanced yet subtly contrasted, the whole business of mixing and matching will seem less of a matter of trepidation.

It is reassuring, too, to recall that people have throughout history mixed patterns and textures with, if not abandon, then at least a sense of richness. Look at the intricacies of oriental rugs, the extraordinary linen-fold panelling, rich plasterwork and tapestries used together in the 16th and 17th centuries; the complicated but beautiful ceilings and floors of Robert Adam, with the various damasks, silks, embroideries and plaster-work of the 18th and 19th centuries; the pattern-on-pattern of the Victorian age; the sinuous complications of Art Nouveau; and the jazzy mixtures of the 1920s.

DISPLAYS

Furniture and furnishings make a room comfortable and, with luck, good to look at. The pictures, objects and accessories are the elements that give the room personality – although it is important to remember that, if you are to achieve a truly personal room, the objects themselves must be personal, liked for their own sake, thought about deeply, lovingly chosen and put together with care and enthusiasm. Buying objects because they are fashionable or because they were displayed in the store alongside the furniture is not at all the same thing. Just as you buy paintings for their own sake and validity or for their subject matter, rather than because their colours suit those you have chosen for your room, you should select objects because you *like* them. Mind you, serendipity can creep in here as anywhere else: happy accidents, after all, have a lot to contribute to the character of a home.

There are two quite separate schools of thought concerning the possession and display of artworks and objects. One school opts for simplicity, the other for

1 *A collection of pictures always adds interest to a hallway. Here an entire alphabet of characters is hung close together, reading as a single composition.*
2 *A tabletop of disparate objects leads the eye up to a collection of framed prints, creating a corner full of delight and surprise.*
3 *Even homely objects can be worthy of display. A collection of carpet beaters makes an unusual frieze, baskets look suitably rustic on top of a wooden dresser, and a fine clock is the centrepiece for a collection of delicate coloured prints.*
4 *Architectural fragments, portrait busts, paintings and engravings are arranged in splendid profusion.*

clutter. The difference is between offering up one or two exquisite, interesting and/or rare objects and presenting a magpie collection of objects and possessions which can generally be termed 'memorabilia'. The difficulty with the former proposition is that the few objects must either be really beautiful or extraordinarily well displayed; the trouble with the latter is that the clutter must be organized in an interesting way or else it looks like nothing more than, well, clutter. This means you have to assemble the items carefully and thoughtfully according to their colour, shape, texture or theme. Thematic collections of small objects – for example, glasses or butterflies, birds' eggs or stones – should always be grouped together rather than scattered all over the house. To take another example, old coloured glass is often shown to particular advantage against other pieces of glass, so group such items on window sills or on glass shelves stretched across a window. Larger objects, however disparate, can be contrasted with each other, but their arrangement looks best if they have something in common with each other (e.g., colour); as ever, balance is all-important. If arrangements are grouped on low tables that are used also as adjuncts to chairs and for the casual dumping of books

5   7   8

6   9

5 *The shape of the brimming pitcher of wine in the painting has suggested an abundant arrangement of richly coloured ceramics and lacquerware.*
6 *In among the colanders, sieves, graters and ladles, holly and mistletoe add a festive touch.*
7 *The polished gleam of copper pans makes an inviting and practical kitchen display.*
8 *Beautiful objects have drama and importance when displayed singly. This modern ceramic piece, standing in a sculptural alcove, has all the calm tranquillity of a Grecian urn.*
9 *A riot of painted plates and teacups has a dolls-house cheerfulness.*

and drinks, leave appropriate space so that the composition will not be ruined.

If arrangements are on a glass shelf, try lighting them with an uplight from below: this gives extra sparkle. If they are on a solid shelf, try lighting them from above with a downlight or spot, or with a small strip of lights (see page 154). It is important to realize that collections of objects can be as idiosyncratic as you want them to be. In fact, assemblages of quite ordinary things – like old spectacle cases, watches, keys, snuffboxes, toast-racks or whatever – can often be much more interesting and decorative than much grander objects.

Hanging Pictures Although some people who own serious art collections see a wall as a means to an end – a convenient space for display – most of us want to use that space to its most decorative advantage, and therefore need to find some unifying factor to bring together our disparate collection of prints and paintings, posters and objects. A miscellaneous series of prints, for example, can be given a unity it would otherwise lack if each is mounted with the same distinctive colour – say buff, deep red or dark green – and framed in the same way. Again, you can group similarly sized and shaped

frames together – ovals with ovals, small squares with small squares. One of the easiest ways to get good groupings without making an awful mess of the walls while experimenting is to lay out on the floor all the pictures you want to hang. After you are satisfied with the arrangement you can measure out the spaces for the hooks on the wall itself, using pencil or chalk that can be rubbed away easily.

In general, you should be careful not to hang things too high or too far apart. Do not fix anything so low over a sofa that people will knock their heads on it – although, when your seating is at a very low level, there is no reason why paintings cannot be hung much lower than usual. Vertical arrangements will make walls seem higher; horizontal ones will make them seem longer.

Posters are best slipped into special holders so that they do not tear or curl up at the corners. They can be balanced by size, subject or colour, depending upon which seems most appropriate to the room.

Wall hangings can be made from just about any piece of decorative fabric, from fragments of old robes to pieces of abstract modern cotton. Hang very heavy fabrics or rugs on slim curtain rods suspended from hooks, or stretch them like canvases over a frame.

Plants

There is almost no gap in any room which cannot be filled and improved by a plant. There is no piece of furniture that cannot be balanced and somehow freshened by a spread of leaves, and there are no hard lines and formality that cannot be softened and lightened by foliage. If books furnish a room, the same can be said of plants. Tall plants, small plants, flowering plants and exotic indoor trees add a quite different dimension to any space – a liveliness and freshness that are gratifyingly cheap in relation to the year-round pleasure the plants give.

On the whole, small and medium-sized plants look best massed together or at least grouped in twos and threes. You can get a good effect by grouping different sizes of plants of the same species together, or by putting a shorter, bushier plant at the foot of a taller, skinnier one. A bushy indoor tree set in front of an uncurtained window can make it look full-dressed, and you can get the same effect by hanging plants from a traverse rod from just above a window. Two standard plants set in front of a pair of windows can strike quite a grand and harmonious note.

In the summer, hanging plants strung from the ceiling of a porch give the whole area a cool greenness just when it is most needed. Windows crossed with shelves in either glass or wood and massed with a mixture of upright and trailing plants can look very attractive indeed. This is a particularly good solution for windows that are otherwise difficult to curtain or dress.

Tall plants and indoor trees make subtle room dividers, and planters can be set on casters or wheels for easy movement. One especially effective set-up I have seen was a green balustrade of plants at the edge of a dining platform in a living room; another living-room set-up employed a group of Kentia palms to form a gentle division between the dining and sitting areas, so that the room was for all the world like an exotic Edwardian conservatory.

Conservatories, in fact, are currently enjoying a well deserved revival. They are marvellous adjuncts to a room, especially if they are stocked with scented jasmine and stephanotis, lilies and gardenias, and give off that heady, warm damp smell of well watered foliage. If you do not own one and have neither the space nor the

1 A sunny arrangement of coneflowers and foliage, highlighted by the warm glow of a pair of table lamps, makes a natural focal point in a country living room.
2 Classical white pedestals of varying heights and cachepots are an elegant way of displaying decorative house plants such as aspidistras and weeping figs.
3 Trailing plants either side of this stark white stairwell, complement the rational 'feel' of this home and add colour.

3

5

4

6

money to add one, you can always at least simulate the impression of one by setting the panelling at one end of a room with mirror glass and massing plants in front of it so that their reflections have the effect of doubling the number of plants there. Extra appeal can be added by hanging plants from the ceiling: these, too, can be dramatized by placing uplights beneath them, or you can put uplights behind planters to shine up through the leaves and create interesting shadow effects.

There is a choice of planters to suit any room: stone and terracotta, chrome and brushed steel, comforting baskets and graceful wooden Versailles boxes. Even when rooms are dark and receive little natural light there is no need to be deprived of greenery, for using the new and sophisticated bulbs that simulate natural light it is quite possible to give foliage all the light it needs.

7

4 Palms set either side of a wood-framed mirror appear to add depth to a modern bathroom.
5 A tall yucca acts as a room divider and also helps to integrate kitchen and living space.
6 A single spindly cactus, set in a Moorish-style alcove, makes an amusing statement.
7 An arrangement of ginger jars and glass vases on an ornate mahogany table are framed by overhanging palms, jasmine and fuchsias.

Room Schemes

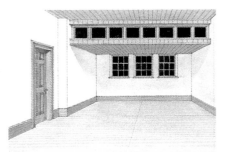

Stage I (*see page* 92)

Stage II (*see page* 112)

Stage III (*see page* 128)

Kitchen: Stage IV

Stage I (*see page 93*)

Stage II (*see page 113*)

Stage III (*see page 129*)

Living Room: Stage IV

KITCHEN

In a way, dressing up the two parts of the room was easy once the main ingredients had been put into place. The wooden ceiling made it a simple task to screw in hooks to hold bunches of dried flowers and herbs. The kitchen shelves just begged for a variety of good-looking canisters and casseroles, always particularly important when the room is going to be used for eating (albeit at a distance) as well as for cooking. The row of old prints, hung vertically, was something of a stroke of genius, since the vertical lines exaggerated the height of the dining area. Moreover, the prints made the area seem very much more of a *room*, and the frames went beautifully with the golden tones of the pine. To these were added other, larger prints and paintings, as well as cushions.

LIVING ROOM

Now that the room looked altogether lighter and warmer, the final exercise was to add liveliness and freshness, using texture and pattern, art, accessories and plants. Rose, apricot and blue cushions were added to the seating as were a few others covered in painted linen in the same colours, which are repeated in a different design in the overcloth on the round table. Further textural interest is introduced through rush log baskets, the iron grate filled with logs, and the old cloisonné urns on the mantelpiece and internal window sills. Paintings were hung above the mantelpiece and on other walls. The room is kept full of flowers and plants to add conservatory-like freshness. By keeping the white shutter semiclosed the dreary outlook is gently disguised.

145

Room Schemes

Stage I (*see page* 94)

Stage II (*see page* 114)

Stage III (*see page* 130)

Bedroom: Stage IV

Stage I (see page 95)

Stage II (see page 115)

Stage III (see page 131)

Studio Apartment: Stage IV

BEDROOM

To add more softness to the room a pile of snow-white lace-trimmed pillows was added to the bed with, behind them, much the same kind of fabric treatment as used on the windows, although on a larger scale. The general effect of this backdrop was almost to create the illusion that there was a third, bigger, window. The bedcover introduces more of the warm rose colour of the bricks surrounding the fireplace, a hue repeated again in the heap of pillows on the chair as well as in the flowers (in their blue vase) by the bed. Notice how every flash of colour, however soft, stands out against the calm, neutral background. Other odds and ends – the dressing mirror, candles, boxes, photographs, paintings and the jokey firedogs in the grate – add a warmth of their own.

STUDIO APARTMENT

The apartment was now reasonably furnished and ordered. Four transparent Plia chairs had been purchased for use at the desk/dining table; these could be hung on a large hook (not in the picture) next to the chest of drawers when not in use. At the sink area in the kitchen a cheap adjustable desk lamp was clamped to the side of a storage unit. To liven up the colouring, the owner found a 1930s geometric rug as well as some vivid cotton in the same colouring which he had made up into a tight cover and extra pillow covers for the sofa-bed. Books, records, tapes, television and stereo equipment fill the shelving units, prints are hung on the walls, odds and ends are placed on various surfaces, and the space is generally freshened by plants.

In some countries it is illegal to install or to alter electrical systems without a professional qualification. Always check regulations before you attempt electrical work.

LIGHTING

Domestic lighting fulfils a number of functions in the interior. In practical terms, it is a supplement or substitute for natural daylight activities, enabling ordinary tasks to be performed safely; it can provide additional brightness in a work area or dark corner, as well as an even level of background illumination. However, just as important is lighting's ability to generate mood and atmosphere. Subtle interplays of light and shade soften and enhance the decoration of a room. Directional light picks out architectural detail, displays, objects and pictures. And the design of the light fitting can in itself be a source of style and interest.

TYPES OF LIGHTING

Broadly speaking, all domestic lights have two components: the light source itself (bulb or lamp) and the light fitting. When choosing lighting for your home, you should consider not only the style of the fitting but also the quality and distribution of the light that it produces. Depending on the fitting, light can be distributed
● evenly in all directions
● principally in one direction with some diffusion
● in a concentrated beam

Background Lighting

Background lighting essentially acts as a replacement for daylight; typically it is supplied by a ceiling-mounted fitting or a pendant. Alternatives include wall lights, uplights and table lamps, all of which can produce something more interesting than a single bright light overhead, whose effect can be dull and uninspiring.

Task Lighting

Areas such as kitchen counters, workbenches and desks – anywhere that specific tasks are to be performed – need an extra level of light. Task lighting should be positioned so that shadows do not fall across the work surface: directional lights which can be angled to suit needs – such as downlights, angled desk lamps and spotlights – are often a good choice.

Another form of task lighting is utility lighting. Practical rather than aesthetic, utility lighting is the type used to illuminate dark and potentially dangerous areas, such as stairways and exterior paths.

Accent Lighting

By picking out decorative displays, accent lighting creates a sense of drama. Strongly directional spotlights are particularly effective: they can be angled to highlight a collection of

Bulbs and Lamps

1 *General purpose tungsten bulb*
2 *Tungsten striplight*
3 *Parabolic aluminized reflector lamp*
4 *Halogen display bulb*
5 *Halogen reflector (cool beam)*
6 *Halogen reflector bulb*
7 *Globe bulb*
8 *Candle-shaped bulb*
9 *Fluorescent long-life bulb*
10 *Reflector bulb*
11 *Fluorescent striplight*
12 *Circular fluorescent tube*
13 *Crown-silvered bulb*
14 *U-lamp*

objects, a set of bookshelves or a group of pictures. Other types of accent lighting include traditional bracket picture lights, concealed lights in display cases and floor-standing uplights.

TYPES OF LIGHT SOURCE

The three main types used in the home are tungsten, tungsten halogen and fluorescent. The differences between them concern the efficiency of their use of energy, their average lifetime and, most important in aesthetic terms, the quality of colour they lend to whatever they illuminate.

Tungsten

The commonest domestic light source is the tungsten filament bulb. This consists of a filament which glows

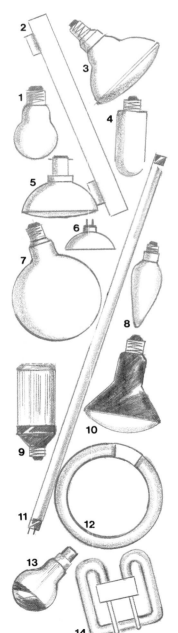

Types of lighting: *background lighting provided by uplights (1); task lighting (2, 4); accent lighting on a stairway (3).*

QUALITY OF LIGHT		
LAMP	COLOUR APPEARANCE	COLOUR RENDERING
Tungsten	Warm	Orange and reds bright, blues dull
Tungsten Halogen	White, crisp	Orange and reds bright, blues less dull
Metal Halide	Cool, white	Slight colour distortion, reds fairly dull
Fluorescent	Warm or cool	Variable
Neon	Range of colours	Variable

inside a pearl or clear glass bulb that is filled with an inert gas (e.g., argon) in low concentration. Compared to daylight, tungsten is a warm light, yellowish in tone, and is well suited to interior use. It does not alter colour relationships significantly and provides a good tonal contrast. Tinted tungsten bulbs are available in a range of pastel and primary colours.

However, tungsten lights are somewhat less practical than other light sources. The bulbs do not last very long, they generate a fair amount of heat, and they do not make efficient use of electricity. But they are inexpensive and can function with dimmers.

Tungsten Halogen

Tungsten halogen has a cool, crisp appearance, whiter and brighter than ordinary tungsten. The lamp is filled with one of the halogens (a family of chemical elements), and this reacts with vapours from the tungsten filament.

Like tungsten, tungsten halogen is effective at colour rendering and at revealing contrasts, but it also has a vital, sparkling quality which makes it particularly suitable for use in uplights, spotlights and accent lighting. There are two main types, mains-voltage and low-voltage; the latter can be used with a transformer. Both can be dimmed.

Fluorescent

Unlike tungsten or tungsten halogen, fluorescent light has a significant effect on both colour and tone. However, there are modern fluorescent lights available that simulate daylight, and special covers can be used to make the light more sympathetic.

The distribution of light

This varies according to the design of the light fitting. Highly directional light is provided by downlights, spotlights and some types of uplights. Table lamps, on the other hand, diffuse light in more than one direction.

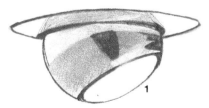

Ceiling Lights

An overhead fixture – either a pendant or one or more ceiling-mounted lights – is one of the commonest ways of providing general lighting. Used on its own, however, overhead lighting can distinctly lack subtlety, be rather obtrusive and have a deadening effect. Wherever possible, supplement it with other types of lighting, and fit a dimmer switch so that the level of light can be adjusted according to need.

Alternatively, consider downlights or spotlights as substitutes.

Pendant Lights
Pendant fittings vary widely in design, price and the quality of light they produce. Glass and ceramic globes and paper lanterns diffuse light evenly in all directions, whereas shades, whether of paper, metal or fabric, tend to direct light downwards, an effect which is emphasized if the pendant is suspended on a long flex (cord). There are also rise-and-fall pendants, where the fitting can be pulled lower – for example, over a dining table – to provide more concentrated light. If the source is visible, you can use a crown-silvered bulb to minimize glare.

Chandeliers are highly effective types of pendant because they support several smaller sources of light, but they are often expensive.

Ceiling-mounted Lights
Generally rather plain and utilitarian, some ceiling lights are mounted on the ceiling rather than suspended from it. The bulb is shaded, often with a glass or plastic globe, half-globe or cylinder, which creates an even light diffused in all directions.

Downlights
Downlights are ceiling lights that are either recessed (fully or partially) or surface-mounted. Functional and unobtrusive, they direct the light downwards. Depending on the type of fitting, they can produce either a narrow concentrated beam or a wider flood of light. Eyeball downlights on swivels can be angled to direct light at a wall or other surface.

Downlights are a useful and attractive way of lighting work areas such as a kitchen counter. They can be used also to provide subtle background lighting,

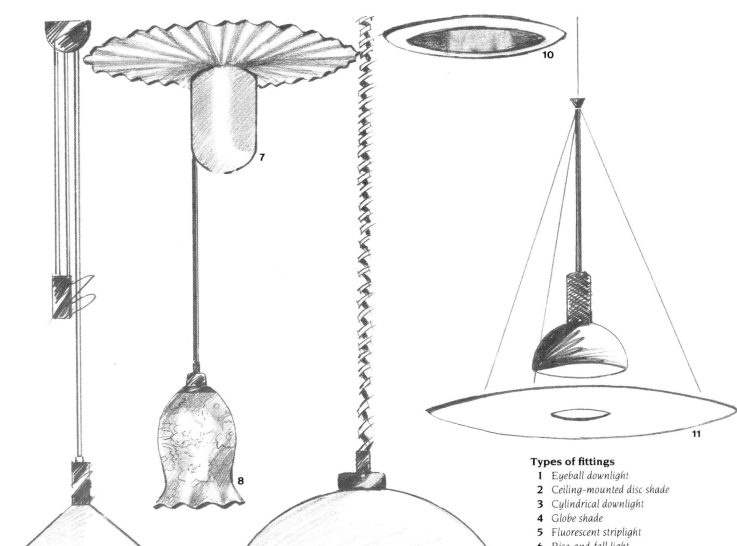

Types of fittings
1 Eyeball downlight
2 Ceiling-mounted disc shade
3 Cylindrical downlight
4 Globe shade
5 Fluorescent striplight
6 Rise-and-fall light
7 Castiglioni ceiling light
8 Victorian-style shade
9 Spiral-flex light
10 Recessed downlight
11 Castiglioni 'Frisbi' light

especially when controlled with a dimmer switch.

Other Types of Ceiling Light
Spotlights can be ceiling-mounted or on a track and used either as background lighting or to accent particular areas.

Ceiling-mounted fluorescent striplighting is suitable only for utility areas. To cut down glare, shade the tube with a diffuser.

1 A modern pendant fitting suspended over a dining table and counterbalanced by ball weights looks like kinetic art. Light is directed at the centre of the table, creating a soft, welcoming glow without glare.
2 Ceiling-mounted lighting need not be strictly utilitarian in appearance. This stylish, graphic-looking ceiling light, fixed over a dining table, echoes the designs of Charles Rennie Mackintosh.

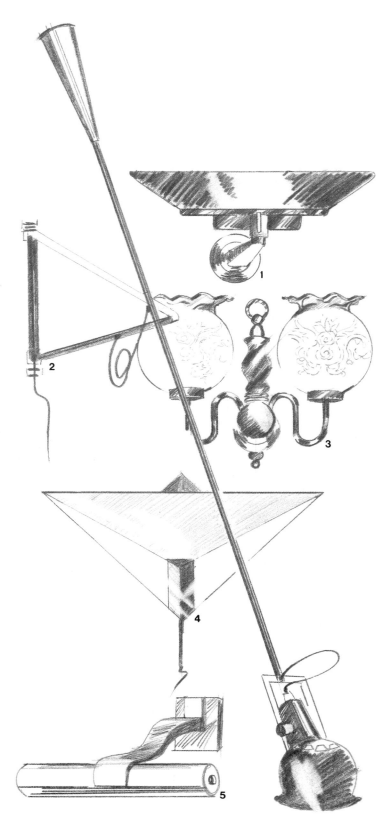

Spotlights and Wall Lights

Spotlights

Spotlights are one of the most flexible forms of light fitting: they can be used not only as accent and task lights but also to provide a general level of illumination. Although generally mounted on the ceiling, spotlights can alternatively be fixed to a wall; they can be used either individually or in series on a track. Also available are spotlights fixed to a stand, clusters of spots on a ceiling fitting, and spotlights with clips or clamps so that they can be attached to a shelf and moved at will.

There is a wide range of sizes and designs. Spots can give you anything from a broad pool of light to a fine concentrated beam. Many are shaded with deep metal or plastic cowls so that the bulbs themselves are hidden; if this is not the case, it is a good idea to use a crown-silvered bulb to cut down glare. Combining a crown-silvered bulb with a parabolic reflector will create a narrow beam of light.

The great advantage of spotlights is that it is easy to position and adjust them, allowing you to angle light in different directions. This effect is best exploited by grouping more than one spotlight in each location – a track mounted on the wall or ceiling is an easy way of achieving this.

Wall Lights

Unlike spotlights and downlights – which, although relatively inconspicuous, are contemporary in style – wall lights come in a range of designs, from traditional to very modern.

Traditional types of wall light include shaded small bulbs which project out from the wall on decorative metal brackets, simulating the look of old-time gaslighting or candle-lit sconces.

Modern types of wall light include curved black-metal halogen uplights, and uplights in ceramic or plaster which can be decorated to blend in with the wall. The distribution of light varies with the fitting, but as a basic rule wall lights provide a sympathetic background light. Wall lights are usually fitted in pairs.

More utilitarian wall-mounted designs include bulkhead fittings – designed for exterior use but with a hi-tech appeal for interiors – and plain globes or half-globes similar to ceiling lights. One of the best ways of lighting a bathroom mirror is to frame it with unshaded lightbulbs, as in a theatrical dressing room. This type of light illuminates the face without creating shadows.

● Never buy a light without turning it on first to see what it does.

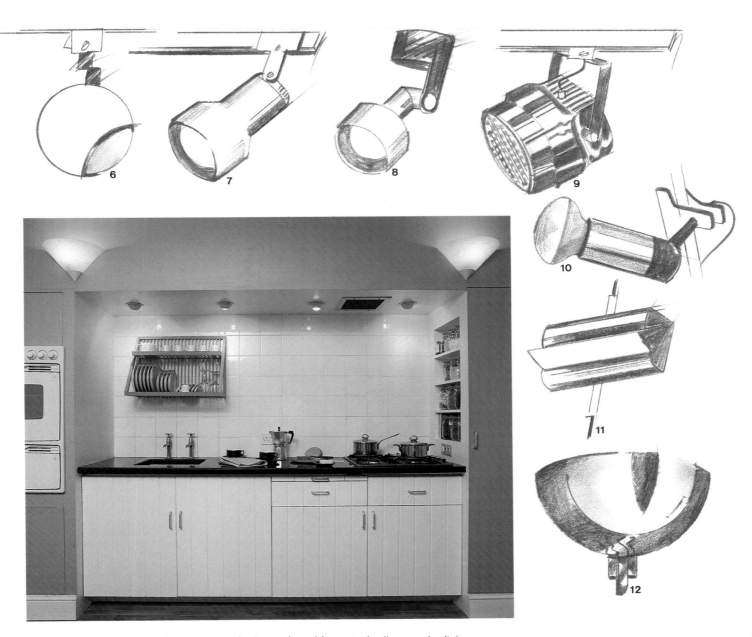

Eyeball spotlights illuminate a kitchen counter; the alcove is framed by a pair of wall-mounted uplights.

SWITCHES

As well as the ubiquitous white plastic variety, a range of more decorative light switches is available, from traditional brass or wood to modern black metal or chrome. You can exploit this diversity to coordinate the style of the details with the rest of the interior.

Dimmer Controls

Whatever the style of lighting or light fitting, the effectiveness of the result can be greatly increased if you are able to vary the light level. Dimmer switches are easy to fit and they are particularly useful in a multi-purpose room – such as a kitchen-diner where light may need to be quite bright in one area but softer in another.

Types of fittings

1 Halogen uplight
2 Wall-mounted desk halogen
3 Double wall bracket
4 Angular wall light
5 Brass picture light
6 Globe spot
7 Track-mounted spot
8 Jointed halogen floodlight
9 Multi-directional spot
10 Spotlight with clamp fitting
11 Adjustable wall shade
12 Chrome hemisphere uplight

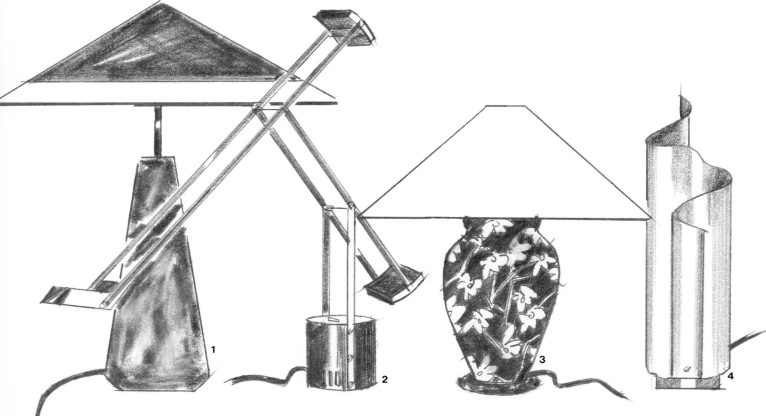

Table and Floor Lights

Lights which can stand on the floor or on a table are a popular choice both for task lighting and for general or background illumination. Decorative as well as practical, they come in a wide range of colours, designs and sizes to suit every type of decorative scheme.

Table Lamps
In many ways the mainstay of domestic lighting, the typical table lamp has a heavy base (often ceramic) which holds the bulb and carries a shade that may be paper- or fabric-covered, made of shell, etc. Even within these specifications, however, there is tremendous variety. The base may be in different colours, patterned or textured, or in different shapes and/or materials. The shade can taper or have straight sides, and can be opaque or translucent. Also, table lamps are available not only in a plethora of traditional designs but also in many modern versions.

Table lamps provide a soft, diffused light at low level. Several of them placed around a room will create pools of light and shadow, an effect that can be very atmospheric. At least some of the light is directed upwards towards the ceiling (quite how much depends on the shade), so table lamps are also a good way of increasing general light levels.

Desk Lamps
The purpose of a desk lamp is to provide a bright, directed source of light for a specific area. The classic design is the anglepoise, a metal light with a deep cowl shade and an angled stand which can be adjusted to many different positions. Other types include modern cantilevered lights, lights which clamp or screw onto a worktop, brass or chrome lights on flexible arms, and traditional-style desk lamps (such as Victorian brass lights with opaque green glass shades).

Floor Lamps
Free-standing floor lamps help to raise the general level of illumination as well as provide local task lighting for reading or other activities.

Except in period rooms, the floor-standing standard lamp can look rather old-fashioned; the modern equivalent is the floor-standing uplight, often fitted with a tungsten halogen lamp to give a clear crisp light. Other modern designs include angled floor lights and spotlights mounted on a portable stand.

Floor lights need not be particularly tall. Uplights in the form of cylinders or flutes or translucent omni-directional lights placed at a low level can be an effective way to light a collection of in-door plants or just to provide an additional lighting accent.

Types of fittings

1 *Modern table light*
2 *'Tizio' task light*
3 *Traditional base and shade*
4 *Sculpted table light*
5 *Anglepoise*
6 *Standard halogen uplight*
7 *Portable uplight*
8 *Chrome uplight*
9 *Curved desk lamp*

Halogen uplights have a classically elegant appearance which suits many styles. Intriguing table lamps provide a soft accent light.

FLEXES (Cords)

The accessories of lighting fixtures do not *have* to be plain and functional. Coiled, twisted, striped or spotted flexes can add visual flair to your lighting scheme. There are many available in bright primary colours to give you a cheerful hi-tech look – especially if they are coordinated with coloured switches and sockets (outlets).

1 *In an elegant kitchen, brass-rimmed downlights provide a general level of illumination and coordinate with the brass light switches.*

2 *Downlights add dramatic accent to a display of sculpture. The fall of light brings out the warm tones of the coir matting.*

3 *The downlights fitted in the bathroom area of this bedroom are a means of dividing two quite distinct areas; they give the bathroom a more intimate and self-contained 'feel'.*

Fitting a Downlight

Downlights are not difficult to fit, assuming there is a power source nearby – there is no need to remove floorboards and to work from above, nor do you have to remove an entire section of ceiling. Downlights can be surface-mounted; however, fully or partially recessed types are more effective and less obtrusive.

The first task is to ensure that there is enough space above the ceiling to take the fitting. If there is too little for a fully recessed light, choose a partially recessed one instead. The particular design will be specified in the manufacturers' catalogues and/or on the packaging. Downlights can be fitted with plastered ceilings, plaster-board or wood panelling. Before you start, plan where the lights will go. If you need to illuminate a worktop, ensure that the fittings are placed close enough together to create overlapping pools of light. They must be positioned directly above the work surface. Otherwise you will find yourself shadowing the work because you are standing between it and the light source.

SAFETY It is vital to switch off power at the mains or fuse box before you begin. Do not switch it on again until you are sure that the light is correctly connected. Always follow manufacturers' instructions when connecting the light flex (cord) to mains wiring, and always use a terminal block. In the United States and Australia, check local regulations before you attempt electrical work.

Materials and Equipment
● downlight(s) and bulb(s)
● template or pattern constructed to diameter of the fitting
● pencil
● padsaw (keyhole saw)
● screwdriver, if necessary
● filler

METHOD
1 Ensure that there is enough space above the ceiling (i.e., between the ceiling and the floor above) to fit the downlight. Required depths are usually listed in manufacturers' catalogues.
2 Switch power off at the mains or fuse box. Draw the template to mark the size of the opening.
3 Cut out the opening with a padsaw. Keep the edges tidy; smooth irregularities with filler.
4 Connect light to mains supply, as instructed, using a terminal block. Fit the downlight into place. If it has clips for fitting, swing both up and push the two longer arms into the hole.
5 Snap the fitting into place and clip on the trim, or fix according to the instructions.
6 Once you are sure that the light is properly connected, add the recommended lamp or bulb and restore power.

Tracks and Wiring

Putting Up Track

A spotlight track is electrified along its entire length so that a series of lights can be fitted. The tracks come complete with mounting clips and are in plastic or metal. There are basic lengths to which extensions can be fitted; some types can be turned around corners by use of flexible connectors.

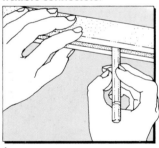

1

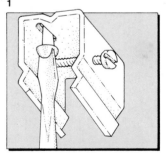

2

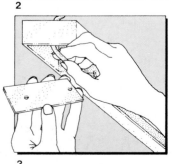

3

1 Decide where you want the track. It must be screwed to a solid surface, such as a ceiling joist. Remember to locate the live end of the track near to the power point. Turn off at the mains or fuse box and mark the position of the track through holes in it. Drill holes at these points.

2 Screw the mounting clips in position.

3 Remove the terminal box's cover plate and feed the cable through it.

4 Clip the track into the mounting clips and secure it by tightening screws. If a different system is used, see the manufacturers' instructions. Connect the cable to the terminals and replace the cover.

5 Slide the spotlights onto the track and lock into position. Restore power.

● In the United States and Australia, you must check local regulations before you attempt electrical work.

1,2 Originally designed for industrial and commercial use, track lighting is a versatile fitting that works well in either traditional or modern interior settings. Its main advantage is that any number of spotlights can be fitted easily to a single track, and directed at different areas.

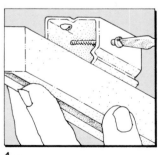

4

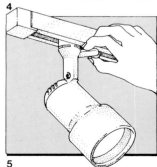

5

Covering Electrical Wires

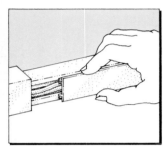

Cover and protect wires in situations where you want to extend your electrical circuit but cannot run the new wiring under the floor or do not want to conceal it behind plastered or finished walls. Covering is available in plastic, metal or wood sections, running at floor-level as a mock skirting board (baseboard) or at ceiling-height as a cornice (crown molding). Plastic types have a clip-on cover.

First plan the route of the circuit around the room. Drill and fix the main body of the covering by screwing through the base or, if the surface is suitable, using contact adhesive. Snap the fittings – couplers, bends and T-pieces – into position. Fit the lid by sliding one end under the cover of the first fitting. Cut 5mm/¼in past the first fitting, spring under the next fitting and snap the lid into position along the main body. Repeat the process between every fitting.

Making a Lamp Base

With a little ingenuity, you can improvise your own table lamps from a variety of containers, provided that whatever you choose is sturdy enough to support a bulb-holder and shade. Old bottles, narrow-necked jugs, interesting vases – all can make attractive bases. All you need to buy is the bulb-holder, flex (cord) and plug;

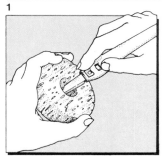

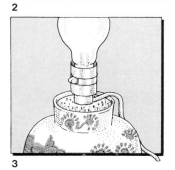

perhaps also a cork stopper if the neck of the container is too wide.

If you want to thread the flex down through the base, you will have to make a hole in the bottom of it. However, if the base is a treasured vase or a particularly brittle container that you do not want to drill, there is no reason why you cannot leave the flex coming out at the side. In which case, you may want to use a more decorative type of flex for the lamp – for example, striped or coloured (see page 157).

1 If the bottle or jar is light, weight it down with pebbles or sand.
2 Wedge the bulb-holder into the neck of the container. If the neck is too wide, take a cork disc and, using a craft knife, cut a hole in it in which the bulb-holder can sit.
3 Insert the bulb-holder into the cork and wedge the assemblage into the bottle. To drill a hole in the base, use a spear-point drill bit in a power drill set at a slow speed. Lubricate the drilling area with turpentine or white spirit contained by a sealed ring of putty.

SAFETY When drilling glass, ceramics or other brittle materials, *always* wear protective goggles or special safety glasses.

3 *A marble-based lamp is the centrepiece of this conversation area.*

SAFETY
Living with Electricity
● Have your electrical wiring system checked every 5 years, or at once if you are buying an older property
● Any system more than 25 years old should be replaced
● Do not overload a socket (outlet) with plugs
● Replace damaged flexes
● Replace plugs that are broken or cracked
● Ensure trailing flexes are kept out of the way
● Store electric blankets flat and in a dry cupboard
● Keep electrical appliances away from the bathroom

Working with Electricity
● *Always* switch off power at the mains supply before carrying out any repairs or replacements
● *Always* disconnect an electrical appliance before working on it
● Use a circuit tester to check that you have shut off power to the area of your home you are working on
● Use a circuit breaker plug on household tools, such as drills and sanders
● If you are not sure how to do the job, call in an electrician

PREPARATION

Preparation is one stage of decorating where the rewards are not immediately evident. Although making a good surface can be time-consuming, laborious and messy, proper preparation is essential if you want a successful result.

Almost all decorating finishes require a surface that is clean, even and dry. The first step is to analyze the condition of the surface and assess how much work has to be done to bring it up to standard. In some cases, all that may be needed is to wash and degrease the area and then allow it to dry thoroughly. More often, though, there will be small holes or cracks to fill, existing finishes to be stripped, and some minor repair work. Occasionally, you will discover that what seemed to be a minor fault is in fact the outward manifestation of a major one requiring remedial action before you can continue to decorate.

Major Problems
Symptoms of major problems can include:
● patches of discoloured or mouldy plaster
● wide cracks in walls which continue to widen
● cracking, warped or crumbling woodwork
● excessive moisture

Whenever you suspect an underlying defect it is crucial that you treat the cause, not just the symptoms: simply ignoring the problem could, at worst, lead to the overall weakening of the entire fabric of your home.

Structural decay, as shown up by poor surfaces, has several causes, including dampness, structural instability, infestations of woodworm or beetle and fungal growths such as dry rot. One cause may lead to

another: for example, dampness can create the conditions for dry rot to flourish. If you suspect any of these defects, call in an expert to treat the condition – or, if you are extremely lucky, to allay your suspicions (see page 25).

Walls and Ceilings
Preparation can be dusty and messy, so you should protect furnishings and fittings as carefully as you would if you were already starting to decorate. Clear the room of furniture as far as possible. Remove lampshades, take down curtains and cover floors with dustsheets. Before you start to work, assemble all the tools and equipment you will need.

Painted walls and ceilings that are in good condition may just need to be cleaned

before you begin decorating. First brush or vacuum off loose dirt and dust. Then, using a solution of warm water and detergent or sugar soap, wash all the surfaces with a clean rag or sponge.

Small cracks and holes can be filled with any number of fillers: some are ready-mixed, others come in powder form and must be mixed with water. Choose the filler that suits the surface and degree of damage.

Foam Fillers

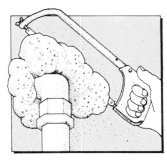

Foam fillers expand and can be used for awkward gaps.

Filling Cracks

1

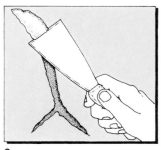

2

1 Rake out loose material and undercut edges.
2 Moisten surface. Press filler into crack. Level off proud of surface and sand.

Filling Holes

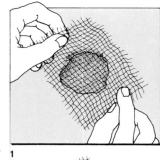

1

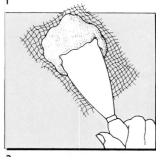

2

1 Prepare as for cracks, cutting round edge for a firm line. Cover with mesh tape, which will act as a backing.
2 Apply thin film of filler.

Filling Gaps

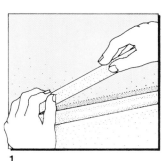

1 Gaps, such as those between skirting boards (baseboards) and floors can be filled using a bunched tissue or newspaper or a strip of expanded polystyrene.
2 Apply sealant to fill and seal the gap. Smooth with wetted fingertips.

Fitting a Ceiling Rose
(Medallion)
To fix a polystyrene ceiling rose, apply adhesive to its back and simply press it into place. If you are using it in conjunction with a light, you can feed the cord down through a hole drilled in the middle. Fill any gaps around the edges.

Architectural Details
Cleaning decorative plasterwork is extremely time-consuming, but it may be the only way to restore its original beauty.

Test a small area by sponging with water. If the paint comes off, soak the plasterwork for 30 minutes and then scrape off the paint using small knives and brushes, working gently into cracks and crevices. If the paint is not soluble in water, try a chemical solvent or a hot-air stripper.

Where architectural detail is lacking, you can buy ready-made cornices (crown moldings), ceiling roses (medallions) and mouldings in fibrous plaster or polystyrene.

SAFETY Do not paint polystyrene details with oil-based paint – this causes a fire hazard. Switch off electricity at the mains or fuse box before tampering with light fittings.

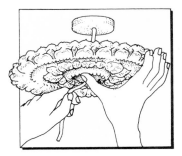

SURFACE TREATMENTS

Emulsion (Latex) If the paint is peeling, strip back to ensure a good working surface. Otherwise, clean with sugar soap and water before painting. New plaster should be primed.
Gloss If the paintwork is cracked, strip right back to ensure a good working surface. Otherwise, clean with sugar soap and water. New or exposed wood or metal should be primed.
Distemper Use a coarse cloth or a scourer and water to scrub the walls. If the layer of distemper is thick, dampen the wall and scrub off. Use

stabilizing solution to cover any remaining areas.
Textured Paint If you are planning to paint the surface, scrub lightly with a mild solution of sugar soap and water. Use a textured-paint stripper to remove it completely and safely.
Wallpaper Dampen the paper with water and use a scraper to strip. Roughen the surface of painted wallpaper with coarse sandpaper or serrated scraper. Washable papers should be stripped using a serrated scraper. Use a steam stripper for 'difficult' papers.

A fireplace is always a focal point and adds to the style and atmosphere of a room. Often, though, you will find either that fireplaces have been removed or that they were never fitted in the first place. Luckily, there are many suppliers of antique and

reproduction fireplaces, so you should find it easy enough to find a replacement to suit the size of the opening, the period or style of the room, and your own budget. Materials for the surrounds include marble, stone, stripped or new pine, cast-iron and tiling.

Stripping Wallpaper

Whether you intend to paint or paper a wall, it is always a good idea to strip the old paper off first. If you do not the dyes or glues in the existing wallpaper may stain through the new surface, the old paper may soften and lift up, the pattern may show through (in the case of relief textures), or (if you are covering washable, metallic, coated or flocked paper) the new finish may simply not stick to the wall.

There are a variety of methods you can use, depending on the type of paper and how firmly it has adhered to the surface. Certain papers can be stripped dry, by simply peeling away the bottom edge and lifting it off the wall. However, this usually leaves a thin backing paper which can be soaked and then scraped off. Generally, though, for most papers you will need to soak the paper with hot water, score the surface and scrape it off or, for more stubborn washable or relief or painted papers, use a steam stripper. In either case, it is important to work gently and methodically to avoid damaging the underlying plasterwork.

Plain painted walls do not need to be stripped before redecoration (unless they have been covered with distemper, which is incompatible with modern paints). Textured coatings, however, cannot be papered over, and so they will need to be stripped.

Remember that textured coatings and relief papers may well have been applied to cover imperfect plaster. If that is the case, stripping will leave you with a surface that requires further work.

Using a Steam Stripper
Steam strippers are fairly inexpensive to hire and can vastly simplify the process of stripping washable, relief or painted paper. Water is boiled in a tank and the resulting steam is fed through a hose to a perforated plate.

Fill the tank with water, according to the manufacturers' instructions, and, when the steam is ready, hold the plate against the bottom of a length of paper for 30–60 seconds, or until the paper appears damp.

● Do not keep the steam stripper in one position for too long or the plasterwork will be damaged.

Materials and Equipment
● broad stripping knife
● serrated scraper, knife or abrasive paper for scoring
● steam stripper
● bucket of hot water
● sponge or brush
● rubber gloves and safety glasses

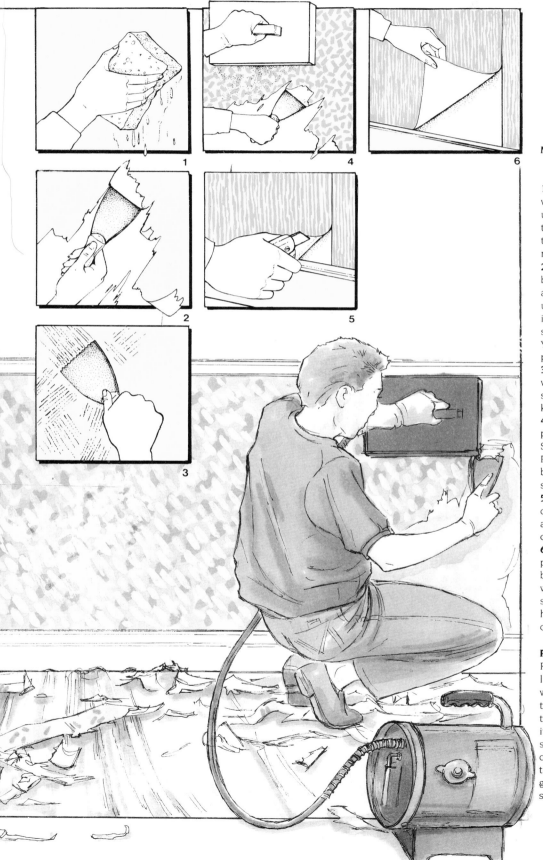

METHOD

1 To strip standard wallpaper, wet thoroughly with a sponge using hot water. Work from the top down, wetting several times, and allow at least five minutes for the water to soak in.

2 Ease the paper off using a broad stripping knife, held at an angle of 30 degrees. Scrape upwards, taking care not to dig into the plaster. The paper should wrinkle and come away. You may also find that you can pull off big strips.

3 To help water soak into washable paper, score the surface with a serrated scraper, knife or abrasive paper.

4 For painted or heavy relief papers, use a steam stripper. Steam rises, so work upwards. Peel off one area of paper with a broad knife while you are steaming the next.

5 Vinyls or easy-strip papers are designed to be peeled off. Using a craft knife, lift the corner of the covering away from its backing.

6 Use your hands to peel the paper away from the wall. If the backing paper comes away as well, strip it off by soaking and scraping. If it remains intact, however, you can simply paper over it.

Removing Textured Coatings

Removing textured paints is laborious and messy. The best way is to paint on a special textured paint remover and, once the coating has softened, scrape it off. Alternatively, you can use a steam stripper. Wash the wall down afterwards, and make sure to wear protective gloves and glasses. Never be tempted to sand a textured coating.

Woodwork and Metalwork

Unlike painted walls, painted woodwork is often better stripped before you redecorate: built-up layers of oil-based paint will prevent your newly decorated woodwork from looking crisp and even. However, if the woodwork is in good condition you can simply clean and degrease it, then lightly sand it down to provide a key for painting.

Metalwork – window frames, for example – can be treated in exactly the same way. If there is rust you should clean this off with an emery cloth or a wire brush.

Wooden floors often require special attention. Boards may need replacing, levelling or fixing down. Also, it is important to fill gaps and sink nail-heads if you are planning to sand, varnish or stain the floor.

Stripping Woodwork

The three main methods of stripping paint from woodwork are scraping, the use of chemicals, and the application of heat.

If you work with chemicals, make sure to wear protective gloves and glasses. If you use a hot-air stripper, do so with care, especially when stripping window frames: excess heat can cause the glass to crack, and there is a danger of scorching the wood or setting the accumulated paint scrapings ablaze.

Heat Stripping

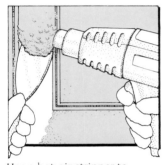

Use a hot-air stripper to soften paint. Move it to and fro, scraping away paint either with a scraper for flat areas or with a shave hook for mouldings.

Chemical Stripping

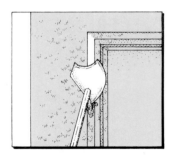

Dab on liquid stripper with a brush. When the paint has softened and bubbled, scrape it off using a shave hook on mouldings (pulling towards you) or a broad scraper on flat areas (pushing away from you).

This is the best method of stripping window frames but it can be expensive, messy and time-consuming.

Sanding

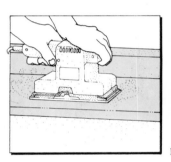

On flat surfaces you can strip paint with an orbital sander, but it can be extremely dusty and messy. For mouldings, use a flexible abrasive block for the job.

1 *Sanded wood-strip floor.*
2 *A stripped wooden fireplace.*
3 *To look their best wood floors require careful preparation.*
4 *Mouldings add period style to a built-in corner cupboard.*

SURFACE TREATMENTS

New Wood   Use cellulose filler for cracks and holes. Cover knots with shellac knotting. Smooth the surface with a fine abrasive paper.
Old Wood   Make sure that there is no sign of rot, and fill cracks and holes. Smooth with a fine abrasive paper.
Painted Wood   If the surface is in good condition, clean with sugar soap and water. Rub down with a medium-grade flexible sanding block or abrasive paper to provide a key for the new paint. Cracked paint should be stripped.
Varnished Wood   Use varnish stripper in order to get back to bare wood.

Stained Wood   Wood bleach can be used to remove stain. If the surface is to be painted, rub with a medium-grade flexible sanding block or abrasive paper. Wood stain protected by varnish must be removed as above.
Painted Metal   Clean with sugar soap and water if in good condition. Otherwise, use a wire brush to remove flaking paint, and treat rust with a primer containing rust inhibitor.
Aluminium/Copper   Clean with white spirit and apply enamel without primer or undercoat. Use flour-grade paper to remove signs of corrosion and scratches.

2

3

Replacing a Floorboard

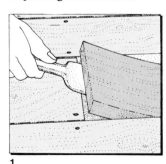

1

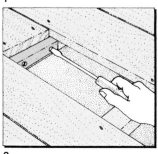

2

1　Lever up the damaged board with a bolster chisel (brick chisel). If you cannot lift a whole board, cut out a short piece. First drill a starting hole and then cut across the board with a padsaw (keyhole saw) alongside, but not cutting into, a joist, pipe or cable.

Loosen nails by slipping a strip of wood under the board and pressing down hard on the end. Repeat the process, jamming the wood strip up as far as it will go, until the board is free.

2　Screw a short wooden batten to the side of the joist, flush with the underside of the floorboards. Cut the replacement board and nail to batten.

Adding Door Mouldings

Flush doors, cupboard fronts and kitchen units can be dressed up by applying ready-made wooden mouldings to provide decorative detail. There are sets available especially for this purpose, allowing you to create the effect of traditional panelling. These come in sizes to suit standard doors, and are available both curved and straight; the corners are mitred. To attach them, drill very fine holes in the moulding and fix with pins.

Alternatively, you can use ready-made wooden mouldings to make your own picture rail or dado rail, fixing it in position with masonry nails or screws.

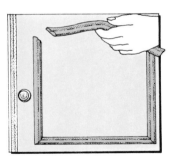

4

Successful Decorating
PREPARATION

METHOD

1 Punch all nail-heads below the surface of the boards, using a nail punch and a claw hammer.

2 Fit coarse-grade paper onto the belt sander, following the operating instructions.

3 Before switching on, tilt the sander so that the drum is clear of the floor. Tilt up at the beginning and end of each row.

4 Sand backwards and forwards, working diagonally at an angle of 45 degrees. Use coarse abrasive paper and overlap each row by about 7.5cm/3in. Follow this by sanding back and forth in the direction of the grain of the board, using first medium-grade and then fine paper.

5 Use an edging sander for edges, following the grain wherever possible and keeping moving while the machine is switched on.

6 For awkward corners, use a hook scraper or a shave hook. Sand by hand any small patches you may have missed.

● Vacuum the floor several times during the course of the sanding. Allow the dust to settle overnight before final vacuuming. Clean with white spirit or turpentine before applying varnish or stain.

SAFETY *Always* wear a dust mask, ear muffs and goggles. Drape the cord of the sander over your shoulder to ensure that it is kept well out of the path of the machine. Always make sure the machine is switched off and disconnected from the mains when you are changing paper.

Sanding a Floor

It takes a degree of skill to operate sanding machines, and it is essential that you protect yourself from inhaling dust and observe a number of vital safety precautions.

Preparation

Before sanding, you must prepare the floor suitably. You should make sure you have prepared for the work before you hire a sanding machine – otherwise you are paying for all the time that the machine stands idle.

If there are many large gaps between boards, it may be worth lifting all the boards, moving them along and inserting an extra piece at the end. Alternatively, one or two large gaps could be filled with wooden fillets, glued and hammered in place, then planed smooth once the glue has dried. (Small gaps can be filled with wood filler.)

All traces of old polish should be removed with steel wool and white spirit or turpentine so that the sander does not become clogged. Nail down loose boards and punch all nail-heads below the surface.

Finally, prepare the room in general by clearing furniture, taking down curtains and covering light fittings. Tape around the doors to minimize the amount of dust percolating through the house. Open all the windows.

Using Sanding Machines

You will need two types of sander: a large belt sander and an edging (rotary) sander. The belt sander is an upright machine with a dust collecting bag and a revolving drum around which abrasive paper is wrapped. The edging sander is smaller and lighter and has an abrasive sheet attached to a rubber pad. Both types of machine can be hired from specialist shops, which also supply abrasive paper and protective gear.

Ask for a demonstration when you hire or buy the equipment. Follow the instruction booklet when fitting the abrasive paper. Always tilt the drum of a belt sander back from the floor before switching on. Once it is on, lower it gently. You must keep moving when you are using it: if the sander is left running while it is stationary it will gouge holes in the floor. Tilt it up at the start and finish of each row.

Materials and Equipment
- belt sander for the main floor area
- edging (rotary) sander for the edges
- shave hook or hook scraper for awkward areas
- nail punch and hammer
- coarse-, medium- and fine-grade abrasive paper
- protective gear (dust mask, ear muffs, goggles)
- vacuum cleaner

ALL ABOUT PAINT

Paint is cheap, quick and easy to apply, and available in a variety of different finishes and in a host of different colours. Thanks to technological advances, modern paints cover well, protect surfaces from weather and wear, and resist fading and discoloration. For all these reasons – both practical and aesthetic – painting is the single most popular way of decorating interiors.

Basic painting techniques are simple to master and the equipment required is not elaborate. With a little extra skill, you can open up a whole new dimension of decorative possibilities using special effects such as sponging, ragging and stencilling.

TYPES OF PAINT

Paint consists of pigment (colour) dispersed in a medium (binder), together with a solvent or thinner which evaporates as the paint dries. Some paints may include other materials such as resin or silica to provide special characteristics. The two main types of paint are oil-based and water-based (commonly known as emulsion [latex]). They are incompatible when wet.

It is always a good idea to buy the best paint you can afford. Cheap paint is difficult to apply and looks streaky; you will end up needing to use more of it than with a good-quality paint.

Oil-based Paints

These come in three finishes: gloss, which has a high sheen and is often used on woodwork; semi-gloss or eggshell, which gives a mid-sheen texture and can be used on walls or woodwork; and matt or flat oil paint,

which provides the basis for many special paint effects.

All oil-based paints are soluble in white spirit or turpentine and require an undercoat. They take longer to dry than water-based varieties of paint.

Undercoat

This oil-based paint is designed to provide a good surface for the application of oil-based top coats. It is soluble in white spirit or turpentine.

Water-based Paints

These are also available in different finishes: silk, satin or sheen and matt. A popular choice for walls and ceilings, emulsion (latex) is quick-drying, soluble in water (tools and spills are easy to clean) and needs no undercoat.

Non-drip Paints

Both oil- and water-based paints are available in non-drip versions which are easy

for the beginner to apply. They need no stirring and should not be thinned. Similarly, trays of 'solid emulsion' can be useful for painting ceilings, stairways or wherever it is important to keep splashes to a minimum.

Textured 'Paint'

This thick, permanent coating dries to a textured finish which is very difficult to remove. It is designed to cover up poor surfaces and should be finished with a coat of emulsion.

Masonry Paint

Essentially an external paint, this can be used on interior brickwork for a durable finish.

Enamel Paint

This is an oil-based paint for small areas of wood and metalwork. It is very dense; only one coat is needed. There is also a textured version which separates as it dries to give a 'crazed' finish.

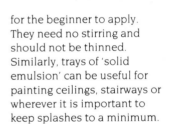

1 Light green paint with a slight sheen is used to decorate walls and ceiling, creating an airy room.
2 A sense of warmth and enclosure is generated by painting all the surfaces in this kitchen the same shade of burnt orange.

Home-made Paints

You can create your own colours by mixing a small amount of artist's colours (oil or gouache) with the appropriate solvent (white spirit, turpentine or water) and adding the mixture a little at a time to the appropriate paint base.

Types of Paint

1 Gloss
2 Floor paint
3 Eggshell
4 Matt emulsion (latex)
5 Vinyl silk (semi-gloss)
6 Undercoat

Applications

	UNDERCOAT	OIL-BASED GLOSS	OIL-BASED EGGSHELL (SEMI-GLOSS)
SURFACES TO USE ON	Use on primed surfaces. Do not use on plastic, copper, brass or stainless steel	Woodwork, metalwork. Can be applied to plastic and copper without using undercoat	Walls, ceilings and woodwork. Ideal for bathrooms and kitchens
EQUIPMENT	Wide paintbrush, roller or spray gun for large areas, small paintbrush for details	Wide paintbrush, roller or spray gun for large areas, small paintbrush for details	Paintbrushes, roller and tray, or spray gun
DILUTING	White spirit or turpentine can be used to thin the paint	White spirit or turpentine can be used to thin the paint	White spirit or turpentine can be used to thin the paint
POSSIBLE PROBLEMS	Can be used as a top coat, but must be covered with matt varnish to avoid marking	Go back over painted surfaces to brush out drips and runs	Patchiness can occur if surface is not thoroughly prepared and completely dry
DRYING TIME	2–6 hours. A second coat can usually be applied after 6–16 hours	4–6 hours. A second coat can usually be applied after 16–24 hours	4–6 hours. A second coat can usually be applied after 16–24 hours
CLEANING	Use white spirit or turpentine to clean brushes immediately after use	Use white spirit or turpentine to clean brushes immediately after use	Use white spirit or turpentine to clean brushes and equipment
NUMBER OF COATS	1 or 2	2	1 or 2
SPECIAL PROPERTIES	It has a high pigment content, and covers well. Chalky texture as top coat	Undercoat is not always necessary. Durable and easy to clean	Smooth finish with dull sheen. Easy to clean and withstands condensation
COLOURS	Limited to a few basic colours	Wide range of colours, some coordinating with water-based ranges	Range of colours

WATER-BASED EMULSION (LATEX)/VINYL	SOLID EMULSION (LATEX)	ENAMEL	TEXTURED PAINT
Walls and ceilings. Vinyl silk/satin can be used as a base coat for paint effects	Walls and ceilings. Do not apply directly onto new/unpainted plasterwork	Metalwork, woodwork. Best for small areas	Walls and ceilings. Particularly useful for covering uneven surfaces
Paintbrushes, roller and tray, or spray gun	Roller for large areas and paintbrush for details. Usually sold in its own tray	Paintbrushes for small areas, roller or spray gun for larger areas	Shaggy (coarse nap) roller and tray
Use water to thin the paint if necessary	Should not be thinned	White spirit or turpentine can be used to thin the paint	Should not be thinned
Oil-based paint and water-based paint are incompatible when wet	Too absorbent to take most paint effects. Not recommended for kitchens and bathrooms	Shows up imperfections of surface, so thorough preparation is necessary	Extremely difficult to remove
2–4 hours. A second coat can usually be applied after 2–4 hours	1–4 hours. A second coat can usually be applied after 1–4 hours	2–4 hours. A second coat can usually be applied after 1–4 hours	1–4 hours
Brushes and other equipment should be cleaned with water and soap	Roller and tray should be cleaned with water and soap	Use white spirit or turpentine to remove paint from brushes	Use white spirit or turpentine to remove paint from roller and tray
1 or 2	2	1 or 2	1 coat, followed by a coat of emulsion (latex) or gloss
No primer required. Dries quickly to a smooth finish	Particularly good for ceilings and stairways because it is non-drip	No primer required. Some brands also contain rust inhibitors. Hard, shiny finish	Much thicker than regular paint. Can be used to create various surface patterns
Wide range of colours	Limited range of colours	Range of colours	Coloured paint is applied to textured surface

Painting Tools and Equipment

The basic tools for most painting jobs are brushes and rollers. Just as you should always buy the best paint you can afford, it makes sense to buy good-quality tools. Maintain them properly during and after use.

Paintbrushes

Brushes can be used with either oil- or water-based paint and are available in a variety of widths for tackling different surfaces. Use wide brushes (10–15cm/4–6in) for walls and ceilings, narrow brushes (2.5cm/1in) for margins and fine trim, and medium brushes (5–7.5cm/ 2–3in) for bigger areas of woodwork.

Special brushes are produced to make the task of painting awkward areas easier. These include cutting-in brushes, with angled tips for painting edges or window frames, and brushes for painting radiators, where the bristles are fixed at right angles to the handle.

Rollers

Rollers are designed for use with water-based paint. Their principal advantage is that they enable large areas to be painted quickly and evenly. Some rollers can be fitted with handle extensions for painting ceilings or other areas which are difficult to reach. Choose a roller where the sleeve detaches from the frame to make cleaning much easier.

There are three main types of roller: short pile (short nap), shaggy pile (coarse nap) and foam. Both foam and short pile rollers work best on smooth surfaces, but short pile rollers will produce a better finish. Shaggy pile rollers are designed to cover textured surfaces. There are also special rollers designed to apply textured coatings. These have relief sleeves which deposit the paint in a pattern.

Paint Pads

As with rollers, paint pads are best used with water-based paint. They consist of a square or oblong pile-covered foam pad attached to a handle. Use pads to cover large surfaces.

Paint Containers

If you are using a brush, you can paint straight from the paint tin, but it is better to use a special paint container. These have handles, which make them more portable than tins; moreover, should you accidentally spoil the paint with dust picked up on the brush, you will waste only what is in the container.

Paint Trays

Rollers must be used with paint trays. The tray has a reservoir which holds a small amount of paint and a slope to facilitate the even application of the paint onto the roller.

Paint Guards

Plastic or metal guards are protective shields which can be placed against a window, wall or floor when you are painting frames or woodwork. Alternatively, you can use a piece of stiff cardboard or mask out the surrounding area with tape.

Care of Brushes and Rollers

Never overload tools with paint. As soon as you have finished, clean your tools by washing them in the appropriate solvent. Use white spirit, turpentine or a commercial brush cleaner for oil-based paints; cold water for water-based paints. Rinse brushes and rollers thoroughly, leave to dry and store flat. Never stand brushes or rollers upright.

● A loaded brush can be left for up to two hours without cleaning if it is covered tightly with foil or plastic kitchen wrap to prevent the paint from drying out.

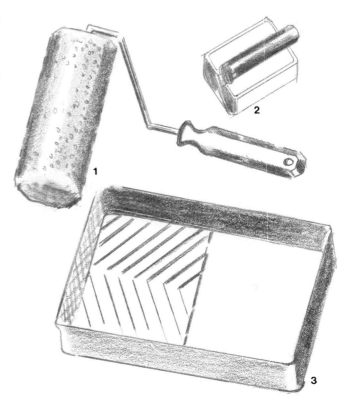

A cornice in a contrasting colour makes a subtle break between walls and ceiling.

Brushes and Equipment

Paintbrushes and other basic equipment can be bought from home decorating stores.

1 Roller for textured coating
2 Paint pad
3 Paint tray
4 Radiator brush
5 Paint guard
6 Regular roller, sheepskin roller and synthetic thick-pile roller
7 Roller frame
8 Medium paintbrush (5cm/2in)
9 Large paintbrush (10cm/4in)
10 Medium paintbrush (7.5cm/3in)
11 Narrow paintbrush (2.5cm/1in)
12 Cutting-in brush
13 Paint container

Order of Painting a Room

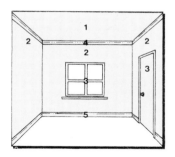

Paint a room in the following order. First, paint the ceiling, working away from the main source of natural light. Then come the walls, and after them paint the window frames and doors. Next paint any mouldings and picture rails, and finish by painting the skirting boards (baseboards).

Painting Walls and Ceilings

The most important principle when painting walls and ceilings is to work to a system. The aim is to cover the area evenly, avoiding visible 'joins' where paint overlaps. Work quickly so that the edges of the painted area will not dry before the adjoining area is covered. If you have to stop halfway through, try to do so at a natural break such as a corner.

Order of Painting a Wall

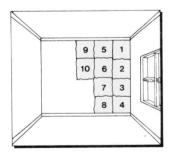

Work away from sources of natural light, especially if you are using a light-coloured paint over a light-coloured ground, or applying a second coat of any colour. Start in the top right-hand corner and proceed from right to left. (If you are left-handed, work in the opposite direction.)

If you are using a brush, work in sections 60cm/2ft square, as shown: complete one vertical strip before moving onto the next, and start each strip at the top. If you are using a roller, work in 60cm/2ft strips.

Painting Platform

Of course, you can paint a ceiling from a stepladder, but there is the disadvantage that you have to climb down frequently to move it along. Alternatively, if the ceiling is not too high, you can simply fit an extension handle to a roller.

Order of Painting a Ceiling

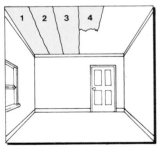

Work in strips about 60cm/2ft wide, away from the source of natural light. First cut-in edges using a narrow brush. Paint one complete strip, then work back in a new row to the end where you started.

However, it is much easier and much less tiring to paint a ceiling when standing on a platform. Set up a pair of stepladders or trestles and lay a sturdy plank or scaffold board across; ensure that the structure is secure before using it.

Cutting-in Using a Small Brush

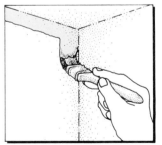

Before painting any section with a brush or roller, paint the edges along, for example, ceiling lines, skirting boards (baseboards), internal corners, window frames and door frames with a narrow brush or a cutting-in brush. Work a little way ahead of the main paintwork – although not too far, or the edges will dry before they are overlapped.

● At all costs, avoid standing on a chair to paint a ceiling.

Applying the Paint

Whether you are using a wide brush, roller or pad, apply the paint in random directions, working out from the corners where the edges have been painted, overlapping and criss-crossing the strokes. When the paint runs out or you complete a section, finish with a light upward stroke to remove brush or roller marks.

WALLS AND CEILINGS
Paint Coverage per Litre (Internal usage only)

Paint Finish	Smooth Plaster or Paper Base	Rough Plaster or Paper Base	Masonry
Undercoat	15m²	12m²	—
All Purpose Primer	7–8m²	7–8m²	—
Matt Emulsion (Latex)	14m²	11m²	14m²
Silk Emulsion (Latex)	13m²	10m²	13m²
Flat Paint	16m²	14m²	16m²
Eggshell	16m²	14m²	16m²
High Gloss	17m²	15m²	17m²
Non-drip Gloss	12m²	9m²	12m²

Multiply by 10 to get the coverage in square feet per US quart.

Stairwell Platform

To paint awkward areas such as stairwells, construct a platform using a stepladder and a straight ladder. Set up the stepladder on the landing, well back from the top step. Lean the straight ladder against the head wall of the staircase, with the bottom resting against a lower stair. The ends of the ladder should be wrapped to protect the wall. Then lay a strong plank or scaffold board across. If the ladders are more than 1.5m/5ft apart, use two boards, one on top of the other for support.

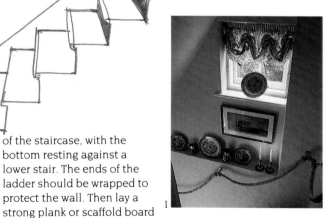

1 *Pale terracotta on a small country stairwell has the soft look of bare plaster.*

2 *Two areas of wall treated in a different manner: pale yellow in a matt finish above the dado rail, and a deeper yellow scumbled below.*

Painting Details

Painting Decorative Mouldings

Cornices (Crown moldings) and ceiling roses (medallions), whether they are the original plasterwork or reproductions made of polystyrene, plaster or anaglypta, should be painted with emulsion (latex) or water-based paint. You will need to exercise some care, especially in the case of intricate mouldings, in order to prevent the design from becoming clogged and obscured with paint. If the cornice is to be the same colour as the ceiling, paint the ceiling first, then the cornice, and finally the walls. If the cornice is to be a different colour, paint it after the walls. If you are going to paper the walls, the cornice should certainly be painted first. The best method is to apply the paint in thin coats with a narrow (2.5cm/1in) brush. Allow each coat to dry before you start on the next.

Some mouldings can look very attractive if elements of the design – usually the recessed parts – are picked out in a second colour. Paint the raised areas first and then fill in the second colour using an artists' brush.

Painting Awkward Areas

The areas behind radiators and pipework are difficult to reach with ordinary brushes. Special crevice or radiator brushes can be very useful in such situations. For painting behind a radiator, an alternative is to use a small roller fitted with an extension handle.

Painting Doors and Windows

If you follow the correct sequence for different types of windows and doors you will ensure a professional result, with all areas being covered evenly and without the formation of hard ridges.

As far as possible, remove fixtures such as handles, knobs, doorplates and window-latches before you begin to paint.

1 *An unusual archway with stained glass panels has been painted white to contrast with the sea-green walls.*
2 *Painting details such as architraves and skirting boards (baseboards) in a deeper shade of the wall colour serves to add graphic interest.*

Painting a Flush Door

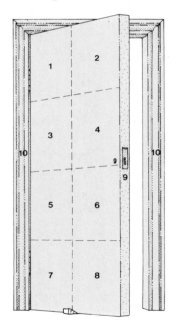

Keep the door ajar with a wedge to prevent it from moving. Paint in sections 45cm/18in square (about half the width of the door), working from the top down, completing each horizontal strip before you start on the next. Always paint to a wet edge in order to avoid hard, dried lines.

Painting a Panel Door

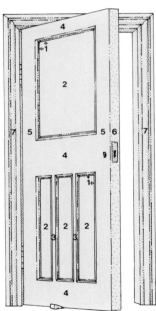

As for a flush door, wedge it open. Then paint in the following order:
1 Mouldings
2 Recessed panels
3 Centred uprights
4 Horizontals (paint top to bottom, following the grain)
5 Outer uprights
6 Door edge
7 Frame

Painting Sash Windows

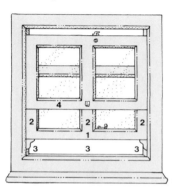 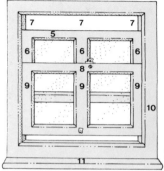

Avoid getting paint onto the sash cords – otherwise they will stiffen and crack. Reverse the position of the sashes to paint as much as possible of the outer sash, the bottom of the inner sash and the inside edges. Then move the sashes back to their original position and paint the rest of the outer frame, inner frame edges and lastly the frame and sill. The most sensible sequence for painting a sash window is as follows:

1 Meeting rail

Painting a Casement Window

First of all paint those windows that open, and start early enough in the day for there to be time for the windows to dry before night falls. The painting sequence of a window should follow the grain of the wood. All casement windows, whether they open or not, should be

2 Outer-sash vertical bars, as far as possible
3 The area beneath the inner sash and the lower runners
4 Lower cross-rail of inner sash and its underside
5 Upper cross-rail of the outer sash
6 Remainder of the outer-sash vertical bars
7 Soffit and top runners
8 Upper cross-rail of the inner sash
9 Inner-sash vertical bars
10 Frame
11 Window sill

painted in the following correct order:
1 Glazing putty
2 Glazing bars
3 Top and bottom rail
4 Outer uprights, or 'stiles'
5 Hinge edge
6 Centred frame, if there is an adjoining window
7 Frame (top and bottom, then sides)
8 Sill

3

WOOD AND METAL
Paint Coverage per Litre (Internal usage only)

Paint Finish	Smooth Planed Wood	Rough Sawn Wood	Radiators and Metalwork
Undercoat	16m²	15m²	16m²
All Purpose Primer	7–8m²	7–8m²	7–8m²
Eggshell	16m²	—	16m
High Gloss	17m²	14m²	17m²
Enamel Paint	—	—	17m²

Multiply by 10 to get the coverage in square feet per US quart.

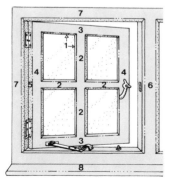

3 The subtle modulation of different greys creates an atmosphere of elegance and tranquillity. The walls above and below the dado are spattered for an unobtrusive but textural finish, and the desk chair has been sponged.

179

Successful Decorating
ALL ABOUT PAINT

METHOD

1 Stir paint thoroughly. Decant paint into paint container, and dip paint brush up to one-third the depth of the bristles. Do not overload the brush, or the paint will drip. Press the brush gently against the side of the container to remove excess paint.

2 If the grain is vertical, paint two or three vertical strips, parallel with each other, leaving between them gaps just narrower than the brush-width. Hold a narrow brush like a pencil.

3 Without reloading the brush, brush out the vertical strokes horizontally across the grain to fill gaps and smooth the paint.

4 Finish with light upward strokes, using a nearly dry brush. Work over the entire section you have just painted.

5 Use a paint guard or shield to protect a glass panelled door or a window. Alternatively, protect the glass with masking tape which you should remove before the paint is fully dry. In either case, allow the paint to cover the glass by about 3mm/⅛in so that the edges between wood and glass are sealed.

6 To paint a skirting board (baseboard), hold a piece of cardboard along the bottom edge so that the brush does not pick up dirt from the floor. Protect fitted carpet with dustsheets.

1

2

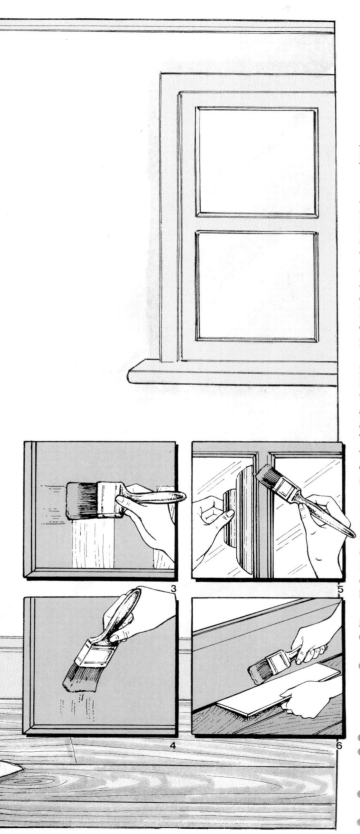

Painting Woodwork

All woodwork should be painted using an oil-based paint, in either a gloss or eggshell (semi-gloss) finish. This type of paint is more durable than emulsion (latex) and gives a thick protective coat which resists scuffs and knocks. All surfaces should be clean, dry and prepared for painting.

The basic principle of painting woodwork, whether it is a door or a picture rail, is to apply the paint *with* the grain, brush out *against* the grain, and lay off *with* the grain. Work in the correct sequence when painting details such as doors and window frames (see pages 178–9).

● Before painting a door, remember to clean the top edge with a rag. Also clean out the keyhole and door-handle slot to remove loose dirt that could be picked up by the tips of the bristles.

Materials and Equipment
● oil-based paint, gloss or eggshell (semi-gloss)
● narrow (2.5cm/1in) brush for fine detail; medium (7.5cm/3in) brush for panels; angled cutting-in brush for frames
● paint container
● paint guard or masking tape for protecting other surfaces
● solvent – e.g., white spirit or turpentine
● rag for cleaning spills

Painting a Wooden Staircase
Wooden staircases comprise a number of upright and horizontal elements which are best painted in a particular sequence. Prepare for painting by removing any stair carpet or covering. Clean the stairs thoroughly.

Work with thin coats of paint to avoid drips and use a selection of brushes of different widths, according to the area you are tackling.

First paint the hand-rail (or varnish it if you prefer). Then paint the newel post and balusters (uprights). Finally, working from the top of the stairs down, paint the stair treads (horizontal parts), risers (vertical parts) and strings (the area of skirting board beside the steps).

Safety Dispose of all paint- or solvent-soaked rags very carefully in order to avoid the risk of fire.

● If you intend to paper a room, paint the woodwork first, overlapping by about 1cm/½in onto the walls. This margin will ensure that slight gaps do not show.

● It is best to paint each particular area of woodwork – for example a window frame – in one painting session. If you stop halfway, the paint will form an ugly edge when it dries, which is very difficult to remove.

PAINT EFFECTS

Traditional methods of painted decoration are enjoying a renewed popularity today, bringing a sense of richness to the interior. Many special paint techniques were originally inspired by the desire to reproduce the look of a particular material. In the past, when marble, fine woods, wallpapers and fabrics were extremely expensive and hard to come by, craftsmen applied their skills to creating excellent simulations.

In addition, decorators learned how to exploit the qualities of different paints to add a dimension of depth to a surface. Layers of transparent washes or glazes, distressed or unevenly applied, can build up a subtle texture that is impossible to achieve with flat colour.

Although certain highly imitative paint effects do require artistic skill for a professional result, most do not. With practice, experiment and a sound understanding of the properties of paints, it is possible to create distinctive decoration at a fraction of the cost of wallpapering, panelling or fabric coverings.

TYPES OF EFFECT

For the sake of clarity, each paint technique in the following section is described individually. It is important to remember, however, that effects can also be combined. Most professional decorators decide how they want the surface to appear and then use a combination of methods to achieve it.

Experiment is essential. Test your ideas on hardboard (masonite) panels or stiff paper before you tackle a wall. The most difficult aspect of using any special paint effect is achieving consistency over a large area; practise until you can work rhythmically and evenly. It is also worth bearing in mind that, although many effects require special tools, good

substitutes can often, for the sake of economy, be adapted from household items.

Non-distressed Effects

There are a number of ways to increase the decorative potential of painted surfaces without using a special distressing or illusionist technique. Plain-painted walls and ceilings can be highlighted by picking out woodwork or plasterwork details in a contrasting or toning shade. Alternatively, decoration can be applied in the form of stencilled patterns painted onto walls, floors or furniture as borders, friezes or single motifs.

You can add depth and intensity to a single-colour scheme by applying several weak layers of wash or glaze

(diluted 1:9, paint to solvent) over a base or ground colour. This method, known as 'colour washing', produces a finish of great luminosity and warmth.

Distressed Effects

Distressed, or broken-colour, effects represent a whole family of related techniques, most of which are defined by the tools used to create them. In all cases, layers of dilute wash or glaze are applied over an opaque background.

There are two methods of achieving the textured finish. The first – additive – is to apply the wash or glaze unevenly using a particular tool – such as a sponge, rag, comb, brush or whatever – so that patches are left where the base colour shows through. The second – subtractive – is to apply the wash or glaze in a continuous layer and then 'distress' it with the tool, revealing areas of base colour. In either case the texture of the finish will depend on the tool you have used: each implement leaves its own characteristic mark. (See pages 184–5.)

Illusionist Effects

Techniques such as woodgraining, marbling and tortoise-shelling are essentially designed to simulate a natural material. Many of these effects are based on broken-colour techniques, with a distressed background being modified or decorated in such a way as to resemble the natural patterns and textures of stone, wood or whatever. Although it is impossible to achieve a highly realistic result without a high degree of artistic skill, more abstract patterning can be equally effective and is much easier. (See pages 188–9.)

Glazes and Washes

All special paint techniques depend on the use of glazes and washes. A glaze is a thinned or diluted oil-based paint; a wash is a thinned water-based paint. The correct ratio of paint to solvent is generally 1:3, but experiment is important. Glazes or washes diluted to a greater degree have more transparency and dry more quickly. Most effects can be

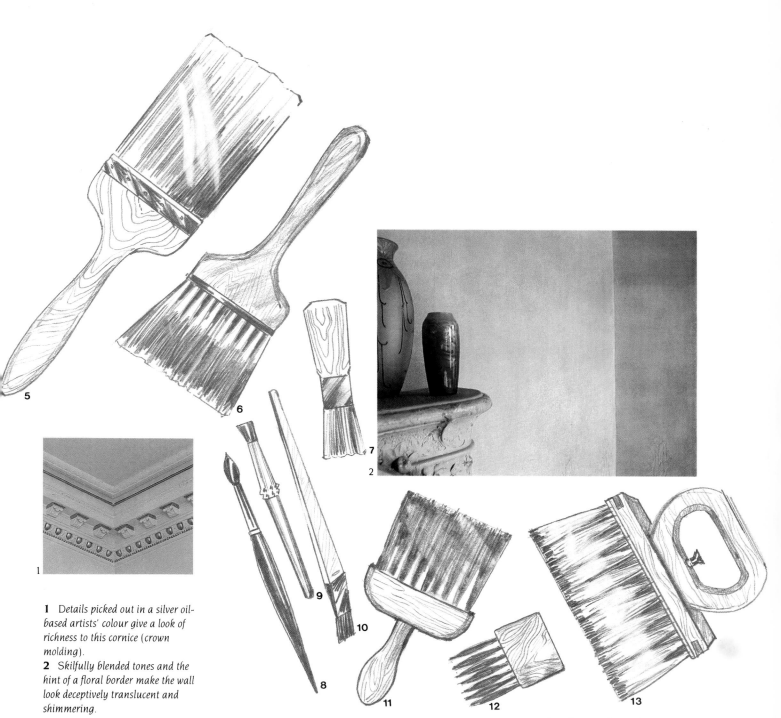

1 Details picked out in a silver oil-based artists' colour give a look of richness to this cornice (crown molding).

2 Skilfully blended tones and the hint of a floral border make the wall look deceptively translucent and shimmering.

achieved using either a glaze or a wash. A glaze produces a more luminous and sumptuous finish; washes are fresh and soft-looking.

Another consideration is the texture of the paint: matt, mid-sheen or gloss for oil-based glazes, and matt or mid-sheen for washes.

Remember that oil- and water-based paints are incompatible when wet.

Making a Glaze
You can buy ready-made glaze, but the following are recipes; all can be tinted using artists' oil colours.
- Transparent oil glaze, thinned 1:1 with white spirit or turpentine
- White undercoat, flat oil or eggshell, thinned 1:3 with white spirit or turpentine
- Undercoat or flat oil thinned 1:1 with

transparent oil glaze and then mixed 1:1 with white spirit or turpentine
- Linseed oil thinned 1:3 with turpentine

Making a Wash
Thin emulsion (latex) paint 1:3 with water and, if need be, tint to the desired shade using artists' gouache. Allow each coat of paint to dry before applying the next.

Brushes and Equipment
1 Natural sponge
2 Feather
3 Sword liner
4 Mottler
5 Dragging brush
6 Badger softener
7 Stencilling brush
8 Small artists' brush
9 Fitch
10 Lining brush
11 Dusting brush
12 Overgrainer
13 Stippling brush

183

Distressed or Broken-colour Effects

The two basic methods of creating broken colour are the additive and subtractive techniques. Many effects, notably sponging, ragging and rag-rolling, can be achieved using either. Others, such as spattering, are inherently additive; while stippling, dragging and cissing, for example, are subtractive.

Additive Techniques
A glaze or wash is applied in a broken film over a dry base coat using a tool such as a sponge or rag. This is the simpler of the two methods, since the drying time of the glaze or wash is not critical. It is best to work in 60cm/2ft vertical strips, taking care not to overlap the prints. Once the glaze or wash has dried, a further one, perhaps in a different colour, can be applied on top.

Subtractive Techniques
A glaze is applied over a dry base coat and then distressed using the tool of your choice while still wet. This method is easier if two people work together – one applying the glaze and the other distressing it. Glazes are more suitable for subtractive methods because they do not dry as quickly as washes.

Base Coats
Choose the colour of the base or ground coat carefully. The background will be modified where the glaze or wash covers it, while in the broken or open areas the colour will of course show through.

Texture is a further important consideration. Matt or mid-sheen is often the best choice – gloss can be obtrusive.

Oil- or water-based ground coats can be used with either glazes or washes, depending on the effect required. Layers of glaze over oil-based paint give a rich lacquer-like finish; a glaze over emulsion (latex) will intensify colour. In the same way, a wash over an emulsion base coat can enhance a soft watercolour look or give a crisp fresh effect; putting a wash over an oil-based undercoat is also effective. In all cases, the base coat must be thoroughly dry before you set to work with your glaze or wash.

Varnish
It is not necessary to seal a surface unless it will be subject to wear – for example, a door or window frame or a kitchen or bathroom wall. Use one to two coats of polyurethane, leaving 5–6 hours between each coat for the varnish to dry.

Varnish enhances and enriches colours but also tends to yellow with age. It is available in matt, mid-sheen or gloss textures; matt is the least noticeable.

Sponging

1

2

Sponging involves the use of a sponge either to dab on a layer of colour (sponging on) or to lift off patches of wet glaze or wash (sponging off). The nature of the print left by the sponge is all-important, and so it is best to use a genuine marine sponge.

First do some test prints on paper. Light colours on a dilute glaze or wash will be subtle and soft; darker shades will give a bolder pattern. If you want to use two or three colours, make each layer fairly sparse and build up from light to dark. Sponging will camouflage a poor surface and can be used as a way of blending.
1 First wet sponge and wring it out. Dip into paint; test print. Dab on colour over dry base coat.
2 Leave first coat to dry. Apply second colour, overlapping prints.

Ragging

Ragging is similar to sponging, and is useful for covering imperfections. It can be either additive or subtractive. Different cloths give different effects, but in most cases the result is fairly insistent and emphatic, so light colours are generally better than strong deep ones. Cloths can be used either dry or wet – wet gives a softer pattern than dry.

Apply colour using a bunched rag. Vary the direction and the way the cloth is bunched. When the cloth is saturated, change for a clean one.

184

Dragging

Stippling

Combing

Making a Comb

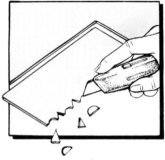

Dragging is a subtractive technique. A dry brush is pulled through wet glaze to produce a fine, rather sophisticated striped effect reminiscent of fabric covering. Dragging is best employed on flat surfaces. It is as effective on woodwork, creating the suggestion of graininess, as on plaster walls. Wallpaper brushes make acceptable alternatives to dragging brushes, which can be expensive.

Glaze works better than wash for dragging. Practise beforehand on a sheet of hardboard (masonite) until you can get the lines steady. Drag through the wet glaze with a large dry brush.

Safety Oil-based paints are highly inflammable. Paint- and solvent-soaked rags can spontaneously ignite if left bunched up in a bag or a confined space. Let them dry thoroughly before you dispose of them.

Stippling is a subtractive technique which produces a delicate, flecked texture. It is particularly effective if a pale glaze or wash is applied over a ground coat of a slightly lighter colour.

Stippling can be tiring to do over large areas. Special stippling brushes are expensive, but you can make do with alternatives: flat-faced brushes such as broomheads, scrubbing brushes, textured rollers and so on. All brushes and rollers should be cleaned regularly in order to prevent the build up of paint.

Apply glaze over base coat and, while still wet, strike the surface with a flat-faced brush, lifting off flecks of colour with the brush.

● Many broken-colour methods are messy. Protect surrounding surfaces, wear rubber gloves and keep a rag on hand to mop up spills and splashes.

Combing is much like dragging. It consists of distressing a wet surface with a comb to create various patterns. The base coat should be robust enough to withstand the combing action. The patterns produced depend on the number and size of teeth in the comb. Although decorators' combs are commercially available, it is easy to make your own. The finish is bold and forthright and suits lengths of woodwork and floors.

Apply glaze to dry base coat. Draw comb over the wet surface to create the pattern.

Cissing

Cissing is, as it were, the reverse of spattering. Apply a glaze or wash to a dry base coat. While the glaze is still wet, spatter on solvent – water, white spirit, or turpentine, depending on the type of paint used. Work on a horizontal surface.

Cut out a design from a piece of rigid plastic, such as the side of an ice cream carton. Vary the spacing and size of the teeth to create.

Spattering

One of the simplest of all broken-colour methods, spattering is an additive technique that involves flecking a surface with dots of colour. The pattern and texture of the finish will depend on the tool: use a stiff brush such as a stencil brush or even a toothbrush. Run your fingers over wet bristles or strike the handle of the brush to release a fine spray. Practise first until you are able to achieve a uniform effect.

● If you accidentally sponge, rag or spatter on a too-thick blob of paint, let it dry and then go over it again with a sponge or cloth dipped in the base colour so as to even out the effect.

Rag-rolling a Wall

Rag-rolling is a variation of a ragging technique in which a cloth is rolled down over a surface to create a finish that displays a great sense of movement and liveliness. As with ragging, the effect is dramatic, resembling the texture of crushed velvet or crumpled silk, and suits formal applications such as in dining rooms. Because the finish could easily become too insistent, it is best to use, rather than bold contrasts, shades of pale colour offset with plain woodwork. Rag-rolling is inherently rhythmic, and for this reason it can be a very effective way of decorating furniture.

Although the finish can be achieved by rag-rolling *on* using a cloth dipped in glaze to apply a layer of broken colour, it is much more subtle to rag-roll *off* – distressing a wet surface using a clean cloth. Because of the need to work quickly before the surface has a chance to dry, it is easier to use oil-based glazes rather than the swifter drying washes. It is also simpler to enlist the help of a partner so that one person can apply the glaze while the other follows closely behind distressing it.

Practice is essential to achieve a fluid movement down over the wall. It is better, if there are two of you, not to be tempted to swap roles from time to time: if a

single person does all the distressing, the pressure and the print will be consistent.

Experiment by folding the cloth in different ways, and try out different dilutions of glaze to get the effect you want. The cloth should be rolled in a variety of directions so that the finish does not look mechanical.

Using the Cloth
As in ragging, the type of cloth will determine the texture of the finish. Soft cotton is a good choice for rag-rolling – the closer the weave, the crisper the print. Whichever you choose, you must have a good supply of clean cloths, as you must take a fresh one frequently when each becomes sodden with glaze. Cloths can be used dry or dipped in solvent; wet cloths give a softer effect and do not clog up as readily.

Materials and Equipment
- oil- or water-based paint for the base coat
- oil- or water-based paint for making glaze or wash
- appropriate solvent: white spirit or turpentine for oil-based paints, water for emulsion (latex)
- artists' colours for tinting glaze or wash, if required
- paint container
- wide paintbrushes
- rubber gloves
- supply of clean cloths
- polyurethane varnish

METHOD

1 Apply base coat using a wide brush. Allow to dry overnight.
2 Make a glaze or wash by diluting paint with appropriate solvent in ratio between 1:1 and 1:3 of paint to solvent; experiment to get the right dilution. Tint with artists' colours if desired.
3 One person should then apply the glaze, working in vertical strips 60cm/2ft wide, so that paint is worked while it is still reasonably wet.
4 Soak rag in solvent if you want to achieve a soft effect. .
5 The second person should then form the rag into a sausage shape and roll it down over the wet glaze. Vary the direction and bunching of the rag to keep the prints irregular. Be careful not to skid across the surface. The more you dab at the paint, the softer the effect you will create.
   Change rags as they become soaked with paint.
6 Complete an entire wall at a time in order to avoid hard edges. Dab into corners using the end of the rolled-up cloth.
7 Surfaces that need protection, such as kitchen walls, should be coated with polyurethane varnish.

● Let discarded cloths dry out thoroughly before disposing of them – they are highly inflammable, particularly when stored in a confined space.

Illusionist Methods

For the beginner, it is best initially to attempt illusionist effects on a small scale, or to divide up a bigger area into workable sections such as panels or blocks. A good way to start is to study a piece of the material you want to represent and to practise copying the pattern and texture onto hardboard (masonite) or lining paper. You can retain the colours, scale and application of the original or you can opt for a more abstract and freer approach. Bear in mind, though, that you are unlikely to attain realism: that is very much in the province of the professional.

Although most of the effects described here can be achieved using water-based paints, for real depth and translucency it is better to use oil-based glazes.

Marbling
Unless you are marbling a black surface, it is easiest to work from light to dark. Apply several layers of a dirty-white glaze tinted with small amounts of raw umber or black. Distress each layer while it is still wet, using a rag or brush. While the surface is still workable, ciss it with white spirit. Choose a darker colour for the veining, and paint on fine lines with an artists' brush; while these are still wet, smudge the lines gently with a cloth or feather. Varnish to protect the painted surface.

Tortoise-shelling
Apply a base coat of yellow oil-based paint thinned 3:1 with white spirit or turpentine. When this is dry, paint on a layer of varnish, tinted brown and thinned 2:1

varnish to white spirit or turpentine. Distress the varnish with an artists' brush, working diagonally. Apply dots of varnish between the marks, and add squiggles of burnt umber and black oil paint following the same diagonals. Smudge gently with a dry brush and protect the surface with varnish.

Antiquing
Antiquing is the process of artificially ageing a surface. On walls this can be achieved by applying a wash or glaze tinted with a small amount of raw or burnt umber, so that the ground colour is softened and deepened. An aged white can be made in the same way.

To age woodwork, apply a light wash or glaze and rub off the excess; then sand down the surface so that the grain shows up in contrast.

Woodgraining

1

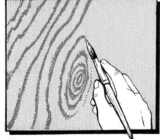
2

Woodgraining can be bold and decorative or it can restore a subtle suggestion of graininess. For a realistic effect, it is important to look at samples of the type of wood you wish to suggest and to practise copying its patterns of grain.

The basis of the technique is dragging. For the glaze, choose a colour slightly darker than the ground coat and drag with a dry brush to make parallel lines.

1 Distress the dragged surface while it is still wet by softening the lines with a dusting brush.

1

2

2 Draw the grain pattern on in chalk. Paint the grain in a deeper shade of glaze using an artists' brush. Print on 'knots', if desired, using cork or bunched blotting paper.

Remember that woodgraining is an effect that attempts to imitate nature, so avoid monotonous lines.

6

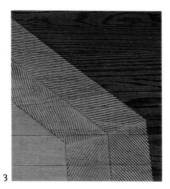

3

5

4

1 *Marbling decorates a hallway.*
2 *Rich tortoise-shelling*
3 *Bleaching, marbling and combing.*
4 *Aged walls decorated with painted cracks.*
5 *A combination of marbling and painted murals.*
6 *Supremely skilful trompe l'oeil.*

Distemper
One way to give walls a sense of depth and age is to paint them with distemper, which dries to give a soft, chalky finish. Distemper is no longer commercially available, but you can make your own. Bear in mind, however, that distemper is not compatible with modern paints: if you later decide you want to paint a distempered wall you will first have to strip it.

Recipe for Distemper
1 Mix decorators' glue according to the manufacturer's instructions. Leave to set – it should cool to a jelly.

2 Half-fill a small bucket with cold water and add a 3kg/11lb bag of whiting. The whiting should rise to the surface. Let it soak for an hour and then stir.
3 Reheat the glue until it is runny. Add it to the whiting mixture, stirring constantly. To tint, add powder-colour dissolved in cold water to the whiting mixture before you add the glue.
4 Use the distemper full-strength or, for a wash, diluted with water.

● An alternative to distemper, but which creates a similar effect, is thinned flat oil-based paint.

189

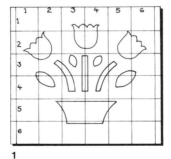

Stencilling

Stencilling is an extremely versatile technique and, with careful planning and a little practice, is quick and easy to do. Almost any surface, as long as it is not glossy or shiny, can be stencilled, including walls, floors, furniture and fabric.

A huge range of effects can be created, depending on the scale and design of the motif – from fresh and charming floral prints or traditional patterns to crisp, geometric designs. Stencilled borders or friezes can stand in for architectural detail where this is lacking; all-over stencilling adds a richness of pattern; handmade designs give interiors a personal touch.

Stencil Motifs
Pre-cut stencil kits are widely available and come in a variety of designs, but it is easy and satisfying to make your own. Inspiration can come from the patterns that already exist in the room – you can borrow motifs from curtain or upholstery fabric, repeat a detail of a cornice (crown moulding), or copy a pattern from a ceramic or rug. Geometric motifs are easier for the beginner, but with practice you can attain to simple freehand shapes.

After you have drawn out your design, experiment with different colour combinations, taking into account the colour of the background. Pin up colour sketches where you intend to stencil to assess how the tones work together.

Planning Patterns
The basic motif can be displayed on its own, as the central feature of a surface such as a table top or cupboard door, or it can be repeated in a continuous pattern, or in a line as a border or frieze. All of these applications require thorough planning to get the spacing right and you may need to make adjustments to the scale of the stencil for it to be effective.

Materials
The traditional method is to cut stencils from oiled stencil card, but using modern transparent acetate can make life easier. Because acetate is see-through, registration is much less necessary; also it can be wiped clean and keeps for longer. But film is more expensive than card and is sometimes fiddly to use.

There is a wide range of stencil paints available. Japan paints (oil-based) or acrylic paints (water-based) are the best, as they are very fast-drying, but emulsion (latex) is also a good choice for walls. Spray painting is a reasonable but inferior alternative to painting with a paint brush.

For furniture and floors use gloss or coloured wood stain, and then varnish to seal; for fabric use special fast-drying fabric paints.

Registration Marks
Because you will need to cut separate stencils for each colour, you must ensure that all of the overlays line up.

On acetate, it is a good idea to draw in the key elements of the rest of the design in dotted lines on each overlay, as an aid to registration. Alternatively, draw crosses at the four corners of each overlay. If you are using stencil card, lay the cut-outs over each other and punch through them with a nail to give a registration hole at each corner.

Making a Stencil
1 Draw or trace your design, then break down the pattern to incorporate bridges – uncut areas linking the openings to prevent the stencil from collapsing. Scale the pattern up or down if necessary, using either a photocopier or a grid system.
2 If using acetate, place the drawing under the film, secure with masking tape over the top. If using card, turn the drawing over and transfer to the card using carbon paper.
3 Cut out small areas before larger ones, so that you do not find yourself trying to cut fiddly details out of an

Equipment Checklist
- tracing paper for sketching or tracing outlines
- drawing paper or graph paper
- pencils, drawing pens, markers
- ruler, compass, setsquare (T-square), plumb line
- acetate or oiled stencil card
- cutting knife
- cutting mat
- masking tape
- stencil brushes
- stencil paint
- solvent
- varnish, if stencilling floor or furniture
- cleaning rags and paper towel
- old saucers or foil containers

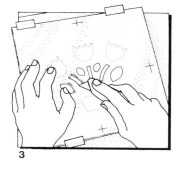

intolerably weakened stencil. Use a scalpel or craft knife, and cut towards you; for curves, turn the stencil, not the knife. Mistakes can be repaired using transparent adhesive tape.

4 Cut a separate stencil for each colour. Using dotted lines, sketch in the key elements of the rest of the design on each overlay. Make registration marks at the edges or corners.

5 Use paint sparingly to prevent seepage. Work most of the paint off onto dry paper towel, then dab brush on scrap paper until no blotches appear and the brush is almost dry.

6 Apply paint gradually, working inward from the outer edges. Use the brush lightly in circular movements. To check progress, gently lift the stencil. Complete one colour at a time and allow to dry before proceeding.

Eliminating Bridges
To eliminate bridges, break down the pattern into two or more stencils which can be superimposed to form a complete design.

● Work as cleanly as possible. Avoid getting paint under the stencil or on your hands. Drips can be mopped up with tissue moistened with solvent. Keep background colour on hand to touch up any mistakes.

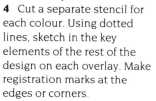

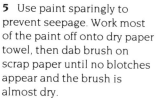

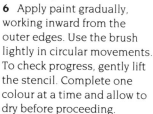

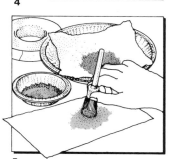

Turning Corners

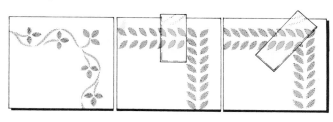

You can adapt a pattern so that the corner appears as an intentional part of the design.

The simplest method, if you cannot adapt the pattern, is to block the corner. Stop where the inside edge of the new border will go. Mask with acetate what you have just stencilled, then continue stencilling at right angles.

Borders

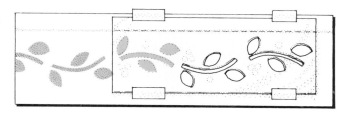

Using a spirit level (carpenter's level), draw a horizontal chalk line on the wall. Make a corresponding line on the stencil for registration. Fix the stencil in the right position with masking tape while you apply the colour.

To turn a corner, gently bend the stencil round, using acetate to mask off where it meets the other wall.

For a professional result, mitre the corner. Draw a diagonal line into the corner. Mask along the line on the side at right angles to the one that you are stencilling. Stencil up to the line and then, when the paint is dry, move the mask to the other side of the line and stencil down the other side.

Fabric Stencilling
The best fabric for stencilling is flat and even-weaved, such as pure cotton; avoid fabric with a pile, such as velvet or knitted jersey. Wash and iron the fabric first and then pin it to a smooth surface. Apply the paint through the stencil to the straight grain of the fabric, working in manageable sections. Once dry, heat-seal with a warm iron.

Painting a Child's Mural

Although mural painting sounds as if it must demand artistic expertise, if you take a careful step-by-step approach you will find that attractive and successful results are well within your reach. Very complex scenes, as well as *trompe l'oeil* – the height of decorative painting, aiming literally to 'deceive the eye' – do require great skill. But simpler figurative or geometric designs are easy to do and make particularly cheerful solutions for children's rooms.

Preparing the Surface
The wall should be in good condition: smooth, clean and nonabsorbent. Prepare by painting on an even base colour. Gloss does not make a suitable base for mural painting; emulsion (latex) is acceptable, but matt or mid-sheen oil-based paint is best.

Transferring the Design
The method shown here involves drawing a grid over the original picture, constructing to scale a larger grid on the wall, and then transferring the design square by square. The size of the grid's squares over those of your original illustration will depend on the complexity of the design. If it is very intricate, you will need a grid of 1cm/½in squares; if it is simple, the grid can have up to 5cm/2in squares.

An alternative method is to use a slide as your reference: project the image onto the wall and draw around the outlines. In either case, however, you will have to establish the horizontal and vertical outlines of the mural by using a plumb line and spirit level.

Materials
Emulsion (latex) paint or interior resin-based paint is the best choice for the beginner. You can use up left-overs from previous decorating jobs, sampler pots, and artists' colours for small areas and for tinting emulsion. You do not have to buy all the colours you need: basic shades can be mixed together to make inter-mediate tones. Remember to mix up enough for all the areas that are to be done in a particular colour – it is difficult to duplicate a shade if you have to remix.

Equipment Checklist
● drawing materials
● ruler and setsquare (T-square)
● chalk or charcoal
● plumb line and spirit level (carpenter's level)
● paint
● paint containers
● selection of brushes
● solvent
● stepladder, if necessary
● felt-tip pen for outlining
● clear matt polyurethane

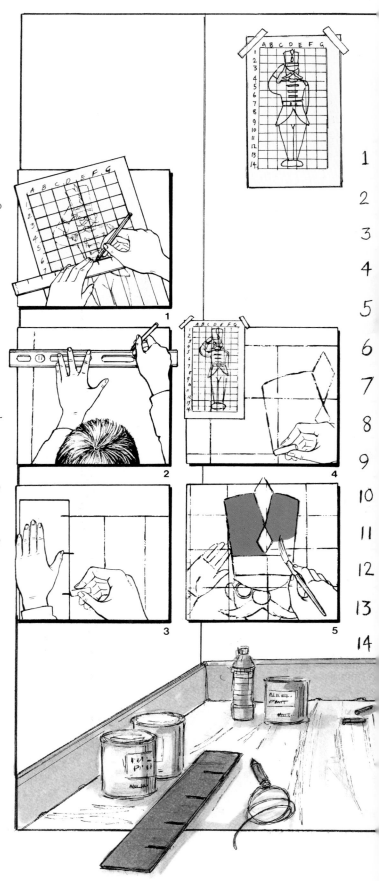

METHOD

1 Draw grid over original picture using ruler and setsquare. Label the grid with numbers and letters.

2 Transfer the outer lines onto the wall, using a plumb line for the verticals and a spirit level (carpenter's level) for the horizontals. Draw in lines with light-coloured chalk or charcoal.

3 Draw grid on wall, using a strip of card marked with grid squares. Use chalk or charcoal.

4 Mark the design on the wall, transferring it one square at a time from your design. Pin the original to the wall so you can refer to it constantly. Use a cloth to rub out incorrect lines.

5 Paint in areas of colour, working if possible from the top down. Complete larger areas first, one colour at a time, then paint details. Do not paint a second area adjoining a first until the paint on the first has dried. Some colours may need two coats. Highlights or special effects, such as stippling or shading, should be added last.

6 For a sharp crisp finish, outline in black, using a fine brush and ink or a felt-tip marker. Test the ink first to make sure it will not run when the varnish is applied.

7 Allow the mural to dry thoroughly, then wipe off the chalked grid lines using a damp cloth.

8 Seal with matt polyurethane varnish or, if you used emulsion (latex) paint, emulsion glaze.

● If you make a mistake, paint over the area with the background colour and leave it to dry. Then paint over again in the correct colour(s).

WALLCOVERINGS

As well as the many different paint effects, there are many other wall and ceiling coverings which you can use to create an interesting foundation for a decorative scheme. Wallpapers, paper-backed fabric and hessian (burlap), tiles, wood panelling and mirrors can all be applied relatively easily to a surface, adding a textural dimension often lacking in painted finishes.

WALLPAPERS

Printed Papers

The range of printed wallpapers is immense – not only in terms of colour and pattern but also in terms of cost, quality and practicability. In general, the cheaper papers tend to be thin and difficult to hang; also, they do not last long. Higher-quality papers are thicker and better-printed. At the extreme end of the market, there are very expensive hand-printed papers, including reproductions of antique designs printed from the original blocks.

Aside from plain white lining paper, which is designed to provide an even surface for decorating, the special attraction of wallpaper lies in the pattern. The range of designs available has enlarged considerably in recent years: it includes traditional varieties, such as Regency stripes and floral motifs, as well as cheerful figurative prints for children's rooms and sophisticated modern geometrics. Many papers are

coordinated with fabrics and wall tiles and some are available with contrasting or complementary friezes.

All printed papers are treated to repel moisture and promote maintenance, but the degree of protection varies. 'Spongeable' papers can be wiped down; 'washable' papers, coated with plastic film, can be washed with water. Vinyls – wallpapers coated with thick plastic film – can actually be scrubbed; they are designed for use in kitchens and bathrooms.

Textured Papers

The chief advantage of textured papers is that they are useful for covering irregular surfaces. These relief papers are generally embossed with wood and pulp, and are designed to be painted. Other types include the once-fashionable flock paper with a cut-pile surface and relief simulations of panelling or plasterwork.

Other Paper-backed Coverings

Today you can obtain hessian (burlap), grasses and other natural fibres with paper backing, allowing you to hang them like ordinary wallpaper. Often in neutral shades, these provide a subtle textural interest but tend to be difficult to clean and not very robust.

Order of Papering a Room

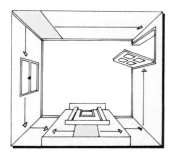

There is a correct order for papering a room if you are to disguise any slight overlaps which may occur. For papers with small or random patterns, it is usual to start in the corner adjacent to the window wall and work away from the source of natural light towards the door, so that overlaps do not cast shadows and are thus less immediately noticeable.

ESTIMATING THE NUMBER OF ROLLS

British Wallpaper

Wall Height	Distance Around Room (including doors and windows)												
	30ft 9.1m	34ft 10.4m	38ft 11.6m	42ft 12.8m	46ft 14.0m	50ft 15.2m	54ft 16.4m	58ft 17.7m	62ft 18.9m	66ft 20.1m	70ft 21.3m	74ft 22.6m	78ft 23.9m
8ft/2.45m	5	5	6	7	7	8	9	9	10	10	11	12	12
9ft/2.75m	6	6	7	7	8	9	9	10	10	11	12	12	13
10ft/3.05m	6	7	8	8	9	10	10	11	12	13	13	14	15

Calculations based on roll measuring 20½in × 34ft/52cm × 10.3m

American Wallpaper

Wall Height	Distance Around Room (including doors and windows)												
	32ft 9.7m	36ft 11.0m	40ft 12.2m	44ft 13.4m	48ft 14.6m	52ft 15.8m	56ft 17.1m	60ft 18.3m	64ft 19.5m	68ft 20.7m	72ft 21.9m	76ft 23.2m	80ft 24.4m
8ft/2.45m	8	9	10	11	12	13	14	15	16	17	18	19	20
9ft/2.75m	9	10	11	12	14	15	16	17	18	19	20	21	22
10ft/3.05m	10	11	12	14	15	16	17	19	20	21	22	23	25

Calculations based on roll measuring 18in (when trimmed) × 24ft/45.7cm × 7.3m

Wallpapers

1, 2   Metallic
    3   Borders
    4   Relief
    5   Flock
    6   Border
    7   Linen
    8   Flock
    9   Suedette
  10   Woodchip
  11   Leatherette
  12   Hessian (burlap)
  13   Silk
  14   Coarse woven
  15   Patterned
  16   Trompe l'oeil
  17   Moiré
  18   Patterned
  19   William Morris design
  20   Paint effects
  21   Victorian design
  22   Bamboo trellis
  23   Large floral
  24   Borders
  25   Small floral
  26   Festoons
  27   Bows
28, 29   Large floral
  30   Borders

Successful Decorating
WALLCOVERINGS

Hanging Wallpaper

When you buy your wallpaper ensure that an extra roll with the same batch number will be available. Otherwise, if you need to buy more you may end up with a roll bearing a different batch number and the shades of colour may vary. Wallpaper should be hung on a sound, even, dry surface. Very poor surfaces may need replastering; alternatively, you may just have to line or cross-line with lining paper.

Establishing a Vertical
Once you have decided on a starting position, you need to establish a vertical so that the lengths of paper are correctly aligned.

Measure out from the corner of the wall a distance that is 1cm/½in less than the full width of the paper, and mark it top, middle and bottom.

Hang a plumb line from the top of the wall aligning with the mark nearest the corner and mark along it at intervals. Join up the marks using a straightedge. This pencilled line is the vertical you will use for aligning the first length of paper. The same process must be repeated each time a corner is turned.

Pasting
Some wallpapers are available pre-pasted, but if you are pasting the paper

yourself you will need a trestle table or a folding pasting table on which to lay out lengths of paper. To avoid getting paste on the table and the consequent risk of spoiling the next length of paper, some decorators let the paper overhang the table by 2cm/1in, but it can be difficult to paste edges if they have no support. Keep a clean sponge and water on hand, and wipe away any paste which does get onto the table.

Most papers need to be left for a while to allow the paste to soak in. Papers with definite patterns should be pasted and hung one length at a time, so that soaking times do not vary – a length left for too long will stretch irregularly and may not match the previous one.

Materials and Equipment
- rolls of wallpaper: buy enough for the job, and record the batch number
- wallpaper paste, as recommended by the manufacturer
- pasting table
- plumb line and bob
- pencil
- straightedge
- stepladder
- paperhanging shears
- sharp-pointed scissors for trimming
- pasting brush and bucket
- paperhanging brush
- sponge

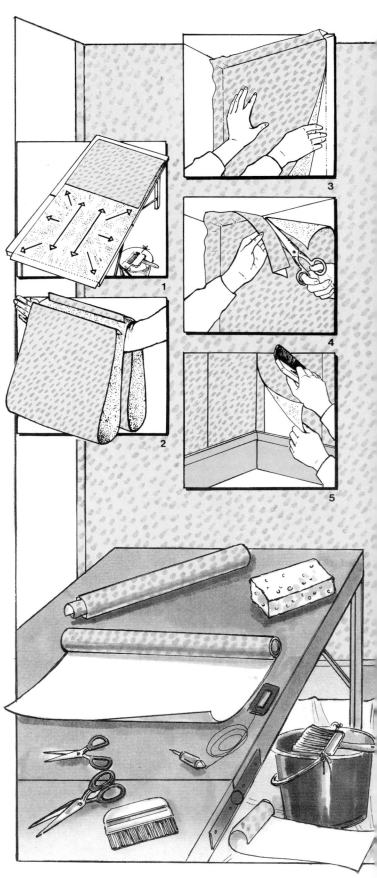

METHOD

1 Apply paste down centre and work outwards. Fold pasted end in and paste second half.

2 Fold paper ends-to-middle and carry to the wall draped over your arm. Turn over ends of paper.

3 Position first length against pencilled vertical, overlapping the ceiling by 5cm/2in and running to about 1cm/½in from the adjacent wall. Brush from the centre out.

4 Score along the ceiling line with the back of the scissors, peel back paper and cut along crease. Brush paper back in place and repeat at skirting level.

5 To turn an internal corner, measure the distance to the corner at the top, middle and bottom of the wall, adding 1cm/½in to the widest distance to allow for overlap. Cut and paste in position. Measure width of offcut from corner and mark vertically this distance from the corner onto the side wall. Paste the offcut, aligning the uncut edge with the vertical line so that the cut edge covers the overlap.

6 To turn an external corner, measure the distance to the corner at the top, middle and bottom, adding 2.5cm/1in to the widest distance to allow for turn. Paste in position but do not brush down. Mark a vertical (using a plumb line) 2.5cm/1in less than the width of the remaining piece on the adjacent wall. Hang offcut to vertical line, and brush overlap down.

7 To paper around a doorway, cut away any excess before pasting and make a diagonal cut into the corners of the door frame. Score around the door frame, peel the paper back and trim. Brush in towards the angle.

197

Wallpapering Ceilings and Details

Papering a Ceiling

The basic method is the same as that for papering walls. Work away from the light, marking a line across the ceiling the width of the paper, less 1cm/½in for overlap. Cut a length of paper, allowing 10cm/4in excess (5cm/2in at each end). Paste and loop the paper into accordion-like folds. Position the paper according to the line and brush down from one end, supporting the folds with a roll of wallpaper. Score and trim overlaps.

Papering a ceiling is very difficult for a beginner working alone. It is far better to get a helper to support the paper while you work.

Papering Around a Switch

To paper around a flush plate, first make sure you turn the electricity off at the mains supply or fuse box. Hang the paper down to the switch and cut diagonally from the middle to each corner.

Partially unscrew the switch plate and pull away from the wall. Trim off excess paper, leaving 3–4mm/⅛in to brush behind the plate. Screw the plate back in place and restore electricity.

To paper around a circular switch make star-shaped cuts out to the edge of the switch, score around the edge and trim off the surplus paper. This method can also be used to paper around ceiling roses (medallions).

● Try to catch bubbles early on by looking sideways at each length before positioning the next piece. Peel the paper back to the bubble and brush out. If the paste has dried, use a sharp knife to cut a cross through the bubble. Peel back the four flaps and paste.

Papering an Archway

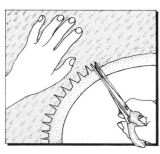

Paper the facing wall first, allowing an extra 2.5cm/1in of paper around the inside of the arch. Cut v-shaped pieces out of this hem so that you are left with a 'saw-tooth' effect. Turn in the 'teeth' so that they lie flat on the inside of the arch. Then measure the width of the arch and cut two lengths of paper, one to run up each side so that they meet at the centre top.

SAFETY Always turn the electricity off at the mains (or fusebox) before unscrewing light switches or sockets (outlets). Never brush metallic or foil wallcoverings behind switches or sockets.

Fitting Around a Fireplace

Cut off excess paper. Make a diagonal cut to the corner and score a line along the top. Snip into the paper to fit around mouldings. Peel back the paper and cut along the scored lines.

Patching Damaged Paper

Tear off the damaged paper, ensuring that the paper left around the hole is firmly stuck down. Select a piece of matching paper; if the paper has a pattern, hold it over the hole and adjust its position until the pattern fits into place. Tear a patch roughly to size, and peel off a narrow 3mm/¹⁄₁₀in strip from the back around the edges. Paste in place, aligning the pattern.

1 *Wallpaper in a muted stripe makes a sympathetic background for a period room. The paper is continued below the dado rail, and care has been taken to match the stripes exactly.*

Borders and Friezes

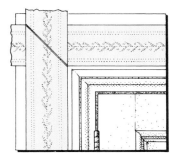

Borders and friezes can be applied to any sound surface (not over heavily embossed paper). Use a pencil line as a guide for position and cut a length of border to fit across the entire length of wall. Paste the border and loop it up so that it is easier for you to position correctly. Brush out, letting out the loops as you work along.

Corners – for example, around a door or window frame – should be mitred. Paste the borders in place, overlapping the ends where they meet, and then draw a diagonal line across the corner, using a straightedge. Cut along the line, through both layers, using a sharp knife. Remove the excess pieces and smooth the others back into place.

● Mark the exact position of screw holes by inserting a matchstick or toothpick in each, leaving 0.5cm/¼in protruding. This will pierce the paper as it is brushed on.

Matching Patterns

Wallpapers with definite patterns are either 'straight' (aligned horizontally) or 'drop' (aligned diagonally). Because lengths of paper are laid side by side across the wall (butt-jointed) and not overlapped, the patterns must match along each length of paper.

Cut the first length of paper about 10cm/4in longer than the depth of the wall; this allows a margin of 5cm/2in at both top and bottom for trimming. Before cutting the second length, match the pattern with the first, again allowing a 10cm/4in excess. Number each length consecutively as it is cut and mark which end is the top.

To avoid wastage when cutting 'drop' patterns, it may be necessary to cut alternately from two rolls at once. Even so, wastage is unavoidable.

Special Effects
You can create your own wallpaper by using thick writing paper, marbled paper or even photocopies of interesting prints to line a wall. This is best attempted on a small area and the surface should be sealed with a coat of polyurethane (which will yellow with age). An alternative is to stencil your own design on plain wallpaper and seal.

Large Patterns

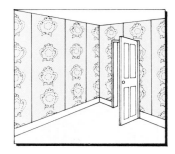

If the paper has a large pattern, it should be centred on a focal point, such as a chimney breast, or on a wall which is the focus of attention in the room.

From the starting point, work in sequence around the room. Whichever way you go, plan to finish in the least important corner or at a doorway, since it will almost certainly be impossible to match the pattern on the last length. If your wallpaper has a large pattern, ensure that the first length features a complete motif near the top of the wall so that broken motifs are near the floor.

2 *Borders lend distinction to a papered room, particularly if the paper has been applied to the ceiling as well as the walls. Here, a paper with a tiny sprig motif has been enhanced by a bold border fixed around the window and defining the bath alcove.*

2

Tiling and Cladding

A variety of hard materials can be used to cover walls and other built-in surfaces. Many of these improve insulation and most are easy to maintain as well as being highly decorative.

Ceramic Tiles

The most popular form of hard wallcovering, ceramic tiles are available today in a huge range of colours, patterns, finishes and sizes, from expensive handmade originals to mass-produced types. Cost varies accordingly.

Tiles are generally glazed, but unglazed and textured varieties are available, too. Most tiles have squared or bevelled edges, but you can buy them with one or two rounded sides for use as edging; also, special coping tiles are made for covering joints (for example, around a bathtub). Some tiles incorporate spacing lugs (pegs) to ensure the joint lines between all the tiles are uniform in thickness.

Tiles are ideal for bathrooms or kitchens, or wherever surfaces need to be wiped down regularly. All tiles are fixed with ceramic tile adhesive and are easy to hang. But, although they have tremendous practical advantages, there is no reason why tiles should look utilitarian, or be used purely for utilitarian purposes.

Manufacturers produce tiles as an element of an entire decorative range, so that you can coordinate their motifs with curtain fabrics and/or wallpaper, or simply achieve a precise colour match.

Plain tiled walls can be enlivened by a contrasting or patterned border, by cheerful coloured grouting, or by insetting occasional handmade or antique tiles. Simple patterns can be created by alternating colours or by laying tiles in a diagonal or herringbone design.

Mirrors

Mirror tiles and sheets of mirror are both effective ways of maximizing light and space in a small area such as a bathroom. Mirror tiles are cheaper and easier to install than sheets of mirror. Both require a flat surface; a large expanse of mirror may need to be mounted professionally. And both need to be kept clean to look their best.

Wood Panelling

This is a traditional way of adding richness and warmth to a room. Today the most common type is tongue-and-groove panelling, mounted on battens (furring strips). As well as its textural qualities, wood is a good insulator and is long-lasting, but it is not a cheap way of covering a wall. However, panelling can be very effective in limited

applications – for example, up to half-height as a dado (wainscot), or to cover the side of a bath. It can also be varnished, stained or painted.

A less expensive way of achieving a similar effect can be gained by using manufactured boards, such as plywood, blockboard or hardboard (masonite) faced with veneer. Cork, too, can be used as a wall covering, although it does not wear as well as wood. Available in rolls or tiles, it can be protected by coating with polyurethane varnish. Some cork tiles are supplied with a protective coating already applied to their surface for greater durability.

Preparation for Tiling

Before you start, make sure all the surfaces are sound, level and dry. Small cracks and irregularities can be filled with a commercially available filler; a really bad surface will need replastering or lining with plasterboard (drywall). If the walls are papered, you will have to strip them; a painted finish can be simply sanded down to give a key.

Tiles can easily be laid over existing tiles as long as these are sound and firmly fixed.

Bathroom treatments *red and white border (**1**); 'crazy' tiling inset with mirror (**2**); diagonal pattern in white (**3**); redwood panelling (**4**).*

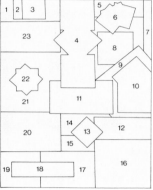

Wall Tiles and Cladding

1 *Glazed mosaic*
2 *Hand-pressed terracotta*
3 *Glazed Mexican*
4 *Dutch style*
5 *Wood-effect laminate*
6 *Glazed Mexican*
7 *Relief border*
8 *High glaze*
9 *Paint effect laminate*
10 *Dutch style*
11 *Patterned*
12 *Hand-pressed terracotta*
13 *Glazed Mexican*
14, 15 *Checkerboard with floral border*
16 *Glazed relief with border*
17 *Tongue-and-groove pine cladding*
18 *Relief border*
19 *Cork*
20 *Glazed terracotta*
21 *Glazed mosaic*
22 *Glazed Mexican*
23 *Relief pattern*

Tiling a Bathroom

Tiling is a particularly good solution for bathroom surfaces. However, most bathrooms present a number of challenges such as recesses, sills, ledges and pipework. The first step is to decide where you want to tile. In a small room, it often looks better to extend the tiling all the way up to the wall rather than stop at half or three-quarter height.

Making a Tile Gauge
The next step is to plan the position of the tiles. The best way to start is to make a tile gauge: mark tile-widths along a length of wooden batten and use this to judge where tiles are going to have to be cut to fit around a window, sink or other obstruction. Try to avoid gaps that are less than half a tile wide.

Starting Position
Using a spirit level, establish a horizontal line no more than one tile width up from the floor, and temporarily nail a wooden batten below it. Work out how many tiles will

fit along the wall, leaving large enough gaps at either end. Using a plumb line, draw a vertical line down the wall to mark where the first whole tile will go. Fix the whole tiles first; when the adhesive has dried, the gaps can be filled with cut pieces.

Materials and Equipment
- tiles – most straight-edged, some with rounded edges
- combined adhesive and grout (water-resistant if necessary)
- notched spreader or trowel for applying adhesive
- tile gauge, made from length of wooden batten
- battens (furring strips)
- pencil, metal rule and spirit level (carpenter's level)
- spacers, if tiles are not bevelled or have no spacing lugs (pegs)
- pincer-action tile cutter
- tile saw
- pincers or pliers
- tile file, sandpaper or carborundum stone
- grout, coloured if desired
- squeegee or sponge
- rubber latex sealant

METHOD
1 Use a small trowel to apply adhesive. Work at an angle of about 45 degrees and in patches 1m/3ft square. Using a notched spreader pull the adhesive into ridges to ensure good suction. Do not cover your pencilled line. Place the bottom edge of the tile against the wooden batten and lower into place ensuring that its

vertical edge is aligned with the vertical line marked on the wall. Press firmly. Position next tile. If tiles have no lugs, insert spacers. Finish one horizontal row before starting on the next. When the whole area of adhesive is covered, check straightness with a spirit level. Sponge off excess adhesive. Allow to dry.

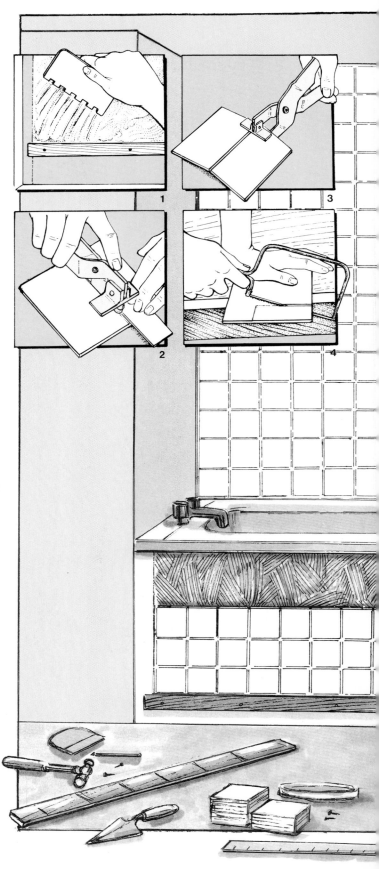

5

6

7

2 To fill gaps, measure the area to be filled with a metal rule. Draw line on tile to mark where it should be cut, and score through glaze using the wheel on a pincer-action cutter.

3 Break the tiles using the pincer-action cutter. When handles are brought together over the scored mark, the tile breaks cleanly.

4 To cut awkward shapes, score a line deeply through the glaze. Then cut the tile with a tile saw. Work slowly and gently. Alternatively, use pliers or pincers to 'nibble' the shape away bit by bit.

5 Smooth the rough edge of a cut tile with a suitable file held at an angle of 45 degrees. Work downwards, away from the glaze. Alternatively, use a small carborundum stone.

6 For joints between surfaces, such as at ledges or sills, fix tiles on vertical surfaces first and then lay tiles with rounded edges along the horizontal surface to create a finished joint. Many tiles have squared, glazed edges which form an equally finished joint. Special edging strips (plastic beading, or moulding) are also available.

7 Allow 12 hours for adhesive to dry before removing the batten and tiling the bottom row. Allow a further 24 hours before removing the spacers and beginning to grout. Mix grout with water to a creamy consistency. Rub into joints using a squeegee or damp sponge and wipe off surplus with a damp cloth. For a really professional look, run a rounded stick along the grout lines to point up.

203

Tiling Details

Cutting a Hole in a Tile

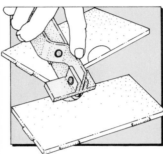

To accommodate a pipe or similar obstacle, first measure the hole and make a pattern, or template, out of thick cardboard. Use this pattern to score the circle on the tile, and then score a straight line to bisect it. Snap the tile in half and cut out each semicircle with a tile saw or tile cutters.

Fixing Sheets of Mosaic

Tiny squares of mosaic or mirror tiles are available in sheet form, with a paper backing. These are easy to fix – each tile comes with its own pad of adhesive already applied and grouting is not required. You must ensure, however, that the wall surface is even and flat. If necessary, the wall should be lined with a 1cm/½in-thick sheet of plywood or chipboard (particleboard) screwed in the right position.

2 *Fragments of broken tiles, both plain and patterned, set randomly in a crazy border, make an original design between bands of deep blue hand-glazed tiles.*

1 *Brilliant white grouting lines make an effective contrast to the deep green tiles on the work surface. Different tiles, with a softer, Provencal-style pattern, have been chosen for the wall area below the kitchen cabinets. Tiling is a particularly practical choice for kitchen surfaces.*

Tiling a Recess
To tile a window recess or a ledge around a bathtub, lay the tiles on the horizontal surface first before you tile the sides and top. Plan the tiling so that the cut tiles are at the rear and the whole tiles are at the front. Use tiles with glazed edges for a border.

Grouting Effects
You can make a feature of grouting by adding dye either to grout powder or to ready-mixed grout. To change the colour of existing grouting, make sure the lines are clean and dry and follow the manufacturer's instructions.

Cladding

Wood Panelling

The most popular form of wood panelling is tongue-and-groove, which is usually fixed to battens (furring strips) nailed to the wall. Boards can be laid horizontally or vertically, depending on the look you want to create. Note that you can never panel over damp walls.

Store the boards for a few days in the room where they will be used to allow their moisture content to adjust. Boards not left to adjust properly could shrink and pull apart after fitting. Panelling should be stopped slightly short of the ceiling to allow airflow and expansion.

3 Pine panelling encloses a tiny lavatory; the warmth and texture of the surface contrasts with the polished brass fixtures.

Fixing the Panels

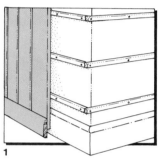

1

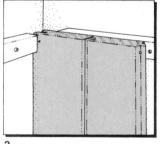

2

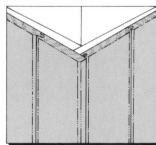

3

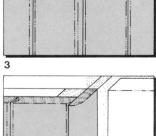

4

1 Battens should run at right angles to the direction of the boards. They should be fixed directly to the wall using masonry nails or screws and wall plugs, spacing the battens by about 0.5m/20in. The new panelling can then be nailed on, with a new skirting board (baseboard) fitted at the bottom.
2 The method of fixing shown here is secret-nailing. Start by butting a groove end into the corner. Then nail at an angle through the tongue. Tap the groove of the next board over the tongue, protecting with an offcut if necessary.
3 For internal or external corners, the tongued edge of the last board is cut off to butt against or overlap the grooved end of the next board. For a professional look, the corner can be finished off with a decorative moulding to hide the nails.
4 Remove architraves or window frames and add battens around the opening, leaving a margin so that a strip of moulding can be applied to cover the battens and the edge of the end board to finish.

Light switches can be framed in the same way. Alternatively, employ an electrician to bring them out flush with the panelling by putting packing behind the plate covering. Do not attempt this yourself.

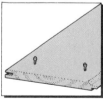
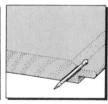

Fixing Methods

There are three basic ways of fixing boards to battens (furring strips). The simplest is face-nailing, where nails are driven through the face of the board. The nail head can be sunk with a nail punch and the hole filled, or it can be left flush with the surface.

Secret-nailing takes longer but the result is invisible. The nail is hammered diagonally through the tongue of the board and is covered when the groove of the next board slots into place.

There are also special metal clips which can be used to fix boards. These fit onto the groove of a board and are nailed to the batten.

To fix the first board, you will need a starting clip. Nail this into the corner and then cut off the groove of the first board and slide the end onto the spikes of the clip.

Fabric Finishes

Fabric-lined rooms are luxurious. There are paper-backed materials, which are applied like wallpaper, but more excitingly fabrics can be draped, gathered or shirred to create a soft, intimate atmosphere. Alternatively you can stretch fabric over wooden battens to give an upholstered look. All of these effects are particularly good at disguising poor surfaces and correcting proportional defects in a room.

Although covering walls in fabric is an extravagant way of using material, you do not

1 *In this bedroom, a simple wooden frame has been constructed and covered in shirred fabric to give the impression of a four-poster bed.*

need to opt for the most expensive. Inexpensive lightweight cottons, such as muslin or cheesecloth, are ideal for shirring or gathering.

Simple Drapery
Lengths of material draped over poles or rods can make decorative frames for beds, alcoves, mirrors, windows and doors.

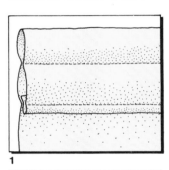

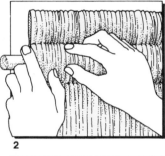

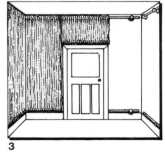

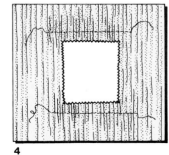

Gathered Wall Coverings
Choose a fabric which is light enough to gather up easily. Calculate the amount required by first measuring the height and width of the wall. Allow 1½–2 times the width for gathering, and add 10cm/4in to the height for hems. Then divide the fabric width (less selvedges) into the total width and multiply the number of widths by the total height to find the length of fabric you require.

1 Make casings at the top and bottom of each fabric length. Fold 5cm/2in of fabric over to the wrong side and machine stitch 2.5cm/1in below the fold. Then turn the hem under and machine-stitch in position.
2 Gather fabric by inserting rod, dowel or curtain wire into the casings at top and bottom. Rods, dowels or wires should extend to the full width of the area. Fix rods or dowels to wall with wardrobe (closet) or curtain rod brackets; wires can be tacked in position.
3 Short panels may be required over doors and around windows.
4 To hang fabric over an obstacle – such as a light switch – first mark the area and cut to within 1cm/½in. Then trim the edges and work a row of gathering stitches top and bottom. Unscrew the switch plate, pull up gathers to fit and fix plate back.

Making a Tented Ceiling

This method of tenting is suitable for square or nearly square rooms.

1 Decide where to position the tenting – level with a door frame, window frame or picture rail, for example. Draw a line around the room at this point and fix wooden battens at the required height. Mark the central point of the ceiling with a dot.

2 Make a paper pattern by cutting out a large triangle, with a base measuring the distance between two corners and two equal sides which are the distance between the central dot and a corner. Cut the triangle in half and insert a rectangular piece between the two halves. The rectangular piece should be the width of the base of each half triangle.

Cut out four fabric pieces according to the pattern, adding seam allowances.

3 Stitch pieces together. Press seams open and finish off, for example, by pinking. Make a casing around the central opening, insert drawstring and pull tight. Stitch two rows of gathering around the perimeter and pleat up fabric until it is the width of the battens. Suspend tenting from cup hook securely screwed into a ceiling joist at the central point. Fix the perimeter to battens and trim with braid or ribbon to finish.

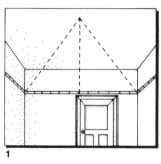

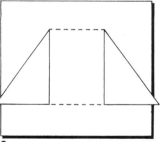

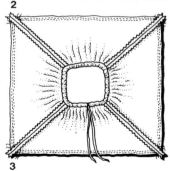

2 *Lined furnishing fabric has been fixed and draped to create a dramatic headboard for this bed. A similar effect can be used behind sofas positioned against walls.*

Joining Fabric Wall Coverings

Some fabrics, such as hessian (burlap), are available paper-backed. They can be hung and butt-jointed like wallpaper. Unbacked 'furnishing' hessian can be stuck by applying wallpaper paste to the wall. To join, overlap edges by about 2.5cm/1in then cut through the double thickness, down the whole length, using a sharp craft knife or scalpel held against a metal straightedge. Peel back both strips and remove the excess. Smooth back into place with a brush.

SAFETY Always turn the electricity off at the mains (or fuse box) before unscrewing light fittings.

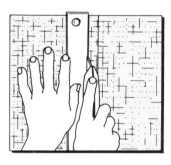

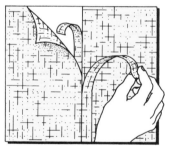

Covering Walls with Fabric

Although fabric can be stuck directly to walls (paste should be applied to the wall, not the fabric), the result can look flat. For a softer, more upholstered effect, fabric should be fixed by stretching it over a framework of wooden battens to provide an even surface. For a really professional finish line the walls first with a layer of polyester wadding (batting) stapled in position.

Calculating Fabric Quantities

Measure the height and width of the area you want to cover. Divide the total width by the width of the fabric (less selvedges) and multiply by the height, plus 5cm/2in.

Plain or randomly patterned fabrics are easiest to work with. Fabrics with definite patterns need to be matched across the wall, and so to get them right you will have to accept that there will be more wastage.

Positioning Wooden Battens

Horizontal battens will be needed at the top and bottom of the wall; vertical ones should be spaced evenly, taking into account windows, doors and other obstacles. If you intend to hang pictures or mirrors on the finished walls, establish where they will go and fix the battens in these places.

Trimming

Fabric can be fixed so that the joins between panels are invisible. But alternatively you can also make a feature of the joins, by covering the staples with contrasting or coordinating trim. Ribbon, braid or fabric-covered strips will give a smart, tailored appearance and introduce graphic interest to a room lacking architectural detail.

Fabric-fixing System

As an alternative to using wooden battens there is a product which enables fabric to be clipped in position without stapling or gluing. This consists of metal or plastic track which you mount around the wall. Previously seamed fabric is stretched and gripped in place by the track. This system enables fabric to be taken down easily for cleaning.

Materials and Equipment
- fabric, cut in lengths
- polyester wadding (batting), if desired
- wooden battens
- screwdriver
- countersunk screws
- hammer
- tacks
- staple gun and staples
- pencil
- straightedge
- braid, ribbon or other trim
- cardboard strips for invisible joins, if desired
- glue

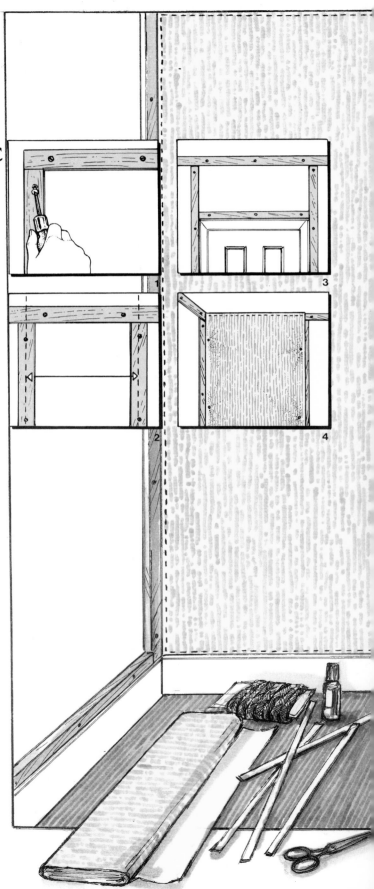

208

METHOD

1 Fix horizontal wooden battens first. The bottom batten can be fixed just above the floor or skirting board (baseboard). Screw in place with countersunk screws.
2 Space vertical battens one fabric width apart, less selvedges (see arrow). Pencil lines on wall where the fabric joins will go and centre battens on these lines.
3 Frame obstacles such as doorways, windows, switches and sockets (outlets). The fabric will be stapled to the outer edge of the battens.
4 Position first fabric panel and tack temporarily, driving tacks in halfway. Staple top edge. Pull fabric taut and staple bottom, then sides, removing tacks.
5 Make invisible joins by placing the second panel wrong-side up over the first. Insert a thin cardboard strip the length of the panel and staple in position.
6 Pull the panel to right side, leaving 2.5cm/1in turned over.
7 Finish off by covering bare staples with braid, ribbon or fabric strips glued in place.

FLOORS

Always on view and taking up a large proportion of the surface area in any room, the floor has a great impact on the decorative scheme in terms of colour, texture, pattern and style. But a floor must also fulfil certain practical requirements – requirements that vary from room to room and household to household. It may be required to wear well; be warm, safe or non-slip; be easy to maintain, resilient or sound- or heat-insulating. In addition to these considerations, new floors and floor coverings represent a large investment of either time or money or, usually, both. Whatever you choose may well have to outlast several changes of the rest of the room's decorative treatments.

From wall-to-wall carpeting to quarry tiles, wood strip to sheet vinyl, there is a great variety of types and styles of floor covering from which to choose. Careful assessment and sound research is necessary if you are to find the solution that suits your tastes and needs.

Combinations of different types of floor surface can be very effective: coir matting with kelims; slate with stone; polished floorboards with area rugs. And, because of the practical demands of different areas, it is unlikely that you will want to extend the same type of flooring throughout your home. For these reasons it is important not to consider each room in isolation: the view from area to area and details such as the junctions between different floor coverings will contribute to the success of the overall result.

bleaching or painting.

To install a new wood floor, it is important to select the right type and quality. Common varieties include pine, beech, mahogany, oak, walnut, maple and elm, but there are other, more exotic, species as well. Different widths of board are available, depending on the type.

Wood for flooring must be properly dried and seasoned. The moisture content should suit the conditions of the room where the boards will be laid (6–8 per cent moisture content if there is underfloor heating; 10–14 per cent if there is central heating), as otherwise shrinking or swelling may occur. Ideally, wood should be left unwrapped in the room where it is going to be fitted for at least two days.

When laying a new floor, you must establish first

where cables and pipes run to avoid nailing through them. Boards can be nailed to joists; tongue-and-groove boards can be slotted together and secret-nailed to joists or to a wooden subfloor.

Ready-made Wood Floors
Manufactured wood floors are available in different woods – usually either in a hardwood or in a softwood with a hardwood veneer – and in different colours. They can be laid in simple patterns. Most are presealed and designed to interlock.

Strip or parquet floors should be laid on level plywood or hardboard (masonite) subfloors; wood block and mosaic on concrete screed, ply or chipboard (particleboard). Fixing is either by adhesive or by interlocking and secret-nailing.

WOOD FLOORS
A wood floor is a classic surface that wears well, improves with age and complements modern as well as period decoration. Costs vary: renovating existing floorboards is one of the cheapest flooring solutions; installing new parquet can be expensive.

Wood floors come in different forms: boards (of varying widths), ready-made strip or parquet, mosaic tiles or panels, and blocks. Many

types of wood, both hardwoods and softwoods, are suitable; a local supplier can advise on different varieties. Also sheets or boards of manmade woods, such as hardboard (masonite), chipboard (particleboard) and plywood, can be used to create stylish and economical floors.

Boards
Existing floorboards can be prepared and sanded, and then finished off by sealing,

1

Manufactured Boards

Although these cheap, manufactured boards are essentially designed to make an even surface for wood, tiles or other covering, they can also be used in their own right. They are not particularly resilient, however, and are badly affected by water.

Hardboard (masonite) can be painted or sealed to promote durability. Lay it smooth side up, beginning at the mid-point of the room, and fit a border around the edges to finish.

Tongue-and-groove chipboard (particleboard) can be fixed with adhesive and secured with nails around the edges of the room.

Plywood is available in tongue-and-groove boards or in squares, and can be painted, stained, or varnished to a high gloss.

Finishes

Apart from presealed manufactured floors, all new and renovated wood must be treated in some way to prevent the surface from degrading. The simplest method is to seal it with several coats of transparent wood sealer – but bear in mind that polyurethane tends to yellow with age. An alternative is to apply several layers of wax polish.

To lighten dark floors you can bleach wood using a solution of household bleach and water. Rinse off well. A similar 'limed' effect can be created by using a whitewash or white oil-based paint.

Floors can also be stained. As well as natural colours, a wide variety of bright stains is available today. Work quickly, using a soft cloth to rub the stain into the grain.

1 *A gleaming polished wood floor.*
2 *Duck-egg blue floorboards.*
3 *Trompe l'oeil oriental rug painted on a wooden floor plays a visual trick.*

Liming Floorboards

For liming, you can use special limed wax, white paint thinned with white spirit or turpentine, or gesso; mix the gesso so that it is reasonably runny. You will need a supply of clean, dry cloths. Limed boards should be sealed with a two-part varnish for durability.

1 Paint the gesso along the length of the board, working 90cm/3ft at a time. Work board-by-board to avoid unsightly lines.
2 Wipe the paint off with a clean rag, pulling strokes along the length of the board and leaving paint in the cracks. Leave to dry.

Painting Floorboards

If floorboards are not attractive enough simply to be sealed, you can paint them. Make sure the surface is dry and clean, apply several coats of undercoat to act as a primer, and then apply a topcoat of oil-based gloss, eggshell or special floor paint. Deck or marine paint can also be used, and is very durable, but it is hard to apply and takes a long time to dry. In addition, it is available only in a limited range of colours.

Simple patterns can be created by alternating colours, by stencilling a border, or by scoring a design into the floor with a knife so that colours do not run.

1

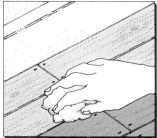

2

211

Laying Wooden Mosaic Tiles

Wooden mosaic tiles are manufactured panels made up of blocks of wood in a basket weave pattern. Solid or veneered, they are designed to be easy for the amateur to lay.

After you have bought the tiles, unwrap them and leave them for at least two days in the room where you plan to lay them. This allows the wood to 'condition', or adjust to the temperature and humidity of the room.

Mosaic tiles can be laid in any room – they are designed to be multi-purpose – but it is essential that the surface is properly prepared: it must be clean, dry and level. For best results on floorboards, cover them with hardboard (masonite).

Most mosaic tiles are already sanded and sealed. If you buy unfinished tiles, sand them after laying. After 1 or 2 weeks, apply three or more coats of the appropriate sealant to protect.

Establishing a Starting Point

Tiles are laid from the mid-point outward, so the first task is to find the central point of the room. Stretch a chalked string from the mid-points of two opposite walls and snap it to transfer a chalked line to the floor.

Repeat this with the other two opposite walls, and you have established the central point of the room – the point

where the two lines cross. Dry lay the first tile here, and then dry lay further tiles along each chalk line until you reach the edges.

If there is a small gap (less than half the width of a tile) left at the margin, adjust the starting point. Remember to leave a margin of 1cm/½in around the perimeter of the room as an expansion gap.

● It is advisable to have a bowl of warm water and a rag to hand, so you can clean off adhesive that gets on the tiles or on your hands.
● Keep any extra tiles. In time, some of the floor tiles may become damaged and it might be necessary to replace them. This can be done relatively easily by cutting around the damaged tiles and lifting them using a chisel. Scrape off any adhesive from the hole and glue new tiles in position.

Materials and Equipment
● mosaic tiles
● adhesive
● notched spreader
● string and chalk
● wooden batten
● trimming knife
● tenon saw
● cardboard
● hammer and panel pins (brads)
● wood moulding or cork strips
● sander, if necessary
● sealant, if necessary

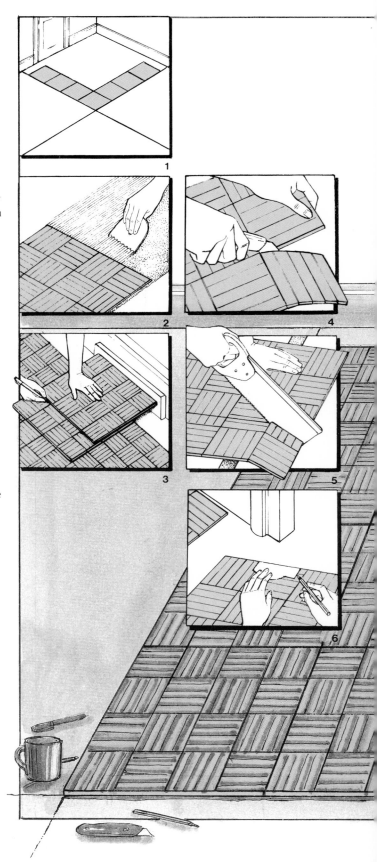

METHOD

1 Establish a starting point by using chalked lines as guides (see main text). Dry lay tiles.

2 Using a trowel or notched spreader, apply adhesive to the floor and lay tiles from centre outwards.

3 To fill gaps, place a whole tile squarely over the last one in the row. Then place another tile over the top, butting it up against a 1cm/½in wooden batten (to allow for the expansion gap) held against the skirting board (baseboard). Using the opposite edge of this top tile as your guide, mark a cutting line on the central tile of the 'sandwich'.

4 Try to arrange the tiles so that at least some trimming is along the edges of the 'fingers' of the wood. This means you have only to cut through the backing with a trimming knife.

5 When you have to cut through the wood, use a tenon saw and cut face upwards.

6 To fit around a doorway, cut away part of the architrave and slide a complete tile underneath. Otherwise make a template or pattern out of cardboard and transfer the shape onto the tile. Cut with a padsaw (keyhole saw).

7 To fit tiles around a pipe, cut through the backing to separate the fingers of wood that will be affected. Mark the shape on cardboard and cut out.

8 The expansion gap is a margin of about 1cm/½in around the perimeter of the room which gives the wood space to expand. It can be covered by nailing wooden mouldings to the skirting board with panel pins. Mitre the joins at the corners.

9 Alternatively, fill the gap with cork strip. Secure with adhesive.

213

Sheet Flooring

Manmade materials such as vinyl, rubber and linoleum are available in sheets up to 4m (13ft) in width and also in tile form. The particular advantage of sheet flooring is that a large area can be laid with the minimum of seams. Sheet flooring is useful also in small areas such as bathrooms where you may have to cut difficult shapes.

Vinyl
Vinyl – polyvinyl chloride (PVC) – is waterproof and resistant to chemicals. Quality varies: there are cheap thin types which can be cold and hard, as well as more expensive warmer cushioned vinyls which include a higher percentage of PVC. Vinyl comes in a wide range of colours, patterns and textures. There are modern, clean-looking geometric designs, heavier-weight industrial types flecked with quartz crystals, and simulations of tiles or natural materials with relief surfaces.

Linoleum
Slightly thicker than vinyl, linoleum is strong and similarly resistant to chemicals. It consists of a baked compound of natural materials pressed onto a jute, hessian (burlap) or fibreglass backing sheet.
    Linoleum makes a tough flooring for kitchens, bathrooms and hallways. It is

available in a range of colours and patterns, including marbled or stippled effects. It is also easy to cut, so it can be used to make original floor designs. Shapes can be cut from a contrasting linoleum and inlaid to define areas.

Rubber
'Borrowed' from industry, rubber flooring has a utilitarian, 'hi-tech' look that suits modern interiors. It is very tough: non-slip, soundproof and resistant to burns, it comes in a range of plain colours and some patterns. Many types are textured with round studs.

Care and Maintenance
Vinyl flooring can be damaged by burns or grit. Keep it clean with warm soapy water, rinsing off thoroughly. At all costs, avoid using harsh detergents, white spirit, turpentine or wax polish. Linoleum is likewise easily damaged by strong detergents. Keep it clean by sweeping and washing; shine with an emulsion polish or a recommended linoleum dressing. Make sure that water is not allowed to seep under the linoleum – this will cause it to rot.
    Rubber is very resilient, but there is a tendency for grime to build up on textured types – around studs, for example. Wash with mild detergent; avoid strong chemicals.

Laying Sheet Flooring

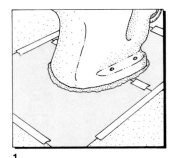

1

2

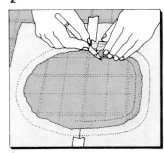

3

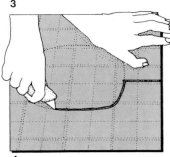

4

The easiest way to lay sheet flooring in a small area, such as a bathroom or utility room, is to make a paper pattern or template for the whole floor. Stiff paper is best.
    This method relies on the use of a scriber, a wooden block 4cm/1½in wide. When the paper is laid, trim 1cm/½in around the edges and around obstacles. Place one edge of the scriber against the skirting board (baseboard) and trace a pencil line onto the paper all around the room.
    Then place the paper template on top of the sheet flooring and tape it in place. Place one edge of the scriber against the pencil line on the template and draw a pencil line onto the sheet flooring, this time using the 'outer' edge of the scriber as a guide. The flooring can then be cut.

Cutting Around a Lavatory
1 Cut a paper template (in two halves for easy fitting) and lay it roughly around the obstacle. Stick it to the floor with tape.
2 Press the scribing block against the base of the obstacle and trace the outline onto the paper.
3 Lay the paper pattern over the flooring and transfer the outline, using the scribing block and pencil.
4 Cut the flooring along this line, making a cut at the back for access.

Rubber flooring complements a 1950s retro look.

A 'tiled' floor created the easy way — with sheet flooring.

WHAT TYPE OF SHEET FLOORING TO USE AND WHERE?

	Fitting	Suitability	Durability
SOLID VINYL	Fairly straightforward to lay. It is flexible and is suitable for any dry, flat surface. Should be warmed before laying as it becomes brittle in cold temperatures.	Ideal for kitchens and heavy-use areas such as hallways and utility rooms. Not usually suitable for bedrooms, living rooms or stairs.	Resilient and practical. Waterproof, resistant to oil and fat, but not burns and abrasive substances. Do not use harsh domestic detergents.
CUSHIONED VINYL	Fairly straightforward to lay. Easier to manipulate than solid vinyl flooring.	Like solid vinyl, not usually fitted in bedrooms or living rooms. Ideal in kitchens and bathrooms. Suitable for utility rooms, hallways and conservatories.	Similar qualities to solid vinyl. Good for soundproofing and warm underfoot.
LINOLEUM	More complicated to lay than vinyl. Lay on dry, level floor, preferably chipboard (particleboard) or hardboard (masonite).	Can be used in most rooms. Ideal for hallways and utility rooms, but not stairs.	Tough, good resistance to household chemicals, but will rot if water gets underneath.
RUBBER	Lay on subfloor or concrete. Most types need to be stuck down with adhesive.	Excellent for heavy-use areas. Good for bathrooms and utility rooms. Not suitable for kitchens.	Very tough. Non-slip, resistant to water, and is good for soundproofing.

Laying Sheet Vinyl Flooring

Most types of sheet flooring, including sheet vinyl, are available in large widths, so it is possible to cover fairly extensive areas without seams. If you do need to use more than one width, avoid laying the flooring so that a join bisects a doorway. Ideally, lay sheets parallel to a window so that seams are less visible.

Patterned vinyl looks better if the pattern is aligned with the doorway – few rooms have walls which are perfectly square to each other.

Vinyl can be loose-laid (i.e., not stuck to the floor). In particular, cushioned-back vinyl has an interlayer, which makes it very stable, but 'lay-flat' vinyl can bubble up or lift in the middle. The answer to this problem is to trim for a snug fit (not a really tight fit, because this is more likely to encourage buckling). Also, before laying the vinyl, reverse the roll and leave it in a warm room for at least two days to make it supple.

Flatten out any kinks. Once the vinyl has been laid – allowing 5cm/2in overlap at each edge – brush with a soft broom to eliminate any air bubbles which might be trapped underneath.

Other types of vinyl need to be stuck, either around the edges or all over. To stick vinyl all over, roll the sheet back and do half a room at a time. Follow manufacturers' recommendations.

● A large room may need more than one width of vinyl. Always use lengths cut from the same roll. If you are laying a large sheet of vinyl, enlist a friend to help you,

Materials and Equipment
● roll of sheet vinyl
● sharp knife
● sharp scissors
● adhesive, if necessary
● straightedge and measuring tape
● chalk or pencil
● soft broom
● wood block

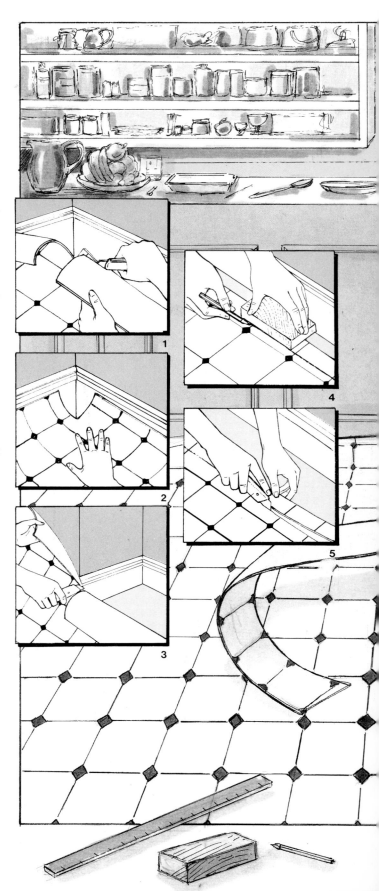

METHOD

1 Lay the vinyl out roughly, making diagonal cuts in each corner. Remove excess from edges, using a sharp knife and leaving a 5cm/2in overlap all around. Brush with a soft broom to remove air from beneath.
2 To fit an internal corner, lift the sheet and make a diagonal cut across the corner with scissors. Press the vinyl back into the angle.
3 To fit an external corner, such as at an alcove or doorway, cut downward, ending up diagonally in the corner. Trim excess, leaving 5cm/2in overlapping the wall to allow for mistakes.

4 Fit the vinyl against the longest wall first. Pull the flooring away from the wall, keeping the alignment. Take a softwood block and place it over the gap, overlapping onto the vinyl. Draw the block and a pencil along the flooring, with the block pressed against the skirting board (baseboard), to make a trimming line.

5 Pull the vinyl away from the wall and trim. Slide back to fit. To trim thin flexible vinyl, press it into the angle of the floor and wall and crease the edge with a wood block. Make the cut along the crease with a knife, guided by a straightedge.

6 Next, trim the other edges. Measure a distance of 20cm/8in from the wall and mark the vinyl. Pull the vinyl back from the wall and make a second mark, measuring back 20cm/8in from the first mark towards the edge of the sheet. Slide the vinyl back to the wall. Make sure the adjacent edge is straight. Make a wood block the width of the distance between the second mark and the end of the sheet and use this to guide a pencil marking the contour of the wall.

7 To fit flooring around a doorway, make a paper template or pattern to the shape of the mouldings and then transfer this shape to the vinyl. Alternatively use a profile gauge.

8 To join lengths, overlap the edges of both pieces, aligning the pattern. Cut through both thicknesses, using a straightedge. Remove the surplus strips and stick the edges of the pieces to the floor using double-sided tape (use adhesive instead if the vinyl is to be stuck down).

Successful Decorating
FLOORS

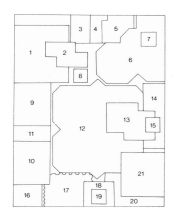

Floor Tiles

   1 Glazed Spanish
   2 Slate
 3,4 Vinyl
   5 Linoleum
   6 Terracotta
 7,8 Glazed Mexican
9,10 Distressed slate
  11 Slate
  12 Marble
  13 Plain glazed
  14 Quarry
  15 Glazed Mexican
  16 Vinyl wood strips
  17 Glazed mosaic
  18 Plain glazed
  19 Glazed Mexican
  20 Cork
  21 Terrazzo

Tiling

Floor tiles come in every conceivable form: hard, soft, warm, cold, light, heavy, easy to lay, difficult to lay ... Sizes, colours, patterns and textures likewise vary widely.

It is important when using heavier rigid tiles or slabs (such as ceramic and quarry tiles, marble, slate or terrazzo) that they are laid on a floor that can bear their weight and which is absolutely level. Floorboards should be covered with hardboard (masonite) or plywood; concrete should be covered with cement or sand screed. You may have to call in a surveyor or engineer to check if a floor can bear the load, particularly in upstairs rooms and hallways.

TYPES OF TILES

Ceramic Tiles

Made from baked clay, ceramic tiles are very hard and strong. Popular colours are the natural shades of yellow through brown, but other colours are available as well. Textures vary from smooth and shiny to knobbly; there are also patterned, hand-painted and unglazed varieties of tiles.

Ceramic tiles are heavy, cold, noisy and hard – an object dropped on them is more than likely to break.

Lay the tiles on level floors such as screeded concrete or plywood-covered floorboards.

Quarry Tiles

Normally square or rectangular, quarry tiles come in a range of warm, natural shades. They are made from unrefined alumina clay high in silica (quartz). Because they are water- and grease-resistant, they make practical floors for kitchens and hallways, although they are hard, cold and noisy. Lay on screeded concrete.

Brick Tiles

Bricks for indoor use (paviors) are hard-wearing, water- and grease-resistant, and warmer than either ceramic or quarry tiles. They can be laid only on ground floors, in a mortar bed. They come in a range of colours, including not only the standard red, brown and yellow, but also blue, purple and green. They often look best in a rustic setting or when linking interior rooms to the garden – for example, as a hall or kitchen floor.

Marble Tiles

The most practical way of using marble is to lay it in thin sheets or tiles, because marble slabs are very expensive and very difficult to work with. Tiles should be laid in cement on concrete or on a perfectly level strong wooden floor.

Like other hard tiles, however, marble is cold, heavy and noisy.

Slate Tiles

Suitable for ground floors only, slate slabs are very heavy, expensive, unwieldy, cold and noisy; they must be laid in cement on concrete. Despite all these disadvantages, slate is a very beautiful material, typically in shades of grey and with a rippled surface. It can be effectively combined with other materials – marble, wood, etc. – and is impervious and durable.

Stone Tiles

Stone floors have a mellow, ageless quality that suits contemporary settings as well as period ones. A variety of types of natural stone can be used for flooring. These include granite, sandstone, York stone and limestone, either in slabs or, more economically, cast with cement. Some types will stain easily.

Terrazzo

Terrazzo consists of marble or granite chips set in thin tiles or slabs with concrete or cement. Smooth, tough and elegantly flecked with colour, terrazzo must be laid on screed. It can be expensive.

Mosaic Tiles

Made of various materials, including marble, clay and glass silica, mosaic tiles are nowadays available with a peel-off backing to facilitate laying (which must be on smooth screeded floors).

Cork Tiles

Made from pressed and baked natural cork, these tiles make a warm, comfortable, quiet and durable floor. Make sure you buy flooring-grade tiles; lay them on a smooth floor, using adhesive. Cork must be properly sealed.

Vinyl, Rubber and Linoleum Tiles

These materials are available in tiles as well as sheet form. Because they are softer, cheaper, quieter and warmer than most hard tiles, they are a popular choice for utility areas such as kitchens and bathrooms. They are also extremely easy for the amateur to lay.

Quarry tiles integrated with painted floorboards tease the eye. It is, however, a very practical and stylish solution.

Laying Ceramic Tiles

Ceramic tiles are ideal for kitchens and bathrooms, but they are heavy, and so you first have to check that the floor can bear the weight.

Because the tiles are hard and rigid, they must be laid on a flat, stable surface that is also clean and dry. Also, the floor must be well ventilated. Strengthen wooden floors by first covering with sheets of plywood at least 1cm/½in thick, laid in staggered rows and fixed with screws at 30cm/12in intervals. Ceramic tiles can be laid straight onto concrete, assuming it is level.

Calculating Quantity
To work out how many tiles you need, measure the length and width of the room using the dimensions of the tile (adding on the width of a join) as the unit of measurement. Round up both distances to the nearest tile-width and then multiply the two figures together to give the total number of tiles you need.

Alternatively, you can work out the floor area and then divide by the area a pack of tiles will cover, thereby establishing the total number of packs you will need. (Many tiles come in packs which state the coverage.) Whichever method you use, remember to allow for extras in case of damage. For a complicated area it may be best to draw up a scale plan.

Finding a Starting Point
First establish the mid-point of the room (see page 212).

Dry lay the tiles from the middle to the wall and from this point out to the furthest corner from the door. Arrange the tiles so that at least half a tile width is left around the edge, then lay a wooden batten along the last row of tiles and nail temporarily. Lay another batten across the adjacent wall, at an angle of 90 degrees. The point where the battens meet is your starting point for tiling.

● Make a tile gauge using a length of wooden batten marked with the tile widths and spaces.

● Remember that tiling will raise the level of the floor. You may have to plane off the bottoms of doors.

Materials and Equipment
● ceramic tiles
● recommended adhesive
● trowel
● notched spreader
● string and chalk
● spirit level (carpenter's level)
● wooden battens
● hammer and nails
● spacers or pieces of stiff cardboard
● heavy-duty tile-cutter
● squeegee or sponge
● grout
● clean cloths
● rubber gloves

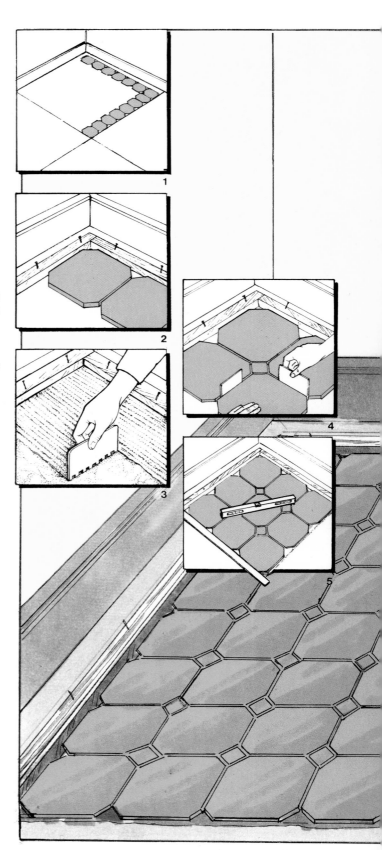

METHOD

1 Find the mid-point of the room and dry lay tiles out from it, along one wall to the corner furthest from the door.

2 Nail a batten along the last row of tiles. Lay a batten along the adjacent wall at 90 degrees and nail. Where the battens meet is the starting point.

3 Remove the tiles. Using a trowel and notched spreader, lay a bed of adhesive over an area about 1m/1yd square. Follow manufacturers' instructions: you may need to apply adhesive to the tiles as well as the floor.

4 Place tiles in position, twisting slightly to improve the bond with the adhesive. Insert spacers or pieces of cardboard to keep an even gap for grouting. Work towards the door.

5 Ensure that tiles are level and square – use a spirit level to check as you go along. Lay all whole tiles first and leave for 24 hours to allow the adhesive to set. Remove battens.

6 Finally, lay edge tiles. To cut an edge tile, lay it over the last whole tile in the row, covering it exactly. Place another tile on top, pushed against the wall over the gap. Draw a line where the top tile crossed the one below. This is the line for cutting. Allow a margin for grouting.

7 Ceramic tiles are thick and difficult to cut. Hire or buy a heavy-duty tile-cutter.

8 After the adhesive has hardened (about 24 hours), use a squeegee or sponge to grout the floor. Work into the joins, finishing flush with the tiles. Clean up joins with a cloth.

9 Wipe off excess grout. Buff with a soft dry cloth. Avoid heavy traffic on the floor for 48 hours.

Successful Decorating
FLOORS

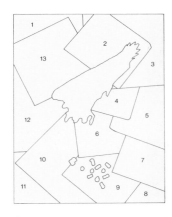

Carpets

1   Cord
2   Deep shag pile
3   Twist pile
4   Velvet
5   Coarse loop
6   Patterned velvet
7   Deep pile velvet
8   Rubber underlay
9   Coarse berber loop
10 Berber twist pile
11 Velvet
12 Cord
13 Patterned velvet

Carpet

Carpet is warm, comfortable and easy to clean and it comes in a wide range of colours, textures and patterns. Price also varies, according to the fibre or fibres used, the method of manufacture and the general performance.

Different grades of carpet are suitable for different locations, from light-use types for bedrooms to heavy-duty varieties for stairs. Durability is a function of the density and weight of the pile, with short, dense-pile carpets being the hardest-wearing type.

Carpets generally have either a woven or a foam backing. Laying woven-backed carpet is a professional job, but laying foam-backed carpet can be done by the amateur. An alternative to orthodox carpet is supplied by carpet tiles, which can be loose-laid or stuck down.

Carpet terminology can be confusing. As well as the fibre composition, carpets can be classified according to the method of manufacture and the type of pile. However, the most important indication of quality is the type and amount of fibre used.

Types

As well as the natural carpet fibre, wool, a number of synthetics are used to make carpets. Most modern carpets use mixtures – either of wool with an artificial fibre such as nylon, or of several synthetic materials.

Wool is expensive, but luxurious; it is often mixed with a percentage of nylon to promote durability – 80:20 wool to nylon is an all-purpose grade. Nylon is very durable and is often used in mixes. Good-quality nylon can be expensive. Acrylic is similar to wool in appearance but is more difficult to clean. Polyester is cheap and is often used to make shag-pile carpet. Viscose rayon is again cheap, but it gives a poor performance overall. Polypropylene is cheap, durable and water-repellent. It is used in mixtures.

Method of Manufacture

In woven carpets the pile and the backing are made together. Types of pile include smooth, uncut-loop, low-loop, long-loop and mixtures of cut and looped pile for sculpted effects. In tufted carpets fibres are inserted individually into a prepared backing which is then sealed with adhesive to hold the tufts in place. The pile may be cut, looped, or both. With non-woven carpets fibres can be bonded onto backing with adhesive; needlepunched and fixed with adhesive; or electrostatically flocked to the backing.

Carpet Terms

Axminster is a type of woven carpet, where the pile is inserted in tufts into the weave, allowing many different colours to be used. The pile is cut, but may be short and smooth, long and shaggy, stubbly or sculpted.
Berber is a term for fleeced carpets with a nubbly pile.
Body carpet is carpet produced in narrow widths less than 1.8m/6ft for use on stairs, halls, and so on.
Broadloom is carpet produced in widths over 1.8m/6ft, commonly 2.75m/9ft and 3.7m/12ft.
Brussels weave is a term referring to dense uncut looped pile.
Carpet tiles are squares of carpet with sealed edges, available in different sizes, colours, patterns and fibres and with different backings, including PVC, rubber and felt. Useful for areas of heavy wear, since damaged squares can be lifted easily and replaced, or tiles can be moved regularly to distribute wear evenly.
Cord is a low-loop woven carpet with a ribbed appearance. It is very durable.
Shag pile is a long-pile carpet with loops of 2.5–5cm/1–2in. It is hazardous on stairs and is prone to tangling.
Wilton is a smooth cut pile carpet. It is woven from continuous yarn, so only limited colours are possible.

A beautiful Axminster carpet, displaying a range of tones.

Types of Underlay

Good-quality underlay is essential for all woven-backed carpets. Foam-backed carpets should be laid on felt paper so the foam does not stick to the floor. Underlay evens out the carpet's upper surface, is a good insulator and protects the carpet from dirt, damp and excess wear.

Foam or rubber underlay is resilient but is not suitable for areas of heavy wear, such as stairs. Avoid laying it over damp floors or underfloor heating. To test good-quality foam, rub it between your fingers and thumb: if it crumbles, it is second-rate.

Felt underlay is made of jute or animal hair, or a mixture. Hair is stronger and wears better. You can also obtain rubberized felt.

Bonded underlay is made from a mixture of wool and synthetics, bonded to rubber.

Laying Carpet

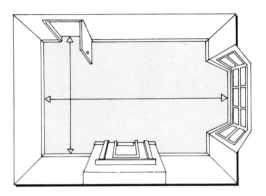

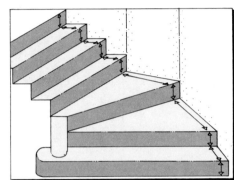

Laying Woven Carpets

Woven carpets should be fitted professionally: a cut in the wrong place would be an expensive mistake. Moreover, carpet will wear out prematurely unless it is tensioned correctly.

The carpet must be laid over thick underlay and secured to the perimeter of the room by gripper rods. At doorways, a metal binder bar is used instead of a gripper rod: the carpet is hooked onto pins and the edge covered with a metal strip.

Measuring for Carpets

Most carpet suppliers will measure rooms, but to do this yourself, measure the length and width of the room, including alcoves, and add an allowance for places where the carpet must extend under doors. Multiply the dimensions together for the number of square metres or feet you must buy.

Narrower carpets are sold in terms of length, rather than of square metres or yards. Measure the length of the room (by the 'length' is meant the opposite direction to that in which the carpet will be laid) and divide the result by the width of each carpet strip. Multiply this by the other dimension and you can easily calculate the length of carpet you need.

To measure for stair carpeting, first measure from the front to the back of a single tread (horizontal part) and multiply by the number of treads. For treads around corners take the longer measurement. Bottom treads are often longer, so take account of this. Next, measure the height of a riser (vertical part) and multiply by the number of the risers. Add in amounts for half-landings or landings, together with an allowance if the carpet is to be moved to distribute wear.

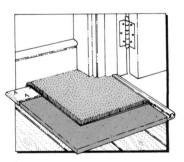

Patching Fitted Carpet

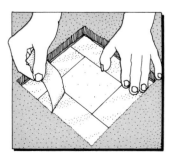

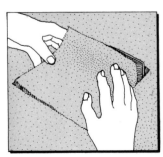

1 Place new piece over damaged area. Cut through both layers at once.

2 Apply adhesive around the edges of both the hole and the patch. Leave to dry.

3 Stick double-sided tape to the underlay or floor. Remove the backing.

4 Place the patch in position and press down firmly. To finish, trim loose fibres.

Laying Carpet Tiles

Carpet tiles are easy to lay. Because they do not need to be fixed down, they can be taken up and moved around to distribute wear; irrevocably damaged tiles can simply be replaced. Carpet tiles need no underlay, but it is important that the surface should be clean, dry and level.

As with ceramic tiles (see page 220), you can calculate how many carpet tiles you will need by measuring the length and width of the room using the width of the tile as the unit, and then multiplying the two figures (rounding up for part tiles). Buy extra tiles in case of damage.

Follow manufacturers' instructions for laying, as techniques vary. Begin by laying from the mid-point of the room (see page 212). Some carpet tiles have an arrow on the back to indicate the direction of the pile. You can either lay all the tiles with the same direction of pile or lay them so that it alternates at right angles to give a checkerboard effect.

Carpet tiles are usually loose-laid, but you can place a strip of double-sided tape around the perimeter of the room to keep the assemblage firmly in place. It is also a good idea to stick the first tile down with tape or adhesive so that it remains in place when the rest are being laid. Push each tile up against the previous one for a snug fit.

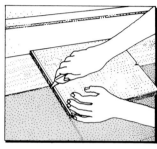

1 After all the whole tiles have been laid, you must cut edge pieces. Place the tile in position upside-down, butting it against the wall. Nick it at each end using a trimming knife. Measure any irregular gaps carefully and make a template or pattern in order to ensure that you cut the tiles correctly. You could also use a profile gauge.

2 Cut through the tile, holding the knife against a metal straightedge. Turn the tile over and fit it so that the cut edge is against the wall. You can cut rounded shapes using a template.

● If tiles dislodge, such as in a busy hallway lift them up and apply carpet adhesive to the underside.

Laying Foam-backed Carpet

Unless the floor is already covered with hardboard (masonite), the carpet should be laid on a paper underlay that stops short of the walls to allow a margin for double-sided carpet tape. Lay the carpet with the pile running away from the window. Try to avoid seams, but if you find you must join widths secure them with carpet tape and butt the pieces together.

● Carpet tape is available in different widths. When you are fitting a single piece of carpet the narrowest width is sufficient. It can be stuck to both wood and concrete.

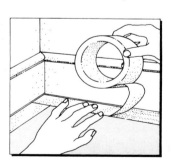

1 Lay the carpet tape around the perimeter of the room. However, at this stage, do not peel off the backing strip. Cut your piece of carpet roughly to size, leaving a 5cm/2in overlap. Make diagonal cuts at the corners to allow the tongues to lap against the base of the wall.

2 To fit carpet around a chimney breast, make freeing cuts in line with the sides of the chimney breast by folding the carpet over a board and cutting through the back. Allow the tongues of carpet to fit into the recess. Trim off excess across the face of the chimney breast.

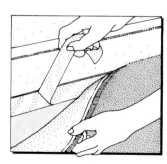

3 Press the carpet under the base of the skirting board (baseboard) with a bolster chisel (brick chisel) or a similar tool, and trim off excess with a trimming knife. Peel the tape backing off and press the carpet back into position. Finish with a threshold strip in doorways.

Rugs

An interesting rug transforms the floor into a focal point. From fine antique Persian carpets to relatively inexpensive rag or braided mats, there is a design and a price to suit every decorative scheme. As well as the wealth of traditional handmade types, there are also manufactured rugs produced in contemporary designs – an exciting and original way of dressing up a modern room.

The three basic types of rug are: flat-weaves, such as kelims and dhurries; pile rugs (often from the Middle or Far East); and braided, hooked or rag rugs assembled from scraps of different materials. Prices vary according to the age and rarity of the design, composition (with cotton the cheapest and silk the most expensive) and method of production – for example, a good handmade Persian carpet will be very dense, with about 125 knots or tufts per square centimetre (800 per square inch), and therefore very expensive.

Flat-weave Rugs
These rugs are woven and have no pile. They are generally cheaper than pile carpets, and are usually made of cotton or of wool and cotton, although silk is also used. The two main traditional types of flat-weave rugs are kelims and dhurries. Kelims are produced in

Turkey and Afghanistan. Patterns are geometric and the vegetable dyes used produce rich, warm colours that mellow beautifully with age. Most kelims are woollen.

Dhurries are Indian flat-weaves, usually made of cotton, although up-market silk versions exist. Designs tend to be modern interpretations of traditional motifs; borders are common. The increasing popularity of these rugs means that they are available in a huge range of colours and patterns. Dhurries are easy to maintain – they can even be reversed – and are fairly cheap.

Serapes are coarse flat-weave rugs from Mexico. They are often fringed, and come in a variety of bright cheerful colours and patterns.

Pile Rugs
Traditional pile rugs are made by knotting tufts of wool (or silk) – the more knots per square centimetre the better the quality. Many of these carpets are very expensive and 'collectable'. Although there are some adequate reproductions, it is hard to match the clear, distinct patterns of originals. Typical designs and colours vary according to the region and the period.

Chinese rugs are thick, often sculpted, and they feature pictorial motifs such as flowers, dragons and

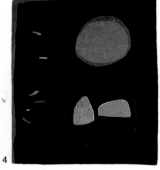

Types of rub: *antique kelim from Persia (1); William Morris design (2); Turkish carpet (3); modern tufted rug (4); 1930s pile rug (5).*

butterflies. Yellow, pink, black and blue are common colours for Chinese rugs.

Persian carpets, from central Asia, display stylized or geometric motifs in rich reds and blues.

Turkish carpets are likewise produced in rich, glowing colours. Many are prayer rugs, typically with a design showing an arch supported by pillars.

Today, hand- or machine-made pile carpets in graphic, contemporary designs are produced. Although those by 'name' designers and one-offs commissioned from hand-weavers are obviously expensive, cheaper mass-produced versions can be very reasonable.

Other Types

Flokatis are inexpensive shaggy-pile wool rugs from Greece, usually white or off-white. Ryas are shaggy-pile Finnish rugs in contemporary designs. Numdahs are cheap felt rugs from India which have birds, animals or flowers embroidered on an off-white background.

Braided, Hooked and Rag Rugs

These are cheerful, hand-made rugs produced using scraps of fabric or wool. Antiques – especially early North American ones – can be expensive, but their modern equivalents are much more reasonable.

Braided rugs are made by plaiting and coiling material. They are usually oval but can be round as well. Hooked rugs consist of a looped pile worked in a pattern or naive design. Rag rugs consist of irregular stripes in bright cheerful colours.

● Care for rugs by moving them regularly to avoid excessive wear or fading in one spot. Clean them by beating them with a carpet-beater, rather than by vacuuming. Never use strong detergent, steam or excess water to wash out stains. If necessary, have the rug treated by a specialist. Frayed edges can be mended by blanket-stitching, but if the rug is valuable you should seek expert help for any repair work that must be undertaken.

● Secure rugs on hard floors by placing them over rubber or webbed underlay. Underlay will prolong the life of the rug as well as preventing it from sliding underfoot.

6

6 *A Portuguese rag rug in shades of rose, apricot and cream reflects the colour scheme in this New York apartment and adds textural interest.*

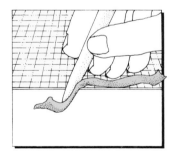

1

Making a Rag Rug

Choose rags made of the same type of material and of the same weight. Wash the pieces and cut them into strips 10cm/4in long and 2.5cm/1in wide.

For the backing you will need a piece of hessian (burlap), cut to the required size, with 5cm/2in allowed all round for finishing. Work with the wrong side facing you.

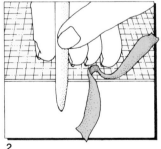

2

To insert the rags in the backing you will need a round-pointed peg.

1 Poke a hole in one corner and push one end of a strip through until it protrudes by just under half.

2 Poke a second hole four threads along (about 1cm/½in) and insert the other end of the strip through this hole.

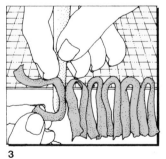

3

3 Poke one end of another strip into the same hole as the last. Make a further hole four threads along and push the other end of this second strip through. Continue working in straight rows, 4cm/1½in apart. Check the density after a few rows. Finish edges by applying latex-based adhesive and folding over a double hem.

227

Matting

Cheap and practical, matting is woven either from a variety of natural fibres or from coloured plastic strands. It makes a simple cheerful alternative to more expensive surfaces. Some types can be laid wall to wall, most can be used like rugs to cover existing floors.

Natural matting is woven in different patterns, including rib, checkerboard and bullseye. This choice of patterns, together with the warm, earth shades of light biscuit brown, honey gold and dark brown, make matting a sympathetic foil for all kinds of flooring. But the particular attraction of matting lies in its texture.

Because it is comparatively cheap, matting is a good solution for floors in temporary accommodation. In warm climates, scatter mats can be laid over hard floors in bedrooms and living rooms to increase comfort. Wall-to-wall matting makes a good base for rugs, and all types of matting are excellent choices for areas which connect directly with the outdoors – not just for doormats but as the principal flooring in halls and conservatories.

TYPES OF MATTING

Coir
One of the cheapest, most widely available and most popular types of matting, coir is made from coconut fibre. As well as making thick, dense doormats, coir is available in various ribbed weaves, narrow and broadloom, which can be laid like carpet and provide a good all-purpose surface that suits modern as well as traditional interiors.

In addition to the natural honey colour, coir matting comes in a range of other shades, including black; this range, while limited, extends coir's decorative applications. There are also types which include coloured sisal in attractive patterns, but these are more expensive.

The disadvantages of coir are that it can be uncomfortable underfoot and dusty, and it will eventually become slippery on stairs – although there are more expensive types that are backed with latex or vinyl to increase durability.

If you are using coir for a doormat, it is a good idea, if circumstances permit, to stop the hall flooring short of the entrance and to create a well that can be filled entirely with the matting.

If you are using coir for a scatter mat, cut it slightly oversize and allow it to adjust to the conditions for at least 24 hours.

For wall-to-wall laying, choose a broadloom type, stitch lengths together and

Coir matting in an American country living room.

bind the edges with jute tape; alternatively, butt the edges together and join them with double-sided tape or carpet adhesive. Do not tack the edges down – this will cause bumps and ridges.

Sisal
As durable as coir, sisal is made from the leaves of various types of agave plant. Available in a range of interesting colours, it is sometimes woven into mixtures with coir. The applications and method of laying are similar to coir.

Rush, Seagrass and Maize
Matting made of these various fibres has an ethnic, natural charm and comes in a wide range of fineness of weave and depth of colour,

Binding Coir Matting
Bind the edges of coir with hessian (burlap) strips 5cm/2in wide. Sew the hessian to the right side of the matting using strong thread and a running stitch. Fold the hessian over to the back and slip-stitch to the matting. Mitre the corners.

maize matting being the smoothest and palest. These types of matting are readily available and cheap and, unlike rugs, need no underlay. Small sections or strips can be sewn together with twine to make a larger covering. None of these fibres will resist heavy wear, and they can be dusty.

Plastic
Woven plastic matting comes in rectangular pieces or in rolls, and a wide range of bright paintbox colours is available. There is also a type of plastic matting made of honeycomb duckboard; this is more substantial but also more expensive. Plastic matting is cheap, durable and comfortable, but it can be damaged by strong chemicals.

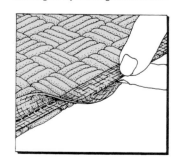

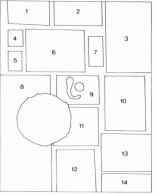

Matting

1 Sisal
2 Herringbone coir
3 Seagrass
4 Ribbed coir
5 Sisal
6 Dyed coconut
7 Tufted coir
8 Bullseye rush
9 Sisal
10 Dyed herringbone coconut
11 Dyed herringbone sisal
12 Dyed coconut
13 Sisal
14 Bleached herringbone coir

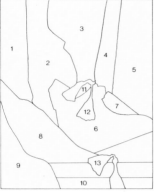

Curtain Fabrics

    1 Satin
    2 Moiré
    3 Puckered silk
    4 Velvet
    5 Damask
    6 Textured cotton
    7 Cotton
  8,9 Glazed cotton
   10 Trompe l'oeil cotton
   11 Cord tie backs
12,13 Tassel tie backs

Curtain Treatments

The practical purposes of curtains are to provide privacy and warmth, to exclude light completely or partially, and to screen unwelcome views. But the type of window treatment you select for a particular location depends also on the window itself, the style and decoration of the room, and the amount you wish to spend on it.

Tailored formal styles extending to the floor suit large windows in living and dining rooms; sill-length curtains in lighter fabric can be chosen for kitchens, bedrooms and bathrooms. In period settings, you can experiment with traditional pelmets (cornices) or elaborate swags and tails.

Headings
The heading defines the style of the curtain. It will determine the fullness of the curtain, how it hangs, and how it is suspended. If the curtain-top is not covered by a pelmet (cornice), the heading will also be a feature in its own right.

Deep, tailored headings which keep the fabric hanging straight in full folds include pencil pleats, box pleats and pinch or triple pleats. Narrower headings, which give a softer, less formal look, include standard gathered headings, smocked headings and cluster pleats.

Today all of these styles can be achieved by the use of special heading tapes sewn to the back of the curtain. Tapes are available in different weights to suit different fabrics. By pulling cords threaded through the tape the fabric is gathered into a particular pattern. Alternatively, the fabric can be gathered by inserting pleater hooks, which serve also to attach the curtain to the track or pole.

Simpler sewn types of heading for lightweight unlined curtains or sheers include cased headings and shaped headings. A cased heading is a sewn channel along the top of the curtain (or at both top and bottom) which enables a wire or rod to be threaded through, shirring the fabric. Also, fabric can be cut and sewn into scallops or castellations which are then threaded through rings or directly onto a pole or rod.

Tracks and Poles
Tracks, which are available in plastic or aluminium, make discreet fittings for curtains, especially if the heading extends a little way over the top. They come with guide hooks into which curtain hooks are slotted, they can be shaped to fit around a bay or bow window, and they can be fitted with a cord set and pulleys so that the curtains can be drawn from one side.

Poles – either of metal or of wood – can be highly decorative. They come with supporting brackets, matching rings or inset runners and hooks. Poles can be mitred to fit around angled windows.

Other means of curtain suspension include fine metal or brass rods for attaching sheer curtains or curtains with cased headings, and plastic-covered sprung wire for the same purpose.

Types of headings and tapes:
*gathered heading using standard curtain tape (**1**); pencil pleats (**2**); pinch pleats (**3**); smocked heading (**4**); box pleats (**5**); cartridge pleats (**6**); scalloped heading hung from rings (**7**); cased heading on covered wire (**8**).*

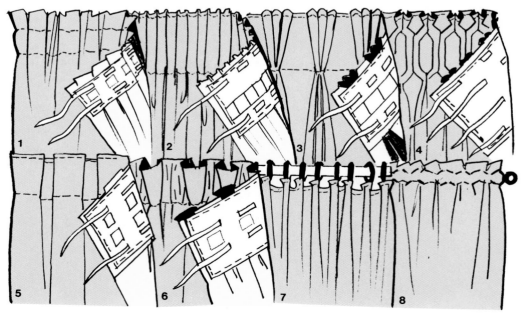

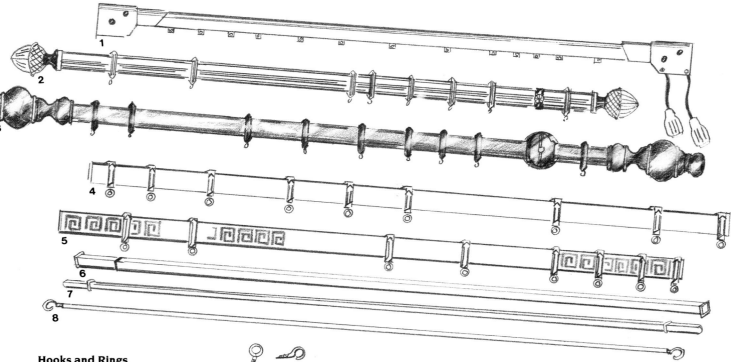

1

2

3

4

5

6

7

8

Hooks and Rings
There is a variety of designs of hooks and rings to suit different types of headings, tracks and poles. Hooks and rings are both available in metal and plastic; there are also wooden rings for use with wooden poles. Some designs are unobtrusive; others are meant for display.

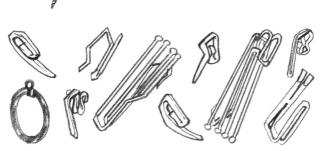

Types of tracks and poles: *corded track with pulleys (1); metal pole with finials and rings (2); wooden pole with finials and rings (3); plastic track with glide hooks (4); plastic track with motif (5); expandable pole (6); fine rod for net curtains (7); expandable wire with eyes (8).*

Putting up a Track
1 Measure the window or recess and mark the desired fixing height at intervals across the window. Join the marks, extending the line to the width of the track. Use a spirit level (carpenter's level) to check that the line is straight and horizontal.
2 With a pencil, mark along the guide line where the brackets will go, spacing them evenly. Drill and plug the holes, screw the brackets in place and clip or slot the track onto the brackets.

● To position the track on the ceiling you must fix the brackets to joists.

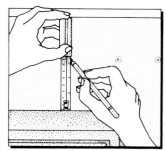

1

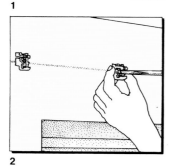

2

Putting up a Pole
1 Construct a guide line, as for a track. To mark the positions for support brackets, measure in from the ends of the pole (note that the screw hole is often slightly above centre). Drill and plug the holes, and drive in screws, leaving the heads projecting. Fit brackets.
2 Centre the pole on the brackets, leaving one ring outside the brackets at either side. Push the finials into place. Drive a screw into the base of each bracket. The screws bite into the pole, and prevent it from becoming dislodged when the curtains are pulled.

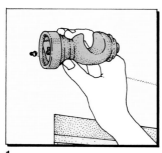

1

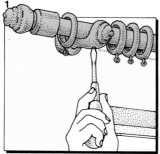

2

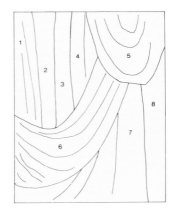

Sheer Fabrics
1 Loose-knit polyester
2 Plain voile
3 Patterned nylon
4 Silk and polyester mix
5 Iridescent polyester
6 Crushed polyester
7 Cotton Chantilly lace
8 Patterned muslin

Sheers and Unlined Curtains

The typical sheer curtain is the net curtain, long used in conjunction with outer curtains to provide daytime privacy and to filter strong sunlight. Almost any kind of light, semi-transparent fabric can serve the purpose – muslin, lace, voile and lawn are all attractive options. Sheer curtains are often suspended from a rod or wire by means of a cased heading, but they can also be hung from a special track or they can be fixed top and bottom as panels – on French doors, for example.

Making Sheer Curtains

Net and other types of semi-transparent material are available in many different

Lightweight, filmy material draped over a pole frames French windows leading onto a balcony.

widths (90–270cm/36–108in), so you can almost always avoid joins. The sides are usually finished but, if not, hem by 5mm/¼in. The bottom edge too may require hemming: stitch a 5cm/2in double hem (turning the fabric by a total of 10cm/4in).

1 Turn a 5cm/2in double hem at the top and machine-stitch close to the edge of the turning and again 2.5cm/1in above the first seam, so that you form a channel. Machine-stitch both lines in the same direction.
2 Thread plastic-covered wire or a rod through the casing and gather up the curtain. The fabric at the top will form a soft frill.

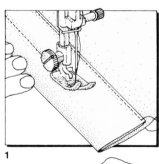

1

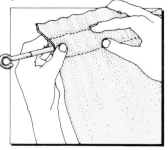

2

Making Unlined Curtains

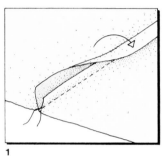

1

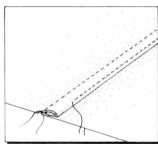

2

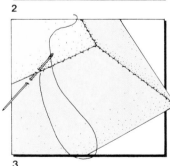

3

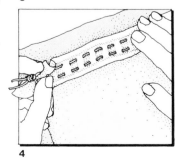

4

1 Join widths with flat fell seams. Machine right sides together, trimming one seam allowance and folding the wider one over the narrower to enclose it.
2 Press and machine-stitch down the seam, close to the edge. If you do not want stitching to show on the right side, use a simple flat seam. Finish by pinking or machine-stitching, and press open.
3 Turn 2.5cm/1in double hems down the sides and 7.5cm/3in double hems at the bottom, mitring the corners (see page 237). Slip-stitch into place.
4 Turn down the top edge of the curtain, and attach heading tape to cover the raw edge. The corner should be angled slightly. At one end of the tape, knot the ends of the cord and turn under. At the other end, free the cords and machine-stitch along the top, bottom and sides, stitching underneath the free cords. Pull the cords so that the fabric draws up to the required width.

● To prevent puckering, remove or snip selvedges. Make sure half-widths of fabric are positioned toward the outer edges of the curtains. To help the curtains hang properly, weight them with special discs or continuous weighted tape sewn inside the hem before you finish stitching it.

Making a Loose-lined Curtain

The easiest method of lining curtains is loose-lining. It is suitable for almost all curtains except those which are made of heavy fabric or those which are very wide.

When you have cut the fabric, pull out a thread across the top of each drop to ensure that you have a straight edge. Check that the pattern aligns at the top of each drop. When cutting out lining fabric, use a setsquare (T-square) and rule to chalk a line across, which you can follow to ensure a straight edge. Lining fabric should be 23cm/9in shorter and 12.5cm/5in narrower than the curtain fabric.

Matching Patterns

Cut out all the fabric lengths (drops) so that the patterns match across the finished curtain. There should be a complete motif at the top of each drop, and both curtains should match.

To join drops, first fold under the seam allowance of one drop and press it. Place this over the seam allowance of the second piece, matching the pattern. Pin in place.

Tack (baste) by stitching across the join, turning the needle through the bottom piece, then stitching across the join again and running through the fold on the top. Turn the top piece back and, with right sides together, machine-stitch along the tacked seam. Remove the tacking, making sure not to pull fabric threads, and iron to finish.

Materials and Equipment
- curtain fabric
- lining fabric
- thread
- heading tape
- ruler and setsquare (T-square)
- tailors' chalk
- pins and needles
- sewing machine
- scissors
- iron (for pressing)
- curtain weights
- curtain hooks

METHOD

1 Join widths of curtain fabric, using flat seams and matching the patterns (see above). Clip seams, press open and repeat for the lining. Mark the mid-points of curtain panels and lining panels with pins or chalk.

2 Place lining and fabric right sides together, with the lining 7.5cm/3in down from the top and side edges aligned. Machine-stitch 1cm/½in seams up to 7.5cm/3in from the bottom of the lining; the surplus fabric will make a pleat at the back. Clip seam turnings.

3 Turn up and press 5cm/2in to the wrong side of the lining and machine-stitch a 2.5cm/1in double hem.

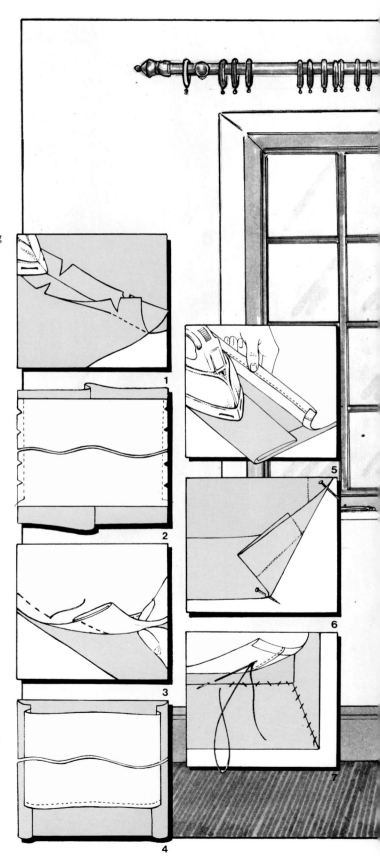

4 Turn curtain right-side out and press, matching the mid-points of curtain and lining panels to create equal margins of curtain fabric on each side of the lining face.

5 Press a double 7.5cm/3in hem in place on the curtain fabric. The lining should finish 5cm/2in above the curtain edge.

6 Mitre corners by marking where the turnings converge with pins. Unfold the corner and then fold up diagonally through both of the pins.

7 Refold the side and hem edges so that a mitre is formed across the corner. Slip-stitch the mitre. To weight the curtain, sew weighted tape or discs into the hem. Slip-stitch the hem.

8 Turn down the top edge of the curtain, angling it slightly at each corner. Attach the heading tape to cover the raw edge. Knot the cords at one end of the tape (on the wrong side), but leave the other ends free. Machine-stitch the tape along the sides and ends (turning the ends under) but do not sew over the free cords. Both lines of sewing should be in the same direction.

9 Pull up the cords to gather the curtain. Knot the ends into a bow or use a cord-tidy. Do not cut off the surplus – whenever you want to clean the curtain you will need to untie the knots so that you can pull the curtain flat.

10 Thread the required number of hooks through the pockets in the heading tape, spacing the hooks evenly. Hang the curtain onto the track's hooks or gliders.

11 To set the folds, tie strips of fabric around the curtain at intervals down its length and leave for a couple of days.

WINDOW TREATMENTS

A window is a natural focal point, and so a window treatment can set the whole style of a room. The range of effects you can create is very wide: from the delicacy of lace panels to the crisp, contemporary look of Venetian blinds; from tailored, pleated full-length curtains to soft, billowing festoons; from grand, traditional swags and tails to the natural charm of split-cane blinds.

CURTAINS
Curtain Fabrics
Curtain fabrics come in a variety of fibres and in different weights, finishes, textures, colours and patterns. In general, the shorter the curtain, the lighter the fabric can be; curtains which hang full-length in straight folds need heavier fabric. Simple cased headings and loose gathers and ties work best if the material is lightweight; tailored pleated headings are more successful in a stiffer, thicker fabric.

Cotton is still the principal fibre used in furnishing fabrics; today it is often blended with artificial fibres such as polyester. Cotton prints well, wears well and comes in a wide range of weights, weaves and finishes. In addition to plain weave cotton, you can obtain cotton brocades, lawns, damasks, chintzes, ginghams, sateens, satins, and velvets.

Linen is sturdier than cotton and more loosely woven. A blend of linen and cotton, known as 'linen union', is the most common linen furnishing fabric.

For furnishing use, wool is usually blended with other fibres. Both light wools and tweeds can be used to make curtains, especially if extra warmth is desired.

Other fabrics involved in curtain-making include linings, interlinings and buckram. Cotton sateen, in colours as well as neutral shades, is the most common type of lining material. Thermal lining comes either in a cotton and acrylic blend or in an aluminium-coated form. Black-out lining, which excludes all light, comes in neutral shades. Interlining consists of a layer of padding stitched between the lining and curtain.

Calculating Fabric Amount

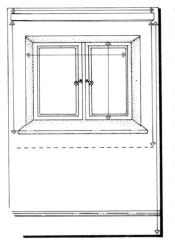

Before measuring, fix the track or pole in position. Use a metal rule to take measurements, as a fabric one can stretch.

Curtain length is a matter of taste. The three standard lengths are to the sill, to the floor or to just below the sill (to the top of a radiator, for example). But curtains can also look luxurious if they are allowed to fall onto the floor in rich, deep folds or flaring like the base of a column.

To establish the length, take the following measurements from the base of the glider or ring: to 5mm/¼in above the sill; to 1cm/⅖in above the floor (or lower if desired); or to 2cm/¾in above a radiator. Add 25cm/9in for hem and heading, plus extra for any pattern repeat. Remember to make allowance for headings which stand up above the track.

A curtain's width is a function of the style of heading used. Measure the length of the track, rod or pole (not the width of the window) and multiply by the required fullness for the heading. Add 15cm/6in for side turnings, and account for any overlap in the middle. It is important not to skimp on fabric width – certain types of heading demand more material than others to work successfully. If you need to economize, choose a simpler style of heading.

1,2 Either in conjunction with outer curtains or as the sole window treatment, lace is a highly effective fabric. Because it is so delicately patterned and lightweight, it does not need to be gathered tightly – it can simply be hung flat. Lace is also excellent for disguising a dreary view.

1

2

Linings and Loop Headings

Locked-in Lining

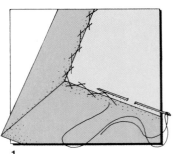

1

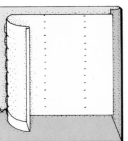

2

3

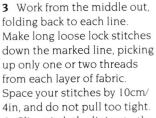

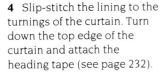

4

This is the professional way to line curtains. The lining is stitched to the curtain fabric with vertical rows of loose stitches. This results in the fabric hanging better. The technique is particularly recommended for curtains made of heavier material. You need equal amounts of curtain fabric and lining.

1 Turn and press 5cm/2in single-side turnings. Turn up 15cm/6in on the hem and press. Mitre the corners (see page 237) and sew edges in place, using herringbone stitch or slip stitch.
2 Using chalk, mark vertical guide lines on the reverse of the main curtain fabric, 30cm/12in apart. On the lining, trim 2cm/¾in from the top and then turn and press 2cm/¾in to the wrong side at the sides and 5cm/2in at the hem. Place the lining on the curtain fabric, 2cm/¾in down from the top, right-side out and with the mid-points aligning exactly.
3 Work from the middle out, folding back to each line. Make long loose lock stitches down the marked line, picking up only one or two threads from each layer of fabric. Space your stitches by 10cm/4in, and do not pull too tight.
4 Slip-stitch the lining to the turnings of the curtain. Turn down the top edge of the curtain and attach the heading tape (see page 232).

Detachable Lining

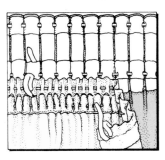

A detachable lining is useful if you need to have the curtains or drapes cleaned regularly or if you like to change them often. Like other types of lining, it will help to screen light more effectively

and improve the curtain's insulating properties. However, a detachable lining does not improve the way the curtain hangs.

The curtain and the lining are made separately, the method used being in both cases as for unlined curtains (see page 235). That done, the top edge of the lining is enclosed in special lining tape. Hooks are inserted through buttonholes in the top of the lining tape, looped onto the bottom cord of the main heading tape, and turned over to slot through the glider. Some gliders have special slots for hooks.

Interlining

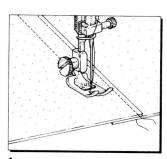

1

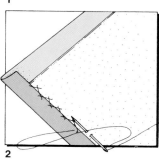

2

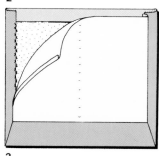

3

2

Interlining consists of a soft layer of wadding stitched between the lining and the curtain fabric. Available in different weights, interlining makes curtains warmer, blocks light, and keeps the fabric hanging in soft, rounded folds. You need the same amount of fabric and lining as for locked-in lining. The amount of interlining you need is the same as for a finished, flat curtain.

1 Overlap widths of interlining by 1cm/½in and sew them together either by machine-stitching two parallel rows or by herringboning. Place interlining to the wrong side of the fabric, 7.5cm/3in down from the top and centred. Lock-stitch, spacing rows of stitches at 40cm/16in intervals across the curtain.
2 Turn the edges of the fabric over the interlining at the sides and bottom, and herringbone-stitch in place.
3 Apply the lining to the interlined curtain with lock stitches, but avoid stitching over the same rows. Slip-stitch the lining to the curtain. Turn down the top edge and apply heading tape.

1 Traditional, full-gathered curtains add period style.
2 Stylish pelmets (cornices) can be made using heading tape. A coordinating trim adds decorative detail.

Making a Loop Heading

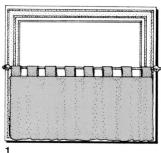

1

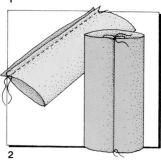

2

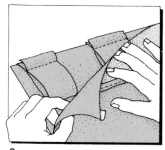

3

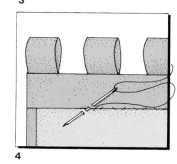

4

A loop heading is suitable for café curtains or for hanging panels of fabric.

1 Make up the curtain in the same way as for an unlined curtain (see page 235), leaving the top edge unfinished, with 1cm/½in extra allowance for turnings.
2 To establish the length of the loops, measure the circumference of the rod or pole and then add 5cm/2in for ease plus 2.5cm/1in for seams. Each loop should be 5–7.5cm/2–3in wide. Cut out, fold in half lengthways and make a 5mm/¼in seam down the long edge. Turn right-side out and press flat, with the seam at centre back.
3 Fold the loops in half widthways, and pin them to the right side of the curtain, raw edges matching. End loops should be 2cm/¾in from the edges, with the rest spaced evenly. Tack (baste) in place 1cm/½in from the top. Cut a strip of curtain fabric 7.5cm/3in deep and the same width as the curtain. Turn 5mm/¼in to the wrong side along the lower edge, press and tack. Place the facing against the top edge of the curtain, with the right sides together. Pin, tack and stitch 1cm/½in in from side and top edges, catching the loops.
4 Trim and turn the facing to the wrong side and press. Slip-stitch the bottom edge. Thread onto the pole.

Special Effects

Curtains can be given added impact if you dress them with pelmets (cornices) and fabric tie-backs. Both of these details are practical as well as decorative – pelmets hide the curtain heading and track, while tie-backs hold curtains in place when they are open.

Other effects can be created using fabric; you can drape lengths of material over a decorative pole, or you can make swags and tails, either to frame a window or to add a special flourish.

Pelmets (Cornices)
There are two types of pelmet: flat, shaped ones, usually attached to a pelmet board, and gathered ones (valances) which are headed or gathered like curtains and suspended from a special rail mounted just above the curtain track.

Flat pelmets have three layers: facing fabric (which can coordinate or contrast with the curtain), stiffener and lining. The lower edge can be shaped.

Gathered pelmets have a softer appearance, the folds of fabric flowing elegantly into the curtain drapery. As with flat pelmets, the lower edge can either be left straight or can be curved or castellated to frame the window. Gathered pelmets are made by attaching heading tape to pleat up the fabric in the required pattern.

Making a Pelmet

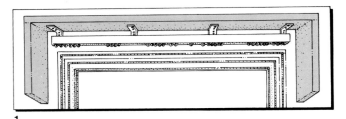

1

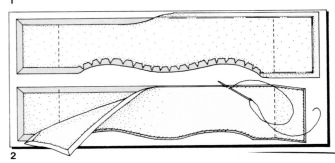

2

1 Make a flat pelmet from 1cm/½in plywood, 10cm/4in deep, and long enough to extend 5–7.5cm/2–3in at either end of track. Fix it to the wall using brackets.

You will need enough fabric to cover the front and sides of the board. Make a paper pattern of the pelmet shape: either draw one half of the design on folded graph paper which you can then open out to achieve a symmetrical shape or use a ready-made template or pattern. Allow 1cm/½in for the seams.
2 Cut out the pelmet stiffener to the shape of the finished pelmet, and place on the wrong side of the facing fabric, peeling off the backing.

Fold over the edges of the turnings, clip the curves, and press into place.

Press in the seam allowance on the lining, clipping curves, and lay the lining on the pelmet, wrong sides together. Slip-stitch in place. Fix the pelmet to the board with Velcro or with tacks concealed by braid.

Swags and Tails

Swags and tails are essentially draped pelmets (valances) but, unlike flat or gathered pelmets, they can be used on their own – for example, for hall windows, or wherever curtains are not desired. The swag is a draped length of fabric fixed to a board; it hangs in a graceful curve across the top of a window. At either end are pleated tails, which frame the window. A wide window can be dressed using a series of swags, with shorter tails at each tie-point.

Where the tail meets the swag it is usual to add some type of trimming, often a bow or rosette. Swags and tails can also be frilled, fringed or lined in a contrasting fabric and decorated with braid, cords or tassels.

1 *A pelmet and half corona, both trimmed with red bows, enhance a cool blue bedroom.*
2 *Tie-backs play a significant part in unifying this scheme.*

Making a Swag

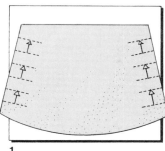

1

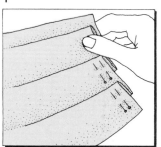

2

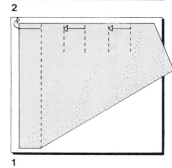

1

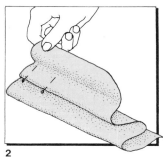

2

1 Cut out a pattern, as shown in the diagram. Mark pleat lines 10cm/4in apart. Cut out the main piece of fabric and lining following the pattern. (If the curtain fabric is not too heavy, you can use it for lining, too.) Sew the lining to the main fabric down the sides and along the bottom, right sides together. Trim corners, finish seams and turn right-side out.
2 Transfer the pleating points to the main fabric. Starting at the top, pin and then sew in place. Turn under the raw edge at the top and tack to the top edge of the pelmet board.

● Practise first using an old piece of material.

Making Tails
Line the tails in the same fabric, in a contrasting colour or a lining fabric.

1 Cut out the pattern, as shown in the diagram, and mark pleating lines across the top. Cut out the main piece of fabric and lining and sew them together, right sides facing, around the sides and bottom. Trim the corners and turn right-side out.
2 Fold the fabric into the pleats. Pin and sew in place. Turn under the raw edge at the top and tack to the top edge of the board. Reverse the pattern and make the tail at the other side.

Making a Tie-back

Like pelmets, tie-backs can be made of fabric, shaped in various ways and coordinated or contrasted with the curtain fabric. They can also be trimmed (with braid, piping or frills) or plaited. A simple finishing touch, tie-backs are particularly useful for curtains that do not draw.

2

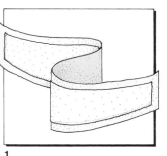

1

2

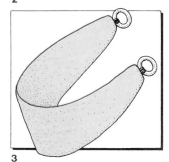

3

To calculate how long the tie-back should be, hold a tape measure around the curtain, and drape it loosely. Position a hook on the wall, and screw it into place.

Make a pattern of the shape you want. For a symmetrical shape, place the pattern on a double thickness of fabric, with the centre of the pattern aligning with the fold. For each tie-back you will need two pieces of fabric, 1cm/½in larger than the pattern all around.

1 Cut a piece of fusible interfacing to fit the pattern, and iron to the wrong side of one piece of fabric.
2 Place the second piece of fabric over the first, right sides together. Pin, tack (baste) and stitch all round, leaving an opening of about 10cm/4in for turning.
3 Trim the corners and seams and turn the tie-backs right-side out. Slip-stitch the opening and stitch onto each end a curtain ring to loop onto the hook in the wall.

Fabric Blinds and Shades

Fabric blinds make versatile, practical and attractive alternatives to curtains. Unlike curtains, they do not provide much insulation against heat loss, but they are more economical to make since you need much less fabric. Styles range from plain, utilitarian roller blinds or shades to extravagant festoon blinds.

Measuring
The size of blind you require will depend on whether the window is recessed or not. If the window is flat, take width measurements across the frame; if it is recessed, measure between the flanking walls or from the outside of the recess to the other side. On large horizontal windows, a series of blinds looks more balanced and works better than one large one.

Festoon blinds require twice the width of fabric if they have a heading, and 1⅓ times the depth; otherwise, you need merely 1⅓ times the depth.

Roller Blinds and Shades
The most widespread type of fabric blind, the roller blind, consists of a sturdy or stiffened fabric wound onto a usually wooden roller. The roller incorporates a spring so that the blind can be lowered to any position and then released to snap back

into its rolled-up state. A lath is slotted through a casing on the lower edge of the blind to hold it straight.

You can buy roller blinds ready-made or have them made-to-measure. Alternatively, kits are available which consist of a roller, brackets for holding the blind in place, a lath and a cord pull (you use your own fabric); the roller supplied can be sawn shorter if it is too long for the window.

Roman Blinds
Classic and elegant, Roman blinds are less severe-looking than the flat version. The blind is attached at the top to a wooden batten; vertical cords threaded through rings attached to the back of the blind allow it to be pulled up into soft horizontal folds. The bottom of the blind is stiffened with a wooden lath. Roman blinds look best if they are lined. They can be very effective if trimmed with contrasting banding.

Festoon Blinds and Shades
Festoon blinds can be made in different ways, but all types pull up into soft, billowing folds. Depending on the type of fabric and trimming, the festoon can look theatrical or elegant. Trimming with ruffles, flounces or fringing will accentuate the opulent flowing lines and will add simple decorative detail.

One type of festoon blind is a cross between a curtain and a Roman blind. Like a curtain, it is headed, lined, weighted and hung from a track using hooks; like a Roman blind, it is pulled up by means of cords which run through rings sewn on the reverse side. Other festoon blinds have cased headings or are attached to rails.

Suitable Fabrics
For roller blinds, choose any firm closely woven cloth, such as cotton furnishing fabric. Specially stiffened fabrics for roller blinds are available, but you can equally well buy a lightweight cheap fabric and apply spray-on stiffener to it (see right). Avoid fabric that might sag, stretch or bunch up untidily. Plain colours,

242

small repeat designs and even large prints can all be very effective.

Most types of curtain fabric – including cotton, chintz, sateen and linen union – are suitable for Roman blinds. Fabric with an overt texture can look very attractive, but it is important to select patterns with care – stripes and geometric designs work better when pleated up horizontally than do large, figurative or circular motifs.

Festoon blinds with curtain headings can be made from any type of not too heavy curtain fabric sturdy enough to pleat up well. Lining is recommended. By contrast, festoons with cased headings can be made in lighter, semi-transparent material and left unlined.

Avoid prints that are too busy and fussy. Geometrics, stripes, plain textured weaves and simple floral prints are all good prints to use.

Spray-on Stiffener
Lightweight material, including lace, can be used to make a roller blind if you treat the fabric with stiffener.

You will need to hem the sides by 1cm/½in to prevent fraying. The fabric might shrink after the stiffener has been applied, so allow extra. Test a small area first: spray it with stiffener, leave it to dry, and see what happens. Avoid loose-weave fabrics that might stretch after hanging.

Decorative Edges
To add interest and soften the plain lines of a roller blind, finish it by adding a decorative edge.

First stitch a casing for the wooden lath, about 12.5cm/5in up from the bottom edge of the blind. Stiffen the hem with iron-on fabric facing. Make a paper pattern of the required shape and cut it out. Finish the cut edge. To keep a castellated edge hanging straight, slot a rod through.

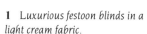

5

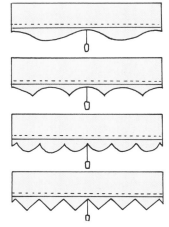

1 Luxurious festoon blinds in a light cream fabric.
2 Floral patterned roller blind makes a cheerful kitchen view.
3 Roman blinds look crisp and elegant in geometric fabrics.
4 The effect of Japanese screens, created by plain Roman blinds.
5 Sheer fabric festoons, for a turn-of-the-century atmosphere.
6 A roller blind painted with a country scene.

6

243

Making a Roman Blind

Roman blinds can be fitted to either recessed or unrecessed windows. If the window is recessed, you can hang the blind inside or outside: inside the recess, the board can be fixed to the recess ceiling; outside, secure it to the wall using brackets.

Calculating Amounts
Fix the heading board in position temporarily to measure up. To calculate the length of fabric required, measure from over the top of the board to the sill, adding 15cm/6in to the length for hem and top fixing. Add 7.5cm/3in to the width for the side turnings. The lining should be 10cm/4in shorter and 10cm/4in narrower than the blind fabric.

The blind is pulled up by means of cords running through ringed tapes sewn to the back. The tape is attached in vertical rows, one at each side with others between

them at intervals of 25–30cm/ 10–12in. Also, you will need cord and a screw eye for each row of tape: to calculate the amount of cord required, measure twice the length of the blind, add the width, and then multiply this figure by the number of rows of tape.

Materials and Equipment
- blind fabric
- lining
- ringed blind tape
- cord
- screw eyes (one for each row of tape)
- thread, pins and needles
- scissors
- sewing machine
- wooden batten (5 × 2.5cm/ 2 × 1in) for the heading board
- wooden batten (2.5 × 0.5cm/1in × ¼in)
- cleat for securing cords
- hammer and tacks, or stapling gun and staples
- angle brackets
- screwdriver

METHOD

1 Trim or snip selvedges to prevent puckering. Join any widths with flat seams; place part-widths to the outside, matching pattern if necessary. Repeat with lining fabric. Mark the mid-points of the lining and blind fabric and, with right sides together, align the top and sides and machine-stitch 1cm/½in side seams. The surplus fabric will form a pleat at the back. Press the seams open.

2 Turn right sides out, matching the mid-points, and press so that the blind fabric forms equal margins at the sides. Turn up the main fabric by 1cm/½in at the bottom, then turn up 10cm/4in to make a hem. Pin in place.

3 Mark guide lines for tape rows. Attach tapes, the first two covering the two side seams and the others spaced evenly between. Rings should align horizontally across the blind; the

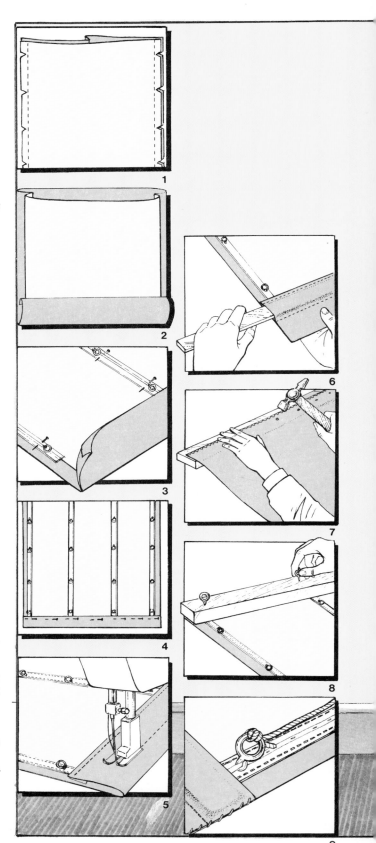

bottom ring should be 1cm/½in from the hem edge. Tuck the tape ends into the hem.

4 Machine-stitch through all thicknesses along both sides of the ringed tape.

5 Machine-stitch twice across the hem, first to catch in the ends of the tape and, again, 4cm/1½in down to form a casing.

6 Trim the smaller batten to make it just shorter than the width of the blinds and slot it into the casing. Slip-stitch the ends so that the batten is enclosed; continue down the ends of the hem to finish.

7 Zigzag-stitch the top edges of the blind together, catching in the raw edges of the tapes. Lay the heading board on a flat surface and position the edge of the blind 2cm/¾in over the wide side of it. Tack or staple at 10cm/4in intervals.

8 Fix screw eyes into the underside of the heading board at the top of each row of tape. Use a larger eye at the right-hand side, because all the cords will converge here.

9 With the blind still laid flat, tie cords to the bottom rings and thread them through each row and through the eyes at the top, working towards the right.

10 Knot the cords together about 5cm/2in from the last eye.

11 Fix the heading board either to the top of the window using angle brackets or directly into the recess ceiling. Trim the cords so that they are level and knot at the bottom. Screw the cleat to the wall near the bottom of the window to secure the cords. Keep the blind drawn up for a couple of days until the pleats in the fabric are firmly established.

10

11

Other Types of Blinds and Shades

Blinds come in materials other than fabric: metal, paper, wood and plastic are the notable ones. In style they range from the crisp, graphic quality of Venetian blinds to the soft, diffused effect of slatted wood and split cane. Most of the types discussed here are available in a range of standard widths and lengths; the more expensive, such as Venetian blinds, can be made up to your own specifications.

Prices vary widely. Standard pleated-paper blinds are among the cheapest window treatments of all, whereas Venetian blinds can cost almost as much as lined curtains. Maintenance, too, varies – from easy-care types such as cane blinds to Venetian blinds which are notoriously difficult to clean.

Paper Blinds

Made of tough paper or fibre, these blinds are permanently pleated and, since they pull up into the window reveal, can be combined with curtains. They are cheap and easy to dust, but are available only in a limited range. Balastore blinds are paper blinds with pierced holes.

Cane Blinds

Evocative of Mediterranean terraces, cane blinds – made from whole or split bamboo – roll or pleat up. They do not

screen light completely, but they are effective in conservatories or wherever there is no requirement for privacy but where you want to mute strong sunlight.

Wooden Blinds

Wooden blinds are made of slats of wood in either natural shades or dark green (they can also be sprayed). 'Pinoleum' blinds have thin strips of wood woven with cotton in wide widths, and suit inaccessible windows.

Plastic Blinds

Available in a good colour range, plastic blinds consist of thin strips assembled in roughly the same way as the laths of a wooden blind. Easy to clean, plastic blinds suit kitchens and bathrooms.

Vertical Louvres

These vertical blinds, made of canvas, wood or synthetic-fibre strips, are fixed to the

window. They can be pivoted to allow different degrees of light to filter through, or they can be drawn across. They particularly suit contemporary settings and large picture windows.

1 *Vibrant yellow pleated-paper blinds diffuse light effectively in a modern kitchen.*
2 *Tiered louvred shutters have a traditional appearance.*
3 *Black Venetian blinds screen a utility corner.*

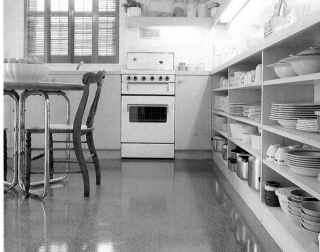

Venetian Blinds

Venetian blinds – slatted, adjustable blinds that pull up to the reveal – are available in plastic, metal and wood. The metal variety comes with either standard or fine slats and in a range of colours and finishes, including striped and gradated versions; there are also types pierced with holes. Operation of the blinds is by use of cords or rods. Wooden Venetian blinds are made of cedar or pine.

The great advantage of Venetian blinds is that they can be adjusted to allow varying degrees of light to filter through: fully open, they are almost invisible. Also, they can be used to cover very wide windows and made to any specification. Originally designed for office use, they suit modern interiors, but in neutral colours they can be unobtrusive enough to combine well with curtains in more traditional settings.

Shutters

Internal wooden shutters have a traditional, rustic appearance. They can be fixed to half or full height, and are usually louvred to allow light to filter through.

4 *Fine Venetian blinds make a shimmering window treatment.*
5 *Vertical louvres particularly suit large expanses of window.*
6 *Bamboo blinds add character to a modern bedroom.*
7 *Natural wooden louvres.*

Glossary

Where meaning differs, the US term is cross-referenced to the British term.

Accent lighting   The use of lights such as spots or wallwashers to highlight architectural features, objects or displays.

Acetate (cellulose acetate)   Strictly speaking, any of a family of esters used in fabrics, etc. The type used in, for example, stencilling comes in thin, tough transparent sheets.

Advancing colours   Colours which, when painted on a surface, seem to make that surface come towards you; they can be used to make a room seem smaller. 'Hot' and 'warm' colours – reds, oranges and yellows – can have this effect.

Alkyds   A family of synthetic resins used as binders in oil-based paints.

Anaglypta   An extremely heavily embossed wallpaper, used for wall or ceiling decorations.

Antiquing   Any of various painting and varnishing techniques used to artificially age a surface.

Background lighting   Essentially, the use of artificial lighting sources as a replacement for natural daylight, providing a general level of illumination.

Baseboard   See *skirting*.

Batten   A wooden or metal strip. In the United States larger battens are referred to as furring strips (*q.v.*).

Bauhaus movement   This movement took its name from a workshop (the Bauhaus) founded in 1919 by Walter Gropius. The movement aimed to design articles that were suitable for mass-production and yet were elegant and functional.

Beading   Wood or other material supplied in the form of a thin strip and used for edging, ornamentation, etc. See also *moulding*.

Blind nailing   See *secret nailing*.

Blistering   The formation of air-bubbles in a layer of paint or varnish, or under a wallcovering.

Blockboard   A thicker form of plywood (*q.v.*). Two layers of softwood, their grains at right angles, are sandwiched between two outer layers of veneer.

Burlap   See *hessian*.

Casement   A type of window having, typically, one fixed pane, a small top pane that can be opened, and one large pane that can be opened (usually hinged at the side).

Cavity wall   A wall constructed in the form of two outer layers sandwiching a gap of air. Extra insulation can be provided by filling the gap with, e.g., expanded polystyrene beads.

Ceiling rose (medallion)   A roughly circular ceiling decoration, usually placed centrally on the ceiling. The rose is often of plaster, and in many cases a lighting fixture may be suspended from it.

Cellulose acetate   See *acetate*.

Chipboard (particleboard)   A substitute for wooden boards created by bonding together fragments of wood using a synthetic resin. Chipboard can be bought either plain or veneered in wood or plastic laminate.

Cissing   A technique analogous to spattering (*q.v.*). Rather than spattering on a wash or glaze, however, you completely cover the base coat and then flick it with specks of the appropriate solvent for effect.

Coir matting   Matting made from coconut fibres.

Colour washing   Painting on several weak layers of wash or glaze over a base colour in order to produce an extremely luminous colour effect.

Combing   A decorative paint technique. Paint on a base coat and, when this has dried, cover it with a glaze. While the glaze is still wet, 'tease' it with a comb.

Corbel   A bracket of brick, stone or plaster; usually an internal feature.

Cornice   See *pelmet*.

Cornice (crown molding)   A decorative band of plaster, wood or other material set horizontally at the junction of a wall and a ceiling or of a wall and a roof.

Crown molding   See *cornice*.

Cutting-in brush   A paintbrush specially designed for painting along the edges of, for example, ceiling lines and window frames.

Dado (wainscoting)   The lower part of a wall whose upper and lower parts have been divided by a horizontal rail (a dado rail). By analogy, the lower part of a wall, if decorated differently from the upper (e.g., with different wallpaper).

Dhurrie   Also spelled 'durrie', an Indian flat-weave rug, usually made from cotton, and displaying geometric designs.

Distemper   A type of paint made by mixing glue and water with size, whiting etc. Ready-made distemper is now out of commercial production, but you can make it yourself.

Distressed effects   Decorative paint techniques that make use of broken colours rather than solid ones. Examples are ragging and sponging (*qq.v.*).

Double glazing   The setting of two parallel panes of glass in a window frame to reduce heat loss, external noise, etc. Equivalent to the fitting of a storm window (*q.v.*).

Double hem   A hem in which the fabric is turned over not once but twice by the same amount, so that the raw edge is completely enclosed.

Dragging   A decorative paint technique for walls and ceilings.

After a coloured base coat has dried you apply a glaze and, while this is still wet, you drag an almost-dry paintbrush across it.

'Drop' pattern A wallpaper pattern in which the repeated images match up diagonally rather than horizontally.

Dry laying Setting down tiles without using adhesive so that you can adjust pattern and positions before starting to fix the tiles into place.

Dry rot Severe form of decay in which, due to the presence of certain fungi, wood (or any other vegetable matter) dries out and crumbles. Dry rot spreads readily.

Drywall See *plasterboard*.

Efflorescence A powdery white substance that can appear on the surface of new brickwork or a newly plastered wall. Soluble salts in the brick or plaster react with moisture and force their way to the surface.

Eggshell (semi-gloss) paint A type of oil-based paint with a mid-sheen finish – halfway between matt and gloss.

Emulsion (latex) paint Water-based paint used principally to cover walls and ceilings.

Enamel paint Very dense oil-based paint used for small areas of woodwork and metal; only a single coat is required.

Faux bois Decorative paint technique which simulates the effect of wooden surfaces.

Fender A low screen that stops burning coals and logs rolling out of an open fire.

Fibreboard Plant (usually wood) fibres compressed to form thin sheets, often used for insulation and as a wallcovering. Compare *wallboard*.

Fibreglass Any material made out of thin, closely matted fibres of glass. Fibreglass blankets are much used for insulation. Sometimes called 'glass wool'.

Flat fell seam The most widely used seam in upholstery and curtain-making, whereby raw edges are completely enclosed.

Flat paint Oil-based paint which is matt (*q.v.*).

Flat seam The simplest way of stitching two pieces of fabric together, but not advisable where a strong finish is required. Compare *flat fell seam*.

Flokati A type of shaggy-pile woollen rug, usually white or off-white, made in Greece.

Frieze A band of plaster, paper or other material usually placed horizontally all around the four walls of a room, often at or above cornice (crown moulding) height.

Furring strips Large battens (*q.v.*) of wood or metal.

Glaze A transparent, or semi-transparent, thinned oil-based paint applied over a base colour, so that one or both are enriched and intensified. A number of decorative techniques – e.g.,

combing (*q.v.*) – depend on the use of glazes.

Gloss paint Oil-based paint that provides a shiny finish. Gloss is used mainly for woodwork and metalwork, for interior and exterior surfaces.

Graining See *woodgraining*.

Grosgrain Heavily ribbed silk (or, nowadays, rayon) tape used as a trim for upholstery or clothes and as banding on fabric-covered walls.

Grout Often called 'grouting', a filling that is inserted between tiles after they have been stuck in place. The grout ensures that the entire area is properly sealed. It can be coloured for graphic decorative effect.

Gypsum board See *plasterboard*.

Hardboard (masonite) A type of board usually used for surfacing. Made from compressed vegetable (usually wood) fibres, it is shiny on one side (the outer side) and textured on the other.

Herringbone stitch A simple type of stitch widely used for fastening hems.

Hessian (burlap) A coarse fabric woven from jute, hemp or similar fibre. It can be used as a wallcovering and is available with a paper backing.

Hygrovents Porous earthenware tubes inserted in walls to attract water, which then evaporates away through them.

Insulating board A type of board applied to ceilings and walls in order to reduce noise penetration and improve heat insulation.

Kelim A type of flat-weave rug, usually woollen and in rich earth colours, made in Turkey and Afghanistan.

Key (1) A surface of suitable roughness for the application of a coat of paint, plaster or whatever. (2) A substance applied in order to create such a surface.

Lacquer (1) A hard, glossy coating. (2) The substance used to produce such a coating, consisting of natural or synthetic resins dissolved in a volatile liquid; as the solvent evaporates it leaves the coating behind.

Lambrequin A deep valance (*q.v.*) that frames a window, extending some distance at either side.

Latex paint See *emulsion paint*.

Load-bearing wall A structural wall supporting a load (usually the wall above). Before you remove or alter a wall of this type you must install a lintel to carry the load. Compare *partition wall*.

Local lighting See *task lighting*.

Lock stitch This is used to hold the lining and interlining of a curtain loosely to the main fabric.

Mahlstick Often called a 'maulstick', a stick used by artists to help steady the hand.

Glossary

Marbling A decorative paint technique designed to simulate the appearance or general effect of a marbled surface.

Masking tape Sticky tape that can be peeled off easily without lifting off the surface beneath it. It can be used to provide a straight crisp edge when you are painting a flat surface, or to protect the glass when you are painting a window frame.

Masonite See *hardboard*.

Matt paint Water- or oil-based paint whose finish shows little or no sheen.

Maulstick See *mahlstick*.

Medallion See *ceiling rose*.

Mitre More correctly, 'mitre joint', a joint whereby two pieces of wood, plastic or other material are joined by cutting bevels at complementary angles at the end of each piece.

Monochromatic colour scheme A colour scheme in which all the colours used are variants of a single colour.

Moulding (1) A narrow piece of wood or other material used as a decorative edging; essentially, a synonym for beading (*q.v.*). (2) A decorative element, usually on a wall or ceiling (often where a wall joins a ceiling), commonly made out of plaster or similar material. See also *cornice*.

Mural A picture or pattern painted directly onto a wall. The term is often used today to mean also anything that gives the general impression of being a true mural – such as the self-adhesive 'mural panels' you can buy in some stores.

Numdah A type of cheap embroidered rug made in India.

Ogee A moulding with an S-shaped cross-section.

Paint pad A rectangular pile-covered foam pad attached to a handle and used to apply paint (usually emulsion) swiftly and smoothly to large surfaces.

Parquet A form of wooden floor covering, usually polished. Traditionally, laying parquet involved the use of small pieces of wood. Today parquet is available in tile form.

Particleboard See *chipboard*.

Partition wall An internal wall that divides up areas but does not carry any direct load. Compare *load-bearing wall*.

Pelmet (cornice) A decorative surround, usually made of fabric or wood, which covers a curtain heading, and adds definition to window treatments.

Plasterboard (drywall, gypsum board) Board used for surfacing walls and ceilings. It consists of standard-sized sheets of plaster sandwiched between external paper coverings.

Plywood A type of board made by gluing together several thin layers of wood. Often used to make sub-floors.

Polyesters A family of plastics with diverse uses. Polyester fibres are used (usually blended with natural fibres) in fabrics, while resinous forms are used in varnishes and certain paints.

Polystyrene A plastic used in both solid and expanded forms for wall or ceiling tiles, packaging, etc. The expanded form is used also for insulation and as a stuffing for cheap furniture. Should you be thinking of buying polystyrene-stuffed furniture, first check that it does not constitute a fire hazard.

Polyurethane (1) A synthetic resin used in the manufacture of paints and varnishes. (2) Synonymous with any transparent synthetic wood varnish, usually but not necessarily containing polyurethane. These yellow with age. (3) A foam used in cheap upholstery. Unless specially treated it is highly inflammable, and furniture containing it is banned in several countries.

Polyvinyl chloride See *vinyl*.

Primer A first coat of paint applied to a surface in order to provide a good key for subsequent coats, to seal and protect the surface, and to prevent it from absorbing the outer coats.

PVC See *vinyl*.

Ragging A decorative paint technique whereby you dip clothes into washes or glazes (*q.v.*) and use the crumpled fabric to make prints on a surface. In much the same way, you can completely cover a base colour with a wash or glaze and then selectively reveal the base colour using crumpled fabric.

Rag-rolling A variant of ragging (*q.v.*) whereby you roll a cloth down over a surface. Either roll a cloth dipped in glaze over a background colour or use a clean cloth to distress a wet surface.

Receding colours Colours that, when applied to a surface, make it appear to recede from you. Receding colours – the 'cool' colours such as blue and grey – can be used to make a small room seem larger.

Room divider Any unit – such as a bookcase, set of shelves or screen – that can be used to divide a larger room into much smaller areas.

Rose (medallion) See *ceiling rose*.

Rya A type of shaggy-pile rug made in Finland.

Screed (1) A layer of material (e.g., concrete or cement mortar) used to even off the surface of a floor prior to the application of a hard or heavy type of flooring. (2) As a verb: to bring a material flush with the surface around it.

Secret nailing Also known as 'blind nailing', a technique of driving nails into wooden boards so that their heads are underneath the surface and are hidden by an adjoining board.

Selvedge On a piece of fabric, a finished border that will not fray.

Semi-gloss paint See *eggshell paint*.

Serape A coarse flat-weave Mexican cloak, often fringed, used as a rug.

Shirring (1) Gathering or puckering a piece of fabric into rows, using elastic or stitching. (2) Adorning a wall with panels of shirred fabric.

Sisal matting Matting made using fibres derived from the leaves of various types of agave plant.

Skirting (baseboard) A border, usually of wood but sometimes of plaster or plastic, covering the base of a wall where it meets the floor. Can conceal wiring.

Slip stitch A type of stitch used for joining two folded edges or to hold a folded edge to a flat edge – e.g., a curtain hem.

Soffit The underside of, for example, an arch, door or window frame.

Spattering Simple distressed paint effect achieved by dipping the bristles of a stiff brush in paint and flicking it at a surface.

Sponging Decorative paint technique using a sea sponge or equivalent either to dab a top coat (or coats) of a wash or glaze over a base coat or to remove selected areas of an overlying wash or glaze.

Stencilling A way of decorating surfaces by dabbing paint through a motif (or motifs) cut

out of acetate or similar medium onto a surface.

Stippling Creating a 'speckled' effect using one of two similar techniques. Either cover a base coat with a glaze or wash and, while it is still wet, strike it with a flat-faced brush, so that flecks of the base colour are revealed, or simply apply speckles by dipping a brush into a glaze or wash and then stab with it at the base coat.

Storm window An extra window fitted externally to reduce heat loss, noise, etc.

Straightedge A metal or wooden strip one of whose surfaces can be used to draw an exactly straight line.

Sugar soap An alkaline preparation, available in crystal form to be mixed with water, which is used to clean and degrease painted surfaces.

Swag A loop of draped fabric, suspended across the top of a window, either as a pelmet (*q.v.*) or on its own as a window treatment. A wide window may have a series of swags.

Tails Lengths of pleated fabric attached to either end of a swag (*q.v.*), framing a window.

Task lighting Lighting placed to perform a particular function. Task lighting can be anything from a bedside lamp to a strip light in a kitchen. Also called 'local' lighting.

Template A cut-out pattern (perhaps in card) used so that

the same line can be reproduced many times over.

Tie-back A length of fabric, cord or similar attached to a window frame and used to loop back a curtain.

Tongue-and-groove panelling A type of panelling that is easy to assemble. Each board has on one side a tongue and on the other a groove into which a tongue can fit.

Tortoise-shelling Paint technique that seeks to imitate – or at least give the overall effect of – natural tortoise-shell.

Trompe l'oeil A type of highly realistic decorative painting which aims to 'deceive the eye'; for example, balusters painted at the base of a wall.

Undercoat A type of paint or stain applied to a surface to provide a good key for the final top coat.

Valance A frill of fabric. Valances can be used to cover curtain fittings (i.e., as a fabric pelmet (*q.v.*) or to trim the base of a chair or bed.

Veneer A thin sheet of material fastened to the surface of a board or plank. Veneers are typically of wood – often of valuable wood – but synthetic materials of many kinds are also used.

Vermiculite Any of various minerals largely made up of hydrated magnesium, aluminium and iron silicates. Expanded by heat, they are much used for

insulation (often in granular form).

Vinyl (polyvinyl chloride, PVC) A thermoplastic found in many applications: floorings, tiles, fabrics, etc. However, the exact properties of any vinyl-based product depend on the nature of the 'plasticizer' – the material used in conjunction with the PVC.

Vinyl wallpapers Wallpapers that have a plastic coating so that they can be scrubbed. They are especially suitable for kitchens, bathrooms and children's rooms.

Wainscoting An additional surface, usually of wood, applied to the lower part of a wall to a height of perhaps 1m/3ft 3in.

Wallboard Board made out of compressed plant (usually wood) fibres or plaster sandwiched between paper and used as a surface for walls and ceilings and in insulation. Compare *fibreboard*, *plasterboard*.

Wet rot Caused by various types of fungi, a condition in which wood decays. The surface of the wood feels 'clammy'.

Whiting Powdered and cleansed white chalk used, for example, in distemper and whitewash.

Woodgraining A painting technique which seeks to imitate – or at least to give the overall effect of – the grain of wood.

Woodworm Condition in which wood is invaded by the common furniture beetle.

INDEX

ACKNOWLEDGEMENTS

EWA in the acknowledgements is an abbreviation of Elizabeth Whiting & Associates. The publisher thanks the following photographers and organizations for their kind permission to reproduce the photographs in this book:

1–2 1 Dennis Krukowski (designer David Webster), 2 Dennis Krukowski/Conran Octopus (Mary Jean and John Winkler); 4–5 Ken Kirkwood/*Homes and Gardens*/Syndication International; 8–9 Bill Stites; 10–11 EWA; 30–31 Jan Baldwin/*Homes and Gardens*/Syndication International; 32–33 1 Dennis Krukowski (designer David Webster), 2 Simon Brown/

Conran Octopus (Graham Carr), 3 Jean-Paul Bonhommet, 4 Roland Beaufre/Agence Top (designer Jacques Granges); 34–35 1 Ianthe Ruthven, 2 Dennis Krukowski (designer Tonin MacCallum), 3 Bill Stites/Conran Octopus (Mary Gilliatt), 4, 5 Jean-Paul Bonhommet, 36–37 Dennis Krukowski/Conran Octopus (designer John Paul Beaujard); 38–39 1 Karen Bussolini (stencils by John Canning), 2 Roland Beaufre/Agence Top (Suzy Frankfurt), 3 Bill Stites/Conran Octopus (designer Mary Gilliatt), 4 Karen Bussolini (paint by John Canning), 5 Roland Beaufre/Agence Top (designer Henri Garelli), 6 Jean-Paul Bonhommet; 40–41 1 Lars Hallen, 2 Jean-Paul Bonhommet, 3 Jack Parsons for *Sante*

Fe Style by Christine Mather and Sharon Woods published by Rizzoli, 4, 5 Lars Hallen; 42–43 1 Lars Hallen, 2 Karen Bussolini (stencils by John Canning), 3 Pascal Hinous/Agence Top, 4 Tom Lorimer/EWA, 5 Spike Powell/EWA; 44–45 1, 2, 3 Dennis Krukowski/Conran Octopus (designer John Paul Beaujard), 4, 5 Jean-Paul Bonhommet, 6 Spike Powell/EWA; 46–47 Jean-Paul Bonhommet; 48–49 1 Ken Kirkwood, 2 Richard Bryant/Arcaid, 3 Ken Kirkwood/Conran Octopus, 4 Jean-Paul Bonhommet; 50–51 1, 2 Tim Street-Porter/EWA, 3 Simon Brown/Conran Octopus, 4, 5 Lars Hallen; 52–53 1 Neil Lorimer/EWA, 2 Jean-Paul Bonhommet, 3 Ianthe Ruthven, 4 Richard Bryant/Arcaid; 54–55 1 Claude Pataut/La Maison de Marie Claire (stylist Marion Bayle), 2 Pascal Chevalier/Agence Top, 3 Jean-Paul Bonhommet, 4 Claude Pataut/La Maison de Marie Claire (stylist Anne-Marie Comte); 56–57 Jean-Paul Bonhommet; 58–59 1, 2 Bill Stites/Conran Octopus (designer Mary Gilliatt), 3 Richard Paul, 4, 5 Jean-Paul Bonhommet; 60–61 Bill Stites/Decorating Remodeling, 2 Jacques Primois/La Maison de Marie Claire (stylist Sophie Belmont), 3 Dennis Krukowski (designer Tom O'Toole), 4 Jean-Paul Bonhommet; 62–63 1 Simon Brown/Conran Octopus, 2 Jean-Paul Bonhommet, 3 Pascal Chevalier/Agence Top, 4 Jean-Paul Bonhommet, 5 Bill Stites/Conran Octopus (Mary Gilliatt); 64–65 1 Carol Athay/EWA, 2 Michael Dunne/EWA, 3 Dennis Krukowski (designer Tom O'Toole), 4 Bill Stites/Conran Octopus (designer Mary Gilliatt), 5 Fritz von der Schulenburg/World of Interiors; 66–67 1 Richard Bryant/Arcaid, 2 Jean-Paul Bonhommet, 3 Dennis Krukowski (designer Douglas C. Rowe of Greenbaum the Interior Design Center), 4 Michael Dunne/EWA, 5 Bill Stites/Conran Octopus (designer Mary Gilliatt); 68–69 Spike Powell/EWA; 70–71 Tom Lorimer/EWA, 2 Dennis Krukowski/Conran Octopus (Mary Jean and John Winkler), 3 Pascal Hinous/Agence Top (David Hicks), 4 Bill Stites/Decorating Remodeling, 5 Ianthe Ruthven (stencils by Lyn de Grice); 72–73 1 Michael Dunne/EWA, 2 Judith Watts (Mary Gilliatt), 3 Michael Dunne/EWA, 4 John Nation/Decorating Remodeling; 74–75 1 Karen Bussolini (floor by John Canning), 2 Richard Paul, 3 Jean-Paul Bonhommet, 4 Spike Powell/EWA, 5 Ianthe Ruthven; 76–77 1 Spike Powell/EWA, 2 Tom Lorimer/EWA, 3 Spike Powell/EWA, 4 Michael Nicholson/EWA, 5 Karen Bussolini (architect Peter Kurt Woerner), 6 Richard Paul, 7 Spike Powell/EWA; 78–79 1 Bill Stites/Conran Octopus (Mary Gilliatt), 2 Dennis Krukowski/Conran Octopus (Mary Jean and John Winkler), 3 Michael Dunne/EWA, 4 Spike Powell/EWA; 80–81 Jean-Paul Bonhommet; 82–83 1 Annet Held, 2 John Hollingshead, 3 Jean-Paul Bonhommet, 4 Dennis Krukowski (designer Anne Eisenhower), 5 Karen Bussolini, 6 Roland Beaufre/Agence Top (designer Jean-Louis Riccardi); 84–85 1 Richard Bryant/Arcaid, 2 Dennis Krukowski (designer Tonin MacCallum), 3 Neil Lorimer/EWA, 4 Simon Brown/Conran Octopus, 5 Rodney Hyett/EWA, 6 Pascal Chevalier/Agence Top (designer Henri Garelli), 7 Karen Bussolini; 86–87 1 Andreas von Einsiedel/EWA, 2 Jean-Paul Bonhommet, 3 Dennis Krukowski (designer David Webster), 4 Carol Athay/EWA, 5 Karen Bussolini (John Canning), 6 Jean-Paul Bonhommet, 7 Carol Athay/EWA, 8 Lars Hallen, 9 John Hollingshead/Homes and Gardens/Syndication International; 88–89 1 Ken Kirkwood, 2 Jean-Paul Bonhommet, 3 Dennis Krukowski/Conran Octopus (designer John Paul Beaujard), 4 Rodney Hyett/EWA, 5, 6, 7 Jean-Paul Bonhommet, 8 Dennis Krukowski (designer Barbara Ostrom), 9 Simon Brown/Conran Octopus (architects de Blacam & Meagher); 90–91 1 Karen Bussolini (Roto Roof Windows), 2 Roland Beaufre/Agence Top (painter Alain de Condé), 3 Guy Bouchet, 4 Richard Paul, 5 Lars Hallen, 6 Richard Paul, 7 Simon Brown/Conran Octopus, 8 Lars Hallen, 9 Richard Paul; 96–97 1 Jean-Paul Bonhommet, 2 Annet Held, 3 Rodney Hyett/EWA, 4 Spike Powell/EWA, 5 Richard Bryant/Arcaid, 6 Tom Lorimer/EWA, 7 Spike Powell/EWA, 8 Dennis Krukowski (designer Tonin MacCallum); 98–99 Lars Hallen, 2 Michael Dunne/EWA, 3 John Hollingshead/UK, Family Circle, 4 Jean-Paul Bonhommet, 5 Dennis Krukowski (designers Saunders and Walsh), 6 Rodney Hyett/EWA, 7 Spike Powell/EWA; 100–101 1 Jean-Paul Bonhommet, 2 Karen Bussolini (architect Abraham Rothenberg),

3 Dennis Krukowski (designer Tom O'Toole), 4 Bill Stites/Conran Octopus (Mary Gilliatt), 5 Jean-Paul Bonhommet, 6 Tim Street-Porter/EWA, 7 Tom Lorimer/EWA; 102–103 1 Rodney Hyett/EWA, 2 Lars Hallen, 3 EWA, 4 Jean-Paul Bonhommet, 5 Dennis Krukowski/Conran Octopus (Mary Jean and John Winkler), 6 Dennis Krukowski (Suzy Frankfurt), 7 Pascal Hinous/Agence Top (designer Jean Dives); 104–105 1 Karen Bussolini (paint by John Canning), 2 Dennis Krukowski (designer Tonin MacCallum), 3 Pascal Chevalier/Agence Top (designer Jean Dives), 4 Tom Lorimer/EWA, 5 Jean-Paul Bonhommet, 6 Michael Dunne/EWA, 7 Pascal Chevalier/Agence Top, 8 Alfredo Anghinelli/EWA, 9 Ianthe Ruthven; 106–107 1 Clive Frost/World of Interiors, 2 Andreas von Einsiedel/EWA, 3 Jean-Paul Bonhommet, 4 Tim Street-Porter/EWA, 5 Ken Kirkwood, 6 Silvio Wolf/Abitare, 7 Jean-Paul Bonhommet, 8 Syndication International, 9 Spike Powell/EWA, 10 Jean-Paul Bonhommet, 11 Lars Hallen; 108–109 1 Pascal Chevalier/Agence Top (designer Christian Badin), 2 Tom Lorimer/EWA, 3 Lars Hallen, 4 Ianthe Ruthven, 5 Tim Street-Porter/EWA, 6 Jean-Paul Bonhommet; 110–111 1, 2 Dennis Krukowski (designer Tonin MacCallum), 3 Rodney Hyett/EWA, 4 John Hollingshead/Homes & Gardens/Syndication International, 5 Dennis Krukowski (designers Irvine & Fleming), 6, 7 Michael Dunne/EWA; 116–117 1 Jean-Paul Bonhommet, 2 Spike Powell/EWA; 3 John Hollingshead/Homes & Gardens/Syndication International, 4 Jean-Paul Bonhommet, 5, 6 Lars Hallen; 118–119 1 Simon Brown/Conran Octopus, 2 Simon Brown/Conran Octopus (architect Richard Gooden), 3 Richard Hyett/EWA, 4 Jean-Paul Bonhommet, 5 Camera Press, 6 Michael Dunne/EWA; 120–121 1 Michael Dunne/EWA, 2 Claude Pataut/La Maison de Marie Claire (stylist Marion Bayle), 3 Dennis Krukowski/Conran Octopus (Mary Jean and John Winkler), 4 Michael Dunne/EWA, 5 Dennis Krukowski/Conran Octopus (Mary Jean and John Winkler), 6 Jean-Paul Bonhommet, 7 Pascal Chevalier/Agence Top (stylist Françoise Dorget), 8 Richard Paul; 122–123 1 Simon Brown/Conran Octopus (architect Robert T Bayley), 2 Lars Hallen, 3 Camera Press, 4 Michael Newton, 5 Rodney Hyett/EWA, 6 Lars Hallen, 7 Rodney Hyett/EWA; 124–125 1 Annet Held, 2 John Miller/Homes and Gardens/Syndication International, 3 Michael Dunne/EWA, 4 Karen Bussolini (designers Gilvarg/Epstein), 5 Tom Lorimer/EWA, 6 Rodney Hyett/EWA, 7 Jean-Pierre Godeaut/La Maison de Marie Claire (stylist Sophie Belmont), 8 Fritz von der Schulenburg, 9 Jean-Paul Bonhommet; 126–127 1 Roland Beaufre/Agence Top (Mr Delafaille), 2 Richard Paul, 3 Pierre Hussenot/La Maison de Marie Claire, 4 Richard Bryant/Arcaid, 5 Michael Dunne/EWA, 6 Jean-Paul Bonhommet; 132–133 1 Dennis Krukowski (designer Tonin MacCallum), 2 Richard Bryant/Arcaid, 3 Philippe Girardeau/La Maison de Marie Claire (stylist Josée Postic), 4 Antoine Rozès, 5 Jean-Paul Bonhommet, 6 Shona Wood/Conran Octopus (Polly Powell); 134–135 1 Karen Bussolini, 2 John Hollingshead, 3 Dennis Krukowski/Conran Octopus (designer John Paul Beaujard), 4 Dennis Krukowski (designer Richard L. Ridge), 5 Jean-Paul Bonhommet, 6 Dennis Krukowski (designers Saunders and Walsh); 136–137 1 Roland Beaufre/Agence Top (Oscar de la Renta), 2 Antoine Rozès, 3 Roland Beaufre/Agence Top (designer Jean-Louis Riccardi), 4 Karen Bussolini (designer Abi Babcock, paint by John Canning), 5 Philippe Girardeau/La Maison de Marie Claire (stylist Phuong Pfeufer), 6 Roland Beaufre/Agence Top (designer Christian Badin), 7 Michael Dunne/EWA, 8 Ianthe Ruthven; 138–139 1 Collier Campbell, 2 Karen Bussolini (designer Jean P Simmons), 3 Tom Lorimer/ EWA, 4 Roland Beaufre/Agence Top (Oscar de la Renta), 5 Michael Dunne/EWA; 140–141 1 Ken Kirkwood, 2 Roland Beaufre/Agence Top (painter Alain de Condé), 3 Jean-Paul Bonhommet, 4 Richard Bryant/Arcaid (designer J Harris), 5 Roland Beaufre/Agence Top, 6 Ken Kirkwood, 7 Pascal Chevalier/Agence Top, 8 Karen Bussolini (architect Peter Kurt Woerner), 9 Tom Lorimer/EWA; 142–143 1, 2, 3 Jean-Paul Bonhommet; 4 Andreas von Einsiedel/EWA, 5 Jean-Paul Bonhommet, 6 Shona Wood/Conran Octopus (designer Jonathan Bartlett), 7 Roland Beaufre/ Agence Top (Oscar de la Renta); 148–149 Dennis Krukowski (designer

Tonin MacCallum); 150–151 1 Clive Helm/EWA, 2 Rodney Hyett/EWA, 3, 4 Jean-Paul Bonhommet; 152–153 1, 2 Jean-Paul Bonhommet; 154–155 Simon Brown/Conran Octopus (architect Trevor Horne); 156–157 John Hollingshead; 158–159 1 John Hollingshead, 2–3 Jean-Paul Bonhommet; 160–161 1 Michael Dunne/EWA, 2 John Hollingshead, 3 Jean-Paul Bonhommet; 162–163 Shona Wood/Conran Octopus (Polly Powell); 166–167 1 Michael Newton, 2 Garry Chowanetz/EWA, 3 Simon Brown/Conran Octopus (designers Jerry Hewitt and Angela Hewitt-Woods), 4 Shona Wood/Conran Octopus (Helen Preston); 170–171 1 Camera Press, 2 Michael Dunne/EWA, 3 Michael Newton/Conran Octopus; 174–175 John Hollingshead/UK, *Family Circle*; 176–177 1 Spike Powell/EWA, 2 Simon Brown/Conran Octopus (architect Ian Hutchinson); 178–179 1, 2 John Hollingshead, 3 Simon Brown/Conran Octopus (architect Ian Hutchinson); 182–183 1 Simon Brown/Conran Octopus (artist Elyane de la Rochette), 2 Dennis Krukowski/Conran Octopus (designer John Paul Beaujard); 184–185 1 Jessica Strang, 2 Shona Wood/Conran Octopus (designer Anthony Paine), 3 Simon Brown/Conran Octopus (Paul Hodgkinson—design by Simon Design Consultants), 4 Shona Wood/Conran Octopus (Michael Snyder); 188–189 Roland Beaufre/Agence Top (designer Madeleine Castaing), 2 Michael Dunne/EWA, 3 Karen Bussolini (paint by John Canning), 4 Simon Brown/Conran Octopus (paint by John Ebdon), 5 Ianthe Ruthven, 6 Jean-Paul Bonhommet; 190–191 1 Karen Bussolini (stencils by John Canning), 2, 3 David Cripps/EWA, 4 Spike Powell/EWA; 194–195 Michael Newton/Conran Octopus; 198–199 1 Dennis Krukowski (designer Tonin MacCallum), 2 Pascal Hinous/Agence Top; 200–201 1 Andreas von Einsiedel/EWA, 2 Jean-Paul Bonhommet, 3 Simon Brown/Conran Octopus (Paul Hodgkinson—design by Simon Design Consultants), 4 Karen Bussolini (architects Andrew Robinson & Marsden Moran), 5 Michael Newton/Conran Octopus; 204–205 1 Tom Lorimer/EWA, 2 Michael Dunne/EWA, 3 Annet Held; 206–207 1 Ken Kirkwood/Conran Octopus (designer George Powers), 2 Andreas von Einsiedel/EWA; 210–211 1 Ornella Sancassani/*Abitare*, 2 Lars Hallen, 3 Karen Bussolini; 215–216 1 John Vaughan, 2 Ralph Bogertman/*Decorating Remodeling*; 218–219 1 Michael Newton/Conran Octopus, 2 Dennis Krukowski (designer David Webster); 222–223 1 Michael Newton/Conran Octopus, 2 Roland Beaufre/Agence Top, 226–227 1, 2 David Black, 3 P J Gates, 4 Helen Yardley, 5 Jean-Paul Bonhommet, 6 Omberto Gigli; 228–229 1 Dennis Krukowski/Conran Octopus (Mary Jean & John Winkler), 2 Michael Newton/Conran Octopus; 230–231 1 Annet Held, 2 Jean-Paul Bonhommet, 3 Michael Newton/Conran Octopus; 232–233 1 Michael Dunne/EWA, 2 Jean-Paul Bonhommet; 1 234–235 1 Michael Newton/Conran Octopus, 2 Pascal Chevalier/Agence Top (designer Henri Garelli); 238–239 1 Brian Harrison/*Ideal Home*/Syndication International, 2 Ian Kalinowski/*Options*/Syndication International; 240–241 1 Michael Dunne/EWA, 2 Spike Powell/EWA; 242–243 1 Jean-Paul Bonhommet, 2 Di Lewis/EWA, 3 Shona Wood/Conran Octopus (Helen Preston), 4 Antoine Rozès, 5 Roland Beaufre/Agence Top (Suzy Frankfurt), 6 Dennis Krukowski (designer Beverly Ellsley); 246–247 1 John Hollingshead/*Homes and Gardens*/Syndication International, 2 Dulux, 3 Rodney Hyett/EWA, 4 John Hollingshead/*Homes & Gardens*/Syndication International, 5 Jean-Paul Bonhommet, 6 Tim Street-Porter/EWA, 7 Rodney Hyett/EWA.

The Publisher would like to thank the following companies for supplying fabric and wallpaper samples for the jacket photography:
Laura Ashley, Coloroll, Jane Churchill, Designers Guild, Heal's, John Lewis, Osborne & Little, Sanderson's, Sandpiper Papers (Mary Gilliatt's Edwardian Garden Collection), and Warner and Sons Ltd.

The publisher would also like to thank the following for their assistance: ICI Paint Division, Wexham Road, Slough SL2 5DS; Crown Decorative Products, Darwen, Lancs; The Flowersmith, 34 Shelton Street, London WC2.

Material for photography was supplied by the following companies:

p.171 Types of Paint
1,3,4,5 Crown Decorative Products; 2 International Paint
p.195 Wallpapers
1,2 John Oliver; 3,24,30 Designers Guild; 4,10 Crown Decorative Products; 5,8 Nairnflock; 6,20 Osborne & Little; 7,12 Tektura; 9,11,13,14,19,29 Arthur Sanderson & Sons; 15,18 Habitat; 16,21,22,23,26,27,28 Warner & Sons; 17 Jane Churchill; 25 Laura Ashley
p.201 Wall Tiles and Cladding
1,21 Boydens; 2,3,6,8,12,13,20,22 Fired Earth; 4,7,10,11,14,15,16,18,23 World's End Tiles; 5,9 Formica; 17 Barkers; 19 Wicanders
p.218 Floor Tiles
1,2,12,14 World's End Tiles; 3,4,16 Amtico; 5 Forbo-Nairn; 6,7,8,9,10,11,13,15,18,19 Fired Earth; 17 Boydens; 20 Wicanders; 21 Reed-Harris
p.222 Carpets
1,12 Tretford Carpets; 2,5,7,9 Allied Carpets; 3,4,6,10,11,13 Brintons; 8 The Gates Rubber Company
p.229 Matting
1,2,4,5,6,9,10,11,12,13,14 David Douglas; 3,8 Habitat
p.231 Curtain Fabrics
1,2,6,9, Arthur Sanderson & Sons; 3 Osborne & Little; 4,5,8,10 Warner & Sons; 7,11,12,13 Laura Ashley
p.234 Sheer Fabrics
1 Ado International; 2,4,5,6 Paris Voile; 3 John Aird & Co.; 7,8 Warner & Sons

Author's Acknowledgements

I have so many people to thank for this book: Elizabeth Wilhide gave so much of her time, help and energy in a particularly generous way. Hilary Arnold, who conceived the project in its present form, makes working with Conran Octopus a great pleasure, not just I think for me, but for everyone. Polly Powell kept me on the straight and narrow as gracefully as possible and became a new friend, and I have always to thank Alison Cathie and Ray Roberts for their strong support. I could not even begin to encompass my various projects without the efficiency, care and thoughtfulness of Amelia Anderson and Mary Rooke, who are both so talented in design in their own way. Nor could we have illustrated the book so well without the inspiration, intuition and sheer hard work of my art editor, Karen Bowen, editorial assistant, Jane Harcus and picture researcher, Shona Wood.

Barbara Pierce, Alathea Michie, David and Bobby Margolis were also very generous with their suggestions, enthusiasm and patience in various ways. And I particularly want to record my gratitude to Felicity Bryan and Bob Levine who have been so caring, and so very supportive.